SOURCE BOOKS ON EDUCATION
VOL. 45

READING
AND LEARNING
DISABILITIES

GARLAND REFERENCE LIBRARY
OF SOCIAL SCIENCE
VOL. 512

READING AND LEARNING DISABILITIES

Research and Practice

Joyce N. French
Nancy J. Ellsworth
Marie Z. Amoruso

GARLAND PUBLISHING, Inc.
New York & London / 1995

Library of Congress Cataloging-in-Publication Data

French, Joyce N., 1929–
    Reading and learning disabilities : research and
practice / by Joyce N. French, Nancy J. Ellsworth, and
Marie Z. Amoruso.
        p.   cm. — (Garland reference library of social
science ; vol. 512. Source books on education ; vol.
45)
    Includes bibliographical references and indexes.
    ISBN 0-8240-4790-7 (alk. paper)
    1. Learning disabled children—Education—Read-
ing.   2. Learning disabled children—Education—
Reading—Bibliography.   I. Ellsworth, Nancy J.
II. Amoruso, Marie Z.   III. Title.   IV. Series: Garland
reference library of social science ; v. 512.   V. Series:
Garland reference library of social science. Source
books on education ; vol. 45.
LC4704.87.F74   1995
371.9'0444—dc20   94-44990
                                                   CIP

371.9
F874r

Printed on acid-free, 250-year-life paper
Manufactured in the United States of America

Contents

Contents

Preface

You, the reader, have probably come to this book searching for answers and solutions to many of the same questions that we, the writers, sought when we undertook the compilation of the bibliography and the writing of this text. The field of learning disabilities has been plagued with many unknowns, none perhaps more vexing than how to teach students with learning disabilities the reading skills and strategies they need in order to succeed today and in the future.

Can we provide you with all the answers that you seek? Probably not. We can, however, provide information, indicate directions, and suggest alternatives. Psychologists and educators have made enormous strides in the past 25 years in our knowledge of learning disabilities and of reading. We are beginning to acquire expertise in how these two fields intersect. However, there are still uncertainties, areas needing clarification and substance. We also know that there is no one solution to the problems teachers and students address every day.

This book is divided into two parts: a text dealing with questions and issues related to enabling students with learning disabilities to acquire and use literacy skills and strategies; and an annotated bibliography of current references related to this topic. In the first part we have addressed topics that have been raised by teachers and that are identified in the research literature. We explore the characteristics of students with learning disabilities and how these students function in school. We also examine the act of reading and the role of the reader in the process from the perspective of the good reader, comparing and contrasting it to what we know about the student with learning disabilities. We identify the role of instruction and the variety of instructional alternatives because of their impact on moving the student with learning disabilities into the role of a good reader. The act of reading is broken down, unrealistically but for the practical purpose of close examination, into reading words, understanding words, and comprehending text. In each of these areas we analyze the skills and strategies of the good reader and compare them to those of the student with learning disabilities. Finally, we suggest instructional alternatives and strategies, the heart of any educational program.

The annotated bibliography was developed from electronic databases and traditional reference sources. The entries are presented in alphabetical order by author rather than in content categories. Authors of articles write about a major topic, but they also include numerous subtopics. This makes for informative reading, but not for clear categorizing. The index will provide guidance regarding the various topics included in particular articles. Because of the rapidly developing and changing nature of this field, the items in the bibliography are generally from 1988 on. However, a few earlier items have been included because they are landmarks in the field. Finally, we have tried to select articles that are accessible and readable. A bibliography, above all, needs to be useful.

Finally, of course, we must consider our readers, preservice and inservice teachers. This book has been written as a guide to understanding and implementing appropriate reading instruction for students with learning disabilities. In addition, it is our hope that administrators, a major support for what goes on in classrooms, will review these findings.

We wish to thank Joseph Groppuso for his help in designing the format of this book.

We would like to give special thanks to Theresa M. Bologna for her thoughtful contributions. We appreciate her professional expertise and her support for this project.

Joyce N. French
Nancy J. Ellsworth
Marie Amoruso

Reading
and Learning
Disabilities

CHAPTER 1

Learning Disabilities:
A Changing Field

Children with learning disabilities are perplexing. Although they do not learn as we would expect them to, they evidence no obvious cause for their failure to learn despite adequate intelligence. In addition, a number of these children have behavioral characteristics that are troublesome both at school and at home. Learning disabilities affect many children, adolescents, and adults, influencing both their schooling and their adjustment to society. The impact of these learning disabilities on their acquisition and development of literacy skills is striking, as documented both in the United States and abroad. The international perspective reflected in current discussions of learning disabilities (Wong, 1992a) emphasizes the extent to which they cut across political and linguistic boundaries.

To complicate the picture further, some children with learning disabilities are also intellectually gifted or show significant talent in a specific area of endeavor. Several eminent historical figures appear to have exhibited the classic characteristics of learning disabilities yet were able to overcome initial failures to reach high points of achievement (Waldron, Saphire, & Rosenblum, 1987). However, most do not achieve what appears to be their potential. Difficulty mastering academic subjects usually forms the basis of children's identification as learning disabled, e.g., a high percentage of these children have been held back in school before being identified (McLeskey, 1992).

The major concern of this book is teaching these children to read so that they may acquire the literacy skills and strategies that will prepare them to comprehend and communicate, both in and out of school. We will focus on reading difficulties experienced by students with learning disabilities and on learning and instructional strategies for the classroom that can effect change. In order to reach this goal we need a grounding in the field of learning disabilities as it relates to the acquisition and development of literacy. We will examine the following areas:

- The interdisciplinary, historical evolution of the field.
- The definition of learning disabilities, for the definition forms a philosophical basis for instruction of students.
- The causes of learning disabilities.
- The evidence for the increasing prevalence of learning disabilities.
- The characteristics of students with learning disabilities that affect the acquisition and use of literacy.
- The settings in which instruction is provided.
- The educational outcomes of these students.
- The emerging research directions that, in turn, will influence both funding and reading instruction.

LEARNING DISABILITIES: AN INTERDISCIPLINARY EFFORT

Throughout the brief history of teaching children with learning disabilities to read, progress has been made through the coordinated efforts of people from many disciplines. Prominent among these are medicine, education, speech and language, and psychology. A short review of the evolution of the field will help provide a framework for understanding the problems of defining learning disabilities, recent emphasis on the interaction of environmental factors with characteristics inherent within the individual, and the models of reading instruction employed in teaching these students.

Researchers have sought a medical explanation for the reading problems of children with learning disabilities on the assumption that much of the difficulty is physiological in origin. The hope that understanding the causes and etiology might lead to knowing how best to provide instruction has encouraged this pursuit. Investigations of aphasia, word blindness, and brain injuries revealed that people's brains are indeed structurally different and that these differences can underlie specific learning and behavioral characteristics in the individual.

By the 1930's, clinical studies of children were, in turn, translated into instructional methods. The pioneers of this era were truly interdisciplinary. The work of neurologist Orton was applied to the education of children by Gillingham in the Orton-Gillingham method of teaching phonics which is still used today for children with decoding problems. In the same era, Fernald created a multisensory approach to teaching remedial reading and spelling for intractable reading difficulties.

In the late 1940's, Strauss and Lehtinen identified a group of children with severe cognitive and behavioral difficulties whom they called "brain injured," because their initial subjects had medical histories that documented that condition. Strauss' categorizations of the biological and behavioral characteristics of these children are reflected in the federal definition of learning disabilities. These configurations included soft neurological signs, a history of neurological impairment, and a lack of mental retardation in the family as well as perseveration, hyperactivity, emotional lability, perceptual disorders such as figure-ground distortion, and conceptual disorders. Strauss later hypothesized that children could be diagnosed as brain injured on the basis of behavior alone without hard evidence of biological signs. The importance of these characteristics was apparent to those working with children having severe difficulty learning to read. His work offered an alternate evaluation of children who previously had been viewed as lazy, stupid, emotionally disturbed, or badly behaved, and who often had been excluded from the public schools because of the seriousness of their problems.

Because of resistance to the term "brain injured" and because of lack of scientific evidence of lesions, other terms were proposed. The two most frequently used were the "Strauss Syndrome" and "minimal brain dysfunction" until, in 1963, the term "learning disabilities" was suggested by Samuel Kirk as an umbrella concept that encompassed diverse types of disorders that impaired learning without an identification of the specific area of difficulty. Its focus on the learning process rather than the causes of the disability was readily accepted, for in the reality of teaching the student, education often begins where medicine stops.

Efforts to structure a school environment in which we can provide effective reading instruction for students with learning disabilities have moved ahead through the cooperation of professionals in a number of overlapping fields. Studies of normal language acquisition, the structure of language, and the assessment and teaching of children with language disorders have been valuable because learning to read requires competence in the use of language, an area that is problematic for children with learning disabilities (Sawyer, 1992). Psychologists have contributed to our understanding of the psychodynamic consequences of reading and learning disabilities by observing, evaluating, and describing behavior. Additional contributions reflective of their various disciplines have been made by neuropsychologists, clinical psychologists, social workers, guidance counselors, occupational therapists, optometrists, and audiologists. Parents have furthered our understanding based on their observations of their children's efforts to learn about their environment from the earliest years. They have provided a richness of information that cannot be duplicated in the school setting. This interdisciplinary nature of the field of learning disabilities has contributed to its resourcefulness and productivity while also providing an explanation of some of the differences of opinion as to the most effective ways to teach these children to become active, comprehending readers.

By the end of the 1980's, the field of learning disabilities had become a recognized discipline in the United States and instruction was under way. With legislation that established and funded programs, teachers were trained and classes begun. Initially most classes were at the elementary school level and were self-contained, but later, programs were expanded to include secondary school students. Many poor readers who previously had been instructed through "remedial reading" programs were now identified and instructed as learning disabled.

An Historical Interlude: Remediating Process Deficits

During the 1960's and 1970's researchers and teachers made extensive efforts to diagnose and remediate the underlying auditory and visual perceptual processes considered so important in acquiring beginning reading skills. These efforts were based on the developmental premise that specific abilities provide the foundation for learning and that remediation of deficits in these areas should be the starting point of instruction. Because often these neurologically based processes are inadequately developed in children with learning disabilities, their potential impact on reading was of great interest.

It is difficult to distinguish between the specific processing functions of the perceptual and motor systems, so instructional methods associated with remediating these abilities overlap. Often they are described collectively as process training, perceptual training, or perceptual-motor training programs.

Tests were designed to isolate deficits in specific processes so that these deficits could be employed as the basis of educational planning (e.g., the *Illinois Test of Psycholinguistic Abilities* and the *Developmental Test of Visual Perception*).

Instructional programs for remediation followed, based on the assumption that we should remediate the underlying "ability" before providing instruction to build the desired "skill" such as reading.

These efforts in perceptual remediation were not successful. A number of researchers have reviewed the extensive evidence indicating the ineffectiveness of most process training. Casbergue and Greene (1988) examined the history of research investigating sensory perceptual screening and training programs designed to help the child with learning disabilities to become a proficient reader. The results were "overwhelmingly negative" (p. 201). The Board of Trustees of the Council for Learning Disabilities (1987) is representative of the many groups opposing "the measurement and training of perceptual and perceptual-motor functions as a part of learning disabilities services" (p. 350) because of evidence of its ineffectiveness. In a meta-analysis of 180 research studies of perceptual-motor training and 39 studies of modality training, Kavale (1990a) found that there were *no* benefits for perceptual motor training and modality training, and "they can rightly be judged in an all-or-nothing manner" (p. 883). Finally, Salvia and Ysseldyke (1991) concluded that instruction should not be differentiated on the basis of diagnostic strengths and weaknesses in process areas.

Why this approach has been so unproductive? Casbergue and Greene (1988) suggest that the reason underlying this failure may be that sensory and perceptual training programs train the eyes, not the brain, and are therefore insufficient. As we will see, reading is ultimately a thinking process, one relying particularly on competence in cognitive and linguistic tasks. The process approach based on perceptual remediation misses the critical point here.

Notions related to perceptual difficulties and reading have persisted with great strength, despite the evidence that training programs are ineffective. For instance, perceptual deficits have been viewed as responsible for letter reversals which, in turn, have been cited as an indicator of a learning disability (Mather

& Kirk, 1985). However, programs that focus on visual perception have not been productive in remediating reversals (Bigsby, 1985). In the area of auditory processing and auditory-visual integration, there is conflicting evidence regarding the characteristics of students with learning disabilities (Wood, Buckhalt, & Tomlin, 1988; Zivian & Samuels, 1986). However, programs to change children's abilities in these areas have been ineffective also (Kershner et al., 1990). Linked to perceptual difficulties is the issue of modality preference, the innate reliance on either the auditory or visual modality for processing information. Once again the research findings reveal the failure of programs such as those developed from Kirk's *Illinois Test of Psycholinguistic Abilities*, programs based on the assumption that we are able to train psycholinguistic abilities (Mather & Kirk, 1985).

Unfortunately, process training still is used by "uninformed teachers" (Casbergue & Greene, 1988, p. 197). Mercer (1992) has suggested that it is "likely that the persistence of these methods is due to the inability of individuals and programs to change" (p. 274). Given the widespread reporting of the research findings that document its failure, this is difficult to condone. Kavale (1990a) proposes that motor and modality training "reveal a stubborn resistance because of the seductive statements found in clinical reports. When conjoined with their intuitive appeal and historical foundation, they remain as established practices in special education" (p. 883).

Worse yet, this process training is harmful because it takes the time and effort of the learner. The harm is compounded because children with learning disabilities have been expected to master sensory/perceptual training before reading instruction is begun; in short, the child is not learning to read and falls progressively further behind.

The lack of research support for remediating perceptual processes does not imply that specific abilities of this type may not be significant in the overall development of the child and in learning to read. Currently, research in neuropsychology seeks to understand more about these processes and how they affect learning. It is indeed possible that findings may some day provide answers, but they have not yet been operationalized to enable psychologists to develop associated theory or educators to develop instructional programs (Swanson, 1987).

We must also recognize that even if we could train an underlying perceptual ability, "fixing" one piece of the learning puzzle does not address the intricacies of the total process of learning to read. Successful reading involves the integration of many skills and strategies, a complex accomplishment for us all. For a more complete historical account, excellent sources are available (Hammill, 1993; Moats & Lyon, 1993).

DEFINING LEARNING DISABILITIES

Since the nature of the student population we are teaching is of obvious importance, we will explore what is meant when a student is referred to as "learning disabled." In order to provide a structure for thinking about different interpretations of the term "learning disabilities," we will explore the issue from several perspectives: a traditional definition and a proposed definition, as well as the problems inherent in each. To illustrate these perspectives, we will look at a recent interchange between experts in the fields of reading and learning disabilities about the difficulties of defining learning disabilities.

Traditional Views

The term "learning disabilities" was proposed in 1963 at a meeting of parents and educators representing small, diverse organizations that came together to attempt to be more effective in promoting the interests of their children. The labels in use at the time included "brain injured," "neurologically impaired," and "perceptually handicapped," to name only a few. The term "learning disabilities" was accepted unanimously as a designation of these children, and the participating groups united to form the Association of Children with Learning Disabilities (ACLD), recently renamed the Learning Disabilities Association (LDA).

Agreeing on a definition of learning disabilities has proved to be a more formidable challenge than agreeing on the term itself (Morrison, MacMillan, & Kavale, 1985; Shepherd, 1988). The federal definition, incorporated in Public Law 101-476, *Individuals with Disabilities Education Act* or IDEA (1990), is the most widely accepted. It mandates requirements for federal funding for educational programs. In a number of states, the federal definition has been expanded to specify more explicitly the identification procedures (Frankenberger & Fronzaglio, 1991).

This IDEA definition consists of two parts. The first part, which became effective in 1975 under Public Law 94-142 and was adopted from a National Advisory Committee for the Handicapped report to Congress (1968), reads:

> The term "children with specific learning disabilities" means those children who have a disorder in one or more of the basic psychological processes involved in understanding or in using language, spoken or written, which disorder may manifest itself in imperfect ability to listen, think, speak, read, write, spell, or do mathematical calculations. Such disorders include such conditions as perceptual handicaps, brain injury, minimal brain dysfunction, dyslexia, and developmental aphasia. Such term does not include children who have learning problems which are primarily the result of visual, hearing, or motor handicaps, of mental retardation, of emotional disturbance, or an environmental, cultural, or economic disadvantage.

The second part, which is considered operational, first appeared in a separate set of regulations for children with learning disabilities (U.S. Office of Education, December 29,

1977). It contains two required components that determine whether a student has a specific learning disability. First, the student does not achieve at the proper age and ability levels in one or more of several specific areas when provided with appropriate learning experiences; and second, the student has a severe discrepancy between achievement and intellectual ability in one or more of the following areas: oral expression, listening comprehension, written expression, basic reading skill, reading comprehension, mathematics calculation, and mathematics reasoning.

The *lifelong* nature of learning disabilities has been emphasized by the change in title of the federal law from the Education for all Handicapped Children Act of 1975 to the Individuals with Disabilities Education Act (1990). This change in title highlighted "individuals" instead of "children" and "disabilities" instead of "handicaps."

We have come to realize that learning disabilities are not outgrown, as was once assumed, but remain in individuals as adults despite the compensations they have learned to make (Chall, 1987; Hughes & Smith, 1990; Ingram & Dettenmaier, 1987; Rogers, 1991; Ross & Smith, 1990; Wong, 1991a). In adulthood continuing problems often cause serious difficulties in vocational adjustments (Lerner, 1993). For instance, as the needs of employers change and there are fewer jobs for blue-collar workers, young people need greater competence in reading and other literacy skills in order to compete in the job market and take their places in the adult world. The continuing difficulties that many with learning disabilities experience suggests that literacy instruction needs to be provided for all age groups rather than just for school-age individuals with learning disabilities. This information is especially important for those delivering instruction because in the past, literacy instruction has often been stopped prematurely.

Other definitions have been proposed over the years; however, none has gained full acceptance. On the whole they reflect changes in emphasis or wording rather than substantive alterations. Each of these proposed definitions presumes that the individual with a learning disability has difficulty in learning because of a disorder in one or more of the basic psychological processes such as those listed in the federal definition, processes that are inherent in the individual. This assumption is generally accepted in the field (Shinn, Tindal, Spira, & Marston, 1987) and by the public (Simmons & Kameenui, 1986). We will review the important ways in which other proposed definitions differ from the federal definition in order to see how these differences would affect our thinking as teachers helping students with learning disabilities to acquire literacy.

First, the heterogeneity of the behaviors and characteristics of individuals with learning disabilities was specifically delineated by the definition proposed by the National Joint Committee on Learning Disabilities (NJCLD). Additionally, it has been investigated through extensive interviews with adults with learning disabilities (Reiff, Gerber, & Ginsberg, 1993). The heterogeneity of this classification of student is accepted by both researchers and practitioners in the field today.

Second, the inclusion of social skills deficits in the definition had been proposed earlier by the Interagency Committee on Learning Disabilities. After considerable discussion, social skills were not added as a category to the federal definition (IDEA) in 1990 because many felt that although a social skills deficit is characteristic of a number of students with learning disabilities, it is probably a result of the learning disability rather than an inherent disability itself.

Finally, we have recognized that a learning disability can occur concomitantly with other handicapping conditions. Attention deficit disorder (ADD) was finally recognized as a disability under the IDEA in a Policy Memorandum issued by the U.S. Department of Education on September 16, 1991. This memorandum specifically recognized these students as eligible for special education services if their educational performance or learning is impaired. The memorandum was accepted as the alternative to including ADD as a type of specific learning disability as had been proposed. Students with ADD can meet the criteria for eligibility under existing categories of IDEA such as learning disabilities or emotional disturbances, or, if ADD is the primary disability, students are eligible for special education under the category "Other Health Impaired" (Education for the Handicapped Act, 1991). In addition, children with ADD can be taught in regular classrooms under Section 504 of the Rehabilitation Act of 1973, which covers a broader range of individuals with disabilities than the IDEA. The appropriate category for classification and the type of educational services to be provided are determined by unique characteristics of the child needing special instruction (Lerner & Lowenthal, 1989).

Common elements in all of these definitions drawn from the federal legislation and the proposals of the major professional organizations and committees include neurological dysfunction, an uneven growth pattern, difficulty in school-related learning and academic tasks, a discrepancy between achievement and potential, and the exclusion of other causes. Additionally, it has become apparent that differing definitions proposed by a variety of organizations over the years have influenced both the implied and specific changes in recent legislation.

Another View

At the other end of the continuum is the view of learning disabilities that considers learning disabilities from the interactive, holistic perspective of the child and the learning process. This view moves us into the camp of the social constructionists as illustrated by Coles. Coles, a psychiatrist and education critic, proposed an interactive theory of learning disabilities in 1987. He suggested that "complex individual attributes and social interrelationships are the starting point of many learning disabilities" (p. 136). These include "learned academic and problem solving abilities, various prior experiences, interest, motivation, emotions, self-confidence, and attitudes; other powerful 'external' influences include teachers' ability, the dynamics of instructional interrelationships, and organization and construction of a test situation" (p. 136). Coles moves outside the classroom setting and includes the family and the interactions " in which learning failure is created" (p. 209). Here the condition of learning disabilities is not intrinsic to the individual and is not the result of a central nervous system dysfunction but instead is related to a complex of variables arising from the interaction of the individual and his environment (O'Shea & O'Shea, 1990).

A common element of these various definitions is that none of them provides consistent, objective criteria to be used in identifying children with learning disabilities. There is little question but that the development of a valid, theory-driven definition and classification system is a pressing goal (Lyon, Gray, Kavanaugh, & Krasnegor, 1993; Torgesen, 1994). Despite lack of agreement on a definition and on criteria for identifying children who meet that definition, legislation was passed and programs begun. Because learning disabilities became a recognized field so recently and because of the urgency of the agendas of the coordinated advocacy groups, instruction was under way before sufficient research had been completed to document the discriminant characteristics, the causes, and the assessment measures to be employed in identifying who is and who is not learning disabled (Moats & Lyon, 1993).

Problems of Definition

One inherent problem in agreeing on a definition of learning disabilities has been that different definitions serve different purposes. The needs of educational service providers, advocacy groups, and researchers are often in conflict, which is reflected in their varying definitions of learning disabilities. As Stanovich (1992) noted, school personnel need a definition that will obtain special services for low achieving students. However, parents' groups desire a definition that will serve as an advocacy tool to produce legislation and resources that they believe will benefit their children. Finally, researchers require a highly restrictive definition to clarify the variables under examination (Council for Learning Disabilities, Research Committee, 1993). Narrow definitions are often resisted by school personnel who want a broad definition of learning disabilities in order to facilitate services for students at risk of school failure.

Researchers have called for more stringent and comprehensive standards for defining subjects participating in research so that results can be compared across studies. Moats and Lyon (1993) point out that valid assessment practices are important in order to enable studies to be replicated in different settings. Much of the current research is conducted using "school-identified" or "clinic-referred" samples of students with learning disabilities; unfortunately, however, there is a lack of consistency in the identification procedures employed. Without comparable subjects, we end up with a conglomerate of interesting but isolated results from which we cannot generalize validated procedures for defining and identifying students with learning disabilities or for teaching these students to read.

Identification Criteria

It is not just researchers who need clear, reliable criteria for deciding who is and is not learning disabled. Explicit identification procedures are just as important to students, their families, and their teachers. One component of the discussion has centered on the mandate in federal legislation that identification be contingent on demonstrating a "severe discrepancy between achievement and intellectual ability" (U.S. Office of Education, December 29, 1977). The importance of the discrepancy concept in teaching children to read is that it implies that the child has greater ability than he/she has utilized, and thus the child has considerable potential for improvement. While a "severe" discrepancy is required, none of the federal legislation specifies what constitutes "severe." In addition, technical inadequacies of some tests used pose an additional problem (Catts, 1989; Phillips & Clarizio, 1988). Catts (1989) noted that IQ can be "affected directly by the cognitive deficit(s) that underlies readings problems . . . [and] can also be influenced indirectly by the lower reading achievement and experience that may result from this deficit" (pp. 52-53). However, "Correlation between IQ and reading achievement is not nearly as strong as might be expected" (p. 52).

Opinions differ. Some, for example, Algozzine and Ysseldyke (1988), argue that there is nothing to support the use of a discrepancy measure for classification purposes. They note that discrepancies often are used to limit the number of students who receive special education because the numbers make difficult human decisions more acceptable. Experts such as Furlong (1988) would agree.

In contrast, Kavale (1987) states that demonstrating a discrepancy is a necessary but not sufficient criterion in identifying a learning disability, even though the discrepancy concept is difficult to validate theoretically. He suggests that cognitive, linguistic, and social factors also should be considered. In a further refinement, Braden and Weiss (1988) suggest that regression methods of determining a discrepancy between IQ and achievement are superior to simple difference methods for determining a discrepancy for learning disability eligibility. Regression analysis is concerned with showing the relationship between variables in order to make inferences from a sample. Braden and Weiss also pointed out that regression criteria are more likely to produce proportionate ethnic composition in discrepant and nondiscrepant groups, an important political consideration.

Some have proposed using teachers' referral decisions to replace IQ in estimating the ability of students (Shinn et al., 1987; Shinn, Ysseldyke, Deno, & Tindal, 1986). Others have proposed modifications relating to these issues in the current assessment procedures. Berninger, Hart, Abbott, & Karovsky

(1992) suggested a practical two-stage assessment model in which classroom teachers first identify children who are low-functioning in beginning reading skills and then provide early intervention. In the second stage, IQ would be used as a part of a more comprehensive psychoeducational assessment for children whose problems persisted. A proposal that identification be based on "treatment-resisting" versus "treatment responding" children was discussed extensively by Berninger and Abbott (1992). Such proposals place increased focus on the interaction of the individual, the task, and the instructional setting and, at the same time, suggest a view of reading that reflects an interactive model.

These questions of how children with learning disabilities are identified are of great importance to the teacher providing reading instruction. For instance, faced with a child who is struggling to read, the teacher might wonder whether the child possesses at least average ability but with the classical neurological impairments that have been traditionally associated with learning disabilities (Silver & Hagin, 1990) or whether the child is having difficulty for other reasons. The range of current definitions suggests that there may be one or more of a variety of reasons for the difficulty. Many researchers and practitioners believe that understanding more about the learner can facilitate planning instruction that will allow the most effective interaction between the learner and all components of the instructional environment.

An Application to Reading

Because we lack empirical evidence that the present assessment instruments reliably identify which students are learning disabled, discussion of whether students with learning disabilities are really different from other low-achieving readers has been widespread (Coles, 1987; German, Johnson, & Schneider, 1985; Lyon, 1985; Shinn et al., 1987; Shinn et al., 1986; Speece, 1987). It should also be noted that an important reason for this concern is rooted in the legal mandates for funding special instruction for children classified as learning disabled, funding that all children having difficulty learning to read might share. The extent of our difficulty in specifying who is or is not a learning disabled reader is exemplified in Stanovich's (1991; 1992) exchange with Christensen (1992). In an article in *Reading Research Quarterly* (1991), Stanovich pointed out that it has not yet been demonstrated that dyslexic and learning disabled readers function differently from "garden-variety" poor readers who are reading at the same level, that they have a different educational prognosis, or that they respond differently to specific types of instruction. He noted that both types of readers demonstrate a core deficiency in phonological awareness. He also suggested that if a discrepancy measure were needed, employing a measure of listening comprehension instead of IQ might be more relevant to reading.

In response, Christensen (1992) wrote that given the similarity in performance of poor readers in general, we should invest our resources in developing and providing more effective instructional programs for all children experiencing reading difficulties rather than continuing the search to identify a subgroup of neurologically impaired readers. If Christensen's argument were to gain acceptance, there would be considerable implications for the funding of educational research.

Stanovich (1992), in turn, rejoined that sufficient data exists to justify the search for a "cognitively and neurologically distinct subgroup of poor readers" (p.279). He stated that the need to provide effective instruction is not the determinant of whether we should seek scientific advances in the field. In addition, he suggested that many resist neurological explanations because, as Coles (1987) noted, they may be mistakenly seen as specifying causation. Stanovich further explained this by stating that "brain differences may exist that cause processing variations of the type that are related to school and academic behavior, but the contexts in which the differential behavior outcomes occur can have enormous consequences for children" (p.280). For this reason, a neurological difference would not be interpreted as full causation for a severe reading problem; however, environmental influences do not negate the importance of neurological and information processing analyses. Stanovich and Christensen's interchange illustrates the difficulty of achieving consensus on a definition of learning disabilities, which, to be operative, must specify how learning disabled students are to be identified.

The likely impact of theoretical discussions such as these on reading instruction is considerable. An ever-present concern is implications for the concentration of future funding. In the minds of many teachers, the issue is not defining the learning disability but instructing the child. An immediate issue raised by this discussion is whether all poor readers should be taught the same way. These questions have been raised, not answered. However, they are issues which will continue to come up in the future.

CAUSES OF LEARNING DISABILITIES

The lack of agreement on a definition of the term "learning disabilities" in turn confounds discussion of causes, for, obviously, people cannot agree on the causes of a phenomenon if they cannot agree on what it is. Nonetheless, discuss them we will, for teachers are concerned about why some of their students are having difficulty learning to read. For purposes of clarity, we will group the contributing causes of learning disabilities into "intrinsic" and "extrinsic" as we consider them.

Intrinsic Factors

Traditionally we have assumed that learning disabilities are intrinsic to the learner and may be genetic (Healy & Aram, 1986). At the least, it is widely agreed that a number of these children display evidence of defects of the central nervous system (Mercer, 1992). This is important for teachers of students with learning disabilities, for as Lerner (1993) reminds us: "Learning is a neurological process that occurs within the brain. All learning involves the central nervous system, hence a dysfunction in that system can seriously impair the processes of learning" (p. 216). It is interesting to note that in reviewing articles written for non-educators about learning disabilities, Simmons and Kameenui (1986) found that "among the most durable and frequently reported conceptions of learning disabilities is the assumption that the source of a learning disability resides within the individual and is the result of a neurophysiological disorder" (p. 311).

The results of recent medical research in genetics and neurology have documented the importance of the inherent characteristics of the individual on learning. We recognize that establishing the intrinsic, biological cause of a learning disability does not provide sufficient direction for instruction. Nonetheless, these findings will affect teachers' attitudes towards children struggling to learn and the effects of frequent failure on children's behavior. Good teachers are generally concerned about why a child is not learning. If the cause appears to be obstinacy, one type of instructional approach may be advisable. On the other hand, if the cause appears to be that the child has inherent difficulty mastering the reading, another may be more effective. For instance, the teacher might vary the text presented, base the method of presentation on how the child appears to learn best, provide understanding and support, and lengthen the time allowed. Research findings can potentially clarify why some children may, indeed, learn differently from other children and why they may require individualized instruction.

Recent research is beginning to shed more light on intrinsic causes of learning disabilities. Genetic differences occur in two ways, through heredity and accidentally during early gestation.

Both types of genetic differences can affect neurological development.

In an extensive review of current literature, Silver (1994) states that, "the academic difficulties seen in children with specific learning disabilities represent only the tip of the proverbial iceberg, the visual peak emerging from a series of underlying hierarchal dysfunctions" (p. 187). This abnormality in central nervous processing can make the acquisition of reading, even speaking and listening, difficult. Silver surveys the results of studies utilizing computerized tomography (CT) scans, electroencephalograms (EEG), Brain Electrical Area Mapping (BEAM), and positive emission tomography (PET) scans. He also summarizes convincing evidence that the causes of specific reading disability are probably inherited, although the exact locations and nature of which genes are involved are still unknown. Much of this evidence springs from family and twin studies (DeFries, Olson, Pennington, & Smith, 1991). Silver concludes that "educational techniques for effective remediation of a child with [a] specific learning disability may depend upon the pattern of his/her unique pattern of disabilities and abilities" (p. 206-207).

As Silver implies, these medical investigations focus on intrinsic causes of learning disabilities are, in turn, related to research on the education of children with inherent learning difficulties. The educational studies are perhaps more directly helpful to those of us engaged in teaching children with learning disabilities to read.

In recent years major funding for basic research on effective reading instruction for these children has been provided under the National Institutes of Child Health and Human Development (NICHD). Results of research funded by NICHD under the program projects and the Learning Disability Research Centers at Yale University, Johns Hopkins University, and University of Colorado were summarized by Lyon (1991). Three findings shed light on the extent to which characteristics inherent in the individual, as opposed to the environment, underlie learning and reading disabilities. First, phonological coding deficits, a widely recognized constraint on the development of early reading skills, are significantly heritable. Second, deficits in phonological processing appear to be caused by atypical organization of the left hemisphere regions (usually involved in speech and language) of the brain. Finally, studies of visual and perceptual systems suggest that spatial and temporal information is processed less efficiently by disabled readers than by good readers. These psychoneurological explanations of learning and reading disorders may seem abstract to practitioners who have tried to apply them to teaching the children.

How have medical findings related to the causes of learning disabilities been implemented by teachers in the past? Traditionally teachers have sought to identify and remediate areas of deficit within the individual child. One way this "medical model" has been applied is to identify and therefore provide instruction on hierarchies of skills needed by students in order to become good readers, i.e., to progress to higher-level skills. Beginning reading often has been viewed as a "bottom-up" operation in which individual skills are learned, building on previously mastered skills. The philosophy underlying this instructional approach is one of looking for strengths and weaknesses, teaching to the former and remediating the latter. A student whose difficulty in focusing and maintaining attention is affecting progress in reading might be taught self-monitoring metacognitive strategies to help compensate for the attentional difficulty, then taught to apply the strategies to the task at hand. In both systems the intrinsic deficit within the child is acknowledged, but the remediation program recognizes and includes the cognitive and metacognitive aspects of learning to read.

In general, the intrinsic causes of a learning disability do not prevent learning; rather, they suggest the need for individualizing instruction. For instance, a student who has particular difficulty with reasoning skills can benefit from instruction. In fact, identifying the difficulty with reasoning skills may form the basis for understanding the student's failure in content areas. Today students with learning disabilities are less likely to be viewed as dumb, obstinate or lazy, which undoubtedly increases the teacher's instructional effectiveness with these students (Lerner, 1993).

Extrinsic Factors

Other theories of the causes of learning disabilities have been advanced in recent years. In general, they incorporate the notion that there may be neuropsychological differences that affect learning, but they extend that explanation to specifically include developmental and environmental factors as well. The basis of this argument is the notion that developmental and environmental factors affect academic achievement and should be viewed as contributing causes to academic failure. Even in the mid-1980's, Mather and Kirk (1985) reminded us that although children's "developmental learning disabilities are integrally related to academic learning disabilities . . . a unitary factor will not account for all disabilities" (p. 61). In a similar vein, Lipson and Wixson (1986) wrote that "research on reading disability needs to . . . move away from the search for causative factors within the reader and toward the specification of the conditions under which different readers can and will learn" (p. 129). They note that although the knowledge and skill possessed by the individual are critical components of the interactive process, we need additional information in order to teach the child.

The term environmental factors is usually interpreted to include the child's total environment. The effect of the home environment on educational outcomes, including such factors as socioeconomic status (Morrison & Hinshaw, 1988) and parents' education (Melekian, 1990) is being studied more widely. Recent emphasis on the role of extrinsic factors as a determinant of individuals' ability to cope with inherent learning disabilities is a reminder that the school environment also may be viewed as a contributing cause. A recent interpretation of the data from the Carolina Longitudinal Learning Disabilities Project that followed children with learning disabilities from ages six to eleven illustrated the importance of educational experience as a risk factor that affects the relationship between characteristics inherent in the child and academic outcomes (McKinney, Osborne, & Schulte, 1993).

Along a different line, NICHD studies reported by Lyon (1991) revealed that orthographic (non-phonetic whole word recognition) deficits in early reading skills do not appear to be the result of intrinsic causes but the result of ineffective education. This is significant information for teachers who need to know that difficulties in this area will probably yield to instruction.

These environmental factors are important for us to consider, for the extent to which schools' expectations incorporate goals appropriate for a wide range of children and the extent to which teachers provide appropriate and supportive learning situations impact both educational and personal outcomes for students. Examination of the interaction between the characteristics of the learner and the characteristics of the learning environment forms a basis for understanding the ways in which developmental and environmental factors can contribute to success or failure in the academic situation. The text or task required of the student is certainly an important part of the learning environment. From the point of view of teachers, the addition of environmental factors may offer a useful explanation of learning disabilities because of the implied focus on what happens in the classroom.

Each of these explanations of the causes of learning disabilities, the "medical" and the "environmental," represents a generalization and takes on different aspects according to the practitioner. In reality, we can think of them as representing a continuum, with the views of most people being located along that line. Once again, we note the interrelationship between how one defines a learning disability and the causes to which the learning disability is attributed.

Some in the field believe that the underlying causes of difficulty in learning to read make no difference if they cannot be applied directly to planning instruction. Others, however, believe that the way in which one explains why a child is not learning influences the way the child is viewed and is treated, both at school and at home (Gelzheiser, 1987). When the major responsibility for the difficulty is placed on the individual rather than being shared with those structuring the learning environment, the child is viewed as "the problem." These assumptions affect learning to read because of the attitudes they engender in both the student and the teacher, attitudes that influence educational outcomes.

A better understanding of the ways in which factors that constitute risk interrelate with those that are protective of the individual and create resilience is important in identifying the causes of learning disabilities as well as in planning instruction for these students (Keough & Weisner, 1993; Spekman, Goldberg, & Herman, 1993; Spekman, Herman, & Vogel, 1993). One of the lessons learned from the Kauai Longitudinal Study was that protective buffers and mechanisms within that society had greatly influenced the lives of vulnerable children and youth. Most children were found to have made a good adjustment to adult life, earning a living and becoming a part of the social community. They, indeed, had succeeded against the odds (Werner, 1993). This exemplifies the extent to which the context in which the child lives and learns can be a determinant of personal and academic outcomes.

In summary, the lack of a research base providing consensus for defining learning disabilities and specifying identification and instructional practices drives current research, discussion, and disagreement within the field. Given the newness of the study of learning disabilities as a recognized discipline, it is to be expected that much remains to be investigated. While many acknowledge that the umbrella term "learning disabilities" is useful in practice, others question the advisability of the current political system of classification for funding purposes. Nevertheless, there *does* appear to be a group of children who, without apparent inherent reasons, fail to prosper in school and generally fit the federal definition of "learning disabled." It is to the education of these children, particularly in the area of reading, that this book is addressed.

PREVALENCE OF LEARNING DISABILITIES

The majority of students with learning disabilities have been identified because they failed to learn to read; therefore, estimates of the prevalence of learning disabilities are of particular interest to people concerned with the teaching of reading. Estimates of the true number of children with learning disabilities vary depending on the criteria employed to determine eligibility; the less stringent the criteria, the higher the prevalence.

We do, however, have accurate numbers of children receiving special education services. Since 1977, with the implementation of P.L. 94-142, the number of students who are classified and are receiving services has been published annually. According to the U.S. Department of Education (1992), 2,144,377 students were receiving services as learning disabled in the 1990-91 school year. In addition, the percent of students in the total school population classified as learning disabled increased from 1.2% in 1976-77 to 3.6% in 1989-90. Finally, the relative proportion of students classified within special education as learning disabled has increased from 24.9% in 1976-77 to 50.5% in 1990-91.

The implications of such numbers are considerable. Depending on one's perspective, the increase may be perceived as a responsibility of the schools to provide effective instruction to all children and the right of each child to receive effective instruction (Shinn et al., 1986) or as an expensive burden on the taxpayer (Shinn et al., 1987). The perspective taken frequently reflects the self-interest of the speaker.

What are the reasons for this increase? Three explanations seem to be likely. Part of the increase probably is due to the newness of the field. The growing recognition by professionals and parents both of the nature of learning disabilities and of more appropriate interventions for these students appears to have led to the increased identification of a number of students who were not previously provided services.

On the other hand, another reason appears to be misidentification. Legislation guaranteeing special educational programs to children classified as "handicapped" or "disabled" has required significant investment of educational monies, and other sources of funding for children who are having difficulties in school have dried up. The need to provide services for these children has led to the classification of some youngsters as "learning disabled" who would not have been so identified in the past.

Additionally, social/cultural changes in society place many children at increasing risk of learning disorders. There is a growing body of literature that links substance abuse in pregnant women to developmental disabilities in their offspring. Changes in family structure, poverty, and the increase in working mothers also are cited as catalysts for developmental disabilities because these social/cultural changes may lead to insufficient support for children who are experiencing difficulty in school. The crux of these arguments is that either an increase in central nervous system dysfunction or a decrease in social support can cause a higher prevalence of "learning disabilities" and that the combination of both of these factors can be especially powerful (Hallahan, 1992).

As we have seen, "learning disabled" is a rather new designation for some students who are having difficulty in school. Although there is disagreement within the field as to the most accurate definition of learning disabilities and as to specific causes of all types of learning disabilities, larger numbers of students with learning disabilities are being identified and schools are now charged with providing individualized educational programs for these students. Next, we will examine some of the characteristics of students with learning disabilities that contribute to difficulties in acquiring literacy, the settings in which instruction is provided, likely educational outcomes for these pupils, and emerging research directions that will influence both funding and reading instruction.

CHARACTERISTICS THAT AFFECT ACQUISITION AND USE OF LITERACY

The characteristics of children with learning disabilities influence their ability to develop an effective reading system. Understanding these characteristics is key to probing the difficulties these students may encounter when acquiring and using literacy. Reading is a complex linguistic and cognitive task that requires negotiation on the part of each reader. Each reader needs to develop skills and strategies that work for him or her, that enable that reader to read and comprehend text. The methods a child employs to combine knowledge of content and metacognitive strategy usage in order to understand the literal and figurative meaning of text form his or her reading system. This need not be a process that the child can readily describe or one that is readily apparent to the teacher. The recognition of a reading system acknowledges that the child attempts to use available methods to decode and comprehend. It is the efficiency and effectiveness of this system that determines the child's degree of success in reading.

A wide range of characteristics are associated with the category "learning disabilities" that can affect the development and use of a reading system. Because of this range of characteristics, there is no absolute agreement on *why* children with learning disabilities have difficulty learning to read (Spear and Sternberg, 1987). We know, however, that they do have difficulty in this area. Mercer (1992) writes that "85% to 90% of all students with learning disabilities have reading problems" (p. 496). Although the term "learning disabilities" encompasses a rather broad cluster of learning and behavioral problems, no child considered learning disabled would be expected to have all of these characteristics. Some researchers have reported that the differences in performance between learning disabled and behaviorally disordered students are trivial (Scruggs & Mastropieri, 1986a). Inherent neurological processing differences underlie many problems in learning. These intrinsic problems are compounded by difficulties interacting with and learning from the environment, difficulties that are typical of many children with learning disabilities. In addition, it is clear that a number of children are raised in environments that are directly harmful to their growth and education, extrinsic factors that are difficult for all individuals to survive.

Children with learning disabilities are *not* a homogeneous group. Therefore, we can not assume that problems that arise in one cluster of children examined in research are also common to another, despite similar categorization (Shafrir, Siegel, & Chee, 1990; Spear & Sternberg, 1987). This reality makes our task much more difficult and requires that we examine a range of characteristics. We will consider those characteristics of learning disabilities that most directly affect acquiring literacy, for this information provides a background for examining instructional strategies for teaching these students to become competent readers. Specific characteristics that we will look at include language, cognition, and social behavior. Although they are not specific to a learning disability, we will also explore learned helplessness and attention deficit/hyperactivity because they often complicate these children's learning.

Some characteristics are more likely to be displayed at certain age levels. For instance, a language disorder may take the form of delayed speech in the young child, a reading disorder in the primary grades, and a comprehension and writing disorder in the upper grades. Preschool children showing signs of difficulty are typically referred to as being "at risk" rather than "learning disabled," for the federal definition of learning disabilities centers on failure to acquire academic skills in school. Frequently this difficulty in acquiring academic skills first becomes apparent when the child is trying to learn to read. As these children move into the middle and high school years, the cumulative lack of information that results from poor reading comprehension can, in turn, bring about failure to master subject areas. These students experience frequent academic failures over long periods of time and across a variety of tasks and teachers. The further behind the student falls, the more frustration and failure are experienced. As a result, accelerating lack of confidence may lessen the willingness of the student to take the risks involved in engaging in learning (Stanovich, 1988). Thus difficulties in mastering reading skills at the appropriate time can underlie later manifestations of learning disabilities. The interactions are complex and they differ greatly in individuals, but each of these characteristics affects the student's progress toward becoming a good reader.

Language

Language is a means of communication; it is integral to thinking and reasoning; and it is a medium through which information is taught and acquired. There is no question but that a long-term relationship exists between language and academic success because language forms the basis for questioning, clarifying, and reducing ambiguity.

Language problems are extremely important factors underlying the difficulties that many students with learning disabilities experience in the course of learning beginning reading skills. These problems encompass the entire spectrum of communication and verbal behavior, including delayed speech; disorders of vocabulary, word meanings, or concept formations;

the misapplication of the rules of grammar and syntax; and poor language comprehension. Often children with learning disabilities are initially identified because of their limited competence in language (Feagans & Short, 1986; Lerner, 1993). Research studies examined aspects of underlying language problems and established that:

- children with learning disabilities demonstrated "consistent and pervasive pragmatic deficits in conversation . . . attributable to underlying language deficits" (Lapadat, 1991, p. 147) in a meta-analysis of 33 studies.

- "language deficits were found in 90.5%" of the 242 children (Gibbs & Cooper, 1989).

- children with learning disabilities were less able to recall information and draw inferences from orally presented narratives than non-disabled children (Crais and Chapman, 1987).

- learning-disabled children appeared to have difficulty interpreting verbal and visual metaphors, which play an important role in language development (Lee & Kamhi, 1990).

- children with learning disabilities "often interpret figurative expression literally" (Baechle & Lian, 1990, p. 451).

- these children had difficulty understanding and paraphrasing narratives, which "appears to be a critically important skill for academic functioning for LD children" (Feagans & Appelbaum, 1986, p. 364).

Although severe language disorders of children are readily apparent to adults, mild difficulties that nonetheless complicate learning academic skills may remain unidentified. Teachers often describe children with a mild level of language problem as having difficulty maintaining attention, following directions, and using the right words when speaking.

Before considering applications to reading, we will take a look at the typical sequence of development. Competence in *receptive language* (e.g., listening and observing) appears to be prerequisite for the development of expressive language (speaking). A lack of phonological awareness is one of the most important manifestations of poor receptive language skills. Phonological awareness is the recognition that words are made up of sound elements (phonemes) that represent the sounds of speech. Insensitivity to phoneme sounds underlies many of the difficulties encountered by poor readers and spellers (Cunningham, 1989; Liberman & Liberman, 1990; Lyon & Moats, 1988). Although there is general agreement on the importance of phonemic awareness, details of theory differ. Felton and Brown (1990) report that they found subcategories of phonological processing ability, each of which was important, but that they found no evidence of a general phonological processing ability. They conclude that "different aspects of reading may be predicted by different combinations of phonological processing skills" (p. 57). Lenchner, Gerber, and Routh (1990) report that "phonological awareness is probably necessary for decoding, but it is not sufficient" (p. 246). By this, they mean that there are additional systems that must be in place before the child is ready to read. It is interesting to note that studies with other alphabet-based languages also show a linkage between the importance of phonological awareness and reading (Liberman & Liberman, 1990). From the standpoint of the teacher, phonological training should be provided early in schooling, because these skills can be learned (Hurford et al., 1993).

Children with *expressive language* disorders have difficulty producing spoken language. Children may depend on pointing or gesturing to make their needs known. Sometimes students with underlying expressive language problems who speak in short phrases are not recognized as having a language disorder until they have difficulty learning to read. Receptive and expressive language exerts a powerful influence on all language-based activities, including reading and writing; however, in teaching, difficulties in the language aspects of learning to read have been neglected in comparison to those in the visual aspects of learning to read.

Because language learning appears to be developmental (Jansky, 1986), it is important for teachers to understand that the child with a severe underlying language disorder probably is not ready to learn to read and write. In a meta-analysis of 34 studies, Kavale (1990b) concluded that psycholinguistic training is likely to provide benefits with regard to basic language skill areas. In the classroom, teachers can help children become aware of the sounds of their language (speech) through rhymes and word games (Lerner, 1993). In the past many children have been plunged into reading before the necessary underlying language skills have been developed, despite our realization that children's language skills are positively correlated with reading achievement (Whitmire & Stone, 1991).

Young children with developmental language disorders often continue to encounter problems with language-based activities as adolescents and adults (Kamhi, 1992; Stirling & Miles, 1988). As might be expected, most adolescents with learning disabilities perform better in listening comprehension than in reading comprehension (Wood et al., 1988). Tested on reading and writing, these students achieved "better on skills requiring literal use of text and worse on skills requiring application of basic skills knowledge" (Algozzine, O'Shea, Stoddard, & Crews, 1988, p. 158). The interpretive level, applied comprehension, proved to be considerably more difficult to attain.

Bashir and Scavuzzo (1992) point out that "because of the effects of language on cognitive development during the school years, persistent problems with growth and generalization of learned material pose serious obstacles for children with language disorders" (p. 56). Another way to view this statement is that the acquisition of literate language is circular. If students cannot read well, they will have less exposure to written language, and, in turn, read less well. The problem is further compounded because the less reading that is done, the less information the child acquires in content areas (Snider & Tarver, 1987; Stanovich, 1988). The "ripple effect" of the developmental language disability that underlies many learning disabilities complicates the acquisition of literacy and the broader education in subject areas that are the major objectives of schooling.

A different kind of language/reading difficulty is experienced by students for whom English is a second language. Garcia (1994) writes that over 18.8 million Hispanics live in the continental United States. Eleven million of them report speaking Spanish in the home, and a high percentage of their children have difficulty with English. As we might expect, some of these children with limited proficiency in English also are learning disabled in their primary language. Appropriate assessment of such children requires a special set of skills. Recent studies have shown that if a language disorder exists in the primary language, it will also be reflected in the second language.

For these children to gain reading competence in English requires special skills on the part of the teacher. Carrasquillo (1994) writes: "The students who have been identified as limited English proficient with special needs should receive specialized instructional services that account for their linguistic and cultural characteristics as well as their identified disabilities" (p. 183). A comprehensive discussion of both models of assessment and instruction for the bilingual exceptional child may be found in Baca and Cervantes (1989).

Cognition

Educators and psychologists use the word cognition to refer to the mental processes under the umbrella of "thinking." Thinking is differentiated from other mental processes such as perception, the process of receiving and interpreting messages from sensory input. We see visual images such as the letters that make up words or hear sounds that represent the words of a language (perception). Through thinking (cognition), we translate these perceptions into meaningful forms of communication, written and oral. One who reads efficiently receives the sensory and perceptual stimuli while automatically and simultaneously making sense of these impulses and stimuli. This multiple and integrated processing allows us to think about what we read.

Considerable research and theory have evolved from our desire to examine and understand what cognition means to a child who is learning to read. The child with a learning disability brings to the process of reading multiple variations on the fragmented use of the processes defined above. Such fragmentation of abilities prohibits the child from developing an effective reading system. The acquisition and retention of content and strategy knowledge along with the ability to use this knowledge to decipher, interpret, and construct written messages are compromised. Experts in the field of learning disabilities from a variety of disciplines have examined the areas of neurological status and development. This work initially focused on sensory and perceptual deficiencies. With more questions than answers generated, the investigations spread into the general field of language and cognition.

There has been considerable effort expended in investigating the role of "thinking" in the context of learning disabilities. Traditionally, the focus in this field has been on perception and language; however, there has been increasing recognition of the role that cognitive factors play in the performance of students with learning disabilities (Ellis, 1993a).

Concurrently, the role of cognition has also become a significant issue in the examination of reading instruction (Snyder & Pressley, 1990). First, we will look at the characteristics of students with learning disabilities, and later we will explore the role of cognition in reading.

Cognition is frequently viewed from the perspective of information processing (Ellis, 1993a; Snyder & Pressley, 1990; Swanson & Ransby, 1994). Swanson (1987), for example, defines information processing, the key to cognition, as a series of components: memory, strategies, and the monitoring of these strategies. Speece (1987) describes cognition slightly differently, as including memory, attention, and organization. Both Swanson and Speece link difficulties in information processing to ineffective reading systems for the child identified as learning disabled. Samuels (1987) concurred, attributing low achievement in reading not to deficits in attending but to difficulties in information processing. Stanovich (1988) clearly associates difficulties in cognitive functioning, such as rule learning, memory, and metacognition, with the term learning disabled. Current views also link difficulties in information processing with those in reading for students with learning disabilities but with a particular emphasis on the importance of strategies in the process (Ellis, 1993a).

Two of Swanson's additional concerns (1987) focus on a holistic approach to understanding the problems that confront children with learning disabilities as they attempt to learn to read. For almost a decade in a field that is recognizably still in its youth, investigations have focused on "isolated components and strategies" (p. 5). According to Swanson, this approach misses a critical element, the need to integrate the components. He reminds us that "learning disabilities is not simply a deficiency in a certain cognitive area, but rather represents poor coordination of several mental components and/or cognitive areas involved in information processing" (p. 5).

In addition, Swanson proposes that the notion of learning disabilities requires recognition and understanding of the role of the child's experiences, the context in which learning occurs, and the interaction between these two and the information processing components. This analysis approaches Coles' (1987) view that learning disabilities develop based primarily upon the extrinsic causes described earlier in this text.

Three areas of concern to those investigating the role of cognition in learning disabilities are memory, strategy acquisition and use, and metacognition. These areas reflect an approach (Brown & Campione, 1986; Ellis, 1993a) to learning disabilities which suggests that students need to "exercise self-conscious, deliberate, and strategically applied efforts when learning academic content" (Lyon & Moats, 1988, p. 833).

Memory

Memory refers to the process of storing and recalling information for the short or long term. Short-term memory includes those pieces of information to which we are immediately exposed, for example, the new material in a passage we are reading. Long-term memory reflects our general knowledge base, the content of what we know and the procedures that we use to manipulate this knowledge. For example, when baking a cake, content knowledge tells us what a cake is, what the ingredients are, the essence of "cake." Procedural knowledge reminds us how to make, eat and store this cake.

Memory has often been identified as a problem area for many of children considered learning disabled. Colson and Mehring (1990), reviewing research on memory in students with a learning disability, remind us that there is little agreement on the range of difficulties included in this label. Although the ability to store and recall is often compromised in children labeled learning disabled, the extent and nature of the difficulty will vary widely with individuals. We will examine several possible areas of difficulty related to memory.

The difficulty here may be related to the way the items are organized in memory. Swanson (1986) subscribes to the view that inadequate organization of items in semantic memory plays a part in the reader's difficulties in encoding. Such a reader does not effectively activate a subset of appropriate features for recalling a word (semantic memory). The features may be in memory, but because of inadequate or ineffective organization they are not readily recalled. In a later study, Swanson, Reffel, and Trahan (1991) also found difficulty in the retrieval of items from memory. They suggested that students with learning disabilities be "trained in the organization of memory" (p. 143) and be given cues to aid in retrieval. The issue of organization of information, whether content or features of words, arises repeatedly when instructing a child with learning disabilities. Such a repeatedly arising issue looms as critical in the process of learning and instruction.

Another area of difficulty is the speed of processing of information in memory. Howell and Manis (1986) found that readers labeled learning disabled required more time than other readers to retrieve categorical information from memory. The difficulty did not seem to be one of organizing information but of speed and efficiency in processing information. The work of Stahl and Erickson (1986) also supports the notion that speed of processing, or the lack thereof, has often been associated with children's learning disabilities. In a study of twins, Ho, Gilger, and Decker (1988) found that the reader labeled learning disabled had "deficiencies in rapid processing of symbolic, sequential information" (p. 70).

The difficulty may lie in an overload in memory. Spear and Sternberg (1987), in a review of the research that provides a basis for defining the characteristics of learning disabilities, report that the problem does not appear to be one of the organization of long-term memory. They propose that the problem lies in the quantity of material recalled from long-term memory.

More recent work suggests that the problems that were initially viewed as stemming from memory may be related to the ability to understand and use language. Ackerman, Dykman and Gardner (1990) found that the group of children described as severely affected by their learning disabilities had "slow articulation and/or continuous naming rates for sequential alphanumeric stimuli" (p. 326). These children appeared to experience a "tangled tongue." Since they process information more slowly and less effectively, it is harder for them to articulate even those things they do know. Mastropieri, Scruggs, and Fulk (1990) premised their work on the belief, drawn from prior investigations, that memory per se is not the problem for children with learning disabilities. Since these children can remember non-verbal material, they suggest the problem may lie in their ability to use language. The difficulty here may be with the structure of semantic memory as well as with the process of storing and retrieving linguistic information. Mastropieri et al. refer to the "dual deficiency in prior language knowledge (structure) and ability to acquire new verbal information (process)" (p. 92) as a problem area for students with learning disabilities.

There is also a link made between memory and strategy use. "One reason why children with learning disabilities display poor memory skills is their inefficient use of cognitive strategies" (Colson & Mehring, 1990, p. 75). This view of memory systems suggests a link between ineffective memory systems utilized by children who are learning disabled and their use of cognitive and metacognitive strategies to recall prior knowledge to assist them in comprehending and acquiring new material. In Vogel and Walsh's (1987) examination of the strategies used by children with learning disabilities, students' lack of information is linked to their difficulty in "spontaneously generating strategies to attend to, learn, and organize information and, therefore, [they] have problems recalling information" (p. 160).

In this view, the difficulty in strategy use and organization of information is linked to a lack of information and a resulting difficulty in recalling information.

The link between information and memory may also have implications for the reading system acquired and used by the student with learning disabilities. Inefficient reading systems stem from inaccurate or ineffective processing of information in memory. Coles (1987) stresses that the problem is not due to the inability to hold information in memory or to lack of storage room but, rather, is due to the way in which information is processed and stored, how it is rehearsed, the amount of elaboration performed on the information, and the way the items are clustered. These difficulties may be related to lack of prior knowledge of the reading process and/or the reading context. Such prior knowledge can provide an anchor for the information the reader attempts to store in memory. The inefficient and ineffective reading system affects memory as does the inefficient and ineffective memory system. A number of other researchers have proposed similar conclusions based on their own investigations.

We are left with a feeling of uncertainty here. As Colson and Mehring (1990) note, the "diversity among students with learning disabilities may account for a lack of agreement on the types of memory problems found in this population" (p. 75). These authors also direct our attention to the especially "wide range of learning tasks [that] have been included in memory research" (p. 75). One conclusion that does seem evident is that there is considerable overlap between the cognitive areas under consideration. Memory is linked to language and cognitive strategy use. These conclusions by various researchers can be related to an earlier finding of Spear and Sternberg (1987) that "the bulk of available evidence indicates that the deficits of disabled readers are verbal rather than non-verbal and cognitive rather than perceptual in nature" (p. 21).

Cognitive Strategy Acquisition and Use

The word "strategy" has been mentioned several times so far. We use the term, as do many in the field, to suggest a set of steps or procedures for solving an academic problem (Ellis, Lenz, Sabornie, 1987; Harris & Pressley, 1991), differentiating it from a skill, which may be considered a specific activity. Pressley & Associates (1990) suggest that "strategies include 'tricks' that aid in the performance of very specific tasks" (p. 8). Identifying the main idea in reading is a skill, a specific task in reading. How this is done, the steps and procedures that are used, is a strategy. Graham and Harris (1994) suggest that strategies are "goal-directed cognitive operations used to facilitate performance" (p. 147). Knowledge and use of a strategy empower the learner because the procedure can be generalized and applied to new situations and new text. Failure to become proficient in strategy use may have the opposite effect. Chan, Cole, and Morris (1990) suggest that the passiveness often observed in children with learning disabilities may be related to their inability to select strategies that will facilitate their completion of the task at hand. This area is so pervasive in our thinking about students with learning disabilities that Palincsar and Brown (1987) suggest a "reconceptualization of the student with learning problems as one who fails to enlist efficient, task appropriate strategies and/or orchestrate their use" (pp. 66-67). The areas associated with ineffective generation, selection, and use of cognitive strategies are varied. They include:

- failure to plan and organize,
- difficulty in the acquisition, use and generalization of strategies,
- and the ineffective use of problem solving and reasoning strategies.

The failure to *plan and organize* information using effective strategies is frequently cited in discussions of oral and written language as well as of memory and strategy use. Sinatra, Berg, & Dunn (1985) state the case strongly by noting that children with learning disabilities "generally experience major difficulties in both recall and organization of verbal information" (p. 310). They believe this organization is "more crucial to overall comprehension than the recall of specific vocabulary" (p. 313). The inability to organize and integrate information using global strategies is frequently cited by teachers and practitioners in the field (Colson and Mehring, 1990; Meltzer, Solomon, Fenton, & Levine, 1989). There may also be a problem in organizing the use of strategies. Colson and Mehring (1990) stress that "students with learning disabilities fail to adopt an active, planful and organized approach to a learning task" (p. 75). This lack of organization and integrative abilities have been observed in children identified as gifted and as learning disabled (Jones, 1986) as well as in the general population of children identified as learning disabled.

The *acquisition, use, and generalization* of strategies is an area of considerable concern for students with learning disabilities, one that affects many areas of academic performance, including, certainly, reading (Spear & Sternberg, 1987). Chan et al. (1990) present and document an impressive list of items with which students with learning disabilities may have difficulty. These include lack of awareness of appropriate cognitive strategies and failure in maintaining and generalizing strategies that are learned. In addition, they point out that students with learning disabilities may exhibit an "inability to shift from one strategy to another, to abandon inappropriate strategies, to process information with one strategy and then select another, or even to consider several processing approaches in rapid succession in order to arrive at a solution to the problem" (Swanson, 1987, p. 3). In fact, students with learning disabilities "experience special difficulty in applying strategies" (Rottman & Cross, 1990, p. 270).

The question of strategy generalization is critical and has become "a central issue in special and remedial education programming and research" (Ellis et al., 1987, p. 7). According to Ellis et al. (1987) "it rarely occurs spontaneously" (p. 8). Chan (1991), in her review of the literature on strategy training, examines strategy generalization and concludes that students not only do not make use of cognitive strategies, but "when they are no longer prompted to use the learning strategy, they fail to generalize its use to relevant learning situations" (p. 427). Scruggs and Mastropieri (1992) deal specifically with this issue in their investigation of instruction in mnemonic devices for children with learning disabilities. Their intent was to provide the students with experience in using a cognitive strategy that could be transferred to other situations. Indeed, the students were able to generate strategies and apply this approach in novel situations.

Problem solving and reasoning are important for two reasons. "Differences in school performance are related to differences in the use of higher-order cognitive strategies, such as problem-solving and reasoning" (Thornburg, 1991, p. 379). They are also related to the generation, selection, and monitoring of cognitive strategies. Meltzer et al. (1989) found that children identified as learning disabled were deficient in developing and using problem solving strategies. Scruggs and Mastropieri's (1986b) work corroborates this. "Much of the failure of learning disabled students in school-related tasks has been attributed to a lack of ability in applying such problem-solving strategies" (p.63). Shafrir et al. (1990) add another dimension to our view of problem solving. They find that "the metacognitive skill of monitoring errors" (p. 506) may be important in problem solving for some children with learning disabilities and may be a major source of difficulty. In examining the use of reasoning strategies, Scruggs, Bennion, and Lifson (1985) compare the performance of two groups of third graders, one labeled learning disabled and one considered normal. Students in the former group made less use of appropriate reasoning strategies than their peers. When they did use reasoning strategies, they were still less successful than their peers. It is encouraging to note that

Leshowitz, Jenkins, Heaton, and Bough (1993) cite evidence that "students [with learning disabilities] not only can reason with higher order skills, but also can outperform their nondisabled peers after receiving brief intervention programs in higher order thinking" (p. 483).

Metacognition

Metacognition refers to the process of reflecting upon what one is thinking. Have you identified the main idea? How do you know you are correct? Where do you think you went wrong? What can you do to correct the difficulty? As one reads the letters that make up words, phrases, sentences, paragraphs, or extended texts, one thinks about what one is reading, attempting to make sense of the format and the content. The reader remembers the information at hand, recalls other information held in long term memory (prior knowledge), organizes the bits of information, possibly elaborates, expands, and reorganizes. The reader's metacognitive abilities allow the reader to select a method for examining the information and subsequently determining whether the strategy selected helped the reader comprehend the reading material.

The use of metacognitive strategies takes at least two forms: an executive function and a regulatory function. In the executive function, the reader selects possible methods or strategies to help one examine the format and content of what one is reading. In the regulatory function, the reader evaluates the effectiveness of selected strategies to determine the nature of the outcome.

The literature on children with learning disabilities repeatedly refers to the need for students to monitor their own learning and substantiates the "growing body of data [that] points to deficits in metacognitive processes as possible contributors to learning disabilities" (Shafrir et al., 1990, p. 506). This area of self-regulation of learning is particularly important for these students because, not only may they have difficulties here, but it is an important component of success in school (Reid & Harris, 1993).

Because the area of metacognition is so pervasive, touching as it does the areas of language, memory, and strategy use, we find indicators of difficulty in a range of areas. We find metacognitive failures in language areas. Thomas, Englert, and Gregg (1987) report a failure of students with learning disabilities to monitor the process of generating expository text. Graham and Harris (1994) identify failure to monitor the process of writing in general as frequently being associated with students with learning disabilities.

We find a relationship between metacognition and the use of cognitive strategies. Scruggs et al. (1985) suggest that students with learning disabilities have unrealistically high levels of confidence in their ability to use reasoning skills despite their poor performance in relation to non-classified peers. Swanson, Christie and Rubadeau (1993), in comparing the performance of mentally retarded, learning disabled, normal, and gifted children in monitoring success in reasoning by analogy, conclude that "metacognitive awareness of strategies plays an important role in LD children's performance" (p. 80). Chan et al. (1990) document the inability of students with learning disabilities to "efficiently initiate, regulate, and monitor the use of [appropriate cognitive] strategies" (p. 2).

We find metacognition occupying an important position in reading, particularly in relation to cognitive strategies. Meltzer et al. (1989) note that children identified as learning disabled lack the metacognitive strategies needed for reading and study skills. They relate this to general disorganization, lack of monitoring strategy use, and an inability to switch strategies when and if necessary. Bos and Vaughn (1994) also note difficulties in monitoring and memory tasks in reading, citing lack of "effective use of elaborative encoding strategies, such as rehearsals, categorization, and association, when trying to remember words or word lists" (p. 98). Students with learning disabilities also do not use strategies to correct a breakdown in comprehension.

Thoughts on Cognition

Can we help students with learning disabilities improve in these cognitive areas? The answers here seem to be positive, which is important and reassuring when planning instruction. In order to improve memory, for example, Colson and Mehring (1990) suggest providing instruction in the use of effective strategies, based on a cognitive approach to instruction, such as constructing and creating new forms of organization, relating new information to prior knowledge, focusing on meaning, and planning when and how to use the information. Others (Brown & Campione, 1986; Swanson & Ransby, 1994) echo this view, stressing particularly the need to ensure transfer of the strategies. For example, instead of teaching memory in isolation, teach relevant memory strategies in the context of the memory demands of the academic situation. This kind of instruction can be effective for students with learning disabilities (Chan, 1991; Graham & Harris, 1994; Swanson, 1990). This conclusion is especially significant for our study of reading and is widely echoed in the field (Graham & Harris, 1990). One common element here is that cognitive instruction should take place within an academic setting (Brown & Campione, 1986; Graham & Harris, 1994).

As we have seen, there is considerable overlap among the areas of cognition, as well as between language and cognition. Swanson and Ransby (1994) suggest, in reference to students with learning disabilities, that "it is best to view their cognitive difficulties as reflecting interactive problems between and among various cognitive-processing components" (p. 257). Groteluschen, Borkowski, and Hale (1990) translate this into practice by stressing the need to expand strategy training to include metacognitive training. We need to look at the factors, taking a broad view of instruction and keeping in mind that the child operates as a whole. In considering the difficulties encountered by students with learning disabilities in monitoring strategy use and performance in an academic task, it is also useful to remember the caution suggested by Reid and Harris (1993). "There are no hard and fast guidelines for which variables should be self-monitored to yield positive effects . . . efficacy, in turn, seems directly related to the interrelationships of task, learner, and outcome variables" (p. 39).

Recent efforts have broadened our perspective by clarifying that the broad range of abilities and disabilities characteristic of children labeled learning disabled matches the broad range of processing problems that can occur in the perceptual, cognitive, and/or language areas. Leshowitz et al. (1993) note that, historically, children with learning disabilities have been taught basic skills first, with reasoning and critical thinking skills as follow up. They propose that this approach is nonproductive and suggest that when these children are taught to think, they can achieve as well as their peers and sometimes better. Borkowski (1992) encourages further research into the use of metacognitive strategies with the intent of providing the teacher, particularly the novice teacher, with a framework. "A working model provides schema for organizing knowledge, a framework in which to incorporate new information, and springboard for launching future actions" (p. 254).

Social Behavior

The failure to apply metacognitive strategies has implications for social development as well as for one's disposition to learning. Vaughn and Hogan (1990) have described social competence as a construct that is made up of the following components: positive relations with others, age-appropriate social cognition, absence of maladaptive behaviors, and effective social behaviors.

Failure to develop these competencies results in the low peer status of many students with learning disabilities (Stone &

LaGreca, 1990), even prior to being identified as learning disabled (Vaughn, Hogan, Kouzekanani, & Shapiro, 1990). In fact, Gresham and Reschly (1988) found that mildly disabled and nondisabled students can be classified accurately on the basis of social skills measures alone. It is interesting to note that there is no evidence that students with learning disabilities are socially withdrawn; indeed, in school settings they participate as much as their nondisabled peers. On the whole, studies show that they do not differ from nondisabled peers in their knowledge of social norms, but that they differ in their monitoring of these norms to regulate behavior so that it is socially acceptable.

Bos and Vaughn (1994) have suggested that one reason students with learning disabilities have problems with social competence is that they may not realize the extent to which their interactions with others are influenced by their own behavior. The perception that failures are caused by events beyond one's control is typical of a number of students with learning disabilities. Frequent unrewarding social interactions can lead to feelings of helplessness, resulting in passivity and a lessening of active attempts to improve social interfaces.

Learned Helplessness

The passivity of students identified as learning disabled has been widely recognized (Jenkins, Heliotis, Haynes, & Beck, 1986). This passivity, sometimes referred to as learned helplessness, has been linked to failure to use metacognitive strategies. Winograd and Niquette (1988) found that "a perception of being helpless to control events" (p. 39) is linked to lack of metacognition which, in turn, affects one's ability to become an active, strategic reader. Without active engagement in monitoring success and adapting approaches to understanding, comprehension suffers. Competent readers cannot be passive or helpless; yet many students with learning disabilities have been recognized as reluctant to participate actively in the reading process as they depend increasingly upon the teacher for direction. This teacher control, in fact, enables and encourages passivity (Coles, 1987). In time, the less the child succeeds, the less motivated the child is to learn, and the stronger the sense of helplessness (Stanovich, 1988). The fear of failure, based on frequent lack of success from an early age, can produce unwillingness to take sufficient risks to enable learning. These patterns are of concern to teachers because they affect the student's ability to participate constructively in class discussions, to work cooperatively with peers in the classroom, and, ultimately, to learn to read.

Attention Deficit/Hyperactivity

Many of the characteristics of children with attention deficit disorder (ADD) and attention deficit hyperactivity disorder (ADHD) also are descriptive of a subset of children with learning disabilities (Lerner & Lowenthal, 1989). ADD and ADHD are not types of learning disability but are disorders often associated with learning disabilities. Results of studies of the overlap between learning disabilities and ADD vary widely. Conservative measures suggest that between 15% and 20% of students with learning disabilities also have ADD and that about 33% are hyperactive (Shaywitz, Shaywitz, & Fletcher, 1992; Silver, 1990).

These terms (ADD and ADHD) encompass a range of behavioral characteristics. Silver and Hagin (1990) have described the processes affected: "the investment, organization, and maintenance of attention and effort; the modulation of impulses to meet situational demands; and 'an unusually strong inclination to seek immediate gratification.' These primary deficits may lead to limited development of higher order cognitive schema and diminished affective motivation" (p. 420).

What do these characteristics look like in the classroom? In addition to hyperactivity and difficulty maintaining attention, students with ADD/ADHD often have social and behavioral problems, especially if hyperactivity is also involved. Being impulsive, often they do not stop and think before responding. There is frequently an overlap between students with specific reading disability and ADD (Dykman & Ackerman, 1991). When coupled with a learning disability, ADHD can significantly compound difficulty in learning to read (August, 1987). From the standpoint of the teacher, the limited attention span and impulsivity of the child with ADHD necessitate instructional modifications in order for the child to learn effectively.

INSTRUCTIONAL SETTINGS AND PROCEDURES

The settings in which students with learning disabilities are being educated form a continuum that ranges from receiving all instruction in a regular classroom through periodic resource room support through spending much of the day in a class with other special education students. Federal regulations that mandate instruction in the least restrictive setting that will facilitate learning provide the basis for placement decisions.

Most students with learning disabilities are being educated in mainstream classrooms. About (77%) spend the majority or all of their time in regular classrooms. Of these, 21% are in regular classes all day, and 56% receive resource room support for some part of the day. About 23% of students with learning disabilities are placed in special education classes for the majority of the day (U.S. Department of Education, 1992).

Opinion is divided on the optimal placement of students with mild disabilities. Some have maintained that all students belong in regular classrooms, with special education and regular education being merged into a single system. Proponents of this type of restructuring maintain that separate instruction is demeaning to students, is less effective, and that special education relieves regular teachers of their responsibilities to teach *all* students. Others have maintained that students with inherent learning difficulties placed in regular classrooms without adequate supports fall through the instructional cracks. Still others believe that there are some students with learning disabilities whose specific learning and attentional problems require instruction in a setting with fewer distractions than the regular classroom.

The opinions of researchers as to the optimal setting generally substantiate the notion that instruction that is individualized to meet the needs of the student with learning disabilities is the most important thing, not the specific setting in which it is delivered (O'Sullivan, Ysseldyke, Christenson, & Thurlow, 1990). The term "individualized instruction" does not imply that the student will be working alone on a special assignment. Rather, it refers to instruction designed to maximize that student's learning, be it in a large group, a cooperative learning group of his peers, or a remedial tutorial focused on a specific problem. Depending on the purpose, the teacher may be fulfilling the role of lecturer, interactor, collaborator, coach, or tutor, depending on the situation.

In recent years we have learned more about which conditions facilitate successful placement in regular classrooms. Salend (1994) suggests identifying behaviors requisite for success in a specific mainstream class, both academically and behaviorally, and setting these as the student's current IEP goals. When the goals are achieved, the student should be ready for the mainstream class. The positive role models provided by increased contact with non-disabled students may contribute to the achievement of the ensuing individualized education program (IEP) goals for the student with social/behavioral needs.

If students with learning disabilities are to be included in regular classes, teachers of these classes must have the attitudes, skills, and support that will enable students to succeed. It is important to remember that most students with learning disabilities were identified and classified as a result of academic failure in regular classrooms. Therefore, it is understandable that something needs to be different if they are to learn well in large-group, regular education settings (Ohanian, 1990; Simmons, Fuchs, & Fuchs, 1991).

There is no question that some teachers have the ability to provide instructional accommodations more comfortably than others. For instance, Chicchelli and Ashby-Davis (1986) point out that teachers are more able to meet the needs of a wide range of students if they "provide different physical arrangements in the classroom, use a variety of grouping modes, select diversified materials, and utilize a range of instructional strategies" (p. 124).

After investigating the general practice today at the secondary school level, the National Longitudinal Transitional Study confirmed that the majority of students with learning disabilities already spend the majority of their instructional time in regular education classes (Wagner, 1990). In examining what happens to these students, the researchers found that students "are held to the same grading standard as nondisabled students in regular education classes, and generally are not provided direct services, such as tutoring assistance . . . . Neither are regular education teachers routinely provided with substantial direct support for instruction of students with learning disabilities" (p. 27). The concern that frequently instruction is not "individualized" for students with learning disabilities in mainstream classes appears to be well founded.

In a research study examining what goes on in traditional elementary school classrooms, Baker and Zigmond (1990) found that fundamental changes were needed in mainstream classes if they were to be able to incorporate students with learning disabilities. They reported that students spent a great deal of time on worksheets and transitional activities and that little time was spent by teachers on actual teaching. They suggested that more time be devoted to reading, and they suggested that a wider range of instructional practices needed to be incorporated. The authors concluded that the mainstream must change, that it must accommodate individual differences if students with learning disabilities are to learn well in a mainstream setting.

Structural and administrative changes have been proposed or experimented with in an attempt to restructure schools in such a way that students with disabilities can be more successfully taught in regular classrooms. The *Regular Education Initiative* (REI) advocates placement and instruction of students with disabilities in regular classes, under the direction of the regular class teacher instead of a special education teacher (Bryan, Bay, & Donahue, 1988; Jenkins, Pious, & Jewell, 1990; Kauffman, Gerber, & Semmel, 1988; Keogh, 1988; Lerner, 1987; Lipsky & Gartner, 1987; Reynolds, Wang, & Walberg, 1987; & Will, 1986). A more far-reaching administrative placement model is *full inclusion*. The purpose of this model is to teach *all* children in the regular classroom in their neighborhood school, regardless of the type of disability or the level of severity of the disability. Regular educators and special educators would collaborate to design an appropriate educational program for each student (Council for Exceptional Children, 1993; Council for Exceptional Children, Division of Learning Disabilities, 1993; Council for Learning Disabilities, 1993; Learning Disabilities Association, 1993; Stainback & Stainback, 1992). Under this model special education would be eliminated as a separate system.

The education of students with learning disabilities in regular classrooms is seen by many as a less restrictive environment in which, given individualized instruction and adequate supports, educational services may be effectively provided. The cost of such a system is being investigated at this time, and, as we might guess, estimates vary widely. It is clear, however, that when placement in a regular classroom setting is used to avoid the expense of providing an individualized program with needed supports, such placement denies students with learning disabilities the type and quality of education they need in order to learn and, in addition, denies them that to which they are entitled under the law.

EDUCATIONAL OUTCOMES

The evaluation of the outcomes of school programs for students with learning disabilities has been fraught with difficulties. The judgment of success or failure is related to the rationale that underlies both the program and the criteria set for determining progress. In addition, the ultimate evidence of the student's progress requires the passage of time and a continuity of follow-up. For these reasons, comparing the results of outcomes studies is difficult. Nonetheless, it is important that we understand the findings, for this information can help us to plan more effective instruction for students.

We know that the need to improve educational programs is urgent. Students with learning disabilities have greater difficulty achieving in school than others. They perform poorly in comprehension and critical thinking in comparison with others, and they experience frequent academic failures over long periods of time and across a variety of tasks and teachers.

Significantly more students with learning disabilities drop out before completing high school than students in the total school population. Looking only at students who left high school between the ages of fifteen and twenty in the 1985-87 school years, the U.S. Department of Education (1992) stated that 60.9% of students with learning disabilities who left school graduated; the others left without graduating. In comparison, 75.6% of youth in the general population in this age range left school upon graduation. The situation is even more serious, because these figures did not account for students who had dropped out before entering secondary school.

How do students with learning disabilities fare while they are in school? The National Longitudinal Transitional Study (Wagner, 1990) reported that 33% of secondary students with learning disabilities who were enrolled in regular education courses had received a failing grade in one or more courses in the previous school year. Are drop-out and failure rates such as these inevitable? Apparently not. Data from this same study suggest that "combinations of educational programs and policies also can reduce the probability of failing in school, even for students with many characteristics that put them at high risk of failure" (p. 22).

In an unusual longitudinal study, Rogan and Hartman (1990) published comparisons from two follow-up studies on the same individuals who had been identified as having learning disabilities in childhood and who had attended a private school for children with learning disabilities in elementary and middle school. The first follow-up was conducted when participants were twenty-one to thirty-nine years old. The second follow-up was conducted ten years later when participants were thirty-one to forty-nine years old. In analyzing the data, three subgroups were created: students who attended only self-contained special education classes in high school (24%), high school graduates (39%), and college graduates (34%). The authors considered students who had dropped out of high school (3%) separately. The outcomes were generally favorable for those who had completed high school or college. However, for those who attended high school only in self-contained special education classes, the results were mixed. Success was evaluated on the basis of engagement in relatively secure and satisfying occupations, independent living, and having cultivated a variety of interests. Rogan and Hartman concluded that "variables contributing to a favorable outcome were intensive effective intervention during the elementary and middle school years, ongoing supportive tutoring or resource help during mainstream school attendance, counseling or therapy when needed, consistent parental understanding and support, and the absence of severely complicating neurological and emotional problems" (p. 91).

Adults with learning disabilities who were interviewed by Gerber and Reiff (1991) described the persistence of learning disabilities in their adult lives. Although some are unemployed and some are successful professionals, the disabling impact of failure that begot more failure in their educational, social/emotional, and vocational growth remains apparent to them. They named three types of assistance and compensatory strategies that were most effective: sufficient early successes, family and school support, and exceedingly hard work.

In a review of four follow-up studies of adults who had been identified as learning disabled as children, Bruck (1987) concluded that "in many cases learning disabilities are not a lifelong handicapping condition, especially if adequate treatment is provided during childhood" (p. 252). She found that the severity of the childhood disability, socioeconomic status, and IQ affected outcomes. However, early identification and adequate educational interventions were the most important factors in the positive adult outcomes of the students.

Current national focus on evaluating outcomes in education, both for students in special education programs and for all students, lends promise of more helpful information in the future. In recent years a major source of funding for basic research on learning disabilities has been the National Institutes of Child Health and Human Development (NICHD). The two priorities stated for future funding are: 1) "to identify and validate critical variables in the treatment of learning disabilities" and 2) "to develop and/or refine measurement strategies to foster more precise replication in studies of LD populations" (Lyon, 1991, p.76). The second priority should encourage the development of assessments to provide more informative data about educational outcomes of students with learning disabilities. A more complete discussion of directions and alternatives is provided by Ysseldyke, Thurlow and Bruininks (1992).

What kind of framework for exploring reading and literacy instruction does this examination of the general field of learning disabilities provide? From the perspective of the teacher, these students' learning styles and pace are sufficiently varied and inflexible as to require individualization of the curriculum and of instruction. The traditional focus on a model of instruction in which the deficits within the child were identified and hopefully remediated has broadened to a focus on the broader learning environment in the school and the interaction between the individual learner and this environment. The failure of attempts to train underlying perceptual deficits revealed that our research was insufficient to enable us to alter characteristics that are inherent in the learner through such means as perceptual-motor training or modality training. The current emphasis that incorporates the total educational environment is indeed pragmatic, for in large part it is within the control of the school.

CHAPTER 2

Reading and the Reader

INTRODUCTION

We take the act of reading for granted. Most of us do it automatically. We read. We get information. We get pleasure. Most readers will read this text for information. A few will read it for pleasure. Some start reading for information and begin to read for pleasure. But you know why you are reading it. You have a purpose. You don't stop before starting this page and wonder if you can read it. You know you can. Or at least you are pretty sure you can. But, tragically, for many adults this is not the case. It is also not the case for many children. They go to school believing that they can learn this trick, this trick that adults have of being able to read. By the time children have figured out that they are not learning to read or are not reading effectively and efficiently, for whatever the reason, they have also begun to figure out that their parents are disappointed in them, their teachers are losing patience, and their friends and siblings know that they are DUMB. The trick turns out to be very tricky!

We all recognize the importance of reading in our lives. The fact that you are reading this book demonstrates that you have reached the same conclusion we have. The ability to read is, even in this multi-media age, critical for our survival, for our advancement and empowerment, and for our development as human beings. Our mutual concern here is with the difficulties experienced by one special group of children and adults, those in that amorphous population known as "learning disabled." We are concerned with why such children have difficulties in beginning the process of learning to read as well as why they have difficulty using the skills and strategies they do acquire. We are concerned with their failure to develop a reading system that works for them. We are concerned with why we aren't teaching them in a manner that will enable all this to happen, that will enable them to overcome the difficulties they experience.

We begin this process of mutual inquiry and growth by examining the act of reading and exploring what it is we think that good readers do. Current theory and research have contributed a great deal to our knowledge in these areas. This knowledge can provide a framework for our understanding of the difficulties encountered by the student with learning disabilities as well as a scaffold for the development of a set of instructional strategies and procedures we can use in helping students acquire and use literacy skills and strategies.

MODELS OF READING

Over the years there has been much interest focused on the development of a model or models of reading. Theorists and researchers seek an understanding of the processes that children and adults use in the act of reading. This notion of a model depicting how we go about reading can give direction to how we provide instruction, to the kinds and format of materials that are developed, and, of course, to what we teach students. Because of the impact these models have had in the teaching of reading, we need to examine briefly the three global frameworks that have been proposed: the bottom-up model, the top-down model, and the interactive model (Bos & Vaughn, 1994; Horn & Manis, 1985; Levy & Hinchley, 1990; Lipson & Wixson, 1991). In examining these models we need to remember that any view of the reading process must account for what the reader does with the print that is on the page and the meaning associated with that print.

The Bottom-Up Model

The bottom-up model of reading suggests that readers read the letters and words on the page, moving across the lines and down the page, processing these letters and words sequentially, and then figuring out or comprehending the meaning the author has intended. This model has been given several names: an information processing model, a linear model, a bottom-up model; all variations have some important similarities. This view of reading is hierarchical, focuses on individual units of text, and examines and teaches particular, often isolated, skills. The reader deciphers the meaning the author intended. This view of the reading process focuses on print and is driven by that print.

Consider the implications of this view of reading. The reader needs to recognize the letters. The reader needs to associate the sounds (phonemes) of the letters with the visual appearance of the letters (graphemes). The reader needs to isolate sounds and then blend them into words. The reader needs to be able to read irregular words that don't lend themselves to this process of analysis and synthesis and focus on the accurate pronunciation of the printed word. Through instruction and practice the reader achieves automaticity in these skills. Automaticity is a key concept here because it enables speed and fluency, allowing the reader to focus on comprehension. The traditional view of automaticity has been the limited-resource model, originally proposed by LaBerge and Samuels (Naslund & Samuels, 1992; Samuels, 1987). According to this model the reader can only attend to one aspect of the reading process at a time. Since the reader needs to be able to identify the words in order to understand the text, decoding must be automatic or habitual before the reader can attend to meaning. How does the reader develop automaticity? "Practice in reading influences automaticity in decoding as well as the size of the visual processing unit" (Samuels, 1987, p. 20). Perhaps the key word here is "practice" with its implication of developing an habitual response. "The limited-resource models of automatized behavior describe automatic behaviors as invariant and done without attention" (Naslund & Samuels, 1992, p. 141). The development of automatic word recognition requires the careful instruction in and learning of the word recognition skills often associated with the bottom-up model of reading. The building up of this automaticity is described as "extremely effortful and demanding of conscious resources" (Naslund & Samuels, 1992, pp. 146-147). Once word recognition is automatic the reader can give full attention to the message.

Now, how does the reader get the message? The reader needs to know the meaning of the words in the text. Teach vocabulary, traditionally through the use of the dictionary. Since words occur in the linguistic context of a sentence, the reader needs to understand the grammatical structure of the language. Teach parts of speech, grammar, and punctuation. Through this series of steps the reader begins to decipher the meaning of the text intended by the author. Teach comprehension skills, such as identifying the main idea and answering questions on different levels of understanding. There are few unknowns for the reader in this approach. If the child learns the absolutes taught and the writer is clear about the meaning, then the reader can read and comprehend the text since the process in this model is print driven.

The instructional procedures developed from the medical model of learning disabilities, with its emphasis on intrinsic causes, have been highly influenced by this model of reading. Certainly beginning readers rely heavily on the information they receive from print. Their perception of the letters influences the sounds attached to them and impacts the word produced by the reader. The words "bog" and "dog" might be confused because of a perception of the "d" as a "b." Much instruction for beginning readers is derived from this model, teaching individual units of text and focusing on the skills needed for mastery in these areas. The role of the teacher is to teach appropriate skills, provide materials using those skills, and include sufficient opportunities for practice to mastery.

A nagging question however, has been raised. Does this account for all the conditions under which reading occurs? What about, for example, the good reader who skips words and still "gets" the meaning? What about the reader who can't read many of the words, doesn't know all the letters and sounds, and still can answer the questions at the end of the passage? We've all had such children in class. Why is it that two competent readers read the same passage and do not agree on what it means?

The Top-Down Model

As the name implies, the top-down model of reading views the process from a very different perspective. Reading, instead of being focused on print, is focused on meaning, with the reader playing an active role in the process. Instead of starting with the graphic text information, this view of reading begins by emphasizing the prior knowledge and experience the reader brings to the text that relates to the writer's message. It is this prior knowledge that enables the reader to interpret the text. The writer's message is interpreted in light of what the reader knows about the concepts, the language used, and even the grammatical constructions and orthographic information embedded in the text. The focus of this approach (also referred to as the "psycholinguistic model" of reading) is on what the reader does to match or compare and contrast his knowledge of the concepts to the text using cognitive and linguistic strategies. The graphic elements of the text are used as needed to confirm or reject a hypothesis about meaning based on prior knowledge. If a reader is reading text about domestic animals the confusion between "b" and "d" in the word ending in "og" wouldn't arise. The reader, based on prior knowledge and the experience, possibly, of owning a dog, would predict that the word would be "dog."

What are the implications of this model of reading for the reader and for the teacher? The reader needs to activate prior knowledge, relate it to the text, and use this knowledge to generate hypotheses about the content of the text. The emphasis right from the beginning is on meaning. Teach the student to identify what he already knows about the topic, possibly by brainstorming what is known about the subject. Teach strategies for using this knowledge, such as generating questions that might be answered in the text. The reader needs to predict the meanings of words that might be in the text and develop meanings of unknown words based on the text and on prior knowledge of the content. Teach the student word meaning within the framework of a concept. Teach the student strategies for using context and orthography to identify word meaning. The reader needs to confirm or reject the hypotheses made based on text information. Teach the student to ask questions while reading about what has been read and what will be read. The reader needs to identify when the text is not making sense. Teach the student to check the text carefully if it doesn't make sense or doesn't fit in with what is already known by rereading, by checking key words, by carefully decoding unknown words. Teach the student some alternatives. The comprehension of the text may result in an elaboration of what is already known and/or an adjustment or correction in the prior knowledge. The meaning of the text is foremost in this model with the reader being the active participant in interpreting this meaning.

This process is not hierarchical, is not print driven, and is, therefore, not word bound. Rather, the reader makes choices and decisions during the process of interpreting meaning. Reading is a process of solving problems. These choices and decisions involve strategies that the reader has developed or has been taught in addition to the skills traditionally associated with reading. Skills and strategies work together to enable effective and efficient reading. For example, the reader can be taught the traditional skill of how to decode a multisyllabic word. The reader also has a set of strategies for figuring out when he can't comprehend text. One of those strategies may involve rereading words that were not comprehended the first time. The reader chooses to reread the word, in this case a multisyllabic word, decides to decode it using the skill taught, and assigns meaning to it, using the morphemes (the smallest clusters of letters with meaning), recognizing that the word may be important in the text. The strategic use of skills as well as the graphic information have been used to aid comprehension.

In this model we see the reader in a very different light. The reader uses cognitive strategies and is not word bound but is meaning driven. The reader, rather than processing text in a linear fashion to derive meaning, manipulates it to interpret meaning. Rather than viewing reading as a perceptual/linguistic process, it is viewed more as a cognitive/linguistic process. The emphasis is on reading as thinking, reading as problem solving.

How can beginning readers possibly do this? They need to be able to read the text, the words. They need to know what the words "say" and what they mean. Maybe sampling the graphic features of the text as an aid to comprehension is not sufficient for beginning or poor readers. Maybe this is why students with learning disabilities have so much difficulty reading with this approach to instruction. It's too vague for them. There are also other possible problem areas for students with learning disabilities. They may come to the text without a sufficient store of appropriate prior knowledge because they have had limited opportunities to read. They may come with a difficulty in interpreting language, certainly important in this approach. Finally, facility in using strategies and solving problems is important. As we have seen, these may present difficulties. The reader with learning disabilities is faced with obstacles on every front in this view of reading.

The Interactive Model

The interactive model addresses the concerns raised in both of the other two models. Even though versions of this model may vary, they recognize that readers can interact with text in different ways, depending on the reader, the text and the task. The reading process is viewed as both print and meaning driven with an emphasis on the reader as an active agent controlling the process.

When the reader has little experience with the topic, and possibly with the form of the text, there may be more reliance on the graphic features of the text during the process of interaction. For many of us, because of a lack of prior knowledge and experience, texts about quantum physics or brain surgery would have to be processed very carefully. We would have to attend to and use most or all of the graphic information in the text, particularly if we were actually going to perform brain surgery. We would, in many instances, be deciphering the text to obtain the author's meaning. The reader's purpose may enter in here too. Even if you know a lot about brain surgery and have performed it many times, you might still attend to all the graphic information, wanting to get every single detail straight in your mind if you were going to try even a slightly different procedure. The more knowledge the reader has about the text, the less graphic information the reader needs to process and the more emphasis may be placed on matching meaning with prior knowledge. Again, purpose may be a variable. If you have no intention of performing brain surgery or of training a dog but would like an overview of these topics, perhaps to find out something specific, you might proceed from a meaning perspective.

There is also some thought that the two processes might proceed simultaneously, particularly for skilled readers (Levy & Hinchley, 1990). Hypotheses might be developed and directed based on graphic information. The reader reads the title and first paragraph of a text and develops very different hypotheses depending on whether a frequently repeated word is read as "bog" or "dog." The hypotheses might direct the reading of the graphic information. If the selection is known to be about the care and treatment of dogs, the reader will certainly read "dog" correctly and will probably read the word "house" as it was intended, not as "horse."

The question of automaticity is also relevant here. Certainly as skilled readers we do not decode every word. We automatically retrieve a substantial portion of the words we read. In contrast to the limited-resources model of automaticity, Naslund and Samuels (1992) view "automaticity as building up a store of information in memory, not as habituation of responses" (p. 145). They cite evidence of the effect of context and of the familiarity or unfamiliarity of text and/or subject matter on decoding, even for skilled readers. The items to be learned are encoded in memory through repeated exposures; the more exposures, the more varied memories are stored and then retrieved. "Automatization is said to occur when behavior reflects a shift from reliance on step-by-step procedures (e.g., an algorithm) to reliance on retrieving encapsulated information from memory (e.g., direct access of word meaning from letter strings)" (p. 144). This learning occurs not from repeated drill and practice but from developing memory traces through repeated exposure to words and the elements that make up words as part of experience with "letter strings corresponding to lexical (meaning) entries and syntactical entries" (p. 148). All of these elements are experienced together and become part of the memory that is retrieved during reading. This view of automaticity suggests that it develops within increasingly complex and varied contexts and that children need this kind of experience. This view also relates to reading as a top-down or interactive process.

There is certainly agreement among many theorists and researchers that the interactive model reflects what happens in the process of reading. Some of the details may still be under discussion, but the basic features of this model are consistent.

The reader interacts with the text in a multitude of ways, and the purpose of this interaction is to construct meaning based on the content, graphic features, syntactic features and structure of the text in conjunction with the knowledge and experience of the reader.   The construction results from a set of skills and strategies that the reader uses purposefully and strategically. The model recognizes many of the elements found in the first two models such as the reader's background knowledge and experience and the skills useful for dealing with the graphic elements of the text. However, this model also stresses reading rate, motivation, word knowledge, reading environment, and the preparation and form of the text as integral components in the process.   Certainly the reader is an active participant in the process, using linguistic and cognitive cues and strategies. Similar to the top-down model, this model recognizes the importance of language, including vocabulary, in the prediction-confirmation for meaning task; however, the reader is not merely predicting/confirming in a problem-solving manner to interpret the author's meaning, Instead, the reader's predictions are an active interaction between what the text actually states and what the reader knows about the subject to construct meaning. This model does give attention to a linguistic awareness (decoding), although not necessarily as a hierarchical prerequisite to decipher the author's intent, as in the bottom-up model.

Current Thinking

The complexity of the task of reading is apparent. It is not simply a matter of learning vowels and consonants as beginners may suppose. It is not just a matter of learning basic decoding skills. In looking at the larger picture of how students learn, Brown and Campione (1986) stress that we are no longer concerned with static findings about basic processes but are concerned with how students acquire and use knowledge and procedures in various learning situations, in this case the acquisition and use of literacy. This view of learning is consistent with current views of reading as a process involving strategic use of cognition and language. The goal of reading is to construct meaning; meaning is essential in every aspect of the process.

A search of the literature would produce other proposed theoretical models that would have elements found in each of the three global ones presented; however, there is a central common element in these models: thinking. Reading, ultimately, is an act of thinking. Thorndike, in 1917, entitled his famous article "Reading Is Reasoning." This cognitive aspect has become eclipsed at times as we focused on the lower-level basic skills involved. A review of the current research indicates that the perspective has come full circle now with the current emphasis on the cognitive and linguistic aspects of the reading process.

In fact, this emphasis on reading as a process has given form to our thinking about how students acquire and use literacy, the processes involved, the strategies used, and the outcomes suggested. However, we all must be concerned, as are these theorists and researchers, with how students acquire and use knowledge of content and of strategies and procedures in various learning situations within the academic setting and of the interaction between.

The framework provided by these models of reading channels our thinking into a broad view of literacy. This view encompasses the print and the meaning aspects of text and includes the perceptual, cognitive, and linguistic processes. Overall, it stresses the active, strategic nature of the reader. This view allows all of us, irrespective of theoretical leaning or philosophy, to acknowledge that a central element of most current theories seems to be that good readers have easy access to and efficient interaction between their cognitive and linguistic processes as they encounter text and construct meaning. The student's difficulty with access and the inefficiency of the interaction between the cognitive and linguistic aspects can be better understood after we briefly observe the good reader.

GOOD READERS: A PROFILE

The phrase "good reader" can certainly refer to a wide range of readers. In fact, that is generally how we are using it. The population can include beginners, those beginners who seem to be natural readers. They will exhibit many, but not all, of the characteristics we identify. The population definitely includes those beyond the beginning level who are comprehending much of the text without undue strain and effort. The key here may be that the good reader we are profiling is that reader, no matter what level, who is reading confidently, purposefully and with comprehension. This means that not all good readers will exhibit every behavior on the list. A behavior might not be age appropriate or might not be needed to accomplish that reader's purpose.

Why explore the characteristics of the "good reader" when our common concern is with those who are not "good readers?" This exploration can provide a framework for understanding how the models of reading actually work when reader meets text and succeeds. It gives us all, teacher, student, and parent, a sense of where we're headed and how we can get there. A student or parent might legitimately ask why a child is being taught a particular strategy. We need to know that it is something good readers seem to find useful and, according to the research, is appropriate for the student with learning disabilities. In examining good readers, we will also begin to indicate ways in which poor readers may experience difficulty and ways in which the characteristics of students with learning disabilities may limit their access to literacy.

In listing indicators of a good reader, three cautions need to be emphasized. First, it is important to remember that good readers do not use one strategy or skill to the exclusion of any other, instead a variety are available and are accessed as needed (Pinnell, 1989). Second, it is also important to recognize that although we describe the process as occurring before, during, and after reading, in fact, readers probably move and back forth within these stages, exhibiting different indicators at various times. For example, during the act of reading this book, you will undoubtedly reflect on the content and concepts, applying what you are reading to yourself and your students. This is very likely, even though we traditionally think of reflecting as occurring after the act of reading. Certainly the tasks indicated as occurring before reading are critical as the reader approaches the process of reading; they are equally critical throughout the whole process.

Third, in talking about the traits of a good reader, the implication often is that all of the variables are within the reader. Current reading theory and research indicate that there are variables operating outside the reader that influence the efficiency and success of the reader (Lipson & Wixson, 1986). The frequency with which words appear in text affects the ease and speed of learning the words. The kind of text, expository or narrative, the length, and the difficulty of the syntax and language all impact on the reader's success. A "good" reader with one text may not be such a "good" reader with another text. In applying this view of the reader operating within a setting to the disabled reader, Lipson and Wixson (1986) conclude that "disability no longer is seen as an absolute property of the reader, but rather as a relative property of the interaction among specific reader, text, and contextual factors" (p. 122). Although we will consider the good reader in an abstract, theoretical way, we need to remember that we must consider the characteristics of the text and the demands of the task in planning instruction.

In general, good readers interact with text before, during, and after the process of reading. They *preview* the content, *monitor* the process, and *reflect* upon what they have read. They are active readers, risk takers, who have developed self-confidence and self-control.

When previewing, good readers activate prior knowledge, predict content and vocabulary, identify key words, and use graphic and/or pictorial cues. They approach the task with confidence, partly because they have been successful in the past and partly because they know they will be able to identify a substantial portion of the words and will be able to guess at others from the text and from the content. During the process of reading they are constantly being selective and strategic, monitoring the process and the results. They may use context, syntax, phonic and/or structural clues; they may skip difficult words, utilize signal words, read ahead, ask questions, revise predictions and predict again. During and after reading they may reflect upon their reading interaction in a variety of ways by making inferences, critiquing content and style, relating content to their own experiences, and applying the learning as needed.

What do good readers do as they approach the task?

• Good readers recognize that the goal of reading is the communication and construction of meaning using both information from the text and the reader's prior knowledge (Bos & Vaughn, 1994).

"The primary goal of both reading and writing is the communication and construction of meaning" (Pinnell, 1989, p.164). How does the good reader reach this goal of constructing meaning? "The ability to read competently depends upon sufficient text comprehension to construct appropriate meaning" (Idol & Croll, 1987, p.124). The emphasis is on comprehension in order to construct meaning. Yet, many children having difficulty with reading "come to regard reading as a process of decoding isolated words with acceptable punctuation" (Brown & Campione, 1986, p.1063). This may be because this process is what they think adults believe is important. After all, look how much time adults spend teaching them decoding skills! It may also be because this is what they can't read and this is where they are having problems. In fact, for students with learning disabilities, the area of word identification may be a particularly critical one, one on which a great deal of effort is expended. Reading, for these children, becomes a process of identifying words. On this very basic, fundamental level, we find a critical difference between good and poor readers.

The problem for poor readers is compounded by the fact the their knowledge structures may be inadequate or inappropriate. This problem may, in fact, increase in significance as the student goes through school, faced with more complicated academic tasks and more complex reading materials. Undoubtedly, one contributing factor is that students with learning disabilities who have a reading problem do little reading. The materials utilized during instruction usually are limited in content since they reflect the level of decoding ability. The less reading that is done and the less exposure to meaningful text, the less information the child acquires (Snider & Tarver, 1987; Stanovich, 1988).

The information acquired through both experiences and reading text form the reader's schema, "organized structures of stereotypic knowledge. They are higher-order cognitive structures that assist in understanding and recalling events and information" (Bos & Vaughn, 1994, p. 57). We add new information to these schema and at the same time use schema to aid in the understanding of new information. Inadequate and inappropriate schemata are a significant problem for the students with learning disabilities (Vogel & Walsh, 1987) and are another point of separation from good readers.

- Good readers are active readers and are risk takers.

They think about the text as they progress through it; they question the text; they question themselves; they make guesses about the words, word meanings, plot directions. Good readers are "purposeful, active and flexible"

(Winograd & Niquette, 1988, p. 40). This is not the case with poor readers. Pinnell (1989) observes, for example, that "sometimes poor readers simply sit, waiting to be corrected or to be told a word" (p.167). Kletzien (1991) points out that good readers need to take a risk, to be willing to take a chance. This can be a problem for some poor readers. In fact, the picture painted of the student with learning disabilities as often passive and reluctant to participate actively, as afraid of failure, does not fit well with the active reader, who is willing to take risks.

• They exhibit self-confidence, a sense of control, and an interest in reading.

This sense of self-confidence, control, and interest permeates all aspects of reading for the good reader from a willingness to take a risk in decoding a word to displaying confidence in strategy use. An example of this sense of control and self-confidence is the good reader's willingness to abandon an ineffective known strategy for a different, possibly more effective one. "If readers feel that they have control over what will happen to them in an academic situation, they will become more likely to attempt to use strategies to compensate for difficulties they encounter. On the other hand, if readers feel that their comprehension depends on the text or on the teacher, they are less likely to try to utilize any strategies that they might know" (Kletzien, 1991, p. 80). Readers who, for whatever reason, do not perceive themselves in control, who view themselves as helpless, are considered "at risk" (Vacca & Padak, 1990). Poor self-image and learned helplessness often go together. As we have seen, learned helplessness is frequently exhibited by students with learning disabilities. It's easier and safer to wait for the teacher to tell you what to do.

What do good readers do as they *preview, monitor,* and *reflect* while reading text?

• Good readers activate prior knowledge of content and of text structure to develop hypotheses and predictions about words, concepts, and meaning to further comprehension of text.

> Idol and Croll (1987) state that "the correspondence between a reader's underlying knowledge structures (schemata) and the textual material determines the extent of comprehension" (p. 215). Good readers use previous experience and knowledge in constructing responses to text (Bos & Vaughn, 1994; Kletzien, 1991). In some instances, however, the reader may fail to recognize and/or utilize that correspondence. This is another point of difference between the good reader and the poor reader. Some research findings have supported the notion "that poor readers may be unable to see relationships between text and inference" (Idol & Croll, 1987, p. 215). Shafrir et al. (1990) suggest that the difficulty experienced by students with learning disabilities in making appropriate inferences might be due to their failure to apply metacognitive strategies, such as detecting errors. In addition, unlike good readers, these students may be unable to connect underlying knowledge structures (which may be inadequate or inappropriate) with new information. In addition, students may over-rely on background knowledge, failing to make sufficient use of the text in constructing meaning (Bos & Vaughn, 1994). We begin to appreciate the complexity of the task.

• They employ a variety of strategies as they interact with text.

> Good readers are strategic, using cognitive strategies as they interact with text to construct meaning (Bos & Vaughn, 1994; Pinnell, 1989). Cognitive strategies are

often thought of as "tools" for thinking, procedures or steps that facilitate learning. Pinnell (1989) suggests that they are "'in the head' processes" (p. 166). Strategies may include organizing and reorganizing information and prior knowledge, questioning, self-questioning, and summarizing. Linguistic strategies, also, are tools, are ways of thinking about the aspects of language that are relevant to comprehending text such as accumulated grapheme-phoneme awareness, knowledge of structural elements (morphemes, words, word forms), and knowledge of text (syntax, semantics). These cognitive and linguistic strategies are generalized and transferred readily, as needed, by good readers. Good readers activate the "controller" during all stages of interaction with the text.

The difficulties in strategy acquisition, use, and generalization already identified are particularly evident in reading, which by its nature requires strategic behavior. Good and poor readers may differ on the number of strategies they have (Vacca & Padak, 1990) or on their ability to use strategies as the text becomes more difficult. Kletzien (1991) reports that good and poor high school readers "used the same type and number of strategies on the easy passage, but as the passage difficulty increased, good comprehenders used more types of strategies and used strategies more often than the poor comprehender did" (p.67). There has been an increasing amount of data supporting the notion that the difficulties students with learning disabilities have in strategy use in general is also evident in the act of reading (Reid & Harris, 1993; Rottman & Cross, 1990). They "do not spontaneously use organized and goal-directed strategies" (Rottman & Cross, 1990, p. 271) or adapt strategies to new text. "It appears that much of poor reader's comprehension difficulty is due to an inactive, non-strategic approach to text processing" (Ryan, Short & Weed, 1986, p. 524).

• Good readers engage in metacognitive and metalinguistic strategies as they read and use text information.

"Metacognition refers to the knowledge we have about our thinking processes or strategies, and our ability to regulate these processes or strategies to ensure successful learning" (Bos & Vaughn, 1994, p. 113). Metacognitive strategies enable the reader to monitor comprehension success or failure, take steps to overcome the problem, and apply the strategy independently to new situations. They can also be applied on a variety of levels, including, for example, identifying words and associating meaning with words. Metalinguistics has the same base of monitoring and controlling as metacognition, but it is applied to elements of language, frequently phonemes and syntax. For example, Fowler (1988) defines metalinguistics as "the most unnatural skill of extracting and manipulating phonemic elements" (p. 91) while also recognizing the importance of manipulating and restating the components of a sentence. It involves both the form and the meaning of language.

"Poor readers fail to monitor their comprehension deeply enough to permit them to detect violations of internal consistency or even just common sense, and they rarely take remedial action even if an error is detected; their comprehension-monitoring faculty is either weak or non-existent" (Brown & Campione, 1986, p.1063). Problems in the areas of metacognition and metalinguistics are widely identified with students with learning disabilities (Bos & Vaughn, 1994; Chan et al., 1990; Graham & Wong, 1993; Rottman & Cross, 1990; Ryan et al., 1986; Shafrir et al., 1990).

• They use a variety of text cues: graphic and pictorial cues, identification of key words, word recognition, phonemic and structural cues, signal words, word meaning, syntax, text structure, and content.

> Good readers do not rely on one source of information but rather recognize and use a variety of sources from the text (Bos & Vaughn, 1994; Horn & Manis, 1985), changing the emphasis depending upon their own background knowledge, the difficulty and unfamiliarity of the text, and the context in which the reading takes place. This process requires a high degree of awareness and of flexibility, both of which may be in short supply for the student with learning disabilities. Reading in this context is a decision-making process in which the problems presented by the text are identified and solved and decisions made on how to proceed. We have seen that the student with learning disabilities can be deficient in developing and using problem solving strategies. We will examine each of these textual cues to identify difficulties students with learning disabilities have exhibited.

Perhaps one of the most important points about good readers is that these variables seem to work together. As previously mentioned, the good reader doesn't use one to the exclusion of the others. Pinnell (1989) describes this process, pointing out to us that "good readers use meaning, their own sense of language structure, and visual information to monitor their own reading" (p. 166). In addition they "cross-reference the different kinds of information they bring to the reading of a text" (p. 166). They may use prior knowledge to predict words that might be in the text and cross-reference predictions with visual information in the text, i.e., the words. They search for and use cues. Good readers "are active problem solvers" (Pinnell, 1989, p. 167), looking for cues from prior experiences, print, pictures, and language structure. In researching the indicators that differentiate good from poor readers, Levy and Hinchley (1990) conclude that there probably is not one way of organizing the skills that characterize the good reader as compared with the poor reader. Rather, it may depend on the reader, the task, and the text. Because of all of these variables, reading, according to Carlisle (1989), is a complex process of interrelated comprehension strategies under the umbrella of reasoning. Finally, as the child is learning to engage in this complex task, there is a recognition that "reading as a language activity is socially mediated" (Bos & Vaughn, 1994, p. 108). There is a sharing of the meanings constructed and the strategies used.

Therefore, the task of studying such a complex and integrated system is a most difficult one. It is a task that calls for the unraveling of the strands that make up the good reader. This will allow us to gain insight into how these strands combine or fail to combine, forming the resulting end product for the reader with learning disabilities.

CHAPTER 3

Instruction: Enabling Effective Learning

At this point, we have focused on students with learning disabilities. We have reviewed their characteristics and abilities and have begun to indicate difficulties our target population might experience. Before moving ahead we need to begin to examine some general issues of instruction. One of the first questions relates to whether instruction can make a difference for students with learning disabilities. Sawyer (1992) represents a common perspective on this question. She suggests that developmental dyslexia can occur "(1) as a consequence of a mismatch between level of maturation attained and environmental stimulation provided, and (2) as a consequence of impaired biological capabilities, unable to benefit from environmental stimulation provided over periods of time that are presumed to be reasonable and even generous" (p. 92). In either case, the match or mismatch between instruction and the cognitive ability to receive that particular instruction is critical. A substantial number of students with learning disabilities are victims of this mismatch and of the impact of inappropriate methods of reading instruction. The importance of the instruction provided to students with learning disabilities cannot be overestimated.

This perspective reflects a view of learning disabilities in which the student is seen as part of an environment, an environment that can be changed, adapted, elaborated to enable the student to benefit from the environment. It also reflects the importance of the interaction of the student with the environment and the need for control and active participation on the part of the student. Felton and Brown (1990) suggest that we must consider "the child's ability to meet the demands of the classroom in terms of the attentional skills required and, perhaps more importantly, the impact of the instructional methods used in teaching reading" (p. 57). This certainly suggests the need for the teacher to plan instruction carefully, using strategies based on current research findings.

How can we apply what we have learned from our examination of the characteristics of students with learning disabilities to the process of providing instruction in reading? We will focus on general strategies for teaching and learning that can be used in teaching a variety of reading skills and content areas. Let's begin with some basic principles of successful instruction.

APPLY LEARNING THEORY TO PRACTICE

Theories and models of learning can help us understand more about how students learn and how we can modify our teaching to make it more effective. Four approaches to learning and teaching are particularly important. We encourage the reader to become familiar with each of these models, for good teachers integrate all of them to construct the teaching-learning process in their own classrooms. First, the *behavioral/operant learning theory* focuses on modifying the learning environment based on observed student behavior and the antecedents and consequences that control that behavior. Second, *cognitive behavior modification* concentrates on self-regulation of the learning processes by the student. Such components as application of strategy steps, modeling by the teacher, verbalization, and reflective thinking are important. Certainly, in view of what we know about possible cognitive difficulties encountered by students with learning disabilities and the concomitant importance of cognitive strategies for developing and using reading skills and strategies, this approach is very relevant. Third, a *sociocultural theory of learning* highlights the social nature of learning. This theory encourages interactive discussions between students and teachers in a supportive structure that will enable students to acquire new strategies, skills, and knowledge. We know that this is an important variable for learning and, at the same time, is an area that may cause students with learning disabilities some difficulty. Certainly, this is a focus we need to include in the learning environment. Finally, *information processing and schema theories* center on the ways in which information is received, transformed, retrieved, and expressed. Sensing, sensory store, attention, perception, memory, executive functioning, and metacognition are important components of this model. They are critical in the development of literacy and are also areas that may produce difficulty and frustration for student and teacher alike. Given that theory should guide practice, these models of instruction can be helpful in deciding when and in what ways different approaches can be applied to improve instruction.

PROVIDE AN INTERACTIVE ENVIRONMENT

A classroom environment that encourages lively interaction will help to engage students in learning. The social context in which learning occurs influences the reading processes, and the social interactions between teacher and student and among students are important ingredients in the context for learning.

Reciprocal teaching is an instructional strategy that exemplifies this principle (Palincsar & Brown, 1987; Palincsar & Klenck, 1992). Teachers and students may take turns leading discussions about shared text materials rather than the teacher typically providing the leadership. The reciprocal teaching approach teaches cognitive strategies through a social dialogue between the classroom participants. First, the students and teacher read the material silently. Next, the teacher models and explains the strategies to be learned by saying out loud the thoughts that the teacher used while employing those strategies. Third, the students read another passage and try to demonstrate the strategies out loud for other students. Guidance and support, called scaffolding, help students perfect their demonstrations. Finally, each student demonstrates competence in the strategies being learned. Palincsar and Brown's strategies include direct, explicit instruction in clarifying and predicting, summarizing, self-correcting errors, self-generating questions, and studying effectively. These researchers demonstrated that students' reading comprehension improved when they were instructed with the reciprocal teaching approach. Because reading entails constructing meaning, it requires active thinking and reasoning on the part of the reader. Instructional strategies that involve students actively during every step of the learning process have much to recommend them, particularly with students with learning disabilities whose performance may be characterized by passivity.

INDIVIDUALIZE OBJECTIVES AND INSTRUCTION

If instructional planning provides for individualized goals, fewer students will be viewed as failures. Altering expectations and instruction to accommodate a broad range of abilities and learning styles can provide an alternative to special classes for teaching many students with learning disabilities to read (Gelzheiser, 1987). As we have pointed out earlier, individualized instruction does not mean each child working alone. It means instruction designed to meet particular needs. The child can work alone or in groups. The key is the focus on the individual needs. In many areas of education we at least give lip service, if not whole hearted support, to the notion of individualizing instruction. Nowhere is it more critical than in the field of learning disabilities. As we have seen, there is no one diagnosis, no one definition, no one set of characteristics that we can use to build a program for these students. We must, by the very nature of the term, develop programs that will be productive for each individual.

ACCOMMODATE A VARIETY OF LEARNING STYLES

We have recently recognized that all students have individual learning styles. If a student's learning style is at odds with the style required to succeed in the educational system, difficulties are likely to ensue. A style of learning refers to the student's attitude, temperament, and general behavior when presented with a learning task. Although researchers have investigated a broader range of characteristic learning styles, we encounter two of them most frequently in students with learning disabilities.

First, the impulsive learning style exhibited by a number of students with learning disabilities poses problems in the classroom. Torgesen (1991) suggests that impulsivity may stem from a lack of alternative cognitive strategies. He believes that we need to help students acquire an array of appropriate cognitive strategies to supplement their inherent styles.

A second way to analyze students' learning styles is by the extent to which they are active or passive learners. Students who approach the learning task with undue dependence exemplify, as we have discussed, a learning style often referred to as "learned helplessness." Because an active involvement is required for efficient learning, a passive learning style hinders students' chances for success. Because of this, Garner, Alexander, and Hare (1991) stress that fostering active comprehension monitoring is of primary importance.

De Bello (1990) compares eleven major learning styles models by presenting an overview of each, their components, the populations for which they are intended, the reliability and validity of their instrumentation, and the ways in which they overlap and differ. He notes that at the present time it is unclear whether one should teach to students' strengths or attempt to expand their learning styles. He concludes, however, that "current research affirms that learning styles-based programs statistically increase student achievement" (p. 219). It appears that consideration of match between the learning styles of students and the style expected in the classroom is helpful in our efforts to teach students with learning disabilities to read.

PROVIDE INSTRUCTIONAL ALTERNATIVES

An important theoretical as well as practical issue related to instruction is whether or, possibly, when the teacher should provide direct instruction in the skill or strategy that is the focus of the lesson or should allow the student to engage in the task in such a way as to discover the point of the lesson. This is certainly an issue faced by teachers each day.

Students with learning disabilities respond well to direct instruction. This approach to teaching stems from behavioral theory that emphasizes the curriculum or tasks to be taught and analysis of behaviors needed to learn those tasks. Other terms that also refer to this kind of teaching include mastery learning, directed teaching, explicit teaching, and sequential skills teaching. Direct instruction focuses on the academic skills that students need to learn and structuring the environment to ensure that students master these skills (Carnine, Silbert, & Kameenui, 1990). This approach to instruction has the following characteristics: academic focus, teacher directed, goals that are clear to students, carefully sequenced and structured materials, sufficient time for instruction, continuous monitoring of student performance, immediate feedback to students, and instruction continued until mastery of the skill in achieved.

Direct instruction may be applied to teaching a specific skill, such as a spelling rule, or it may be applied to more complex processes such as ensuring strategy identification, use, and monitoring. For example, Darch and Kameenui (1987) taught elementary school students with learning disabilities to detect faulty arguments with direct instruction using specific rules and strategies. They report that these students significantly outperformed students taught via a discussion/workbook approach.

This linkage of direct instruction and strategy development is widely supported. Garner, Alexander, and Hare (1991) stress that teachers should emphasize direct, explicit instruction in teaching strategies to children. This includes direct explanations about the processes entailed in comprehension. Extensive modeling also is an important component. Also, teachers should be aware that "explicit information about *when* to use strategies is as important as explicit information about *how* to use them" (p. 295). The authors go on to suggest that it is important to achieve a transfer of control of learning from teacher to student. They suggest that this process might begin with explicit training, then shift to guided practice of strategies on which students have been trained, and finally move to student-regulated practice and independent reading. They cite the "reciprocal teaching" method as one that builds in this planned ceding of teacher control. This approach is often employed to facilitate interaction between the learner and the instructional environment.

Another approach to instruction is to construct the environment in such a way that the student discovers or builds the skill or strategy to be learned. The teacher does not isolate skills through direct instruction but rather allows students to grapple with learning and mastering relevant skills and strategies through immersion in text and in literacy experiences, without direct instruction. Frequently this kind of issue arises when instruction is provided using a whole language approach. As we will see, particularly in the discussion of reading words, there is much controversy about using this approach with students with learning disabilities. The reliance on discovery or constructed learning is not limited to reading words, however, but is also relevant to strategy learning and comprehending. Harris and Pressley (1991) assure us that "educators need not choose between constructed and instructed knowledge, but, rather, recognize that active mental construction is part of all human learning and that instruction therefore must 'provide the material on which learner's constructive processes can operate'" (p. 393).

PROVIDE FOR LINGUISTIC AND COGNITIVE DEVELOPMENT

In viewing the characteristics that affect the acquisition and use of literacy by students with learning disabilities, we begin to see, quite clearly, areas that need to be included in reading programs. Certainly language skills and language development have been recognized for some time as areas of difficulty for many students with learning disabilities. When we add the notion of the foundation of language in the process of reading, we can identify language as an area that needs to be recognized and probably included in programs for many students with learning disabilities.

The impact of cognition is so critical in the acquisition and development of literacy that we must consider whether the various aspects of this variable should be incorporated in instruction. Sawyer (1992), for example, identifies difficulties in strategy use and suggests that "efficient compensatory strategies can be induced if instruction focuses on critical underpinnings for reading strategies as well as on the strategies themselves" (p. 93). She also stresses the need for an enriched language environment. Note the emphasis on incorporating both strategy instruction and language development. It is, in fact, this broad approach to instruction that characterizes much current application of theory.

TEACH COGNITIVE STRATEGIES

Reading, as we have seen, is a strategic process in which the reader must use a variety of thinking strategies to derive meaning from the text. Some of these strategies are directly related to comprehending the text. Others are related to metacognition, knowing about strategies and knowing when and how to apply specific strategies. Finally, we need strategies to help translate printed words into meaning: attentional, perceptual, contextual, and memory processes to activate background knowledge. As Seidenberg (1989) points out, investigations in text processing have helped us "to translate reading and writing skills into explicit strategies that students can be taught directly" (p. 7).

In looking at cognitive and metacognitive strategies, Wong (1991b) provides a clear example, relating them to reading.

> Cognitive strategy is a procedure that enables an individual to reach a goal. For example, one can learn a summarization strategy to record efficient notes from one's reading. A metacognitive strategy is a procedure that involves self-monitoring, self-testing, or self-evaluation. For example, one can learn a strategy that helps one to self-check whether or not one has properly carried out the summarization strategy. This self-monitoring strategy may consist of self-questions such as: "Have I included all the important points from this passage in my summary?" A self-evaluative strategy may have these self-questions: "How good is my summary? Is it sufficiently concise? Have I paraphrased all the important points?" Clearly both kinds of strategies, cognitive and metacognitive, are important in our successful learning and performance. (p. 234)

The question is, will strategy instruction be effective? Can students with learning disabilities who demonstrate difficulty in strategy acquisition, use, and generalization learn and use reading strategies? Recent findings have demonstrated that students with learning disabilities can be taught to behave strategically (Graham & Harris, 1994; Palincsar & Brown, 1987; Swanson, 1990). It appears that students can learn to use strategies even though they may not be able to discover them themselves (Graham & Harris, 1990). We have also learned that strategy instruction can improve reading comprehension (Harris & Pressley, 1991; Newby, Caldwell, & Recht, 1989; Paris & Oka, 1989; Wong, 1986; Wong, 1991b) as well as arithmetic problem solving (Fleischner, Nuzum, & Marzola, 1987). As Scruggs and Mastropieri (1993b) write: "Strategy instruction has been shown to be very effective, particularly in promoting such skills as reading comprehension, listening comprehension, note taking, memory for content, essay writing, and effective test taking" (p. 395). In addition, giving students information regarding the benefits of using reading comprehension strategies increases their effectiveness (Schunk & Rice, 1992; 1987).

In suggesting strategy instruction, we rely heavily on current research. Chan (1991), in discussing the field of learning disabilities, asserts that "research indicates that students with reading disabilities, in particular, benefit from explicit instruction in the use of cognitive and metacognitive strategies" (p. 427). Seidenberg (1989) concludes that the instructional implications derived from this research "can provide a framework for instructional practice for teachers seeking to improve the reading and writing competencies of learning disabled students" (p. 10). A cautionary note needs to be included here. Wong (1991b) states that "the effects of long-term cumulative strategy instruction on normal-achieving children and LD children have not been researched" (p. 252). Benefits that should accrue from such research would be an understanding of how learners modify the learned strategies for their own purposes; the effects across cumulative strategy learning; and how well the learners transferred the learned strategies to other settings and domains.

How do we, as teachers, provide strategy instruction? Thornburg (1991) examines the issue of the teacher structuring and guiding the lesson to enable the student to self-instruct. The teacher describes and models the strategy, "thinks aloud" during the process, guides the student's performance, and fades as the student thinks through the task (Graham & Wong, 1993; Harris & Pressley, 1991). This approach is referred to as "strategy instruction" or "cognitive process-based instruction" and stresses the underlying cognitive and metacognitive processes in learning, in our case, in learning to read (Wong, 1992b). This approach to instruction recognizes the critical role of cognition in learning, at the same time that the teacher is providing direct instruction and enabling the student to construct new learning. "Strategy instruction is neither a panacea nor a holy grail for the field of special education . . . . Used appropriately, however, cognitive strategy instruction is an exciting and viable contribution to the special educator's repertoire" (Harris & Pressley, 1991, p. 401). At present, cognitive strategy instruction typically is not integrated into the curriculum, and many teachers make little use of it. Barriers that prevent broad-scale implementation of strategy instruction are examined by Kline, Deshler, and Schumaker (1992), and suggestions are provided that should prove helpful for those interested in investigating what changes will be needed to accomplish this objective.

The self-perception of the reader as being competent and responsible for his or her own learning seems to be closely related to performance in reading and to the acquisition of cognitive and metacognitive strategies. As we have seen, this mental set is often cited as a characteristic of good readers. Unfortunately, readers with learning disabilities frequently view themselves as not being responsible for their own learning, and they may attribute the responsibility for success or failure to an outside source (Ryan, Short, and Weed, 1986). By providing strategy training, by motivating, and by engaging these students in the act of reading, they may become empowered; thus the responsibility for succeeding or failing begins to shift.

What does cognitive process-based instruction involve? It supports the learner's development of new skills and abilities. It also bridges the gap between the learner's actual level of development and the level needed for independent problem solving, sometimes alluded to as the zone of proximal development. Wong (1992b) explains it to us as "the teacher teaching through modeling and thinking aloud the cognitive processes that underlie the acquisition of knowledge, or the execution of task, or the solving of a problem in a specific academic domain" (p. 150). She goes on to explain that this type of instruction rests on the assumptions that our cognitive processes can be studied and that the resulting knowledge can benefit students.

Graham and Harris (1990) report the need for explicit strategy instruction in which students know what they are doing, why they are doing it, and how and when to apply the strategy to different situations. The obligation of the teacher is to teach strategies and encourage their use. Graham and Harris stress that one of the most important things needed by students with learning disabilities is this kind of strategy instruction. Despite the strides that have been made, Graham and Harris (1994) point out that "the number of academic strategies that have been evaluated using scientific methods is quite small" (p. 147). They go on to urge expanded research in this area.

Earlier efforts to teach general cognitive strategies, devoid of domain content, focused on teaching students to learn in a planned, strategic, and flexible manner. An example of such a strategy would be Feuerstein's Instrumental Enrichment, which utilized twenty instructional instruments to teach thinking skills. The instrument often selected to be used first is an amorphous array of dots for which the student must analyze and then use the underlying structure (Feuerstein et al., 1985). Two important difficulties that students trained on these general strategies encountered were maintenance of the strategies and transfer to specific domains such as improving reading comprehension in the social studies or science classroom.

Interest in the possibility that strategy instruction integrated with instruction in specific content domains might be more effective accelerated, in part as an effort to address these difficulties. Several reasons that favor this type of approach are important to us. First, the problem of transfer of general strategies to specific domains would in large part be avoided, for instruction would be provided initially in the particular domain. Second, motivation to learn the strategy should be higher if students can see the link between the strategy and learning content-area information. Third, domain-specific content knowledge interacts with general problem solving strategies. Given these considerations, the current direction of research in cognitive strategy instruction, including that in reading comprehension, anchors this instruction in content domains (Wong, 1993) ranging from social science to literature.

READ LITERATURE
WITH A FOCUS ON MEANING

Given that the purpose of reading is to derive meaning, it is axiomatic that literature should be a component of any program of reading instruction. Agreement with this statement would be easy for most of us; more difficult, however, would be to plan the logistics of carrying it out in classes with students who are remedial readers or who have limited proficiency in English. Ellsworth (1992) provides a theoretical and practical overview for devising a teaching methodology that encompasses the multiple needs of the children in such a class, including guidelines for selecting the literature to be read.

Many interesting accounts have been published of successful applications of literature with students with learning disabilities. We will mention only a few of them that may be of special interest to classroom teachers. Roser, Hoffman, and Farest (1990) report on their efforts to bring quality literature into a reading program serving primarily limited English-speaking students, concluding that the inclusion of children's literature had a positive effect on both students and teachers. Shapiro and Welch (1991) tell of their success in using poetry with an adolescent with severe learning disabilities after several semesters of trying other approaches. Groshong (1988) recounts Junior Great Books discussions that she used to teach critical thinking skills and independent learning behaviors to fifth graders with learning disabilities. And finally, Hittleman (1988) explains ways in which teachers can use literature to build daily living skills.

At the junior high school level, Glowacki (1990) offers practical suggestions for integrating literature into daily reading instruction that should be helpful to teachers. Farris and Andersen (1990), in a case study, report their personal experiences of adopting a literature-based, whole language program for junior high school students with learning disabilities. They read aloud to students on a daily basis, encouraged the participation of students in selecting the books to be read, integrated written and oral responses to the literature, and engaged in sustained silent reading daily. These teachers report, "A literature-based reading program may not be the answer for all students, but it is a desirable alternative" (p. 12).

SELECT CONSIDERATE TEXTS

We are likely to be disappointed if we expect that a student's independent reading of text that is too difficult will be sufficient to comprehend new information. Because textbooks are the most frequently used instructional material at all levels of school beyond the primary grades, their choice becomes especially important. What are the characteristics of texts that may enhance or interfere with students' comprehension? Let's examine what research tells us of providing learnable text for students to read, i.e., text that students have the requisite skills to comprehend.

Putnam (1993) reports that the four text-based variables that most influence comprehension include text language, text organization, story structure, and text readability. Text language includes semantics, syntax, background knowledge, and the match between the reader's own language and that used in the text. Text organization refers to how logically organized a textbook is for the reader. Story structure refers to how ideas have been interrelated to convey meaning. Text readability is defined as the minimum level of competence required to understand the text. Readability formulae such as the Flesch Index, the FOG Index, and the Dale-Chall Readability Formula based on word length, sentence length, and sentence complexity are often employed as a rough measure of reading difficulty.

Other studies affirm that the factors that make a textbook easy or difficult to understand are complex, extending well beyond traditional "readability" formulae. Ellis and Lenz (1990) suggest that teachers need to select textbooks based on a range of criteria. They point out that using readability formulae as the primary basis for "selecting alternative textbooks thought to be controlled for reading difficulty is problematic" (p. 5).

Armbruster and Anderson (1988) suggest that structure, coherence, and audience appropriateness form the most important bases for evaluating textbooks. They conclude that "content-area textbooks that are 'user-friendly' are relatively easy to read, understand, and learn from" (p. 47), and they offer practical suggestions for reviewing textbooks that should be helpful to teachers.

Kinder, Bursuck, and Epstein (1992) evaluated ten eighth-grade American history textbooks that are frequently used. They considered readability, global and local coherence, use of questions, and introduction of new vocabulary as measures of difficulty. Their suggestions of criteria for selecting considerate texts should be of particular interest to teachers reviewing textbooks in this area.

USE TECHNOLOGICAL
ENHANCEMENTS TO READING

American classrooms are structured around print, a technology that Rose, Meyer, and Pisha (1994) conclude is inadequate to meet the challenges of inclusion, individualization, and student engagement. They propose that we design new approaches for teaching and learning around new technologies, "technologies that are flexible enough to respond to the diversity among children and malleable enough to include all children in the active exploration of a world whose knowledge is no longer fixed in permanent ink" (p. 59). They suggest that electronic multimedia offer this flexibility. For example, format options can include "enlargeable text for beginning readers or students with visual impairments; choices for highlighting words and sentences on the screen to support focused attention; digital or synthetic speech to help with word decoding, instantly translatable into numerous languages" (p. 59) and many other format options. Although electronic multimedia technology is used in few schools today, it has such benefits for students having difficulty learning to read that research and development in this area is increasing. Meanwhile, less sophisticated and less expensive technologies such as microcomputers and audiotape recordings are used extensively.

Computer-assisted instruction to present new information or for review can enable students to comprehend and remember challenging content-area readings more effectively, both at school and at home (Rickelman & Henk, 1991). Majsterek and Wilson (1989) report that the results from reading research "support the use of CAI [computer-assisted instruction] for pupils with LD" (p. 19). They review important considerations for teachers who wish to use CAI in their classrooms. These authors conclude that good results are obtained "when instructional software . . . is designed using effective practices and when the materials are used appropriately to meet the student's educational needs" (p. 25).

Carrasquillo and Nunez (1988) investigated the effects of software that monitors the student's use of metacognitive strategies as a part of improving reading comprehension. They reported that ESL students using the Tutorial-Direct Monitoring Strategy, based on the work of Palincsar and Brown, performed better than students using computer-mediated text who were not using the strategy monitoring component.

Given the benefits that technology can offer students in the area of reading, why is it not more widespread? Hicks (1988) writes: "The first time I taught a course about computers to special education teachers, I was stunned at the apprehension in the teachers" (p. 227). Investigation of teachers' needs is under way. Cicchelli and Baecher (1989) examined teacher concerns about using microcomputers in the classroom. They concluded that inservice activities that match the degree of concern of teachers about using computer technology in their classrooms may reduce resistance to implementation.

Audiotape recordings, a more widely implemented technological enhancement, can help students with reading difficulties to enjoy the same literature as other students and to acquire new information from content readings. One type of audio recording enhancement is verbatim audiotapes of the text. Torgesen, Dahlem, and Greenstein (1987) report that when adolescents used a verbatim recording and completed a worksheet as they read a chapter-length text, they made significant gains on weekly comprehension tests.

A second type of audio recording enhancement is key information tapes in which parts of textbooks are recorded verbatim and other parts are paraphrased to emphasize important information. Paraphrased parts may include advance organizers, reviews, summaries, and cues to students to take notes on important information. Additional research is needed to determine the extent to which specific enhancements contribute to the effectiveness of audiotape recordings in extending reading comprehension (Hudson, Lignugaris-Kraft, & Miller, 1993).

SUMMARY

Effective instructional strategies are of overriding importance for students with learning disabilities, for, by definition, these are students who have failed to learn as expected. We are fortunate that a great deal of progress has been made in recent years through research such as that reported in this book, and it is important to push ahead. As Scruggs and Mastropieri (1994) remind us: "[There is] far too little research intended to identify methods for improving the social or academic functioning of students with learning disabilities" (p. 130).

CHAPTER 4

Reading Words

THE IMPORTANCE OF WORD RECOGNITION

What students do with print and how effectively they do it is important to their growth and success as readers. The ability to read words is critical to the comprehension of the text. You may not need to read every word, but you certainly need to be able to read a substantial number of them. The value of both accurate and automatic word recognition for the development of reading ability, particularly in beginning reading, has been well substantiated (Bruck & Waters, 1990). Adams (1990) maintains that skilled readers will also need automatic access to words. "There is now substantial empirical evidence that fluent word recognition skills are a crucial prerequisite for the construction of meaning from text" (Torgesen, 1986).

Perhaps equally important, the ability to identify words is critical to the sense of empowerment it gives the reader. Beginning readers as well as poor readers of all ages frequently believe that the ability to read words is critical. Faced with new text that is filled with words they don't recognize, they realize the need to identify words in order to comprehend the text. They need a place to begin. Written words can provide that starting point. If these readers are to have some sense of control, some empowerment in the process of acquiring literacy, they need some signs of success in this area.

For many children, word recognition turns out to be a difficult task. Ehri (1987) states that "from our findings and those of others, it is clear that learning to process graphic cues accurately, automatically, and rapidly is one of the hardest parts of learning to read. It is a part that consumes substantial learning time. It is a skill that clearly separates good readers from poor readers." (p. 9). Because of the importance of access to words, findings that this is a significant problem area for students with learning disabilities are of particular concern. Reetz and Hoover (1992), for example, identify reading as the most prevalent problem area for students with learning disabilities and word identification as the most common area of difficulty. As we look at the development of word identification skills and strategies, we can highlight the particular areas of difficulty experienced by students with learning disabilities.

WORD RECOGNITION
AND MODELS OF READING

> Reading is a skill that, to a large extent, is based on
> knowledge of the rules for translating letters and groups
> of letters into sounds but also of the existence of
> irregularities that call for disregarding those rules. (van
> Bon, Boksebeld, Freide, & van den Hurk, 1991, p. 471)

As this quote indicates, the emphasis in learning to read has traditionally been placed upon the reader's processing of the small units of written text, the letters and the words, either reading the words as a holistic unit (sight word reading) or reading the words by analyzing and synthesizing the sounds and letters into words (decoding). Because there are two routes to acquiring skill in reading words, the visual and the phonetic, the process has been called a "dual-access" or "dual-route" model of "parallel coding systems" (Beech & Awaida, 1992; Ehri, 1991; Manis, Szeszulski, Holt & Graves, 1990; Olson, Wise, Conners, & Rack, 1990; Rack, Snowling, & Olson, 1992). Recently, the assertion has been made that these two routes are not necessarily distinct and separate (Ehri, 1991; Rack et al., 1992). It may be that both routes combine in the recognition of some words and that readers may have difficulties with one or both of these routes. In any case, the focus in word recognition has traditionally been on print, on how the reader interacts with the text on the print level. This point of view represents a bottom-up model of reading.

However, it is important to recognize that:

> The identification of words during reading is a complex process that is aided by information from at least two sources. First, readers use information derived from comprehension of what they are reading to identify words as they occur in text. Word recognition is facilitated when words in text are consistent with expectations derived from context. Second, information derived directly from the printed visual symbols for words is also critical to word identification processes during reading. . . . Current models of word identification processes suggest that the information involved in identifying words from print falls within two broad domains: phonological and orthographic. (Barker, Torgesen, & Wagner, 1992, p. 335)

Although the model represented here, the interactive model, differs from the first quotation, the view of word identification is similar: a dual access route. Both routes to word identification are important for good readers. It has been documented that when recognizing words as single, holistic units out of context (sight word recognition) good readers are able to do so more accurately and more rapidly than poorer readers (Amoruso, Bryant, & Boehm, in press; Ehri, 1992). The ability to decode unknown words independently is, as we will see, widely recognized as important to readers.

We have already raised some issues about which comes first, reading the words or comprehending the text. Findings such as those made by Sawyer (1992) are illustrative of the view that, in considering beginners, comprehension is highly influenced by word recognition. As some skill develops, comprehension influences word recognition. Eventually, as skills develop and mature, "word recognition and comprehension [are] essentially independent" (Sawyer, 1992, p. 82). This process is reminiscent of the models of reading we examined, particularly the interactive model, and certainly suggests that readers need some skills and strategies in reading words, skills that they can apply in different situations. "The goal of reading instruction should be to help students acquire a versatile and extensive word recognition repertoire" (Alexander & Pate, 1991, p. 54). As students develop their reading system, they not only need to be able to identify words, they need a variety of ways of achieving that end. However, it is important that all recognize that "rapid word processing is not sufficient for effective comprehension" (Levy & Hinchley, 1990, p. 122). As we will see when we explore issues related to text comprehension, there is a great deal involved here besides the ability to read words rapidly.

PHASES OF WORD RECOGNITION

It appears from the literature that beginning reading acquisition seems to progress through three developmental phases: a logographic phase, an alphabetic phase, and an orthographic phase (Ehri, 1991; Frith, 1986; Rack et al., 1992; Sawyer, 1992). There are some variations in how different theorists and researchers view these stages, differences that will be noted in the discussion. These phases can provide a framework for the study of word recognition, the difficulties encountered by the reader with learning disabilities, and instructional alternatives.

It is interesting to note the agreement among theorists that basic cognitive processes are involved in moving through these phases and in acquiring literacy despite disagreement in other areas (Sawyer, 1992). This is particularly relevant in view of the difficulties that students with learning disabilities may experience in strategy acquisition and use. These word identification phases are often considered to be a continuum, with skills and strategies acquired in one phase enabling the student to move to the next phase. Difficulty in passing from one phase to another might be due to "arrested development of cognitive abilities necessary to pass from one phase to another. Specifically, the abilities to 'merge' old strategies with new learning may be affected" (Sawyer, 1992, p. 90). Here, we see again the importance of strategies to the reader. We have also seen the difficulties students with learning disabilities may encounter in strategy use. The problem highlighted by Sawyer (1992) may be of particular concern to teachers of students with learning disabilities.

Phase 1. The Logographic Phase

There appear to be two graphic sources of information that readers can use to read words (Ehri, 1987). Probably the first to be used is the representation of the word in memory. The other, the representation of the sounds represented by the letters, stored in memory and used to analyze the word, appears to come later in the sequence. Thus, we start with the logographic, or sight word, phase. This phase, identified and named by Frith, is similar to Ehri's (1987, 1992) initial phase, visual cue reading.

Logographic sight word reading is an important phase of beginning reading for all learners. It involves the association of the whole word directly with meaning and the spoken word (paired-associate learning). Since it is a form of rote learning, it often requires much repetition and practice in order to have the word committed to memory (Amoruso et al., in press; Ehri, 1992; Sawyer, 1992). Word reading in this phase is characterized by the memorization of the visual form of the word and a recognition of its meaning. This phase requires a metalinguistic awareness of the terms "word" and "sentence" in order to recognize whole words. The emphasis is on the visual as opposed to the phonetic (Ehri, 1991). The reader attends to visual print cues and stores information in memory about specific words. The mapping of words is linked to meaning and pronunciation. The process is similar to the identification of simple Chinese characters (Amoruso et al., in press; Ehri, 1992; Frith, 1986; Sawyer, 1992). In examining skills and strategies in the logographic phase, we begin by reviewing what good readers do and then explore the difficulties that might be encountered by students with learning disabilities.

What do good readers do in this phase?

• They learn the mapping principle between print and sound, the notion that written words correspond to spoken words and letters to sounds (Manis et al., 1990).

> Metalinguistic abilities help the beginning reader discover the mapping between written words and speech (Sawyer, 1992). It is at this stage or earlier that basic print awareness and word awareness develop (Adams, 1990).

• They acquire a body of sight words that can be read automatically (Levy & Hinchley, 1990; Sawyer, 1992).

> Word recognition in this phase is essentially sight word recognition, the recognition of high-frequency words in isolation and in context. According to the dual-route theory, this involves reading words "by establishing direct connections between the visual forms of words seen in print and their meanings in memory as a result of much practice reading the words" (Ehri, 1992, p. 107). Ehri takes issue with this process of acquisition but concurs with the result. According to Ehri the end result is a store of sight words; the process is one of connecting spelling with pronunciation not with meaning.

• They use strategies for visually interacting with print.

> These strategies include: recognizing the word-to-word correspondence, moving from left to right across the line, and returning to the left for the beginning of the next line (Pinnell, 1989).

• They begin the process of moving from phase one to phase two, the alphabetic phase, using phonemic information.

> The areas of sound segmentation and phoneme-grapheme correspondence are the two areas that might be considered as transition areas between the first two phases. Phonemic segmentation has frequently been identified as one of the distinguishing characteristics of children who are successful in beginning reading (Levy & Hinchley, 1990). Segmental awareness, according to Morais (1987), requires experience with the alphabet and a certain degree of analytic ability.
>
> Learning in the area of phoneme-grapheme correspondence is generally limited to sounds and symbols in isolation (Sawyer, 1992) and is viewed as important to beginning reading (Bruck & Waters, 1990). There may be an interaction that occurs between knowledge of letter cues and acquisition of sight words (Manis et al., 1990). This knowledge might be used as a aid in recognizing sight words (Ehri & Robbins, 1992). According to Ehri (1987, 1991) phonetic cue reading enables the reader to identify words by remembering some letter cues, generally the first or last letter. Ehri (1992) describes this as a "visual route that is paved with phonological information leading into lexical memory" (p. 114). In addition, Sawyer (1992) suggests that the interaction of the skills of learning sight words with skills in sound segmentation and phoneme-grapheme correspondence appear to "trigger" the movement into the next phase.

Children at this stage may also use these beginning phonetic skills to read words by analogy to sight words already known (Ehri, 1991; Ehri & Robbins, 1992; Haskell, Foorman, & Swank, 1992; Manis et al., 1990). They identify the first letter and the rime, the last part of the word, relating this to the known word. Because there are fewer demands on the reader to analyze, segment, and blend sounds than are required in decoding each letter separately, this is seen as a transition to full decoding.

• Readers use a variety of methods to learn letter shapes, names, and associated sounds.

These may include associating sounds with meaningful words using mnemonics, discriminating letters, words, and fonts through association and meaning, and attaching meaning through story writing using inventive spelling (Ehri, 1991; Lipson & Wixson, 1991).

What areas have been identified as possible sources of difficulty in this phase for students with learning disabilities? In reviewing these areas, it is important to keep in mind that probably no one child will experience all these difficulties. The range and variety of difficulties that are found reflect the heterogeneity of the population labeled "learning disabled." Likewise, in each area of difficulty we may suggest several possible causes. Again, different causes may be relevant for different children. The uncertainty reflected in these statement highlights the uncertainties of working with students with learning disabilities. There are no neat formulas we can use.

• These students with may have difficulty identifying and naming letters because of visual discrimination difficulties.

Visual discrimination problems such as reversals and rotations of letters may impact on letter identification. A *b* and *d* are different, as are a *p* and *b*. Feagans and Merriwether (1990) suggest that not only does this area hinder beginning reading, but that "this deficit may have long-term consequences for reading recognition and comprehension" (p. 423).

The problem of reversing letters has frequently been associated with perceptual difficulties (Jordan & Jordan, 1990; Mather & Kirk, 1985) and remediated accordingly. However, questions have been raised about this conclusion. Bigsby (1985) points out that reversals in letters are not due to visual perception but to mislabeling. The problem is linguistic, a difficulty in translating from the visual cue to the name code. Bigsby identifies the need to stress letter to sound mapping. This finding relates to Coles' (1987) suggestion that reversals may be due to poor instruction rather than "any organic deficiency" (p. 30). This may also explain why programs that focus on visual perception have not been productive in remediating problems with letter reversals. Feagans and Merriwether (1990) hypothesize that this difficulty may be associated with lack of strategy use by students with learning disabilities; "they do not spontaneously attend to the correct features in the letter-like forms task" (p. 423). Finally, Mann and Brady (1988) caution that "reversal errors are made by almost all children at some point in their development" (p. 811). The sources of the difficulty with reversals are consonant with the kinds of linguistic and cognitive difficulties exhibited by some students with learning disabilities.

- They may have difficulty with the rote learning and memory task of recalling sight words.

Traditionally, while rote sight word recognition has been used to teach beginning reading to normally developing readers, readers with learning disabilities may have had difficulty with such rote learning and recall. In Swanson's (1988) review of memory subtypes, he points out that there appears to be a continuum of problems that can be experienced by students with learning disabilities. Over 50% of the students studied had difficulty forming multiple connections between information in memory and new information from the material used in the task. This translates into difficulty in the recall of sight words. Considering the difficulties some students with learning disabilities have with memory-related tasks in general, this is not surprising.

Olson et al. (1990) suggest that rather than an intrinsic cause for this problem there may be an extrinsic cause. Reading experience may be an important variable here, related to "the degree of print exposure in the home and reading instruction in the schools" (p. 298). This must be considered in light of Naslund and Samuels' view of automaticity in which automaticity develops through repeated exposure. Lack of reading experience may be a contributing factor in the difficulty encountered in acquiring a store of sight words. The problem may even be circular. The child can't read because he/she does not have an appropriate store of sight words. He/she does not acquire the store of sight words because of limited reading experiences.

- Students with learning disabilities rely heavily on context and meaning as a cue system in acquiring a store of sight words.

Some have also been suggested that "less skilled readers may in fact rely on context to assist word recognition to a greater extent than skilled readers" (Bruck & Waters, 1990, p. 193) in the process of acquiring a store of sight words (Amoruso et al., in press). This suggests that these readers rely on the lexical aspects of words to aid in reading to a greater degree than do skilled readers. In fact, Ehri (1992) finds that a characteristic of good readers is that they abandon the lexical access and use "a systematic connection between spellings and pronunciations rather than an arbitrary connection between spellings and meanings" (p. 108). Readers who have not made the links between phonetic cue reading and sight word acquisition maintain semantic association as a critical cue system for word identification (Ehri, 1991).

- They may have difficulty with the tasks of sound segmentation and phoneme-grapheme correspondences.

These are important transition skills for beginning readers. In fact, Ehri (1991, 1992) considers that these skills work in conjunction with the development of sight words and are part of the acquisition of a store of sight words. Frith (1986), among others, considers problems in these areas as typical of the range of problems of dyslexic readers. She cites evidence of "a causal connection between early failure in sound categorization and segmentation and later reading problems" (p. 75). The problem here may have long-term repercussions. Difficulty in sound segmentation is commonly cited for dyslexic students (Coles, 1987; Rack et al., 1992; Sawyer, 1992).

Problems in this area may be caused by intrinsic or extrinsic causes. Frith (1986) suggests that these difficulties may be due to a breakdown in the phonological domain, i.e., an oral speech problem. The previous discussion of problems associated with language highlighted ways that intrinsic difficulties in speech and language might impact on phonological awareness and development for students with learning disabilities. Olson et al. (1990) suggest that there is certainly a possibility that difficulties with segmental language tasks might be inherited. Morais (1987) also recognizes the importance of segmental awareness for the development of early reading but links it to an extrinsic cause: instruction and early reading experiences. When reading focuses on whole words the student may not develop an awareness of the parts of words. When reading is taught phonetically "the ability of segmental analysis develops much more quickly" (p. 131). Morais cites evidence that dyslexic students can learn sound segmentation; the problem is that it may not become automatic. Speed of processing then is slow, affecting comprehension. Again, we see the possibility of long-term repercussions.

As Freebody and Byrne (1988) point out, students with learning disabilities may well begin reading by memorizing sight words, but in order to progress they will need to be competent in some level of decoding. No matter what model of reading one subscribes to, this is a needed skill. Significantly, it is the failure to make the transition into the next phase that characterizes many students with learning disabilities (Sawyer, 1992). Because of difficulties in the next phase, poor readers, including those with learning disabilities, may hang on to the security they may have found in this first phase (Beech & Awaida, 1992). However, an essential part of their emergence as readers is success in the next phase: the alphabetic phase.

Phase 2: The Alphabetic Phase

The good reader has phonological awareness and acquires and uses grapheme-phoneme correspondences as one of the cue systems through which meaning can be constructed. The beginning of the alphabetic phase (Frith, 1986) occurs while or after children learn about letter-sounds. As Ehri (1991) states, "although there is disagreement about when the alphabetic phase begins, it is definitely underway when readers become able to phonologically recode spellings into pronunciations according to grapheme-phoneme correspondences" (p. 396). The children continue to develop and consolidate a store of sight words while developing expertise and efficiency in recoding new words. Ehri's phase, phonetic cue reading (1992), also stresses the utilization of phonetic features of the written language as an source of information for word recognition, although it may begin as a transition to the alphabetic phase. First, we will examine what good readers appear to do with phonemic tasks and then we will look at the variety of difficulties encountered by many students with learning disabilities.

What do good readers do?

- They apply phonemic awareness strategies (Liberman, 1990).

  Phonemic awareness, phonetic awareness and phonological awareness are often used interchangeably (Ehri, 1989). Morais (1991) defines phonological awareness as an umbrella term that refers to the awareness of "phonological strings (a global, nonanalytical level of awareness); awareness of syllables; awareness of phonemes (also called segmental awareness); and awareness of phonetic features" (p. 6). Sawyer (1992), reviewing Frith's theory, suggests that "phonological awareness might be a critical mechanism supporting the transition from the logographic phase to the alphabetic phase" (p. 90). Perfetti (1991) relates phonemic awareness to the awareness of speech segments and finds that children who have this awareness learn to read better than children who don't. Phonemic awareness strategies are particularly important in the tasks of blending segments and identifying and locating sounds (Adams, 1990; Bashir & Scavuzzo, 1992; Freebody & Byrne, 1988). Liberman, Shankweiler & Liberman (1989) cite "abundant evidence that phonological awareness is predictive of success in reading" (p. 14). Swanson & Ransby (1994) find a causal relationship between phonological awareness and reading. Mather (1992) goes farther, citing evidence that lack of phonemic awareness may be the single most reliable indicator of potential difficulty throughout school.

• They are able to recode (decode) written words (Bruck & Waters, 1990).

Phonological recoding is defined as "translating letters into sounds and blending the sounds" (Ehri & Robbins, 1992, p. 13). Lenchner, Gerber, & Routh (1990) agree, but add an additional element: "a certain level of ability to manipulate phonemes" (p. 244). Effective decoding is certainly a skill the good reader uses, with the goal of automatic word reading (Groff, 1991). This skill becomes particularly important as the text becomes more difficult and more unrecognized and unknown words are included.

Recoding goes beyond segmenting phonemes and recognizing and supplying sound-symbol relationships in isolation. It requires facility in manipulating sounds and symbols, in analyzing and synthesizing (Sawyer, 1992). Alexander and Pate (1991) find that "the conscious control of language units, particularly phonemes, was essential to reading acquisition" (p. 47). The act of manipulation of phonemes is also cited as "among the most difficult phoneme tasks" (Swanson & Ransby, 1994). "A consistently reported finding has been that good readers show greater dependence on phonological recoding in short-term memory than do poor readers" (Levy & Hinchley, 1990, p. 87). Not only can they recode, good readers can do it in a timely fashion, demonstrating automaticity (Bruck & Waters, 1990). Ehri (1992) further suggests that with repeated phonological recodings "word-specific connections linking spellings to pronunciations are established in memory" (p. 122). The repeated recoding develops a store of automatically read sight words. The two phases are closely linked. Finally, inability to decode words efficiently has frequently been linked to poor comprehension (Fowler, 1988; Rack et al., 1992) and may also affect spelling (Aaron & Philips, 1986; Frith, 1986).

What kinds of difficulty have readers with learning disabilities experienced in this phase? This question assumes particular importance in view of the early reliance on this cue system by beginners as well as the support it can give to the construction of meaning by all readers. In addition, there is considerable evidence that recoding is the most common area of difficulty in word recognition for students with learning disabilities (Bruck & Waters, 1990; Catts, 1989; Coles, 1987; Manis et al., 1990; Stanovich, 1988). Good readers increase both their store of sight words and their ability to decode words. Readers with learning disabilities are often characterized by arrested development at the logographic phase, demonstrating an over-reliance on sight words and a delay or deficit in the acquisition of decoding skills. Again, consider the fact that this is a general review. No one student will exhibit all difficulties nor will the difficulties all be caused by the same factor.

• Students with learning disabilities may exhibit difficulties or delay in phonological and/or phoneme awareness (Bashir & Scavuzzo, 1992).

The difficulty may come from one or more of a variety of problems. According to Liberman et al. (1989), difficulty in phonological awareness may be due to a general phonological problem in the capacity for language. Bruck and Treiman (1990) reached a different conclusion. They suggest that dyslexics have problems accessing phonemes in both oral language and in their own spelling, and that they exhibit difficulties in phonemic awareness. However, they "seem to use the same processes as younger normal children" (p. 175) suggesting a delay not a deficit. From another perspective, Felton and Brown (1990) suggest that "because phonological awareness requires metalinguistic abilities, it is very sensitive to the impact of environmental experience and training, particularly the process of being taught to read" (p. 55).

• The student with learning disabilities may have difficulty mastering phoneme-grapheme correspondences.

The key here is mastery. This is a task that is difficult, even for good readers, but is mastered by them (Bigsby, 1985). Sound-symbol knowledge is important if the learner is to use decoding skills and strategies (Sawyer, 1992). Morais (1987) cities evidence for widespread support of difficulty in phoneme-grapheme translation for students with learning disabilities. In fact, this difficulty is considered a hallmark of the "classic dyslexic." According to Hurford (1990), "children with learning disabilities have impairments in processing phonemic material" (p. 567). How significant is this difficulty? "It has been suggested that poor readers' weak knowledge of spelling-sound correspondences is a major determinant of their continuing poor word recognition skills" (Bruck & Waters, 1990, p. 164).

• Students with learning disabilities may have difficulty in phonological processing as related to memory.

One variable that has frequently been linked to the difficulty in phonological processing is that of memory (Bashir & Scavuzzo, 1992; Beech & Awaida, 1992; Catts, 1989; Kamhi, 1992; Mann & Brady, 1988). It is significant to note that the area of memory has been identified as a possible source of difficulty for the student with learning disabilities. We have already seen that there can be problems with the organization of information in storage and recall, with the speed of processing, with overload on items in memory, and with strategy use related to memory. All of these can be potential sources of difficulty when processing vague and abstract phonological information. Brady (1986) concludes that "developmental and individual differences in verbal memory span are related to the efficiency of phonological processes" (p. 138). The link is clearly made between increases in memory span and "the efficiency of phonological processes" (p. 143). Siegel and Ryan (1988) also cite a significant lag for students with learning disabilities in phonemes and phonological processing as well as in short-term memory. An unresolved question, according to Swanson (1989) is "whether phonological skills are a necessary prerequisite of memory performance or whether phonological processing deficiencies develop because of poor memory" (p. 495).

Naslund and Samuels' (1992) view of automaticity as a memory storage and retrieval process is relevant here if the aim is automatic recoding. Their view of the memory process implies a variable that may also be extrinsic to the child. It is not simply a question of practice. "Automaticity reflects the development of a knowledge base pertaining to cues that elicit behavior" (p. 144). There is conscious direction of the behavior, of performance, of the items in memory. This can be influenced by the educational situation and instruction provided. We begin to see implications beyond the ability to link sound and letter.

The link between memory and phonological abilities is frequently cited (Brady, 1991). Torgesen (1988), for example, points out that children with learning disabilities who exhibit memory deficits may have difficulty in coding or representing the phonological features of the language. Catts (1989) cites difficulties in encoding and retrieving phonemes from long-term memory. Rack et al. (1992) also identify a relationship between memory and phonological abilities but view it differently, similar to the way Brady (1991) views it. They suggest that there can be problems in the phonological abilities that "lead to problems in short-term memory, sound segmentation and categorization, and sound blending, and consequently to problems in reading and in spelling" (p. 31).

• Students with learning disabilities have difficulty in processing non-meaningful elements when engaged in decoding tasks.

We already have evidence that in developing recognition of sight words, students with learning disabilities rely more and for a longer period of time on context and the meaning supplied by that context than do normal readers. There is evidence that the same reliance on context may apply to word recognition through recoding. Bruck (1988), in examining the processes used by children to recognize words, finds that "both dyslexic and control children showed the same patterns of context effects, although the dyslexic children relied on context to facilitate word recognition to a greater extent than the control children" (p. 65). She concludes that this supports the notion that a higher-level skill is used to compensate for lack of word recognition skills.

There is also evidence that in recoding words students with learning disabilities may rely more on the meaning of the word as an aid in decoding than do normal readers. Amoruso et al. (in press), in reviewing research in this area, find evidence that disabled readers "could decode only words whose meanings were known to them" and that these students had more difficulty with nonsense words. These authors also note that this is typical of normally developing beginning readers, suggesting that students with learning disabilities may be at a more elementary phase than their peers. "The use of meaning during the decoding *process* may result in improved decoding *ability*" (in press).

• The student with learning disabilities may have difficulty in manipulating the phonetic elements of the text.

Fowler (1988) identifies possible links between phonological processing and/or metalinguistic abilities related to manipulating phonemic elements. In a situation where the student must deal with a string of letters, where the demands on knowledge and memory are high, the student may be slow to respond and/or may be inaccurate (Brady, 1986). According to Brady (1991) this problem relates to the "formation or storage of phonological representations" (p. 137). However, it may not be just the ability to identify sound-symbol correspondence that is the problem for the student with learning disabilities, but it may be a problem with the manipulation and application of those elements (Kamhi, 1992; Rack et al., 1992). These skills in monitoring and managing language elements suggest links to cognitive areas, areas which we have seen may cause difficulty for the student with learning disabilities. In fact, Catts (1989) cites general "agreement indicating that dyslexic individuals often show specific difficulties in the cognitive and metacognitive processing of phonological information" (p. 54).

The child with learning disabilities is in a difficult situation. Failure in this phase may result in the child relying on the much less efficient sight word strategy. Obviously, in the long run this is not a good alternative. On the other hand, if the child has also had difficulty with the task of learning sight words in a program that emphasizes phonics, he or she may rely strongly on using an unsuccessful phonics approach (Manis et al., 1990).

Phase 3. The Orthographic Phase

The orthographic phase is generally considered the third and final phase of word identification.   There are several perspectives on what might be included here.   There is consensus that in this phase readers focus on the larger units of words rather than on the individual phonemes (Ehri, 1991; Frith, 1986).   Frith (1986) defines the orthographic strategy as the "instant recognition of morphemic parts of words taking into account letter order, but not letter sound; rather, if any sound at all, it is the sound of morphemes or of whole words" (p. 72). Alexander and Pate (1991) suggest that "morphological analysis refers to the ability to break words into meaningful parts and then to recombine those parts into a whole (p. 52). Orthographic units, according to Sawyer (1992), are "frequently occurring letter clusters, such as the suffixes *-ed* or *-able* or the syllable units *sub*, *tic*, and *com*" (p. 91).   The common element here seems to be that once the reader is competent and comfortable with the alphabetic phase, he/she begins to work with larger units.

The focus in this phase is generally on these two aspects of word recognition: morphemes and syllables (Henry, 1988). In both areas meaning is linked to the word part (Amoruso et al., in press).   Leong (1988) points out the intimate relationship not only between morphemes and meaning but also, possibly, between morphemes and syntax.   "This complex system may serve to link derived morphology with word meaning and paragraph comprehension" (p. 115).

Affixes and roots may fill a special role in the process of word recognition.   As Amoruso et al., (in press) and Henry (1988) point out, they not only enable access to words through meaning but possibly also through decoding.   These authors suggest that the use of meaningful word parts may play a dual role: 1) that of accessing meaning directly as do sight words, and, 2) that of accessing meaning through phase 2 associations with sounds of the blended word.   In addition, orthographic knowledge may include "permissible letter patterns" (Barker et al., 1992, p. 336), or sequences of letters (Horn & Manis, 1985), which may also assist decoding. Although there are some differences in these various perspectives, researchers all concur that the emphasis is on the larger units of letters and sounds, not on the individual phonemes.

This phase is particularly important because vocabulary demands increase greatly as students go through school in terms of the number and length of words and the number of new words in text (Lenz & Hughes, 1990). There is evidence that syllables are easier to process than individual phonemes (Alexander & Pate, 1991; Swanson & Ransby, 1994). This is certainly helpful as readers deal with longer words and more complicated text. As Cox & Hutcheson (1988) cogently points out, when reading a novel, guessing at a long word is acceptable "but test questions, math word problems, factual material, job applications, and directions on a medicine bottle demand accuracy" (p. 227). In addition, the ability to process these larger units is also important in developing speed and fluency in reading (Barker et al., 1992).

Again, we will examine this phase from two points of view, that of the skilled reader and that of the reader with learning disabilities.

• Skilled readers apply skills and strategies acquired in both of the previous two phases in becoming proficient in this third phase.

They recognize common letter clusters such as affixes and syllables using strategies acquired in the logographic phase. They use phonetic skills to decode regular clusters using analytic strategies (Frith, 1986; Sawyer, 1992) as they are acquiring skill in this phase. The use of onset-rime strategy may be useful to the student at this stage, as well as in the logographic stage, as a way of developing orthographic awareness (Haskell et al., 1992).

• Good readers are able to analyze words into orthographic units without relying on a phonemic analysis.

> Readers develop expectations about print, about how letters are chunked in words into meaningful or nonmeaningful units that can be pronounced (Henry, 1988; Sawyer, 1992). They can analyze words, dividing them into syllables and units without referring to a phonemic analysis, relying on a phonemic analysis only as a last resort (Henry, 1988). They begin to see and to utilize patterns in words (Ehri, 1991). This "ability to decode long, polysyllabic words increases the qualitative differences between good and poor readers" (Lenz & Hughes, 1991, p. 149). The emphasis here is on two features: the analytic ability that was also important in phase 2 and the use of word parts as a strategy for reading words.
>
> It has been suggested that the use of the analogy strategy may not develop until this phase rather than in the logographic phase (Ehri, 1991). Ehri (1991) found that "older readers are more likely to read words by analogy to known words than younger readers" (p. 410). It can be a useful strategy for developing orthographic skills and strategies.

• Skilled readers use the word recognition skills and strategies acquired to construct meaning.

> "All word recognition strategies serve the meaning construction process by being accessible on demand" (Sawyer, 1992, p. 92). Sawyer's (1992) findings support the notion that in this phase the reader, who has always been meaning driven, is now able to focus primarily on meaning. In fact, it may be that morphemes provide a direct route not only to word meaning but also to syntax (Leong, 1989). This view connects to our models of

reading, with the beginner and poor reader focusing on a bottom-up approach and the skilled reader using a top-down approach or an interactive approach.

Now we will explore some of the difficulties cited for students with learning disabilities in this phase of learning to read.

• In this phase also, students with learning disabilities may have difficulty with memory tasks.

Cox & Hutcheson (1988) cites difficulties students with learning disabilities (dyslexia) may have remembering long words. The kinds of memory difficulties already indicated may also be evident here in remembering the various units that constitute morphemes, syllables, and common word parts.

• Students with learning disabilities have limited strategies available for accessing multisyllabic words.

There are several indicators here. Henry (1988) found that frequently poor readers have only one approach to identifying long, unknown words, using a letter-by-letter analysis. This is inefficient and wasteful of the potential of reading words in chunks. In viewing the strategies used by students with learning disabilities in reading multisyllabic words, Lenz and Hughes (1991) also found that they tended to use only one approach. They lacked a strategic, problem-solving approach to reading long, difficult words. Any of the general difficulties cited with strategy acquisition, use, and generalization may be relevant here for some of the population of students with learning disabilities.

On the other hand, students with learning disabilities may over-rely on the use of orthography to recognize words. Horn and Manis (1985) reviewed research and presented results of their own studies, indicating that disabled fifth- and sixth-grade readers made greater use of the orthographic structure of words than did normal readers, possibly to compensate for their inability to decode or remember words.

• Students with learning disabilities may rely more on meaning as an aid in orthographic analysis than normal readers.

Amoruso et al. (in press) reviewed research related to the processing of letter combinations. They found support for the notion that students with learning disabilities can remember trigrams arranged for meaningfulness and tend to divide letters into units according to meaningfulness. The use of meaningfulness calls on a higher-level strategy than remembering the trigram. Amoruso et al. suggest that, according to Stanovich, higher-level skills help compensate for difficulties with lower-level skills. These findings reinforce similar findings for the previous two phases, in which context and meaning are used in the process of word identification.

Because of the importance of this phase in ensuring that the emphasis in reading is on meaning and not word calling, this phase has long-term benefits for the reader. Yet there are readers who, as in previous phases, flounder and fail to make progress.

Summary

In reviewing the information available to us concerning the difficulties encountered by students with learning disabilities as they move through these phases of learning to read, certain common elements begin to appear, elements that we need to consider in planning instructional programs. We also need to keep in mind that there are two sources of information available to the reader in the process of identifying words: the meaning of the word and the text as well as the visual and phonemic information inherent in the word itself.

Students with learning disabilities may have difficulties with the linguistic features of word identification tasks. We have seen this in all three phases, in many different kinds of tasks, from knowledge of the terms "word" and "sentence" to the metalinguistic tasks associated with phonological awareness and the manipulation of phonemic elements.

Students with learning disabilities may have difficulties in tasks requiring memory. Problems associated with memory have been identified at each step along the way, from remembering sight words in initial reading to remembering phoneme-grapheme correspondences to remembering long words.

These students may have a limited repertoire of strategies that can be used in word identification tasks. This difficulty has been cited repeatedly. In addition to processing strategies, students with learning disabilities may have difficulty merging strategies acquired in one phase with new ones that are being acquired in a new phase. Lack of appropriate strategies and rigidity in strategy use is seen, particularly in processing phonemes and in identifying long words.

Students with learning disabilities may be able to use a higher level skill to compensate for difficulty with a lower-level skill. Consistently in the review of difficulties experienced by these students, it has been seen that the use of word meaning and context is an important, perhaps critical, cue system for accessing words.

These general findings, as well as the specific ones cited in the various phases, can provide a framework for instruction, instruction that recognizes the difficulties encountered as well as builds on possible strengths. Next we need to consider instructional alternatives for all of these phases.

INSTRUCTIONAL ALTERNATIVES

There are two related questions here: is instruction needed and can it make a difference? Ehri (1989) is a vocal representative of many who believe that instruction is essential. Dyslexics have phonological deficits because they have not learned to read and write. "Inadequate instruction spawning limited reading and spelling development and limited phonological awareness is the primary cause of dyslexic's reading disability" (1989, p. 356). Both maturation and education are needed, according to Frith (1986), for the development of skills and to "trigger" the change from one phase to another. There is a clear need for appropriate instruction in word identification skills and strategies.

The second part of the question deals with the issue of whether instruction can make a difference for these students. The literature shows that good, appropriate, focused instruction helps. Much of the instruction that has been provided, however (in both special education and in mainstream classes), has been mediocre. The instruction, in many instances, for many children, has not made a difference commensurate with the time and effort spent.

There is evidence that children with learning disabilities can acquire the strategies needed to engage successfully in word identification. These students can learn how to acquire a sight word vocabulary. Difficulty in non-phonetic whole word recognition appears to be the result of poor instruction (Lyon, 1991; Olson, Wise, Conners & Rack, 1990) or lack of exposure to print at home (Olson, Wise, Conners & Rack, 1990).

What happens when we teach phonological skills? Students with learning disabilities frequently learn them. Coles (1987) found, after reviewing a body of language studies of phonological and phonetic-skills deficit, that "instruction rather easily remediated deficiencies in those language skills, without need of extraordinary methods" (p. 135). Any competent teacher, according to Coles, can teach these phonetic skills and they should be taught to readers with learning disabilities. Siegel and Linder (1984) cite the difficulties readers with learning disabilities have with phonological coding but find that it can be taught and will develop over time. We have seen that students can develop segmental awareness and automaticity in using phonemes. As we review instructional procedures we will find a variety of ways children with learning disabilities can be taught word identification skills and strategies effectively.

Perhaps one of the reasons that most of these students can learn phonics is that the differences between this group and a group of "normal" readers is quantitative not qualitative. Bruck (1988) concluded that "dyslexic children do not use qualitatively different processes to read and spell words" (p. 51). It may be, as Brady (1986) suggests, a question of accuracy. "Good and poor readers use the same strategies, but poor readers are less accurate" (p. 150). It may be, as we have seen, a difficulty in acquiring and generalizing strategies. However, these can be taught. These findings suggest the possibility of success.

There may be another consideration here. Treiman and Hirsh-Pasek (1985) compared dyslexic to normal readers and found that "their reading performance was quantitatively different from that of normal children in that it lagged behind, but it did not appear to be qualitatively different" (p. 363). This notion of a lag or delay has been cited several times in connection with phonological awareness, phonological processing, and the reliance on word meaning as a cue for decoding, This idea carries the implication that instruction can be successful. Students can make up some of the lost ground. Sawyer (1992) holds that even the "true" dyslexic, the one with impaired biological capabilities, can benefit from appropriate instruction.

Instructional Content and Strategies

The range of difficulties experienced by students with learning disabilities in identifying words reflects the diversity of behaviors and characteristics seen in this population as a whole. Just as we need to accept the heterogeneity inherent in the classification of students as learning disabled, we also need to accept this diversity in developing instructional programs for word identification. There is no question that an appropriate program can make a difference.

First, we need to establish a framework. Teachers need to plan for instruction in both sight words and recoding. Programs need to be balanced to ensure that students acquire the phonetic skills needed to read new words and the store of automatic sight words needed to read fluently and focus on comprehension (Alexander & Pate, 1991). Because of the link between word identification skills and comprehension, we certainly need to teach decoding skills to students who experience difficulty (Felton & Wood, 1992). Bateman (1991) firmly states that all children, regardless of diagnosis, need a phonetic approach. She cites evidence that specific methods for different populations have not made a difference. We also need to include instruction in strategy development and use and the monitoring of those strategies. Readers need to be active and versatile in their approach to word identification.

So, now we have a goal, a framework. Teach both sight words and recoding. Teach strategy use and metacognitive awareness. The question is how. The major issue here is whether to provide direct, systematic instruction in word recognition skills and strategies or whether to involve the child in meaningful text and teach the word recognition skills based on that text, practicing them in the context of the text. Mather (1992) phrases the issue slightly differently, looking at it from the perspective of whole language instruction. "The key distinction that emerges between whole language theorists and traditional educators involves the role of explicit, skill-by-skill decoding instruction in the teaching of reading" (p. 87).

The lines here have been clearly drawn in the past; however, as we will see, the edges are beginning to blur. There has been and still is substantial support for providing direct instruction in word identification skills and strategies. This is true not only for students with learning disabilities but also for all children. Adams (1990), for example, suggests that all children need this kind of instruction, not just children with learning disabilities. Liberman and Liberman (1990) agree and base their recommendation on the premise that while learning speech is natural, learning the written code is "a cognitive, intellectual achievement in a way that learning to speak is not" (p. 52). Written language is an "artifact," and children with learning disabilities need specific instruction in unlocking the code.

There is much support for this point of view in the literature. We will encounter many specific instances in which researchers conclude that a specific skill or strategy requires direct instruction if the student with learning disabilities is to master and use it. There is also general support. Considerable research has shown that many children with learning disabilities learn best given direct, structured instruction in basic skills as a part of their overall instruction. Stahl and Miller (1989) reviewed over fifty studies on the effects of whole language approaches and basal reading approaches on beginning reading achievement. They report that more systematic phonics instruction was needed by slower readers, although they found that neither approach was clearly superior for all students. Liberman and Liberman (1990) found that direct instruction in hearing sounds and building phonemic knowledge before learning to read benefitted children having difficulty with phonological awareness. Along the same lines, Williams (1994) writes: "To be a proficient reader, one must have these skills [phonics and decoding], regardless of how one acquires them. And many children do not seem able to acquire them without careful, explicit, structured lessons" (p. 70). Groff (1991) looks at word recognition within the context of critical reading and concludes that automatic word recognition is so important to critical reading that we must provide direct instruction in it, not leave it to chance. Students have to be able to read individual words in order to critique the author's message. "Direct, systematic, and intensive instruction in word recognition is called for. The whole language argument to the contrary is unsound, and thus must be rejected" (p. 29).

Why is the whole language argument in relation to learning to identify words deemed unsound? Lyon (1991) reviews research on the acquisition of phonic skills and concludes that "structured and systematic phonic-based instruction that is informed by linguistic theory produces more favorable outcomes than intervention with approaches that rely more on reading context" (p. 31). He goes on to suggest that "disabled readers do not readily intuit and acquire the alphabetic code when learning to read due to deficits in phonological processing. They must be presented with structured, explicit, and intensive instruction in phonics rules and the application of the rules to print" (p. 32). At the same time, some have suggested whole language applications for teaching children to identify words (Oberlin & Shugarman, 1989).

Whole language as an approach to instruction in reading remains controversial in the field of learning disabilities. Lerner, Cousin, and Richeck (1992) point out that "currently, many children with learning disabilities receive their reading instruction in a mainstreamed classroom using whole language methods. The critical question is how do children with learning disabilities fare under this type of reading instruction" (p. 226). Unfortunately, long-term studies of the effects of whole language on students with learning disabilities are not yet available.

In this area, as in many others, educators and researchers do not always agree. In addition, the information that is available urges caution in mandating any one approach to teaching reading to all students. Mather (1992) believes that some students will require more explicit, systematic instruction in reading. She concludes that "students with severe learning disabilities may learn to read in a whole language, mainstream classroom, as long as appropriate supplemental instruction is provided, a variety of instructional techniques are employed, and the intensity and duration of the services are based upon the individual's needs" (p. 87). Thus, the whole language instruction should be supplemented, but the literature base retained, because children with learning disabilities need many types of instruction.

The conclusions of Stahl (1994) seem to be particularly helpful in achieving balance regarding the controversial issue of whether to teach reading to children using whole language instruction. He writes that "good phonics instruction can occur within the context of story reading, as in Reading Recovery, a program that is highly regarded by whole language advocates. Good phonics instruction can also involve direct instruction. However direct instruction of phonics seems most effective when it is well integrated into a reading program that also stresses meaningful interactions with text and writing" (p. 112). As summarized by O'Shea and O'Shea (1990) in their overview of pedagogical theories and practices of reading disabilities, "No theory or method is espoused as a panacea" (p. 89).

It may also be that at different times for different children, different approaches may be appropriate. Alexander and Pate (1991) have reviewed research in this area for normally developing children and find much support for the notion that kindergartners benefit from programs that emphasize meaning and language while first graders need specific skill instruction, particularly for economically disadvantaged students (Alexander & Pate, 1991; Stahl & Miller, 1989). Students need both approaches. "Phonological training should not be offered at the exclusion of more personal, meaning-oriented instruction, but should serve as a component of a well-rounded program" (Alexander & Pate, 1991, p. 55). "It is time to move beyond the simplistic whole language versus phonics debate into a mature stage of reasoned, interactive analysis of word recognition abilities" (p. 56.). This isn't an either/or situation. Rather it seems to be a question of including parts of both approaches, depending on the characteristics of the student and the situation in which the learning occurs. Alexander and Pate rely on an interactive model of reading to support the "potential benefits of both whole language and phonics-based language programs" (p. 44).

This certainly seems sensible. Consider the reading models. Beginners appear to rely on the visual cues of text to a great degree in learning to read. We also know, however, that they interact in a variety of ways with text. They rely on meaning and context. For students with learning disabilities meaning and context seem even more critical in the task of identifying words. Some mixture of the two approaches is reasonable and workable. Johns (1991) also identifies the "recurring debate between meaning-based (whole language) and phonics-based (code emphasis) approaches to teaching reading" (p. 59) and suggests that we go beyond this debate and provide excellent instruction. For at-risk readers this involves several things. Consider the student with learning disabilities. We need to establish a warm, caring, and positive relationship with the student. This is important for our student who is reluctant to take risks and is fearful of failure. We need to get students to read and reread. This is certainly important for our student who needs this exposure in order to achieve mastery. We need to use materials that are interesting to the student and which will ensure success. We need to unify the overall act of reading and the pieces of skills instruction we provide. Otherwise instruction seems isolated with little chance of transfer. Johns advocates using a direct instruction model: teach, model, and have the student practice various strategies to pronounce and understand the meanings of words. The student needs to acquire "a *set* of strategies" (p. 65). Here, Johns combines whole language and direct instruction while also viewing reading as a strategic process. The student with learning disabilities is seen as part of this process, not as watching the process from outside the mainstream.

The question of direct instruction for students with learning disabilities seems well supported, including many informed educators who advocate a broad literature-based approach. Mather (1992), for example, suggests that whole language assumes the students can retain sight words and naturally acquire sound-symbol relationships. This can be a problem for children with learning disabilities. As we have seen, they may have trouble with sight words and/or may not be able to figure out phonics. She reinforces the need for direct instruction in word recognition for these students. The question is how much? "The optimum amount of instruction in letter-sound relationships for any child is the *minimum* amount that child needs to become an independent reader. Children with learning disabilities should be immersed in literature, be active classroom participants, be in a language-rich environment, and most importantly, be taught to read" (p. 92). Mather emphasizes that this does not mean endless drill and workbook pages.

We begin to get a clearer perspective on the question of how to teach children strategies for identifying words.

Learning to Acquire Sight Words

There appear to be several threads that run through the research relating to teaching children with learning disabilities how to acquire sight words. One relates to the difficulties they have with memory tasks and another with their reliance on meaning as a cue system. In theoretical terms these two areas are closely connected and certainly should be closely connected in instruction. One source of difficulty is the failure to make connections between new information and old information. Another source for students having difficulty learning to read is the lack of sufficient opportunity to identify and remember the words in a meaningful reading situation. "Children who are successful readers, read, and by engaging in reading they become even more successful in performing reading tasks. Conversely, poor readers do not read, and they become even less successful as the task demands increase" (Sawyer, 1992, p. 89). As Naslund and Samuels (1992) point out, so cogently, "the rich-get-richer" (p. 151). Finally, we have seen that frequently children with learning disabilities rely heavily on meaning to make the connections between words and print and to remember the printed words. Instructional activities can build on these findings. Let's consider approaches that incorporate effective instructional strategies.

Develop Meaning and Context as Cues

Building meaning for the sight words and establishing a context for them are themes that run through much of the current literature on teaching children with learning disabilities how to acquire a store of sight words. We will examine several alternatives.

In planning instruction for students with learning disabilities, it may be useful to consider how variables can interact. Hargis, Terhaar-Yonkers, Williams, and Reed (1988) studied the rapidity with which students with learning disabilities were able to recognize words and the number of repetitions it took to make that recognition automatic under different conditions. The conditions clarified the interaction between the meaningfulness of the word itself, the use of context in the process of identification, and the decodability of the word. They cite several useful conclusions. Words presented in context as well as those that were meaningful required fewer repetitions for mastery. Decodability was important but not as important as the other two variables. The interactions were particularly interesting. Low-imagery words, those with little concrete meaning, required context with substantial repetition for mastery. It is important to remember that many of the basic words children need to learn are low-imagery words. High-imagery, decodable words required the fewest repetitions for mastery. The problem is compounded because one way to read words in context is to read text. Poor readers can't read text, so they don't get the repetition. The teacher's role then is to ensure that students with learning disabilities encounter words in a variety of readable text, whether written by others, by the teacher, or by peers.

Walker and Poteet (1989) identify the need for elaboration and semantic associations in order to improve memory of sight words. The teacher needs to add semantic context to words and not have children rely on rote memory. In addition, the teacher has to build this elaboration and semantic association and meaningfulness into the lesson.

Sinatra (1992) asserts that to build a sight vocabulary for children having difficulties the teacher must "deemphasize the child's perspective of reading as being a word-centered process to one that emphasizes reading as being a meaning-centered process" (pp. 179-180). Words must be presented in a meaningful context. He suggests four ways of approaching instruction that will provide a context for the student: children's literature, a thematic approach, language experience, and interactive computer software programs. These suggestions capitalize on the strategy children with learning disabilities often use, that of gaining access to the word through meaning. He further suggests that direct teaching of words or phonemes should occur only in the context of reading, not in isolation. It is important to note here that Sinatra doesn't advocate the avoidance of direct instruction. Rather, he places it in the context of meaningful text. Thus, the choice of appropriate text is important in the development of sight words.

Combine Instructional and Learning Strategies

Studies at the Teachers College Columbia University's Research Institute for the Study of Learning Disabilities during the 1980s found that sight word learning could be accomplished with appropriate instruction and with a meaningful context for the words. One potential difficulty with memory tasks that we have already identified is that of overload. The instructional strategy developed at Teachers College recognized that it is possible to "facilitate learning new words among learning disabled readers if their information processing capacity is not overloaded" (Amoruso et al., in press). It is important that words are taught to mastery with discrimination training and decreased response competition in short term recall. "The possibility of an error is greater at the moment of recall when a student has many items to recall and must select from them. Interference with the learning of new sight words was decreased by eliminating mastered words from trials" (Amoruso et al., in press). Here, the emphasis is on how the teacher can provide effective instruction to aid in the use of memory.

Effective instruction needs to be combined with strategies that students can use. Certainly, one of those strategies for students with learning disabilities may be the use of meaning as an aid in learning and recalling sight words. In the Amoruso et al. study, once the words were mastered in isolation they were placed in a meaningful context of phrases and sentences and read and reread. We see a combination of instructional strategies: effective memory training, the use of meaning and context, and the development of automaticity through reading and rereading. The combination of variables may contribute to the effective development of skills and strategies by students. Once mastery has been achieved, this method is similar to a whole-word meaning emphasis program in which "visually distinctive words" are read and then reread in "meaningful contexts" (Ehri, 1992, p. 109).

Encourage and Enable Rereading of Text

The need to read and reread text seems critical in developing automaticity in sight word recognition. It may be important because of the repeated exposure the reader has to the word in a meaningful context or it may be, as Ehri (1992) suggests, because it "involves remembering systematic connections between spellings and pronunciations of words" (p. 137). In any event, the reader needs to develop automaticity in word identification as well as fluency while reading the words in the context of text. Repeated reading of text appears to be a way for students with learning disabilities to accomplish this and to generalize the skills and words learned to other text (Weinstein & Cooke, 1992) as well as to increase fluency and comprehension (O'Shea, Sindelar, & O'Shea, 1987).

Getting students to reread text can present problems in motivation and in teacher supervision. A few alternatives have been suggested here. Torgesen, Waters, Cohen, and Torgesen (1988) studied the effectiveness of three computer programs designed to teach sight words to students with learning disabilities in grades 1 to 3. Words were presented in isolation in three different formats. The three programs were graphics (a pictorial representation of the word) only, graphics plus synthetic speech (pronunciation of the word and the word used in a sentence), and synthetic speech only. All three approaches demonstrated significant growth in speed and accuracy of word recognition although the students seemed to prefer the first two formats. It is useful for us to note that all three conditions involved some kind of meaning association for the words, even though they were presented visually in isolation. The authors caution that any learning that takes place as a result of the computer program must be reinforced in real text in the classroom. The words must eventually be used in context.

Another approach that has been explored is providing a situation in which the student with learning disabilities reads text silently while listening to someone else read the text orally. Van Bon, Boksebeld, Freide, and van den Hurk (1991) investigated the effectiveness for students with learning disabilities of three different reading while listening experiences: reading while listening to different texts each session; reading while listening to the same text repeated; and reading while listening, using different texts with the listeners identifying errors in the oral reading in their own copies of the story. In this study the student is receiving correct feedback on word pronunciation, using context to confirm the pronunciation, and, in one instance, hearing the text several times. The results demonstrated that "what children learn by rereading the same text over and over apparently is highly context-specific and is not transferred to new situations – not even to reading the same words outside the original text" (p. 475). "With all three methods a practice effect was found for texts as well as for single words" (p. 471). The authors did find that "texts and single words from the preceding training session are read faster in the testing sessions than words not practiced before" (p. 475). They conclude that we need more research in order to explore why the conditions yielded similar results. It is interesting for our purposes to consider the three conditions in this study as they might apply to the classroom, since all three had elements of effectiveness.

Learning to Recode Words

One very practical reason for teaching phonics and phonetic skills and strategies is, according to Richardson (1989), that our language is phonetically based. There certainly are many exceptions to this notion, but this is a reality of the English language. We need to examine general areas where students with learning disabilities experience difficulty and to look at total approaches that have been developed.

Develop Phonological Awareness

The issue here appears straightforward. Do we provide instruction in phonological awareness before teaching phonics, either outside of the context of reading or as part of the process of reading? The issue really is whether phonological awareness is an antecedent to or a consequence of reading instruction. Williams (1994) points out that "the evidence to date is that phonemic skill is both an antecedent to and a consequence of reading instruction, that there is a reciprocal relation between phonemic ability and reading instruction" (p. 67). Keep this "seemingly contradictory" (Yopp, 1992, p. 697) relationship in mind as we consider instructional alternatives.

One view is that we need to teach phonemic awareness outside of the context of reading before providing direct instruction in phonics. Lundberg, Frost, and Petersen (1988) provided phonological awareness training to preschoolers without providing training in reading. The program used games and exercises that helped children discover the structure of the language. They found the program affected metalinguistic skills such as rhyming tasks and "tasks involving word and syllable manipulation" (p. 263) with a "dramatic" effect on sound segmentation. They conclude that "phonemic awareness can be developed outside the context of the acquisition of an alphabetic writing system" (p. 263) but we need to provide explicit instruction. A wide variety of games, songs, and activities can be used to link phonological awareness and the structure of language, leading to and sometimes including instruction in letters and sounds (Yopp, 1992).

Another point of view holds that we must teach phonological awareness within context of reading. Morais (1991) found that "the results obtained with illiterate subjects seem to indicate that, as a rule, instruction on some written code is necessary for the acquisition of phonemic awareness" (p. 14). It must be developed within a framework of the alphabetic code. Mann and Brady (1988) state the issue slightly differently. "Awareness of phonemes is enhanced by methods of instruction that direct attention to the phonetic structure of words and may even depend on it" (p. 814). This conclusion suggests that we shouldn't isolate instruction in phonemic awareness; we should develop it through teaching phonics.

We need to consider a variety of tasks that are linked to phonological awareness. Lenchner et al. (1990) reviewed training studies and found that "phonological awareness training affected reading performance, especially if it involved training in both segmentation and blending and direct instruction in letter-sound correspondence" (p. 241). Hurford (1990) linked phonemic awareness, sound segmentation, and phonemic discrimination. He found that in order to teach phonemic segmentation to disabled readers, whether learning disabled or reading disabled, it is important that we teach phonemic discrimination first.

Certainly, all the research is not yet in on what should be included here. But the implication is clear. We need to consider a broad range of items in planning instruction. This examination of developing and teaching phonological awareness is particularly interesting because it highlights in microcosm the range of possibilities being considered in many of the areas related to reading. Suggestions range from teaching the skill in isolation, to putting it clearly in the context of phonics and reading, to broadly investigating and including all important aspects of the task.

Teach Recoding Through Specific, Direct Instruction

As we have seen, there are strong voices raised in favor of direct instruction in word identification skills for students with learning disabilities. Ehri (1991) adds an additional argument here, specifically related to recoding. She points out that many of the skills and strategies taught in explicit, systematic phonics instruction may not be the skills used by competent readers. She illustrates this with a discussion of the frequent inappropriateness of rules taught to children. However, "although phonics instruction teaches beginners rules and operations that are inaccurate and not used by mature phonological recoders, such artificial devices may have pedagogical value in getting readers to attend to and do the things that enable them to become skilled recoders" (p. 401). One thing that may help the process become operationalized for the reader and allow for transfer to new words is to apply the rules to words that consistently follow the rule.

Liberman et al. (1989) are explicit here. For those children who do not discover the alphabetic principle of the language and who have poor phonological processing skills, direct instruction in the use of phonics to read words is critical. They suggest the use of blocks or counters to mark the letters in words in order to teach phonemic awareness and the mapping principle. Then, add color coding for consonants and vowels and use letter cards. The children can use the cards to read real words and write stories. Here, direct instruction links phonological awareness, sound-symbol correspondence, and the reading of real words and the writing of stories. This process reflects a bottom-up view of reading, but it is one that emphasizes the use of real text as a vehicle for practice and reinforcement.

Use Spelling to Develop Recoding and Word Recognition Skill

Teaching phonic word identification for the task of reading through teaching spelling may be an effective instructional strategy. Ehri (1989) has been a strong advocate of this point of view, citing both her own research and that of others. She suggests teaching letter names and shapes, using those to develop first invented spelling and later conventional spelling skills as a "back door to phonics instruction" (p. 360). Through this approach children become aware of the structure of written language. They learn sound-symbol correspondence and sound segmentation as part of spelling and eventually can be taught blending within the context of reading. Learning spelling also enables sight word recognition because students will develop an orthographic image of the word.

Van Daal and van der Leij (1992), working from the notion that learning to spell helps the child move from implicit phonological awareness to explicit phonological awareness, report a study with children with written language disorders who were trained to spell using a computer. Three conditions were used. The group taught to read the word and copy it from the screen using the keyboard made fewer spelling errors and read the practiced words faster than the group who wrote the words from memory. Both of these groups outperformed the group that only read the word on the screen. All groups could receive speech feedback as needed. Van Daal and van der Leij concluded that computer instruction could provide the kind of processing required to improve both spelling and reading problems.

Link Recoding Instruction to Meaning and Context

We have seen that there is support for the notion that students with learning disabilities who have difficulty identifying words from the phonemes frequently rely on context and meaning to aid in the identification of words. The issue here is whether you, as the teacher, capitalize on this compensatory strategy by teaching students to use context and meaning or whether you avoid this strategy because of concern that students will have difficulty moving beyond it. Nicholson, Bailey, and McArthur (1991) suggest that we need to use careful instruction here. We should teach children to use context, but not to the point where it completely compensates for their difficulty in learning and applying decoding strategies. If this happens they may never learn to decode. The authors caution us about "the 'whole language' approach that puts excessive emphasis on the use of context as a strategy for recognizing words" (p. 40). The key here may be the word "excessive." Nicholson et al. clarify this by suggesting that the use of context to improve decoding is helpful. The use of context to compensate for decoding is not helpful.

Teach Strategies That Can Be Widely Applied

An example of teaching students strategies with many possible applications is provided by Haskell et al. (1992) who suggest teaching the onset-rime strategy. "A potential advantage of the onset-rime level of instruction . . . may be that it gives students more flexibility than they would get from individual phoneme instruction when reading exception words" (p. 46). Considering the number of exception words there are in English, this is certainly a reason to teach this strategy. However, there is even more reason to teach it. The onset-rime strategy is very similar to the analogy strategy suggested by Ehri and Robbins (1992) and by Ehri (1991) in which children are taught decoding through familiar word parts by analogy. As we have seen, this can be a transition step between phase 1 and phase 2 and may be the foundation for the orthographic phase.

Include a Metacognitive Component

Mather (1992) identified this component as a critical element in teaching recoding skills and strategies. "When providing instruction, a metacognitive approach to phonemic awareness training may be the most effective" (p. 91). She describes a program developed by Cunningham in which children learned blending and segmentation and reflected on its value and purpose. Cunningham (1989) compared a skill-and-drill group, a metacognitive group, and a control group for both kindergarten and first grade. The skill-and-drill group was trained in how to segment and blend phonemes. The metacognitive group was trained in the application, value and utility of phonemic awareness as well as how to perform the tasks. The control group listened to stories and answered comprehension questions. In both grade levels students in the two experimental groups did better than the control group on tests of phonemic awareness. Children in first grade in the metacognitive group performed better on a transfer test than did the skill-and-drill group. When actually reading, it's important to have metacognitive knowledge of the task. Considering the potential difficulty some students with learning disabilities have in developing metacognitive strategies, it is especially important that we include them in instruction.

Include Instruction in Metalinguistic Knowledge

In a similar vein, Bashir and Scavuzzo (1992), in discussing instruction in phonological skills, stress the need for "systematic approaches to teaching reading that include facilitation of metalinguistic knowledge" (p. 61). These authors combine the need for direct instruction with the need for the child to understand and monitor the linguistic features of the task. Ball and Blachman (1988) define metalinguistic ability as "the ability to reflect deliberately on language in and of itself, as opposed to the automatic use of language to convey meaning" (p. 209). This adds a dimension to instruction that is frequently omitted. The key in the activities Ball and Blachman suggest seems to be to directly relate sound segmentation to knowledge of the grapheme-phoneme correspondence. This focuses "attention on the internal sound structure of the word" (p. 222).

Learning to Use Word Parts

Word parts can, as we have seen, provide an important window into word identification, particularly for long, difficult, content area words. There are several advantages to developing the word identification skills and strategies included in the orthographic phase. Syllables are less demanding phonological units that are phonemes (Alexander & Pate, 1991; Swanson & Ransby, 1994). Morphemes, because of their link to meaning, may be a useful avenue for many students with learning disabilities. They also draw on prior sight word learning and may provide a strategy to compensate for delayed decoding skills (Amoruso et al., in press).

Provide Direct Instruction in Word Parts

There is substantial support for this recommendation, based on both the general support for direct instruction and on specific support for its use in instruction in word parts (Alexander and Pate, 1991; Leong, 1989; Leong, Simmons, and Izatt-Gambell, 1990). Bateman (1991), for example, does not find that specific methods for students with learning disabilities have made a difference. What has made a difference is direct instruction. She cites the need for a phonetic approach, stressing instruction in multisyllabic words.

In providing instruction it seems helpful for the teacher to have knowledge of useful syllable divisions (Cox & Hutcheson, 1988) and affixes (White, Sowell, and Yanagihara, 1989). It is also useful to limit the number of affixes taught and to teach their application to unfamiliar words.

Link Learning Word Parts to Meaning

Amoruso et al. (in press) suggest that direct instruction of affixes and their meanings is needed. This should be done in conjunction with known sight words. The strength of this method is that it develops word meaning and word recognition and provides another decoding strategy. In this study students with learning disabilities could transfer knowledge of word parts and meaning to other words. Amoruso et al. found that "the explicit teaching of the affix-meaning within sight words most likely provided the learning disabled reader a compensatory device that assisted with the decoding *process* and resulted in an increase in decoding *ability*" (in press).

Enable Discovery Learning of Word Parts

Cox & Hutcheson (1988) provides a rationale for the importance of syllable division and specific sequential instructions for syllable division. The stress is on enabling the student to "discover the new information independently" (p. 229), moving from the known to the unknown. With each stage, the steps once discovered are posted as a reference, which is then used as a device for monitoring awareness and accuracy of use, a metacognitive device. This technique deals with the issue of error awareness and correction, already identified as potential problems for the student with learning disabilities.

Develop a Strategic Approach
to Identifying Multisyllabic Words

Students with learning disabilities often do not effectively engage in strategy use in general, as we have seen. We have also seen that they may not use a strategic, problem-solving approach to reading words. In teaching these students to read multisyllabic words, emphasis has been placed on helping students develop a strategy for identifying these words (Henry, 1988; Lenz & Hughes, 1990). We need to ensure, as part of our instructional procedure, that students are aware of both procedures and strategies. Lenz and Hughes (1990) differentiate between the two. A strategy "relates to a person's knowledge of the general approaches to making decisions regarding which procedures should be implemented and modified, and it guides the learning, remembering, and problem-solving processes involved in the application of procedures" (p. 150). A procedure involves the "knowledge of steps or algorithms that can be used in a specific situation" (p. 150).

    Lenz and Hughes (1990) used a strategy training approach in which they taught word identification as a problem-solving process. Adolescents with learning disabilities were provided direct instruction in a series of steps they could use. The set of possibilities included the use of context, the application of structural analysis, and the use of available resources for help. Lenz and Hughes found that instruction reduced oral reading errors and increased comprehension for most students. This approach is certainly an example of addressing the strategy needs of the student with learning disabilities and providing instruction that supports growth.

INSTRUCTIONAL PROGRAMS
AND APPROACHES

In planning instruction we need to consider alternatives in building a program, in linking together the various parts of instruction and learning that students may need. We will consider this from several perspectives. We have looked at the phases of learning to identify words and have concluded that all need to be represented in an instructional program. We will look at sample programs that suggest doing this, including an instructional delivery system that has been with us for a while but has not been fully utilized: using computers for practice and reinforcement in word identification. Finally, we return to the question of whole language/direct instruction by taking a closer look at programs on both sides of the issue.

Incorporate a Range of Phases in Programs

Here we will consider three different programs. They differ in details but all illustrate that programs for students with learning disabilities need to be broadly conceived and include a variety of phases and strategies.

Gaskins, Gaskins, and Gaskins (1992) developed a program for poor readers and readers with learning disabilities based on theory and research. They remind us that readers need a strategy for reading words that goes beyond the use of context; they need to develop automaticity without relying on context as good readers do. They need explicit instruction on phonological awareness, sound-symbol association skills, and word parts. They need a basic sight vocabulary. They also need to use what they already know as a strategy for figuring out what they don't know. Based on these premises, the authors developed an analogous word strategy similar to those strategies used by good readers (Adams, 1990; Ehri and Robbins, 1992). According to Gaskins et al. (1992), "the instructional focus was teaching cognitive and metacognitive strategies that would enable the student to become a strategic, motivated, and independent reader and writer" (p. 203). In decoding, the strategies children are taught should include "context clues in conjunction with the initial letter(s) . . . and the analogy or compare/contrast approach" (p. 206). The program incorporates spelling as well as reading words, developing language experience text, reading text, and listening to text. Decoding is only one part of the instructional program, a critical part, but only a part. The focus is consistently on reading for meaning.

Henry (1988) also describes a broadly conceived program, although one with a different emphasis. She focuses on word parts but also combines skill and strategy instruction as part of a total program building on many of the notions already discussed. Children are taught reading and spelling simultaneously beginning with letter-sound correspondences, moving to syllables and morphemes. They are introduced to the development of language patterns based on Anglo-Saxon, Romance languages, and Greek. Understanding of syllable and morpheme patterns is based on an understanding of language structure. Advanced students also develop strategies for analyzing long words. Direct instruction is used throughout the program. The teacher builds a metacognitive component into the lessons for the students by including "discussing, reflecting upon, and monitoring their decoding and spelling performance" (p. 274). Follow-up is provided through games and through finding relevant words in text. Because children with learning disabilities are being taught to read all kinds of words, they can read interesting, motivating text. Ehri (1991), in critiquing this approach, suggested that the key may be that the children were taught "which rule to apply to which words because they were taught to distinguish the origins of the words" (p. 407). In this instance, skills instruction on several levels is combined with the use of effective strategies.

Houck (1987) gives an example of a total approach for adolescents with learning disabilities. This program uses a setting and materials conducive to motivating readers, recognizing that skill instruction cannot exist in a vacuum. Reading materials are an integral part of instruction and must be motivating, interesting, and useful. Direct instruction must be given in the word identification skills students need such as sight words and word parts. Houck provides many guidelines, including: use students' prior knowledge and abilities, develop strategies as well as skills and have students practice them repeatedly in a variety of situations to ensure transfer, and involve the students in the process of monitoring outcomes.

Utilize Computers

One vehicle that has been explored as a means of providing effective practice and reinforcement is that of computers. One problem encountered by students with learning disabilities is the difficulty encountered in the classroom in providing the corrective feedback needed for both sight words and words that are being decoded (Farmer, Klein, and Bryson, 1992). It is possible to use computers for both of these word recognition areas, particularly if speech feedback is included in the program.

Jones, Torgesen, and Sexton (1987), citing the need for practice and mastery in both speed and accuracy, report on a study conducted with elementary school students with learning disabilities. Practice was provided in phonics with a computer program giving feedback through "high quality digitized speech" (p. 123). They report that there was substantial increase in speed and accuracy in the items practiced and that students could generalize to words on paper copy. Students also demonstrated increased speed of paragraph reading, indicating increased fluency.

In reviewing current research, Farmer et al. (1992) find that the uses of computer programs can improve both word recognition and comprehension. In word recognition, they can be used with whole words, syllables, or on-set rimes. The authors offer several comments based on the literature and on their own research. The teacher needs to monitor the process to ensure that the words used are appropriate and that students are attending and are identifying words that need to be reinforced. There may be an additional benefit besides the skills and strategies targeted in the program. Just the fact that students are having additional practice reading, even if individual words are not mastered, is probably beneficial.

Olson et al. (1990) cite a similar benefit. "Reading generally improves with greater exposure to print, even in children with severe phonological deficits" (p. 303). They developed a computer program designed to get students to read more and to receive immediate feedback on word recognition and decoding skills. The children read interesting stories containing real, useful words. The authors found there was a problem for many children with blending of segmented phonemes so the program gave feedback on whole words, syllables, and subsyllables. Whole word instruction was the least effective.

There are several advantages to using a computer to provide practice and reinforcement. We have already cited the fact that it can be provided more extensively than is usually possible with other methods. Another plus to using a computer is that it is always enthusiastic and patient and always teaches the way it is programmed to do (Olson et al., 1990). Instruction can be individualized and can present the practice lessons in several different ways (Torgesen, 1986).

Whole Language, Direct Instruction, Both?

In looking at this issue, we are concerned not only with how instruction is delivered but with the model of reading it represents. Whole language programs frequently represent a top down or interactive model of reading in which the child begins with whole text and uses cue systems to construct meaning. O'Shea and O'Shea (1990) provide a useful description of whole language. The unit of meaning is the whole story or text, not a part of it, and builds on constant exposure to written language. "The primary system for identifying words lies in the semantic relationships expressed through meaningful stories and children's experiences, whereas syntax and morphology serve as a secondary system that supplements semantic elements. . . . The third and final system, phonology, is taught as a mechanism for analyzing words after the student has learned a set of words and is using other contextual strategies" (p. 87). Learning requires discovery, exploration, and independent experience and expression. Lerner, Cousin, and Richeck (1992) recognize the need for knowledge of sound-symbol relationship and the ability to use this knowledge but as part of a larger system for reading. "Learning proceeds from the whole to the part" (p. 227). It is done as needed and in the context of the whole text. Children with learning disabilities should do authentic reading and writing, not endless work sheets and drills. If we take reading apart into separate skills, it becomes more abstract and more difficult (Hollingsworth & Reutzel, 1988) and the student sees no purpose to it. This view strengthens the notion of using real text.

As O'Shea and O'Shea suggest, "the reading instruction practices derived from the holistic model have a strong intuitive appeal" (p. 88). There is no mention of direct instruction or of systematic instruction in the skills and strategies identified in the three phases of word identification. According to Chiang and Ford (1990), "there has been a disturbing paucity of research on whole language approaches with students with LD" (p. 32). We have found many statements about the need for direct, systematic instruction of the skills and strategies included in the three phases of word identification. In order to develop some guidelines here we need to look at overall research that has been done on these two approaches, and we need to examine several programs that are widely used and researched examples of each.

Wasik and Slavin (1993) reviewed the long-term effectiveness of five programs designed to prevent early reading failure that are frequently used with students with learning disabilities or students who are considered "at risk." Reading Recovery is based on the assumption that reading is an act of constructing meaning. Word identification is taught in the context of the text as needed. Success for All is a comprehensive reading program using real text and teaching word identification skills systematically. In both of these programs children learn to read by reading. Prevention of Learning Disabilities identifies skills needed for reading (prereading, word attack, comprehension, and study skills). The program focuses on "perceptual analysis of print, decoding, and oral language proficiency" (p. 191) and teaches those with which the child is having a problem. There is no emphasis on reading text or on relating to classroom instruction. The Wallach Tutoring Program emphasizes systematic instruction in essential subskills of reading. Phonics is taught outside the context of connected text. Programmed Tutorial Reading identifies and isolates specific sight word and decoding skills outside the realm of connected text.

Research studies related to the programs are reviewed. The Wasik and Slavin (1993) found that "results were more positive when reading instruction was based on a more comprehensive model of reading" (p. 178). It appears that more comprehensive models of reading may work because they include "more complete instructional interventions" (p. 196) and more effectively teach the complexities of reading. Success for All is the only program studied that is designed to integrate completely into instruction in the classroom. It also "produced some of the largest effect sizes" (p. 196). According to this review, reading programs designed for the student with learning disabilities that are developed from a comprehensive model of reading appear to be more effective than those that focus on isolated, basic skills.

Let's take a closer look at Reading Recovery because research is available on it and it is a "rapidly expanding" (Wasik & Slavin, 1993) program. It is used individually with young children deemed at-risk for reading difficulties and those who may fall into the category of "learning disabled" (Lyons, 1991).

"Reading Recovery children are taught to use cues and strategies rather than to memorize skills in order to read fluently" (Hill and Hale, 1991, p. 481). There are important differences between this and other programs in how phonics is taught, according to Hill and Hale (1991). In other programs, first the child learns a letter, then the sound. These are taught in a prescribed sequence. In Reading Recovery, first the child hears the sound in a word and then identifies the symbol. These are taught according to the needs of the text and the child, not according to a set sequence.

Research results reported by Wasik and Slavin (1993) are generally favorable, indicating "impressive" (p. 187) gains that are maintained for at least two years. In a statewide study that compared four approaches to instruction, the Direct Instruction Skills plan, using a traditional direct instruction, sequential skills model, consistently underperformed the other three, more comprehensive approaches, both initially and over time. Lyons (1991) found that students in Reading Recovery who were classified as learning disabled over-relied on visual and auditory information when they began the program, not using the language and meaning of the text. Her study found that these students tended to use multiple cue systems as they progressed through the program, which is what good readers do.

Lyons makes an interesting point in comparing Reading Recovery to the traditional code-emphasis programs often used with students with learning disabilities. She believes that children taught with the code-emphasis approach who were "classified as learning disabled never figured out what reading is all about. . . . They were operating from incomplete and inappropriate concepts about the reading process" (p. 404). They were not learning disabled; they were "instructionally disabled. . . . Their learning disability was environmentally produced" (p. 404). Again, we are confronted with the importance of how instruction is planned and provided and with the critical importance of developing strategic readers.

The lines are certainly drawn. Liberman and Liberman (1990) review research and theory related to word identification and conclude, clearly, that the problem is that students with learning disabilities cannot "access the right phonological structure" (p. 5). Phonics needs to be taught and it needs to be taught directly. Kamhi (1992) concurs. "The deficits displayed by individuals with dyslexia do not extend too far into general domains of cognitive functions, such as reasoning, problem solving, and comprehension" (p. 51). We need to provide fairly limited direct instruction on word recognition skills. Advocates of this view limit the problem and the focus of instruction to one aspect of reading, in contrast to those who see the problem and the resulting instruction in a larger context.

We have surveyed a large body of research that has examined the various word identification tasks and concluded that direct instruction in these skills and strategies seems beneficial to some students with learning disabilities. The issues and contradictions are highlighted when we look at programs that have been developed specifically for word identification instruction. Wasik and Slavin (1993) generally found that results were less positive for tutoring programs focusing on specific subskills than for programs focusing on the process of reading. The emphasis in these programs is on breaking the code, not on teaching reading and reading strategies. Although there are several widely used programs that fit in this category, we will only examine one of them as an illustration of this perspective on teaching.

One program that has used with economically disadvantaged students as well as with some populations of special students is DISTAR. It "incorporates small-group, face-to-face instruction by a teacher using carefully sequenced daily lessons in reading that emphasize decoding skills" (Kuder, 1990, p. 69). Kuder (1990) reports on a two-year study in which students with learning disabilities were either in a DISTAR program without additional materials or a basal reading program supplemented by additional materials. At the end of both the first and second years, there was no difference in the two groups on reading achievement except that at end of the second year the DISTAR group did have "somewhat better word attack skills" (p. 69).

Again, using DISTAR, Kuder (1991) pursued the question of why direct instruction programs appear to work well with some students with learning disabilities and not with others. Based on research supporting the notion that "direct instruction in academic skills can be enhanced when combined with strategy training" (p. 124) and difficulties experienced in language by some students with learning disabilities, he extended the previous study. He studied 26 students with learning disabilities from an inner city who had received instruction in DISTAR. He found that "success in a direct instruction reading program was related to the language abilities of inner city students with reading disabilities. Specifically, improvements in word attack were related to phonological abilities, while progress in word comprehension was related to syntactic knowledge" (p. 126).

The question of the effectiveness of DISTAR for students with learning disabilities, according to O'Connor, Jenkins, Cole, and Mills (1993), has not been adequately researched. They cite the effectiveness of DISTAR with disadvantaged students as well as the lack of research showing effectiveness with young children with learning disabilities. They studied a group of young children predicted to fail or with documented learning disabilities. The study divided them into two groups. The first group used DI Reading Mastery 1, based on DISTAR, using direct, sequential instruction of phonics. This program addressed the need for strategy instruction by including a strategy for each skill taught. The second group was taught using *Superkids,* which does not follow a strict sequence of phonics instruction and uses a "more relaxed attitude toward strategic learning approaches" (p. 313). Both groups improved over the year. When tested a year later, there was still no advantage for either group. The authors suggest using restraint in selecting programs "solely on the basis of design features and their presumed benefits" (p. 322).

At this point, we are left, as are others, with many unanswered questions. Yet the need to provide instruction is a daily reminder that we must make some proposals. Let's consider another alternative. Iversen and Tunmer (1993), citing the need to investigate "whether the inclusion of more explicit and systematic training in phonological recoding skills would increase the effectiveness of the Reading Recovery program" (p. 113), added this component to a training study of at-risk learners. The issue was clearly identified. Should word analysis skills be taught only in the context of real text as the need arises or should they be taught on a systematic basis? The program did not use a skill-and-drill approach but rather a metacognitive approach. The emphasis was on two phonological processing skills: phonological awareness and phonological recoding. Children were taught phonograms (common elements in word families) using the onset and rime strategy. The words came from stories already read. The teacher modeled the process and the child made words with magnetic letters. This was based on developing phonological awareness, "the ability to reflect on and manipulate the phonemic segments of speech" (p. 114). The children were required to use their knowledge of words and ability to manipulate phonemes in identifying unknown words. The emphasis was on "developing metacognitive knowledge and strategies for identifying and spelling unfamiliar words, not on 'knowing' a particular list of words" (p. 118). In addition, the program followed the usual Reading Recovery pattern of reading and writing whole text. They found that the children in the modified Reading Recovery program reached the stage of discontinuing the program faster than those in the standard Reading Recovery program. Those in the modified program also learned to read "much more quickly" (p. 123). Here we see an effective combination of the two basic approaches. Consider how many of the needed skills and strategies have been built into this approach.

It is this broad approach to instruction that seems to have much potential. In examining the effectiveness of instructional programs, Palincsar and Klenk (1992) take a similar view. They identify the areas of metacognitive and strategy deficits as problems for students with learning disabilities when they engage in intentional learning, learning that is the result of purposeful effort on the part of the learner. Students with learning disabilities have difficulty with intentional learning because often they don't understand the nature of learning and lack the strategies and motivation to learn. As a result they often engage in low-level basic skill tasks, using "degraded texts" (p. 212), with little emphasis on reading and writing for meaning. This approach can only make the situation worse, it will not develop the strategies and skills needed for effective reading.

Palincsar and Klenk advocate "redefining the contexts of early literacy learning" (p. 213). They report on the results of a training study conducted with young children who were identified as learning disabled and/or emotionally disturbed. Along with a standard reading program that included phonics instruction, children, engaging in reciprocal teaching, read stories around a theme and wrote using invented spelling. Reading and writing were social interactive processes. As of the writing of the article, the authors were still compiling data from study, but so far they had found that children were more inclined to take risks, ask questions, exhibit interest in learning, and share their knowledge. The children had demonstrated growth in spelling from random and patterned letters to invented and conventional spelling. Their understanding of print was clearly developing. The conclusion was not that phonics instruction should not be provided. Rather, it seemed to be that children with learning disabilities, like all children, need a rich environment in which to acquire, practice, and "reveal the strategies they develop independently as they generate their own text and confront print in meaningful situations" (p. 225). Don't throw out instruction in basic skills. Put it in a "supportive context" (p. 211).

Part of this supportive context should be a context that the child understands and accepts. Reetz and Hoover (1992) compared the reactions of middle school students with learning disabilities who demonstrated word identification problems to a variety of instructional techniques including language experience, direct instruction, multisensory, neurological impress, and basal reader. The response to the first four was equally acceptable. The response to the basal reader was the most favorable. The authors suggest that this may be because the students viewed the basal approach as the most socially acceptable. They also suggest that "it may be important to acquaint students with the importance of remedial methods for meeting their individual needs when these materials diverge from the familiar" (p. 14). This is certainly a caution worth noting.

CONCLUSIONS

Why have we put so much emphasis on beginning reading instruction at the word level, particularly on having children master recoding? Probably one reason is because so many children, whether labeled as learning disabled, dyslexic, or reading disabled, have difficulty breaking the code and reading unknown words. They not only have difficulty, but it takes them longer to learn. There is also a widespread conviction that we need to deal directly with the issue of improving "essential phonological skills" (Brady, 1986, p. 150) if children are to learn to read. Therefore, we as teachers spend more time and effort teaching these skills. Brown and Campione (1986) suggest another reason. "Until recently the processes involved in comprehending prose were not well understood" (p. 1063). Thus, we as teachers emphasize in instruction the area we understand from theory and research.

There seems to be a general consensus (although it is always risky to assert this in the field of education) that there is a need at some level for word recognition skills and strategies.

The question is not whether children need some skills but rather how they should acquire them. Consider the available evidence from research and experience on the specific difficulties encountered by children with learning disabilities in acquiring and using word identification skills. We see the need for instruction in these areas. However, reading is more than word recognition. As we have seen, it is a process that requires interaction with prior knowledge, with the content and structure of the text, and with other readers. Instruction in word identification must be put into a "supportive context." The label for that context is not the important thing. Call it a whole language program. Call it Reading Recovery. Call it a Reading and Writing program. Call it a Strategy Intervention program. The critical element is what is included in the program. Programs need to be meaning oriented and provide a rich language base. Both of these are critical in the development of reading competence and are areas particularly important for students with learning disabilities. We need to include instruction in and experience with cognitive and metacognitive strategies. We have identified how important these are in the act of reading and that students with learning disabilities can benefit from instruction in these areas. It is time to merge these findings into appropriate instructional strategies.

It is also important to remember that there is no one way of accomplishing the goal of engaging children effectively in the task of word identification. As we have seen, the problems and needs of students with learning disabilities are indeed diverse. One of the problems we have identified that is encountered by these students in learning is the mismatch between the learning environment and their needs. The solutions therefore must also be diverse. We need to enable these students to develop their own workable reading system. As Harris and Pressley (1991) point out, learning must be personalized and constructed by the learner for the learner, recognizing the "active and purposeful modifications and adaptations of strategies among students engaged in strategy instruction" (p. 393). This is the construction of a "reading system." The teacher's role is to aid each student in such a way as to enable the accomplishment of this critical part of the larger task of reading, the development of ways to identify words.

Recent literature suggests that teaching decoding may not be a sufficient answer to the variety of problems encountered by students with learning disabilities. With appropriate instruction most children can learn to identify many words, using one or more strategies (Coles, 1987). As Brown and Campione (1986) point out, "decoding is mastered eventually, but reading comprehension scores tend to be permanently, severely depressed" (p. 1063). Spear and Sternberg (1987) vividly describe a group of children whom all of us have seen who, after an intensive phonics program, have learned to decode with "alacrity." "The disturbing thing, particularly to someone who had excessive faith in the curative powers of a phonic approach to teaching reading, was that the children continued to be poor readers" (p. 3). Levy and Hinchley (1990) stress that rapid decoding does not ensure comprehension. "Rather, it may intimately involve more abstract elements of the linguistic system" (Hodgson, 1992, p. 100). We turn our attention now to that other critical area of reading: comprehension.

CHAPTER 5

Understanding Words

The role of word meaning in comprehending text seems, to all of us, to be critical. How can you understand the author's message if you can't understand the words being used? Try reading a text in a field where you have a very limited vocabulary, possibly physics or space exploration, or try a verse from the poem *Jabberwocky*.

> 'Twas brillig, and the slithy toves
>   Did gyre and gimble in the wabe;
> All mimsy were the borogoves,
>   And the mome raths outgrabe.

You could certainly "read" this poem. You could decode the words. But, did you know what it meant? Did you comprehend it? You probably had difficulty with it. The critical words had no meaning to you. What are "toves?" We know the word "toves" is a noun because the article "the" comes before it. However, the meaning of the word eludes us. Probably "slithy" is an adjective describing "toves" because it comes between "the" and "toves" and ends in the letter "y." But, we still don't know what this means. There are so many unknown words that we can't get the meaning from the context. Just as understanding the meaning of words was important in trying to read this passage, understanding the meanings of words is essential to success in school because of the verbal nature of most school learning.

BUILDING COMPETENCE

Several issues concern us with regard to understanding words. First, about how many words are students expected to know? How rapidly do they learn them? We know that during their years in school, children rapidly increase the size of their vocabularies at an exponential rate. According to Bos and Vaughn (1994) the size of the vocabulary of six-year-old children is estimated to be about 2,500 words, and that of the average high-school graduate is 60,000 to 80,000 words that are known and used. These authors go on to point out that "students with learning and behavior problems generally have vocabularies that are more limited, and their word meanings are generally more concrete and less flexible" (pp. 73-4).

Next, what does it mean to know the meaning of a word? There is general agreement that understanding the meaning of a word, in its fullest sense, requires knowing the concept underlying the word. Because words and concepts are embedded in larger domains of knowledge, new words that are learned must be tied to what we already know in order for them to have meaning. Vocabulary is, in a sense reciprocal: understanding word meaning provides an enabling base that allows us to build broader knowledge and concepts and, in turn, the prior knowledge base provides the context for understanding new words that we encounter in the course of that context (Lipson & Wixson, 1991).

Finally, how are vocabulary and comprehension related? Virtually all researchers note a substantial correlation between vocabulary and comprehension and view a primary goal of vocabulary instruction to be the improvement of comprehension. Simmons and Kameenui (1990) believe that by the later elementary grades, reading comprehension, word attack, and vocabulary knowledge constitute a core of skills that are inextricably linked. It may be that it is the general knowledge

Difficulty with word meaning certainly suggests potential difficulty with comprehending and writing text that is useful to ourselves and others, and studies of students with language/learning disabilities often cite these kinds of problems (Blachowicz, 1991; Candler & Keefe, 1988). Additionally, today it is generally agreed that the overall vocabulary knowledge of students with learning disabilities is less adequate than that of their peers (Simmons & Kameenui, 1990).

In our attempt to come to grips with understanding word meanings, it will be helpful to take a look at what good readers do.

• Good readers assign meaning to a word or phrase based on the context in which they encounter it.

There is little question but that context is the means by which most vocabulary is acquired (Scott, Hiebert & Anderson, 1994; Sternberg, 1987). Learning from natural contexts while reading or listening provides an unlimited resource for acquiring new words. In addition, it provides a way to integrate word and text comprehension. As Carlisle (1993) explains, the word is experienced within the literate environment, and the reader develops the concept in which the word is embedded.

The importance of context is illustrated by a study conducted in New Zealand (Elley, 1989) in which oral story reading constituted a significant source of acquiring vocabulary, whether or not the reading was accompanied by the teacher explaining the meaning of a word. The features that best predicted whether a new word would be learned were: the frequency with which the word occurred in the text; the depiction of the word in illustrations; and the amount of redundancy with which the word was used in the surrounding context.

In a different kind of study, Jenkins, Matlock, & Slocum (1989) demonstrated that teaching students to derive word meaning from sentence context, rather than teaching specific meanings, improved students' actual ability to infer word meanings. Medium or high amounts of practice were required, and the instruction proved to be ineffective with less practice. The ability to assign meaning to words or phrases based on the way in which the words are used is an attribute of the good reader.

- Good readers use word parts to help derive word meanings.

  Identifying and attaching meaning to structural parts of words, such as prefixes, suffixes, and roots, helps readers to discern the meanings of complex, unfamiliar words (Graves, 1987). This can be especially true for adolescents because the number of derived words that students encounter in their textbooks increases as they move to higher grade levels (Herber & Herber, 1993).

- Good readers understand the relationships among words. Because these relationships comprise a basis for comprehending abstract concepts, they are especially important in reading in content areas.

  As words become more abstract, the concepts they reflect become more difficult to grasp. A concept consists of ideas that are associated with smaller but related ideas (Herber & Herber, 1993). Typically they represent abstractions, or the essence of things. For instance, the concept of *table* refers to a symbol of concrete experiences. The reader's experience may have been limited to a formica kitchen table or may extend to an elegant antique or a conference table. At a more abstract level, the concept of *table* becomes a part of a broader concept of *furniture*. Even more abstract are those concepts removed from the sensory world such as *honesty, loyalty,* or *oppression*. The good reader discerns these relationships and employs them to aid in understanding the meanings of words (Lipson & Wixson, 1991). These skills are important in initially comprehending word meanings (Graves, 1987) and in remembering meanings (Bos & Anders, 1988). They are also important in understanding the more abstract concepts that are typical of content-area readings (Graves, 1987).

• The good reader uses metacognitive strategies to remember and to monitor understanding of word meanings.

Although the good reader may have a firm grasp of the meaning of a familiar object such as "bottle," the ability to accurately understand and recall the meaning of an unfamiliar technical term for which the reader does not have a concrete referent is likely to be more limited. The fine variations in the understanding of meaning that make the difference between the sophisticated and the novice reader are characterized by Drum and Konopak (1987): "Access to word knowledge cannot be compared to an on/off toggle switch. A more appropriate analogy is the increasing luminescence of a rheostat" (p. 79).

Self-monitoring skills are an important determiner of the extent to which readers independently regulate their own comprehension and remember what words mean (Lipson & Wixson, 1991). As Herber and Herber (1993) remind us, an important goal of instruction in the area of vocabulary is that students become autonomous learners, monitoring their own understanding of the words they are reading. For instance, Graves (1987) pointed out that good readers realize that the same word can have multiple meanings, depending on the context in which they are used. In addition, studies have demonstrated that above-average readers are substantially more advanced in metacognitive knowledge about vocabulary and passage organization difficulty than those with learning disabilities (Wong, 1991b).

Applications of metacognitive strategies will be more fully developed in the section on understanding extended text because, although the research includes word meanings, much of it is focused primarily on the broader competence of understanding text.

What areas have been identified as possible sources of difficulty for students with learning disabilities? As we discuss this question, it is important to remember that no individual student would be expected to experience all of these difficulties. The heterogeneity of the group of students whom we call "learning disabled" reflects a wide variety of characteristics.

• Students with learning disabilities may have difficulty assigning meaning to a word or phrase based on the context in which it is encountered.

Incidental word learning from context is an important aspect of vocabulary development. However, for students with learning disabilities who are faced with severe reading problems, this facility may be lacking (Adams, 1990). An example of difficulty employing context to derive word meanings is that some students with learning disabilities "have adequate vocabularies for their age range but have assigned a small number of attributes to each word" (Mercer & Mercer, 1993, p. 557). If the subtleties of the multiple meanings of words, depending on the context in which they are experienced, are not understood by the reader, comprehension will surely be impaired.

Because most students with learning disabilities read less, they gain fewer of the understandings that come from reading. "Wide reading is agreed to be an important contributor to general vocabulary development" (Blachowicz & Lee, 1991). Unfortunately, students with

(Blachowicz & Lee, 1991). Unfortunately, students with learning disabilities, who are often poor readers, gain less exposure to new words through reading.

- Students with learning difficulties may not make good use of word parts in establishing the probable meaning of a word.

Especially for students with learning disabilities, there is a need to learn the roots of words, prefixes, suffixes, and word origins that can provide a knowledge base to support their vocabulary development (Graves, 1987). Many students with learning disabilities know the meanings of fewer words than their nondisabled peers, and often they are not adept at inferring word meanings from context (Lerner, 1993). As we noted in the previous chapter, teaching students to analyze the structure of words may improve their decoding skills as well as their understanding of word meanings.

- Students with learning disabilities often have difficulty understanding the relationships among words, and therefore they may not make good use of these relationships in understanding abstract concepts.

Proficiency with language and perceiving the relationships between words play a key role in understanding the meaning of words. Students with learning disabilities, who typically have difficulty in these areas, are likely to experience limited vocabulary development and conceptual ability (Lerner, 1993). In content-area subjects, in which both the words and the concepts they incorporate are frequently abstract and may be lacking concrete examples to which to relate them, discerning the relationships between words becomes even more important. In addition, in disciplines such as social studies or science, the problem may not be the difficulty of the words per se and the limited time and practice allowed for mastery (Bos & Vaughn, 1994).

• Students with learning disabilities may have difficulty remembering word meanings and monitoring their understanding of those meanings.

It is not enough for students to learn to derive meanings from the context if they are unable to remember them. As Pressley, Levin, and McDaniel (1987) remind us: "Although providing contexts should facilitate meaning *discovery*, there is no reason to expect inference operations to facilitate subsequent meaning *retention*" (p. 116). Metacognitive strategies to help students remember new vocabulary and self-monitor their understanding can be effective. For students who are poor readers, even recognizing that an unknown word has been presented can be a big step (Graves, 1987).

INSTRUCTIONAL ALTERNATIVES

How, then, do people acquire new vocabulary, and what conditions surround its acquisition? We know that "most of the words students learn they must somehow learn independently" (Graves, 1987, p. 172), rather than through instruction in school. Nonetheless, classroom instruction offers an opportunity for students to gain new understandings of word meanings that they would probably not learn otherwise.

What instructional strategies should we be using to teach word meanings to these students with learning disabilities? Although word meanings and learning strategies that will help students become independent word learners are taught in most reading programs, instruction is often unsystematic and brief. Understanding the meaning of sophisticated, abstract words is integrally related to understanding concepts, and in the following section on understanding text we will explore this relationship in more detail. The teaching and learning strategies employed to expand and enrich students' understanding of words and of extended text are, in general, closely associated. We will consider eight ways to teach word meanings and independent word-learning skills to students with learning disabilities: provide direct instruction, use the context of their school experience, teach word parts, establish relationships between new words and known information, provide ways to remember word meanings, self-monitor understanding, utilize technology, and individualize and combine instructional strategies.

Provide Direct Instruction

A powerful principle of instruction that has been confirmed in the last decade is that if you want a student to learn word meanings, give a high priority to this objective and teach the vocabulary directly (Bos & Vaughn, 1994; Mercer, 1992; Stahl & Miller, 1987). Although we all learn many words from context, it can be helpful for the teacher to teach students essential word meanings that they have not learned in other ways. Scott, Hiebert, and Anderson (1994) found that "less than 5% of reading lesson time is devoted to vocabulary instruction" (p. 263). They also report that researchers who have observed vocabulary instruction in schools have found that it lacks purpose, breadth, and depth. In short, schools are not doing a good job of helping students with learning disabilities to master the vocabulary that will help enable their success in content-area subjects as well as in their daily lives.

There are two purposes of direct vocabulary instruction according to Scott et al. (1994). The first purpose is to teach students the difficult words needed to understand a particular text. They write: "Now there is a growing body of evidence that teaching difficult vocabulary can help" (p. 263). The second purpose is to help students become better independent word learners. As best we know, readers become independent learners through instruction that gradually shifts the responsibility of developing new vocabulary from the teacher to the student. These authors suggest that the shift to independence be planned for within the instructional program.

Teach Students Using Context

"Providing readers broad, rich experiences with words within a framework of contextual reading, discussion, and response is the goal of vocabulary instruction" (Blachowicz & Lee, 1991, p. 194). This philosophy builds on real-life experiences such as exposure to a variety of people, places, and books that forms the ultimate base for vocabulary development. Practical application of this philosophy is illustrated by Blachowicz (1991) who presents a sample lesson for teaching vocabulary in this manner in the context of a middle school social studies class. In reporting an earlier study that highlights essential components of this philosophy, Blachowicz and Zabroske (1990) point out that students must know why and when to use context in deriving word meanings, they must know what kinds of clues may be provided by context, and they must know how to look for and use these clues. The authors provide a specific example of instruction for remedial students that illustrates these principles.

Another effective instructional strategy based on the use of context for learning and remembering words was identified by Bos and Anders (1987). Students with learning disabilities predicted the relationship between individual words and concepts within the text on a semantic feature analysis grid before reading. They shared their prior knowledge and then read the text to confirm the predictions.

In a later study (1990a), these investigators found that elaborated, interactive vocabulary instruction that highlights contextual information produced greater gains than definition instruction that was relatively context free. In describing their instruction, Bos and Anders write that

> long-term learning seems to occur under conditions that provide adequate opportunities for students to (a) activate and instantiate prior knowledge, (b) share that knowledge with each other, (c) make predictions concerning the relationships among concepts, and (d) read to confirm and justify their predictions. . . . The results of this study seem to promote the notion of engaging students in ideas, thereby facilitating long-term learning that becomes schema upon which new learning can occur. (p. 40)

Other researchers have reached similar conclusions. For instance, Leong, Simmons, and Izatt-Gambell (1990) successfully taught word knowledge using both internal and external contextual cues.

In a different application of context, Leverett and Diefendorf (1992) suggest using the context of school reading by identifying difficult words and writing notes to students about them in the margins of reading material. They call this technique a "marginal gloss." This strategy provides immediate, specific information for the student whose vocabulary is weak, and it requires no additional work on the part of the student. Because it occurs in the natural context of the reading to be mastered, the validity of the words on which instruction is focused is assured.

Both text characteristics and student factors affect the ease with which word meanings can be inferred from context. Because the skill of utilizing text cues and other variables to learn vocabulary from context can be learned, a major objective of instruction should be to teach students to use context productively in all of their reading. One important advantage of teaching words by employing the context to help derive meaning is the positive relationship of this activity to "real" reading. When we decide to focus on teaching words by using other strategies, we need to be aware that learning definitions does not teach students the appropriate uses of the words and may not affect their comprehension of passages containing those words.

Teach Word Parts

In planning an instructional program the selection of which structural elements should be taught is important. White, Sowell, and Yanagihara (1989) list and recommend the word parts most frequently used in school books. The same topic is addressed by Graves (1987) who supports teaching "inflectional suffixes, derivational suffixes, prefixes attached to regular English words, prefixes attached to non-English roots, and non-English roots themselves" (p. 174). He points out that the extent to which each type of element is likely to contribute toward identifying a word's meaning should be considered in deciding which word parts to teach and the order in which they will be taught.

After reviewing recent studies of teaching word parts such as prefixes, suffixes, and roots, Stahl and Shiel (1992) suggest that direct instruction of word parts may be especially helpful in content-area reading. In this kind of reading a higher percentage of words contain inherent, identifiable word parts that retain their meaning in different applications.

Establish Relationships Between New Words and Known Information

In teaching students with learning disabilities to establish relationships between new words and their background knowledge, visual arrays are frequently used. Different researchers have employed visual applications in a variety of ways and have called their procedures by a variety of names. The underlying principle is that it is more effective to portray the relationship between related words or ideas by adding a graphical component.

A relationship matrix to organize information was used by Bos and Anders (1990a). They combined this graphic organizer with an interactive instructional method and taught strategies that could be applied in a variety of situations. Their instructional strategies included semantic mapping, semantic feature analysis, and semantic/syntactic feature analysis. These methods were more effective for improving vocabulary and comprehension than was traditional instruction in definitions.

A semantic or content map to visually represent the relationship among terms was also endorsed by Bos and Vaughn (1994). In teaching words as part of a semantic field, a few new target words serve as a springboard for learning sets of related words. For instance, one targeted word can be tied through class discussion and semantic mapping to other related words. Stahl & Shiel (1992) found this approach to be especially effective with low-vocabulary children, for whom a number of the related words may be unfamiliar.

Word webs are a variation on this strategy that is recommended by Lerner (1993). Word webs enrich associations with a word and enhance understanding concepts. A word web can be readily developed by answering such questions as "What is it?" "What is it like?" and "What are some examples?"

McKeown and Beck (1988) also created instructional units with related sets of words belonging to a semantic group (e.g., love) or used in discussing a specific topic (e.g., skiing). Discussions that focused on analysis of meanings and comparisons of words provided a strong conceptual and semantic foundation for learning new vocabulary. These authors also discussed criteria for deciding which words or phrases to include in a visual array. They suggested that the teacher should evaluate the general usefulness of words, their relationship to other classroom lessons, and their relationship to the specific domain of knowledge being explored.

Instruction that is focused on synonyms, antonyms, and classification can clarify the relationships among words. However, Graves (1987) points out that this instruction typically has focused on teaching word meanings rather than on teaching relationships directly. Graves suggests out that we should focus on the relationships themselves, their similarities and differences, and that we should be teaching students to recognize and manipulate these relationships among words.

Instructionally, the teaching of word meanings and concepts is so intertwined that it becomes virtually inseparable (Lerner, 1993). A more extensive discussion of teaching students concepts and the vocabulary embedded in them will be presented in the next chapter which focuses on understanding text in content areas.

Provide Metacognitive Strategies

As in the comprehension of extended text, teaching metacognitive strategies related to word meanings can enable students with learning disabilities to learn more effectively (Carlisle, 1993). These strategies have to do with remembering what has been learned and with monitoring one's performance so as to know when comprehension is breaking down.

Scruggs and Mastropieri (1990) review a decade of research on memory-enhancing strategies with students with learning disabilities. They conclude that "instructional models that effectively link new, unfamiliar information to a previously established knowledge base of concrete, meaningful information are more likely to result in rapid, efficient acquisition of school-relevant content" (p. 10).

When we are teaching strategies to students, it is our hope that these strategies will be applied in a range of contexts. We have learned, however, that this seldom occurs unless students are taught specific ways of doing so. Fulk, Mastropieri, and Scruggs (1992) look at ways in which we can help students apply independently the complex mnemonic strategies in which they have been instructed. These researchers report that intensive training in using mnemonic strategies in other situations facilitated students' ability to transfer a strategy to independent use. The applications of strategies covered a variety of domains, including vocabulary, science, and social studies.

An important factor in remembering the meanings of words is the "establishment of a reliable associative link between the vocabulary word and its definition" (Pressley, Levin, & McDaniel, 1987, p. 116). This philosophy underlies the *keyword* mnemonic strategy, a way to facilitate vocabulary learning and recall for students with learning disabilities (Lysynchuk & Pressley, 1990; Symons, McGoldrick, Snyder, & Pressley, 1990). The keyword approach establishes an association between a word and a meaning that is easy to remember. Often the phonetic and visual imagery components of a word provide the mnemonic cue that links the word with its definition. In an earlier study, Condus, Marshall, and Miller (1986) reported using a keyword mnemonic strategy to teach vocabulary to twelve-year-olds. Students taught with the keyword method recalled more word meanings both initially and after ten weeks. This elaborative strategy may be particularly appropriate for students who have difficulty generating effective memory strategies spontaneously.

Precision teaching is an instructional method for improving vocabulary by teaching students to monitor their own performance based on rate or fluency of response. Stump et al. (1992) recommend this instructional strategy for teaching words out of context. They report that both students with and without learning disabilities showed vocabulary gains.

Use Technology

"Technology-driven changes in the nature of teaching, learning, and literacy spur a new educational research agenda" (Reinking, 1993, p. 29). Computer technology has been integrated into the mission of the new National Reading Research Center established in 1992. A part of this research agenda includes new ways of teaching students word meanings.

In the past, computer-assisted instruction has been employed frequently to teach and review the meanings of new words. For instance, in content-area subjects, computers have been used to teach new vocabulary and to review that which has already been studied. Horton, Lovitt, and Givens (1988) report success in employing this kind of program with high school students learning words from their world geography class. A definition appeared on the screen, and the student selected the word defined from a choice of ten possible answers. A pretest, practice, and posttest sequence was used.

Another successful application involved computerized presentations of text passages in which meanings of unfamiliar words can be called up on the screen when desired to help build vocabulary (Carlisle, 1993). This approach provides a word meaning when it is needed and does not require the memorization of words out of context.

A more sophisticated technology, hypermedia, is recommended by Higgins and Boone (1991) as a basal reader supplement to provide individualized instruction in reading. Hypermedia provides a flexible format that "gives a reader access to related information by means of a simple selection process. The process 'brings up' to the computer screen new windows of related text, related pictures, and computer generated voice that provide the supplementary information, clarification, and elaboration needed by the reader, all within the single medium" (p. 3). These authors found in their study that one helpful application for students with learning disabilities was the ability to access the definition of a word within the context to which it is linked.

Captioned television is also being employed to help students learn vocabulary. Koskinen, Wilson, Gambrell, & Neuman (1993) write that "studies suggest that captioned television is a motivating medium for improving the vocabulary and comprehension skills" (p. 38). The studies reported in this article support the notion that multisensory processing (audio/video/text) enhances learning. Even though there are differences between reading text on the video screen and printed text, "below-average readers appear to benefit from the multifaceted support provided by captioned video" (p. 41). These authors suggest that this method will be especially effective if students read text that focuses on the same concepts introduced in the video captions after using the captioned television. In an earlier study, Neuman and Koskinen (1992) documented the effectiveness of a captioned television instructional program on the acquisition of science vocabulary and concepts of bilingual seventh and eighth graders.

Individualize Instruction and Combine Strategies

Particular approaches to vocabulary instruction may be more or less suitable for individual students, depending on their verbal ability (Bos & Vaughn, 1994; Lerner, 1993). As Mercer (1992) points out: "Because each student with learning disabilities is unique, a combination of approaches and various teaching strategies are [sic] needed to meet the needs of these students" (p. 530).

Students with weak verbal skills, whose oral and reading vocabularies are poorly developed, may not thrive on definitional approaches to vocabulary learning. At the same time, reading alone, without further guidance, may be inadequate to effect significant gains in vocabulary. For these students Carlisle (1993) endorses a program that builds reasoning and language skills, a program that is independent of a particular context. Carlisle provides detailed suggestions for implementing this kind of program. These include: learning meanings out of context, learning words through prereading and reading activities, inferring meaning from context, and teaching word concepts. In discussing its objectives, she writes: "When semantic relations are taught in prereading activities, the goal is to enrich both topical knowledge and vocabulary together" (p. 103). Carlisle suggests that for other students with good verbal ability, speed and accuracy of word recognition may underlie their comprehension problems. For them, programs that provide practice in both word meanings and word recognition may be helpful.

Combinations of strategies are especially powerful, and, in practice, we would seldom use just one (Bos & Vaughn, 1994; Carlisle, 1993). Each method has benefit, and none provides a panacea for meeting vocabulary objectives for students with learning disabilities. For instance, learning to derive meanings of words from context and remembering the meanings of new words are not mutually exclusive. Most students will need to learn both. When the main objective is to enhance students' ability to infer the meanings of unknown words, then contextual strategies would be applied. On the other hand, when the goal is to have students remember the meanings of new words, mnemonic strategy instruction would be most helpful. In such a unit of work, the keyword approach (Mastropieri et al., 1990), semantic mapping (Bos & Anders, 1990b), and enriched instruction (McKeown & Beck, 1988) all could be used to good advantage. Several strategies will be utilized at any given time, and separating them, for purposes of analysis, is to some degree artificial.

As we conclude this section on teaching students to understand word meanings, we would like to stress the need for further research in this area. Lysynchuk and Pressley (1990) point out that "although vocabulary instruction appears to be a key element in education, there is very little research examining the vocabulary instruction currently taking place in schools" (p. 71). As in all areas of education, research-validated instruction will produce superior results. We encourage further investigation along these lines.

CHAPTER 6

Comprehending Text

What is this thing we call "comprehension?" As we might expect, different experts define it in different ways. Garner, Alexander, and Hare (1991) tell us that "comprehension is the successful outcome of reading" (p. 284), and, indeed, this sounds like our objective. From a different perspective, Herber and Herber (1993) tell us that comprehension consists of three things: (1) reading the lines; (2) reading between the lines; and (3) reading beyond the lines. This, too, sounds like what we're working to achieve, but neither of these definitions tells us how to go about it. Finally, McCormick (1992) writes that "the reader must weigh many elements, select the right elements, combine these in the right relationships, and give each the appropriate amount of weight" (p. 75). We would have to agree with each of these definitions of what the good reader accomplishes when comprehending text. However, the problem awaits us. What does a reader need to be able to do in order to comprehend text?

In examining comprehension, it is becoming increasingly clear that we must look beyond the word level. Silliman (1989) suggests that comprehending is a task that requires the use of language, but it demands more than an understanding of language. It requires knowledge of content and an understanding of temporal and causal chains of events and purposes. For instance, when reading a story, the reader needs to understand the function of stories and have knowledge of the structure of a story, i.e., how it is organized, in contrast to the function and structure of content-area text. In addition, today the good reader is viewed as an active, inquiring participant in the reading process, developing hypotheses and predictions, often by formulating questions while reading. The reader will read critically and draw inferences in order to understand the author's implied meanings. Finally, through summarizing and self-monitoring comprehension, the good reader will be able to remember considerable information learned from the text.

Upon consideration, it is apparent that the components required for good comprehension are closely interrelated (Garner, Alexander & Hare, 1991). For instance, good decoding interacts with specific comprehension strategies to yield a more sophisticated understanding of text. Likewise, understanding simple sentences using syntax is a natural transition from learning individual words to comprehending the meaning of extended text. Isolating specific components of comprehension in order to examine them more carefully, as we will do initially, presents them in a different perspective than the integrated use of strategies that characterizes the good reader.

GOOD AND POOR READERS: A PROFILE

Reviewing what good readers do can help us begin to tease out how it is that the poor reader, often a reader with learning disabilities, differs from the good reader. In turn, these understandings can prepare us for our major quest: to investigate research-based instructional strategies for improving the reading of students with learning disabilities, strategies that translate theory into practice.

- Good readers activate and use prior knowledge.

     Having the necessary background knowledge and being able to retrieve it when needed are both important to comprehension, and good readers do these things well. In comprehending difficult expository passages, background information is particularly important. The failure that can result from a lack of it is illustrated in Manolakes' (1988) account of his attempt to understand an article on electronics, a subject of which he has little knowledge. Manolakes concludes: "My inability to understand this article was not due to any lack of experience with those 'comprehension skills' that are part of most instructional programs in reading. Clearly it was my lack of prior knowledge" (p. 202). Without question, limited background knowledge to link with new information hinders comprehension (Herber & Herber, 1993; Olson & Gee, 1991).

However, we have also learned that prior knowledge cannot compensate for other difficulties in the reading experience. McKeown, Beck, Sinatra, & Loxterman (1992) report from their research with normal readers that background knowledge interacts with text structure to such an extent that extensive preparation by teachers to provide background knowledge did not compensate for the inadequacies of the poorly written text. Their results suggest that "background knowledge is most useful if the text is coherent enough to allow the reader to see the connections between the text information and previous knowledge" (pp. 91), a reminder of the interrelated nature of the processes that comprise reading.

The research involving comprehending narrative text has yielded somewhat different results. After reviewing recent studies, Carver (1992) concluded that using prior knowledge appears to account for only a small difference in comprehending narrative text. Carver points out that although there is little doubt that general prior knowledge influences how much of a particular passage will be comprehended, he questions the level of importance often attributed to prior knowledge, especially its importance as compared to general reading ability.

- Good readers utilize knowledge of sentence and text structure and are sensitive to the organization of information in the text.

At the sentence level, syntax helps good readers to understand what they are reading, and it serves as a cuing system for monitoring comprehension (Eckwall & Shanker, 1993; Lipson & Wixson, 1991). Thus syntax is one of the "organizational, text-based strategies" (Kletzien, 1991, p. 81) used by good comprehenders, particularly in reading on the instructional level as compared to the independent level.

Good readers use and understand text structure, whether narrative or expository. This requires the ability to recognize or generate an effective organization of ideas. On the one hand, when a reader perceives and uses the structure of text to enhance understanding, sequencing and organizing the information given in the text has played an important part in recognizing the existing pattern. On the other hand, if the reader is having difficulty perceiving the structure of the text, consciously sequencing and organizing the information within the text may indeed make apparent the underlying structure, thus facilitating comprehension. Sequencing and organizing information is typically practiced both by competent readers as they strive to understand text and by teachers in their presentation of information.

As we might guess, unfamiliar text organizational structures are difficult to follow. In a study of average and poor readers, Day and Zajakowski (1991) found that the structure of text, exemplified by placement of the topic sentence in a paragraph (first, last, or missing), influenced how easily students were able to master finding the main idea.

The practical significance of the interaction between the background that the reader brings to the text and the structure of the text itself has not been sufficiently appreciated. Roller (1990) writes that

> text structure is most important when the subject matter is moderately unfamiliar to the reader, because the reader can use knowledge of the structure to construct the relations between the concepts in the text. In contrast, if the text is on a familiar topic, then the relations between concepts are already known, and if the text is quite difficult, the reader cannot discover the relations in the text even when utilizing the structure. Although structure variables are important only for moderately unfamiliar material, it is from such text that readers most often acquire new knowledge." (p. 79)

In an extension of this line of reasoning, Carver (1992) writes: "Variables derived from schema theory are not likely to have direct relevance to the comprehension process that is involved in typical or ordinary reading - the kind of reading that elementary and secondary students ordinarily do . . ." (p. 173). Nonetheless, often assigned reading in content-area classes is difficult for students, and in this circumstance knowledge of text structure can be a valuable aid to comprehension.

• Good readers employ self-questioning strategies to aid in attending to and comprehending text.

Learners are frequently questioners, questioning both others and themselves. In efficient reading, text-specific or problem-specific questions are derived from the general schema. For example, given the informed expectations of fairy tales in general, the reader can apply text-specific questions to understand what happened to Cinderella as compared to Snow White. Reading comprehension and problem solving both are facilitated by understanding a problem both as a general cognitive structure and as a series of specific, self-generated questions to enable understanding (Bos & Vaughn, 1994; Herber & Herber, 1993).

Another way of stating this principle is that reading is an interactive process between the reader and the text. Marzola (1988) suggests that to derive meaning, "good readers actively interrogate the text, monitoring their understanding by asking themselves questions and clarifying their comprehension before, during, and after reading" (p. 243). Griffey, Zigmond and Leinhardt (1988) report similar conclusions and, in addition, suggest that self-generated questions will be helpful if comprehension failure occurs. Thus, self-generated questions can function as a strategy for text comprehension and can function as a metacognitive coping strategy.

- Good readers read critically and draw inferences.

Similar cognitive processes underlie critical thinking and reading comprehension. As comprehension consists of an interaction between the resources of the reader and the characteristics of the text (Adams, 1990), so the critical thinking skills needed to solve problems consist of an interaction between the resources of the individual and the characteristics of the specific problem. Reading and critical thinking reflect high level intellectual processes, for they require complex interrelationships of a number of factors. The ability to read discerningly has become increasingly important as the profusion of information has increased. Accordingly, a redefinition of literacy is in process that incorporates the broader understandings and competencies needed in our society today. Ellsworth

(1994) suggests that an important component of this redefinition consists of the critical thinking skills that underlie sophisticated reading comprehension.

The importance of the ability to make inferences is clarified by Trabasso (1994).

> When we attempt to understand a series of events, states, and actions in a text, we do not experience them as isolated individual occurrences. Rather we experience them or try to experience them as a coherent sequence of happenings. We achieve this coherence by making inferences. We make inferences about the time and place in which the action occurs, and about who the characters are and what they are like. We make inferences that interrelate or connect ideas about the events. These inferences are primarily of a causal and logical nature. From these inferences, we construct a memory representation of the text that determines how well we can remember, answer questions, summarize, paraphrase, evaluate, or judge the text. In general, the more coherent the mental representation of the text, the better the comprehension and usage of the text. (p. 190-191)

In their discussion of reading comprehension skills as related to content areas, Herber & Herber (1993) suggest that when ideas are "textually implicit," rather than being stated explicitly, it is the job of the reader to establish what authors mean by what they say. In other words, the reader must "infer ideas that can be logically drawn from information presented in the text" (p. 214). This can be a challenge for the best of readers. For example, Lipson and Wixson (1991) explain that good readers are more able to infer the additional information needed to illuminate key relationships between and among ideas, whether or not connectives are explicitly stated.

- Good readers summarize text.

    What is involved in summarizing? Lipson and Wixson (1991) describe it as follows: "To summarize means to eliminate extraneous information so that only the main points remain" (p. 603). Thus, the role of summarization in understanding text becomes apparent. Good readers typically enhance comprehension by summarizing text (Griffey, Zigmond & Leinhardt, 1988; Herber & Herber, 1993; Olson & Gee, 1991). The exercise of reducing the ideas presented to their essentials provides a structure that facilitates understanding. Summarizing has also been shown to improve recall, even when students employ only very simple forms of summarization (Graham & Johnson, 1989).

- Good readers actively monitor their comprehension.

    Mature, fluent readers are seldom conscious of their own comprehension monitoring (Wong, 1991b). Only when a comprehension problem arises, does self-monitoring come into play as the reader slows down his rate of reading and either reads on and attempts to enhance meaning through subsequent text or stops and rereads. Proficient readers seem to be alerted to difficulty because they become aware that their reading does not make sense or does not sound like what they recognize as valid language patterns. This active, metacognitive, monitoring of comprehension has come to be recognized as a requirement for the good reader (Garner, Alexander & Hare, 1991).

Now let's turn to considering the likely sources of difficulty for students with learning disabilities. It will be important to remember that because of the diversity of these students, no individual is likely to show all of the following characteristics.

• Students with learning disabilities may have difficulty activating and using prior knowledge.

Efficient use of background knowledge may be even more important for students with learning disabilities than for good readers because these students frequently possess meager domain knowledge (Garner, Alexander, & Hare, 1991). This problem often accelerates because they tend to fall further behind each year in school (Lerner, 1993). The importance of this difficulty is summarized by Scott, Hiebert, and Anderson (1994): "The fund of knowledge a reader already possesses is a critical determiner of comprehension" (p. 261).

In addition to coming to school with a smaller fund of background knowledge, students with learning disabilities may have difficulty activating the background knowledge that they do possess (Graham & Johnson, 1989; Montague, 1988). As we have already seen, the problem here may be linked to the inadequate or ineffective organization of the information in memory. For this reason, mastering strategies to help organize and tap into that prior knowledge can enable these students to comprehend what they read more fully. In reviewing the literature on memory issues, we saw that one reason students with learning disabilities may have difficulty remembering what they know is their inefficient and ineffective use of cognitive strategies. Ellis and Lenz (1990) provide us with links in these areas when they report that "strategy instruction holds great potential for many mildly handicapped and low-achieving students" (p. 1) in learning to activate background knowledge.

Ellis and Lenz also point out that if students lack the required background knowledge, no amount of activating that knowledge can be successful. In the introduction to a review of instructional techniques for mediating content-area learning, they write that "the power of both single and multiple strategies is often limited by a student's knowledge base" (p. 1). In short, if the students have not built that knowledge base in academic areas, no amount of skill in strategies to activate it can be effective.

• Students with learning disabilities may lack sensitivity to the organization of information in the text and may not utilize the knowledge of sentence and text structure that they do possess.

Syntactic competence has been identified as one of the characteristic areas of difficulty for students with learning disabilities (Bos & Vaughn, 1994; Feagans and Applebaum, 1986; Siegel & Ryan, 1988). It is not clear whether the difficulty is inherent in the child or whether, because of lack of extensive reading, the child with learning disabilities perhaps fails to gain facility with written syntax. Stanovich (1988) suggests that "much general information and knowledge about more complex syntactic structures probably take place through reading itself" (p. 162).

Above average readers are substantially more advanced in metacognitive knowledge about passage organization than those with learning disabilities (Wong, 1991b). In fact, Englert and Thomas (1987) believe that much of the difficulty experienced by students with learning disabilities is due to "failure to apply appropriate metacognitive strategies involving text structure" (p. 102). In addition, these researchers demonstrated that students with learning disabilities required more instruction than average readers in order to master this skill, which is not surprising in view of the fact that the learning disabled have difficulty with metacognition in general.

It seems likely that one cause of the poor comprehension of many students with learning disabilities is these students' underlying difficulty in organizing information. Colson and Mehring (1990) reported that "students with dysfunctional learning patterns often do not spontaneously organize information" (p. 77). Along similar lines, in reviewing studies of language learning disabled children within the context of comprehending narrative text, Silliman (1989) found evidence that "LLD is a manifestation of a broader, more cognitively based, organizational limitation" (p. 136). In short, these students may not independently recognize or use the cues signaling a specific organization, and they may need to have these routines identified for them explicitly. We have identified this as an area of difficulty when discussing cognitive strategies in general; it also is an area with significant implications for comprehension.

Because of the interrelationship between learning to read and to write, it is important to take a look at the way students with learning disabilities progress in their composition skills. A lack of organization in their writing is reported by a number of investigators. Laughton and Morris (1989) found that students frequently did not employ basic story grammar components in narratives that they wrote. Along similar lines, Montague (1988) reported that stories "written by Learning Disabled students are incohesive, unorganized, and incomplete in relation to episodic structure" (p. 7). Finally, Englert, Raphael, Anderson, Gregg and Anthony (1989) found that students' compositions were not only less organized, but they "contained fewer ideas than low- and high-achieving students" (p. 5). Also, students' summaries reflected less knowledge about processes of organizing and categorizing ideas than did those of students who were not learning disabled.

An insensitivity to the *importance* of text structure, as well as a lack of grasp of the actual structure such as the hierarchy of ideas, i.e., main idea and detail, is also characteristic of students with learning disabilities (Englert & Thomas, 1987; Thomas, Englert, and Gregg, 1987).

Montague, Maddux, and Dereshiwsky (1990) suggest that the difficulty may be that the strategy of using story schema may not be activated spontaneously.

Some researchers report that students with learning disabilities do utilize text structure, but that they differ from good readers in a variety of ways. Ripich and Griffith (1988) conclude that students with learning disabilities use story grammar to recall and generate narrative text but that these students do not include the same amount of detail. Montague (1988), after comparing students with and without learning disabilities in grades 4 to 11, concludes that "Learning Disabled students have acquired a rudimentary but perhaps not fully developed schema for narrative prose" (p. 1).

•   Students with learning disabilities may not employ self-questioning strategies to aid in attending to and comprehending text.

Students with learning disabilities often do not spontaneously ask themselves questions about their performance prior to, during, and after completion of a specific reading task, an important component of becoming independent learners. These students may need to have self-questioning behaviors modeled for them (Garner, Alexander, & Hare, 1991). As was noted in the chapter on learning disabilities, these students, who frequently are not risk takers, may have become "passive learners," students who are not actively engaging in the learning process to the extent that we wish they would. For such students the self-generated questioning about the likely meaning of text may represent a major step (Bos & Vaughn, 1994).

•   Students with learning disabilities often have great difficulty reading critically and drawing inferences.

Critical reading and making inferences from the information given in the text are sophisticated comprehension skills, and many students with learning disabilities have problems in these areas. We need to place these particular difficulties within the context of the broader range of difficulties these students typically experience both in and out of school. As we have seen, students with learning disabilities often have difficulty integrating information, a skill need in inferencing; they make less use of reasoning strategies than do their peers; they have difficulty with the problem solving required in inferencing and critical reasoning; and they also may neglect to monitor their success or failure in these activities.

It is no surprise to find the same general difficulties appearing in these areas when students need competence in them in order to be good readers. Winne, Graham, and Prock (1993) report that "readers with learning problems can have difficulty comprehending information and making inferences from text" (p. 53). They point out that teaching poor readers to discriminate and use text clues that aid inferencing is an aspect of comprehension that has received relatively little attention in instruction. In an earlier study, Crais and Chapman (1987) found that students with learning disabilities performed less well on inference questions than age-matched controls. Students' performance seemed to be tied to questions that required integration of information and that changed the wording of sentences in the story. These researchers highlighted the need for specific instruction on how to organize lexical and semantic systems.

The need for specific instruction, and schools' failure to provide it, is discussed by Haney and Thistlethwaite (1991). They write that "critical thinking/reading skills are often neglected for high-risk students" (p. 337), apparently those who may need it most. As already cited, students can benefit from instruction in these higher order skills and strategies. Interestingly, Darch and Kameenui (1987) pointed out that students with learning disabilities do not require different strategies for critical reading than students without learning disabilities; rather they require more examples and practice before mastery. It is clear that instruction and practice are important and that they are often lacking.

• Students with learning disabilities may not summarize text.

Students with learning disabilities often have difficulty summarizing text (Bos & Vaughn, 1994). Englert, Raphael, Anderson, Gregg, and Anthony (1989) report that students with learning disabilities produced "significantly less well-organized summaries that contained significantly fewer ideas than both low-and high-achieving students" (p. 5). Again, the issue of organization of information is cited as a potential area of difficulty. As a result of these problems, Herr (1988) recommends instruction in summarizing and paraphrasing to assist students with learning disabilities in comprehending content-area text.

• Students with learning disabilities often do not self-monitor their comprehension.

A number of researchers have found that students with learning disabilities show problems in self-monitoring their understanding of what they are reading (Chan, Cole and Barfett, 1987; Garner, Alexander & Hare, 1991; Ryan, Short & Weed, 1986; Wong, 1991b). As we have seen, these difficulties with metacognition can be linked to general disorganization, failure to use monitoring strategies, and difficulty in switching strategies. Wong (1991b) adds another dimension here. "The assumption that LD students generally lack metacognitive skills in reading is invalid. Rather, they appear to have less sophisticated metacognitive skills than non-learning disabled peers in reading" (p. 243). Metacognitive difficulties may also be related to students' failure to attend to meaning as they read which could make them unable to manage their own reading (Lipson & Wixson, 1991).

In a review of the literature, Palincsar and Brown (1987) provide a metacognitive profile of the student with learning disabilities that reveals substantial need to improve the use of metacognitive strategies such as monitoring comprehension. This profile includes both the knowledge one possesses about one's own cognitive processes and the ability to self-regulate cognitive activity. Palincsar and Brown make the point that "this focus on metacognitive deficits is to be contrasted with the focus on underlying ability deficits which has played a significant role in special education" (p. 67).

Summary

In this profile of the good reader and the potential areas of difficulty that might be exhibited by the student with learning disabilities, themes recur which we have encountered before. These themes are beginning to have an impact on the educational environment and instructional alternatives for the student with learning disabilities. We have identified the need for effective strategy use and generalization, particularly in the areas of integrating new information with prior knowledge and organizing information in text, as well as for metacognitive skills and strategies in monitoring success and fixing failure. Again, we have seen the importance of teaching skills and strategies within the context of an academic situation, not in isolation, using real text, not work sheets. These are all reminiscent of what we learned in examining issues related to reading words. What remains now is to review suggestions from the literature to determine instructional alternatives.

INSTRUCTIONAL ALTERNATIVES

How can we go from understanding the strategies that characterize the good reader to planning instruction that will enable poor readers to perform more like good readers? This is an important question, for comprehension is often tested but frequently not taught. To begin to answer this question, we will examine effective programs that provide direct instruction in comprehension strategies that students can apply independently. Let's review what the research tells us about teaching comprehension strategies to students with learning disabilities.

One focus of strategy instruction is on teaching students the importance of comprehension strategies, the difference these strategies can make in understanding text. A second focus is teaching students to determine whether the strategies they are using are being effective by monitoring their comprehension as they read. A third is on providing alternative strategies that students can turn to if needed. These principles of good reading are embedded in each of the individual strategies we will examine.

These strategies for improving comprehension translate theory into practice, because each is based on research with students with learning disabilities. Within this framework, Clark's (1988) statement of the limitations of instructional programs in reading is still valid: "No currently existing reading program meets all the instructional requirements of dyslexic students. Therefore, if we educators select any of these programs for our students, we must be prepared to add missing instructional components" (p. 100). This holds true whether instruction is provided in a remedial or special education setting or in a mainstream classroom in which attention is being placed on improving reading comprehension.

The most robust instructional strategies include several component strategies, again reminiscent of findings in programs designed to teach children to identify words. We will discuss some of the more comprehensive models. After we review the individual components, we will examine those typically used with elementary and middle school students, and then we will look at strategies developed for secondary students. These components consist of teaching students to utilize knowledge of text structure and organize information, generate questions to help them attend to and understand the text, read critically and draw inferences, summarize text, and monitor their own comprehension. Teaching students ways to activate and use their prior knowledge will be addressed in the last section of this chapter in which we discuss instruction for secondary students, because much recent research in the area of activating prior knowledge has centered on adolescents.

Use Text Structure and Organization

The close relationship between understanding the structure or organization of text and comprehending its meaning deserves our attention. When the match between the writer's organizational structure and the reader's expectations is poor, as is often true for students with learning disabilities, comprehension is impaired. These students can, however, learn metacognitive strategies that will organize more effectively their understanding of reading material and improve comprehension and recall (Colson & Mehring, 1990; Darch & Gersten, 1986; Freund, 1987; Griffey, Zigmond, & Leinhardt, 1988; Hicks, 1993; Newby, Caldwell, & Recht, 1989; Seidenberg, 1989). Given the potential benefits of this kind of strategy, teachers should prompt students to become actively involved in using what they know about text to enhance learning and comprehension, and should cue them as to when and how they may best do this. Various strategies have been investigated that can help students to use their knowledge of text structure and to organize information. We will review several of them.

Apply Knowledge of Text Structure

The importance of knowledge of text structure on locating the main ideas in stories presenting personal problems requiring decisions was demonstrated by Williams (1988). She found that direct instruction in finding main ideas (including application and practice in new contexts) was effective. In order to improve their comprehension, students needed to learn to make more explicit use of text structure, such as understanding that different genres have different characteristics that can be used to improve understanding. She also pointed out (1991) that even the poorest readers show sensitivity to changes in the macrostructure of text, such as adding a statement of the character's priority when describing a problem that needs to be resolved.

Williams also found that students' patterns of reporting components of the problem schema (goal/obstacles/choices) were different for problems presented with or without a statement of the character's priority for action. The need for more effective strategies to discern the structural subtleties of stories was apparent throughout these studies. Williams (1993) suggests that instruction in using knowledge of text structure is important in of helping students improve their reading comprehension.

Instruction in story grammar to build an appropriate schema for the reader has been reported by others (Eckwall & Shanker, 1993; Lipson & Wixson, 1991). As Bos and Vaughn (1994) remind us:

> Research in schema theory has shown that the knowledge one brings to the reading task affects comprehension, particularly inferential comprehension. . . . Teaching strategies that encourage students to activate their knowledge, or activities that provide opportunities for students to enrich their backgrounds prior to reading, can facilitate comprehension. (p. 171)

In addition to instruction about text, students need both exposure to good models of text structure and experience constructing text themselves if they are to become proficient readers and writers (Englert, 1992; Englert and Thomas, 1987). In her analysis of teaching writing, Englert (1992) points out that strategy instruction begins with text analysis in which teachers introduce the text genre and draw students' attention to the specific features of the text structure. She places this focus on text structure within an overriding framework of interactive classroom dialogues about writing that involve students in the cultural and social activities of the literacy community, a perspective she refers to as "social constructivism." In a response to Englert's (1992) article, Isaacson (1992) reinforces Englert's focus on the ways in which texts are organized. He points out that "text-structure knowledge assists writers in two ways: guiding decisions on (1) how to categorize and label ideas, and (2) how to combine these clusters of ideas to create meaningful texts" (p. 173). He concludes by reminding us that certainly "students with and without learning disabilities can benefit from learning text structures and cognitive strategies" (p. 177).

The importance of text structure in some types of reading has been questioned, however. In an analysis of recent research studies, Carver (1992) found that the match between the reader's schema and the type of text becomes important only when reading relatively hard material. He points out that in everyday reading that is within the reader's ability to comprehend, the structure of the text, as well as a variety of prediction activities and prior knowledge, does not make a difference. He concludes that "students probably have to be forced to shift out of their normal reading process, called rauding, into untypical reading processes involving learning and memorizing before these variables that are important in schema theory become salient" (p. 164).

Organize with Visual Displays

The degree to which readers with learning disabilities master the routines that can help them sequence and organize information influences the extent to which they will be able to understand what they read. The development and use of visual displays that graphically portray the organization of content and depict the relationship between pieces of information in text is one way to do this. There are many types of visual displays, such as graphic organizers, story maps, semantic feature analysis, and semantic maps; and a number of the more effective strategies incorporate several of these components. Different types of visual displays are used before reading, during reading, or after reading.

Graphic organizers may be used before reading (as advance organizers), during the presentation or reading of new information, for review and reinforcement, or for guided or independent practice. Although not all studies have shown graphic organizers to be effective (Griffin, Simmons, & Kameenui, 1991), most research has suggested that a graphic representation of information can facilitate comprehension (Alvermann, 1991; Darch & Carnine, 1986; Freund, 1987; Idol, 1987b; Newby, Caldwell & Recht, 1989; Sinatra, Berg, & Dunn, 1985) as well as increased recall (Mastropieri & Peters, 1987). Visual displays have been employed extensively with both students with and without learning disabilities. We will review some of the studies that have been done with students with learning disabilities.

Direct instruction in using story mapping as a strategy to build structural schemata with elementary school children was used effectively by Idol (1987-a) and by Idol and Croll (1987). Story mapping entails using a pictorial story map as an organizer for readers. Students are asked to fill in the map components either during or after reading. Typically the teacher initially models story mapping, then students complete the story map with prompting from the teacher only as needed. The focus in these studies was on integrating story mapping into the learner's personal repertoire of comprehension skills. In so doing, these researchers put organizing information and utilizing story structure into a strategic category. To explain, Idol (1987a) states that "a technique only becomes a strategy when the learner spontaneously and independently applies the technique as a means of arriving at a solution to a problem" (p. 197). This guideline is helpful when evaluating the success of students' mastery of organizational strategies.

Pictorial displays that illustrated the time-space sequence of text for third graders were investigated by Chan, Cole, and Morris (1990). Visual presentations were coupled with instruction to encourage the children to make pictures in their minds. The investigators found these methods to be effective in improving comprehension.

The relative effectiveness of a visual display, a study guide, and a control condition in helping secondary students learn science information from a textbook was examined by Bergerud, Lovitt, and Horton (1988). They report that the visual graphics adaptation was more effective than either the study guide or self-study.

In support of the use of visual displays, Hedley, Hedley, and Baratta (1994) write that "graphic organizers have the greatest single advantage in that they foster the integration of visual thinking and verbal thinking" (p. 124). They suggest that students learn to utilize graphic organizers and semantic maps from experiencing instruction that employs the techniques. Graphic organizers, semantic maps, and structured overviews are similar ways of visually representing the concepts and vocabulary to be learned.

The effectiveness of using a visual semantic feature analysis chart with adolescents was investigated by Bos, Anders, Filip, and Jaffe (1989). Semantic feature analysis is a prelearning activity that visually organizes the relationships between major concepts and related vocabulary. A relationship chart is used to make predictions about the connection between specific vocabulary words and ideas in the text. Prior to reading a social studies text, students in resource room classes either completed a semantic feature analysis relationship chart or used the dictionary to look up definitions of vocabulary words. Following independent reading, students again used the semantic feature analysis to revise their predictions. Students in the semantic feature analysis condition performed better on a comprehension measure, both immediately following and six months after initial teaching.

Semantic mapping has also been widely investigated with students with learning disabilities. Semantic mapping uses free association as a stimulus to generate a list of words and phrases related to important concepts. After this step has been completed, a network that shows the relationships between them is portrayed in diagrams. Pehrsson and Denner (1988) reviewed the use of semantic maps or webs with students of all ages to develop improved organization and recall.

> With the semantic organizer approach to a guided strategy lesson, the student is guided by the teacher to (a) evaluate the importance of organization to writing and reading, as well as the reasons for developing a specified type of semantic organizer; (b) observe the construction by the teacher of a particular semantic organizer; (c) participate, sometimes by finishing a partially completed organizer; and (d) gradually assume full responsibility for the development of a particular organizer. (p. 28)

One purpose of the semantic organizer approach is to bridge the gap between idea organization and written language structures, i.e., to display the important relationships. Pehrsson and Denner state that this approach can be viewed as both preventative and remedial.

Semantic maps were applied to comprehending history texts by Brownlee (1988). Brownlee found that semantic maps may help in providing a schema for organizing structural elements of the reading. If successful, such a schema could provide students with the incentive to develop and use strategies on their own.

Although research on semantic mapping and similar techniques has yielded promising results, some concerns have been expressed. Scott, Hiebert, and Anderson (1994) pointed out that within this line of inquiry

> a limitation is that most of the research has been done with college students trying to learn difficult technical material, and the students have been required to employ elaborate systems for semantic mapping, systems that are themselves difficult to learn and tedious and time consuming to use. These systems would be daunting for children in the elementary grades. (p. 262)

These authors go on to remind us that simplified semantic mapping as employed in elementary school reading lessons varies greatly and that additional research is needed to determine its effectiveness.

Generate Questions About Text

A variety of types of self-questioning strategies have proved to be effective for students with learning disabilities (Chan, 1991; Chan & Cole, 1986; Elrod, 1987; Mercer, 1992). Trabasso (1994) concludes that "questioning, when done in conjunction with reading or listening to a text, can facilitate enormously the comprehension and subsequent retention of the text" (p. 197). In some studies, such as that by Johnson (1988), students with learning disabilities showed improvement when taught a questioning strategy but normal readers did not. Johnson hypothesized that normal readers were already spontaneously asking questions about the text and so had not benefitted greatly from the instruction.

A strategy such as consciously self-generating questions is, by definition, metacognitive. There is general agreement in the field that this type of metacognitive strategy, properly employed, is helpful for all readers. One result of using such strategies is that, by the very act of employing them, the reader develops an active processing of text.

Another purpose of self-questioning strategies is to help readers relate new information to prior knowledge, an important skill for all readers. A strategy called Question-Answer Relationships (QARs) is an example of this type of application. Simmonds (1992) investigated improving comprehension through QARs that "illustrate the relationship between questions and possible sources of answers both in the text and in the readers' background knowledge" (p. 195). She reported that QARs have been found to accommodate to content area reading material readily and that they "significantly improved the question-answer recognition and location performance of students with learning disabilities" (p. 198). Graham and Wong (1993) compared the effects of direct instruction in QARs and self-instruction in which students responded to modeling of the strategy with self-questions and inner speech mediation. The researchers found the latter more effective in "enhancing and maintaining students' reading comprehension" (p. 270). Marzola (1988) also investigated QARs, along with ReQuest, and Reciprocal Teaching, which are other frequently used questioning techniques. She pointed out that the improvement shown by poor readers probably occurred because they had learned to comprehend "by utilizing the same questioning strategies good readers use spontaneously" (p. 243).

Some investigations of questioning strategies have focused on their use in combination with a focus on the structure of the text. Griffey, Zigmond, and Leinhardt (1988) taught students to use self-generated questions in conjunction with story grammar, which resulted in improved comprehension. Along similar lines, Billingsley and Wildman (1988) examined the use of self-questions in three conditions: self-questions only, structured overviews and self-questions, and a control group in order to investigate adolescents' ability to monitor their comprehension during reading and to recognize passage information after reading. Both experimental groups recognized more passage information than subjects in the control condition. The group using structured overviews and self-questions used the overview to formulate most of their questions and posed fewer unrelated questions.

As with any metacognitive strategy, the extent of the strategy's generalizability to new situations is an issue, because unless this occurs, the usefulness of the strategy is limited. Wong, Wong, Perry, and Sawatsky (1986) investigated transfer as a part of their study. They report that the self-questioning summarization strategy applied to social studies materials improved performance and also transferred to new content areas. These authors conclude that students with learning disabilities made "active, purposeful, and deliberate modifications of the inculcated strategy" (p. 20).

As a method of instruction, teachers are encouraged to model their own thought processes for students about the kinds of questions they are thinking about and why they want to ask them (Bos & Vaughn, 1994; Olson & Gee, 1991; Rhodes & Dudley-Marling, 1988). The advantages of using this kind of instruction are explained by Garner, Alexander, and Hare (1991).

> If teachers settle for teaching a few procedural recipes for text comprehension to children, they have not, in the long run, assisted them very much. Far better is teaching that provides procedural detail, motivational impetus, and models of self-regulation that sustain effective performance in the teacher's absence. (p. 303)

Garner, Alexander, and Hare go on to describe the task analysis required in order to generate a sufficiently detailed sequence of steps to constitute an effective questioning strategy. They provide the following description of a teacher modeling self-interrogation while reading a text on the topic of "Endangered Species."

> Oh, endangered species, I saw a National Geographic program the other night. It said that some great apes were in danger of becoming extinct. I wonder if this article will talk about those apes (modeling retrieval of prior knowledge on the topic of the text, tying old information to new). Oh, headings about the animals discussed. That tells me what I'll read about. Yup, gorillas. And bald eagles, I saw a bald eagle on a camping trip; they're neat (modeling use of headings to structure information read, a general strategy; also, modeling of interest in a subtopic). Oh, I don't know this word, h-a-b-i-t-a-t. But, I can skip it for now and see if the meaning is clear from other sentences; I can always look it up if I can't figure it out myself (modeling an efficient word-identification strategy). I'm pretty good at most words, and I don't need to know every single one to understand what I'm reading (modeling a coping plan). (p. 301)

These authors suggest that teachers encourage students to model effective strategies to other students, noting that both will benefit.

Draw Inferences and Read Critically

Why do many students with learning disabilities fail to draw correct inferences from what they are reading? McCormick (1992) investigated the reasons for erroneous responses to inference questions on both narrative and expository text. The results of her study suggest that 4 of 26 subcategories of possible error sources accounted for 54% of incorrect responses. These subcategories were: 1) overreliance on background knowledge, 2) underdeveloped written responses, 3) answers unrelated to main points in the selection, and 4) answers too specific to reflect global constructs.

Recommendations for instruction in inference skills vary widely. One principle that is reflected in many of the studies is the importance of direct instruction. Darch and Kameenui (1987) emphasize its effectiveness in teaching students how to detect faulty arguments by learning rules and strategies. Although direct instruction is often employed to teach less complex skills, these authors suggest that its use in teaching higher level skills is helpful.

On the other hand, we also find more student-centered approaches suggested by some researchers. The Socratic dialogue format is suggested by Leshowitz, Jenkens, Heaton, and Bough (1993) for teaching students with learning disabilities the scientific method, applying it to advertisements and then to text about everyday information. Students stated the underlying question or problem, engaged in discussion, and prepared graphic representations of the information. Here, they were active learners, generating questions, using graphic organizers, reading text, and basing conclusions on evidence. Thornburg (1991) advocates a cognitive apprenticeship in which students acquire and use problem-solving and reasoning strategies through modeling, verbalization, scaffolding, fading, and eventual ownership of the strategy. An important variable here is that the learning all takes place within real tasks of reading and writing in the area of social studies.

Moving beyond the specifics of the type of instruction, a general overview of instruction is presented by Haney and Thistlethwaite (1991). These authors examine a sample of lessons, presenting a "roadmap" for teachers who will be guiding students with learning disabilities through the process of critical reading. Included are a framework, introductory activities, alternatives for students who find the reading difficult, a critical reading map, and activities for extended study.

Setting priorities for instruction to teach inference skills is stressed by McCormick (1992). These are her priorities. First, students need to be made aware that correct inferential responses necessitate text information as well as prior knowledge; teachers need to help students learn to discriminate text cues that aid inferencing. Second, students must learn to focus their attention on the important ideas in text. Finally, she recommends that we teach strategies for combining several specific prior knowledge cues to create more inclusive generalizations. McCormick suggests that we might begin inference training with pictures in cases where the incorrect inferences drawn appear to be related to limited cues.

The importance of a well-developed knowledge base in making inferences is cited by several authors (Bos & Vaughn, 1994; Herber & Herber, 1993). Based on her research, Carr (1991) reports that "children with learning disabilities can answer inferential questions when they have an adequately developed knowledge base, although not as proficiently as their normally achieving age-level peers" (p. 19).

In an investigation of students' ability to make sophisticated inferences about character, plot, and motivation in short stories, Gurney, Gersten, Dimino, and Carnine (1990) examined the effectiveness of teaching story grammar to high school students. This strategy was an adaptation of story grammar techniques used successfully by Idol and Croll (1987) in the elementary grades. Results of the study with high school students suggested that the story grammar provided a framework for analyzing literature and making inferences, improving students' comprehension.

Winne, Graham, and Prock (1993) remind us of the importance of specific and timely feedback to students. In a study of third- to fifth-grade readers, they found in the pretests that poor readers could make only low-level text-based inferences. Instruction that provided feedback about the correctness of answers, encouragement, rehearsing correct information, and reminding students about why the information is important to learn resulted in better inference-making. However, it was clear that instruction in which students received feedback that is explicit about how to construct inferences produced better inference-making than the multifaceted feedback. These authors conclude that the students lacked pattern-recognizing procedures: "procedural knowledge that identifies a rule, a critical fact, or both as information that should be stored in memory" (p. 64).

Summarize Text

Summarizing a text requires several component skills and strategies that students with learning disabilities need to master. These are highlighted by Lipson & Wixson (1991): "In order to summarize effectively, students need to learn how to identify the prevailing text structure, how to recognize or generate important ideas and connections, and how to produce an overarching statement of topic" (p. 603).

In a more detailed description, Seidenberg (1989) provides an overview of instruction for students with learning disabilities as she discusses "the ability to use a set of decision rules for summarizing texts, to identify important ideas in text, and to integrate separate ideas into larger units" (p. 5). Seidenberg gives six rules that she recommends be used by readers in summarizing texts.

(1) delete unnecessary or trivial information;
(2) delete redundant information;
(3) substitute a superordinate term for a list of items (e.g., the word 'pets' can be substituted if a text contains a list such as dogs, cats, goldfish, etc.);
(4) substitute a superordinate action for a list of subcomponents of that action (e.g., 'John went on a trip' for John left the house, he went to the train station, etc.);
(5) select a topic sentence;
(6) if there is no topic sentence, invent one. (p. 5)

Seidenberg reminds us that improved recall of major text information is most likely to occur when students are taught to carefully monitor and evaluate their own use of summarization procedures.

Several researchers have studied the effectiveness of summarization strategies for improving comprehension. Gajria and Salvia (1992) taught students in grades 6-9 to use a summarization strategy as they read expository prose. They concluded that "direct instruction in the summarization strategy significantly increased reading comprehension of the students in the experimental group. Strategy usage was maintained over time, and students were reported to generalize its use" (p. 508). In an earlier study, Jenkins, Heliotis, Stein and Haynes (1987) used a metacognitive strategy prompting with simple questions such as "Who?" and "What's happening?" They found that "in all instances the strategy-trained students exhibited better comprehension than did the control students" (p. 54). With a different focus but addressing a critical aspect of strategy instruction, Wong, Wong, Perry and Sawatsky (1986) reported that after learning a summarization strategy applied to social studies material, students were able to transfer applying this strategy to general science and biology materials. The intervention included: first, teaching the subjects to identify main ideas in single paragraphs; second, summarizing single paragraphs; and third, applying the preceding subskills to social studies material through a self-questioning summarization strategy. These results are of particular interest, for generalization to different materials or situations is not to be taken for granted.

A self-monitoring component was combined with instruction in summarizing by Malone and Mastropieri (1992). They found that the summarization strategy alone was sufficient when the material was not too demanding for the reader. The addition of a self-monitoring component was effective when the material was complex and difficult. A card on which self-monitoring prompts were written was used for students to check off each completed self-monitoring step. Using either the summarization or the self-monitoring strategy resulted in better comprehension than did a traditional approach to instruction with an emphasis on vocabulary and prior knowledge.

Monitor Comprehension

Typically, efforts to monitor comprehension have been accomplished through metacognitive strategies designed to make readers aware and in control of their cognitive activity. These strategies are important to effective reading, for if comprehension is breaking down, the reader must shift to strategies that will improve understanding of difficult reading material. A growing body of literature suggests that students with learning disabilities may have difficulty using cognitive strategies spontaneously when reading unfamiliar material. The following studies examine instructional efforts to help students with learning disabilities improve their use of metacognitive strategies.

A number of researchers have suggested that teachers should provide explicit instruction in monitoring comprehension (Bos & Vaughn, 1994; Chan & Cole, 1986; Graves, 1986). An example of this type of instruction is provided by Lipson & Wixson (1991) who recommend the following instructions to students to help them monitor their own understanding and respond to problems as they read. First, ignore the problem and read on if the information is unimportant. Second, wait and see, especially if you suspect that the problem will be cleared up by subsequent text. Third, generate a hypothesis, an educated guess as to the meaning, and test it as you read on. Fourth, reread the sentence or use the prior context to help clarify the problem. Finally, seek help from an expert source, such as a dictionary or another person, if the other steps have failed. Although this may sound like just good common sense, poor readers often need direct instruction in monitoring comprehension in order to learn to do these kinds of things.

A variety of metacognitive strategies have been investigated in recent years. Palincsar and Brown (1987) reported that students with learning disabilities who were taught to self-monitor the application of metacognitive strategies improved in text comprehension, among other things. These authors recommend an instructional approach that includes teaching the student to be aware of task demands, use appropriate strategies to facilitate task completion, and monitor the application of strategies. Using a somewhat different procedure, Chan, Cole and Barfett (1987) found that students with learning disabilities who were taught an evaluative technique to monitor text for internal inconsistency by comparing one proposition or statement with others in the text demonstrated improved performance in comprehension monitoring and in reading comprehension.

In a study that highlighted both the benefits of appropriate self-monitoring and the distraction that can result from the requirements of the procedure, Reid and Harris (1993) concluded that "both self-monitoring of attention and self-monitoring of performance can significantly and meaningfully increase the level of observed on-task behavior of students with learning disabilities" (p. 36). A second conclusion, however, was that many students had found self-monitoring of attention to be intrusive when they were trying to study. These authors note that "the procedures used in the self monitoring of attention condition, which required rapid alternation of attention between tasks, may not have been appropriate for many students with learning disabilities" (p. 37). They also caution us that apparent on-task behavior may not correlate with improved academic performance. For these reasons, it is important to consider the characteristics of the student when selecting a self-monitoring procedure so that procedure itself does not create a distraction from the text being read.

Combine Instructional Strategies

In real practice we would seldom teach students a detached strategy. Instructional programs for students with learning disabilities need to be broadly conceived and include a variety of phases and strategies. As stated by Snyder and Pressley (1990): "Strategies are rarely used in isolation. Rather, they are integrated into higher-order sequences that accomplish complex cognitive goals" (p. 9). For instance, reading may begin with previewing, activating prior knowledge about the topic, and self-questioning about what the text will probably say. During and after one's reading, self-monitoring to determine whether comprehension is adequate and deciding what steps to take if there is a comprehension failure helps the reader evaluate whether or not the strategies being used are proving to be successful.

In a study with elementary school students Elrod (1987) used a self-questioning strategy that incorporates several other strategies as the means of turning passive readers into active readers. These strategies included: establish a purpose; skim for relevant cues; predict text content; read; verify/alter predictions; clarify; form questions; summarize; self-check; and monitor. This strategy proved to be successful in improving the comprehension of children with learning disabilities.

The Directed Reading-Thinking Activity (DR-TA) is recommended by Bos and Vaughn (1994) as a set of strategies for teaching reading that encourages students to read reflectively and use prediction. This approach is based on the assumption that students must relate their own experiences to the author's ideas to construct meaning from text. Students set purposes for reading and generate hypotheses about meaning; then students confirm or disconfirm hypotheses, revising them as needed. The process ends when the hypotheses have been confirmed and the purposes for reading fulfilled. Bos and Vaughn point out that this approach does not systematically teach word identification skills, which students with learning disabilities may need.

As students with learning disabilities progress to the middle school level, many who were getting by in the lower grades begin to experience general school failure. Expectations of mastering content-area information through reading accelerate, and by about sixth grade, students whose reading comprehension of content texts is poor often begin to fail. Integrating combinations of strategies for teaching and learning into content areas begins in the elementary grades, but by middle school and high school it is more widespread. We will briefly review several complex metacognitive strategies often used at the middle school level.

A program that includes training in a self-questioning strategy for the identification of main ideas based on principles of summarization was evaluated by Chan (1991). She concludes that "self-instructional training, with its emphasis on the development of self-regulation through self-statements, is particularly appropriate for teaching students with learning disabilities the use and generalization of cognitive strategies" (pp. 427-428). The combination in this program of several of the individual strategies that we examined earlier exemplifies the way these metacognitive strategies are likely to be applied in practice.

In a review of the literature, Colson and Mehring (1990) report that combining self-questioning and story structure training is effective in improving comprehension and recall. Students in the studies they reviewed were actively engaged in strategies to construct and create forms of organization, relate new information to prior knowledge, focus on meaning, and plan when and how to use the information.

In a content-area application, Rinehart, Barksdale-Ladd, and Welker (1991) used a variety of strategies involving advance organizers with seventh grade poor readers. The most effective format was one of oral delivery of the advance organizer by the teacher followed by whole-group discussion.

Finally, Englert and Mariage (1991) report on an instructional program of strategies called POSSE that "significantly affected recall of expository ideas and knowledge of comprehension strategies among students with learning disabilities" (p. 123). POSSE uses reciprocal-like teaching formats to make visible to students their prior knowledge about a topic and the structures in the expository text they are reading. Students are taught to:

Predict ideas based on background knowledge
Organize predicted textual ideas and background
Knowledge
Search for text structure
Summarize main idea
Evaluate their own comprehension.

This questioning strategy can be conducted within the regular curriculum to further elementary and middle school students' reading comprehension and recall.

Instructional Alternatives for Adolescents

The Power of Learning Strategies: A Parable

If you give a starving man a fish, you feed him for a day. However, if you teach the man to fish, you feed him for a lifetime. Similarly, if you teach an adolescent a fact, you help him or her for the moment. But, if you teach this adolescent how to think about learning, you help him or her for a lifetime.

Lerner, 1993, p. 286

Instructing students with learning disabilities in content-area subjects can be particularly difficult because of the discrepancy between these students' strategies for reading and learning and the demands of the curriculum, whether instruction is provided in regular or special education classrooms (Bos & Vaughn, 1994). Students typically are expected to read independently and to demonstrate understanding of what they read, an unrealistic assumption for many. However, content teachers can significantly reduce the discrepancy between course requirements and students' reading skills.

Integrating reading instruction with content-area instruction has been a long-term objective of school-based research and practice. Herber and Herber (1993) find that "the reading process is manageable by most content-area teachers because it fits naturally with the resource materials used in most content areas" (p. 207). By teaching students cognitive strategies that will aid comprehension as an integral part of content instruction, meaningful improvement can be expected (Graham & Harris, 1990, 1994; Griffey, Zigmond, & Leinhardt, 1988; Scruggs, Bennion, & Lifson, 1985). This approach also reflects the general trend we have already noted toward integrating literacy instruction for students with learning disabilities into the academic areas.

Care must be exercised in identifying which comprehension strategies to teach. Pressley (1990) provides helpful guidelines. He suggests that teachers should select only research-validated strategies; otherwise, the risk of wasted time and enthusiasm is too great. Second, the strategies should mesh with the objectives of the curriculum, thus achieving a true integration of the content and the strategy instruction. Finally, strategies should be teachable with materials already available in the classroom so that they are economical and easy to implement.

In this kind of teaching we are implementing a broad model of instruction, a reality-based way of approaching text that reflects what good readers really do. Englert and Mariage (1991) remind us that content "teachers play an important role in teaching students to make use of background knowledge, text structures, and comprehension strategies in expository reading" (p. 137). For many students with learning disabilities this kind of instruction is particularly important, for many have not come along well with their reading.

Use Study Guides to Increase Comprehension

One example of content-area instruction that enhances comprehension is providing study guides to students to help them comprehend the text they are reading. Study guides are sets of statements or questions that center on critical content information. They may be presented as framed outlines, short-answer questions, or matching questions. Study guides can be used in the prereading phase to focus students' attention on looking for important ideas, during reading as a structured way of recording important information, or after reading for review. Guidelines for developing study guides for students with learning disabilities (Lovitt & Horton, 1987) can assist teachers planning to write this type of content enhancement. Lovitt and Horton's guidelines require the teacher to select the most important information, then write study materials for students that will focus their attention on the salient points. Since the study guide is a vehicle for actively engaging the student in the task of comprehending, it can be a useful tool for the student with learning disabilities who may be a passive reader.

A series of studies investigated using study guides in social studies and science classes. Horton and Lovitt (1989) utilized study guides with learning disabled, remedial, and regular secondary students to enhance independent reading assignments in social studies and science. During the guided practice phase of instruction, students read the textbook independently. Then they used the study guides either in a teacher-directed or student-directed condition. These two groups were compared to a self-study condition. The findings indicated that use of either teacher-directed or student-directed study guides produced higher textbook comprehension than the self-study approach. Next, Horton, Lovitt, Givens, and Nelson (1989) examined the effects on social studies textbook comprehension of a computerized study guide in comparison to a notetaking condition. The computerized study guide approach produced significantly higher performance than did notetaking.

In a later study, Horton, Lovitt, and Christensen (1991) investigated the effects of using study guides containing several levels of referential cues compared to using single-level study guides that did not contain referential cues. Three groups of junior high and high school students learning social studies or science participated: learning disabled, remedial, or nondisabled. The investigators report that the multilevel study guides were more effective than single-level guides in helping all groups of students understand their textbook reading in both content areas.

Extend and Activate Background Knowledge

We have already identified the critical importance of background knowledge to a reader's success. This is certainly true in content area reading. "Background knowledge is the strongest predictor of a student's ability to learn new material. The more students know about a topic, the better they comprehend and learn from the text on the topic" (Lerner, 1993, p. 287). For these reasons, strengthening students' background knowledge before providing instruction on a topic is a valuable instructional method with students with learning disabilities. Bolstering the knowledge base of high school students was investigated by Darch and Gersten (1986). They pretaught critical terms, facts and concepts to extend background knowledge before students read independently from a text. These activities were designed to relate the reading to students' previous experiences. These authors found that students given this instruction scored higher on unit tests than did students given the traditional prereading activities. They remind us that it is important that advance organizers such as this be aimed at accomplishing specific purposes, such as preteaching vocabulary, in order to maximize student learning.

As we have seen, even when the fund of prior knowledge exists, many readers have difficulty activating and using it at the appropriate time. Rhodes and Dudley-Marling (1988) provide an example of a teacher instructing students in how to activate their prior knowledge. The first step is called "already-know time" and consists of students thinking and talking to activate their own knowledge of the topic. Students list what they already know so that everyone can see it. Next, students reread their lists of what they already know and think of questions they have about the topic. Finally, students categorize their knowledge to develop a well-organized body of statements and questions that should make it easier to gain new knowledge during reading.

The *Pre Reading Plan* is also a strategy that provides a direct means of activating students' background knowledge (Bos & Vaughn, 1994). It is a group activity that builds on the instructional activity of brainstorming. First, the teacher should ask students to give their initial associations with the concept. They can be cued by the teacher saying, "Tell us anything that comes to mind when ... (e.g., you hear the word 'weather')." Students' responses are recorded on the board with their names. Next, ask students to reflect on the initial associations by inquiring, "What made you think of ...?" referring to the responses recorded on the board. Finally, lead students in a reformation of knowledge activity by asking, "Based on our discussion, have you any new ideas about ... (e.g., weather)?" Given the input from other students as well as their own guided reflection, students form new links between prior knowledge and the key concept to be taught. Bos and Vaughn conclude: "Taking the extra time to conduct the Pre Reading Plan is worthwhile since it requires the students to bring to the conscious level why they made their associations and it gives them the opportunity to reflect on what they have learned through the discussion" (p. 177).

Teach Memory Strategies

Successful learners use effective memory strategies, and a number of formal schemes have been designed to improve memory. These mnemonic devices are strategies that can enhance the learning and later recall of information. Complex strategies for remembering often include components that help students sequence and organize information. Also, they frequently provide some link with background information, for as Lerner (1993) reminds us, "Most of what is learned is forgotten quickly if it is not acted upon or linked with previous learning" (p. 288). These strategies may consist of a variety of techniques that help students recall content-area information by making it easier to remember. Often mnemonic strategies are integrated into the presentation and guided phases of instruction. Much of the research has been done within content areas such as social studies and science, and the findings reflect information that should be integrated into content area instruction.

Bos and Vaughn (1994) present the instructional principles of using mnemonic devices effectively: "The information to be learned needs to be distilled so that the students are learning conceptual lists or frameworks. It is this information that is then operated on when using mnemonics" (p. 296). We find that this kind of instruction is easy to implement in content-area classes.

Constructing mental images while reading is an effective strategy for improving comprehension and for remembering (Lysynchuk & Pressley, 1990; Symons, McGoldrick, Snyder, & Pressley, 1990). The theory underlying this technique is that the dual coding (both a verbal memory code and an imaginal memory code) leaves a more powerful memory trace than a verbal code alone, making it easier to recall information later. One type of mental image strategy is *representational imagery* in which the images represent precisely the content of the prose. A second type is a *keyword mnemonic*, a proxy for the concept to be remembered. A keyword is a word that can be linked to the concept, and it is useful when a direct image cannot be readily generated. These authors say that students seem to be "struck by the effectiveness of mnemonic imagery when they use it (p. 54)" and are particularly enthusiastic about using it.

A word association strategy for helping students remember information in content-area subjects is suggested by Herber and

Herber (1993). To carry out the strategy, the teacher selects a stimulus word that reflects the focus of the organizing idea of the lesson. Students working in small groups are given the stimulus word and asked to list words or phrases that they associate with the stimulus word. Next, each group reads its list and the class compares the similarities and differences across groups. Finally, the class examines the lists to infer categories of information and the ideas that stimulated the associations. The class discusses the connections between categories and the teacher emphasizes the associations that support the organizing idea of the lesson.

Overall, results of studies of applications of mnemonic strategies are very encouraging. Pressley, Scruggs, and Mastropieri (1989) found that recent "experiments provided conclusive evidence that LD students can be taught to execute mnemonic strategies and experience learning gains when they do so" (p. 71). However, most have been conducted in laboratory settings in which instruction was provided individually. At this time, additional research is needed to determine the effects of mnemonic strategies used in classroom settings.

Combine Instructional Strategies in Content-Areas

A number of comprehensive instructional models used at the secondary level that reflect this orientation of integrating comprehension strategy instruction into content areas are reflected in the recent literature, and we will review five of them. They include: (1) Ellis' Integrated Strategy Instruction (ISI) model; (2) the Strategies Intervention Model (SIM) of the Kansas University Institute of Research in Learning Disabilities; (3) Scruggs, Mastropieri, Bakken, and Brigham's Inquiry-oriented Science Learning; (4) Bos and Anders' Interactive Instruction Model; and (5) Hudson, Lignugaris-Kraft, and Miller's Content Enhancement Model. The underpinnings of much of this line of research are to be found in work that has been pursued at the University of Kansas over many years. As might be expected, considerable overlap exists between these five models.

We will discuss only the first one, Ellis' Integrated Strategy Instruction, in detail in order to provide a fuller picture of this type of instruction for the reader. Each model, however, has been extensively developed and deserves full attention. Although the focus of these models is broader than improving reading comprehension, each model contributes to our understanding of ways to provide instruction that will enable students with learning disabilities to succeed in comprehending content-area reading. Indeed, this broader, integrated focus exemplifies our current philosophy that reading comprehension is best taught within the context of the reading expected in the student's daily life.

Integrative Strategy Instruction (ISI). Ellis presents a framework for using strategy instruction to improve reading comprehension and ultimate mastery of content. Having participated in the Research Institute at the University of Kansas, his involvement in the field is extensive. He views the ISI model as emerging, as being in the process of growing and changing.

The ISI model (Ellis, 1993a) is designed to teach adolescents with learning disabilities information processing strategies that will make them more efficient learners and readers at the same time that they are learning a specific content area. "Teacher-directed instructional procedures, cooperative learning, and direct explanation and dialectical strategy instruction are integrated into four key instructional processes" (p. 358). The first step is *orienting*, in which the teacher demonstrates the strategy to students. The second is *framing*, in which the teacher demonstrates applying the strategy to a specific learning objective. Third, in *applying*, the student utilizes the strategy independently. Finally, in *extending*, students learn to extend the strategy to other problem-solving domains (Ellis, 1993a, p. 358). This instruction enables students to learn content more strategically while they learn to self-mediate their own cognitive processes. Unlike most models, Ellis' provides an integrated curriculum design with instruction in both the strategies and the content area interwoven inextricably.

In explaining the ISI model, Ellis says that teachers must attempt to make as overt as possible the covert processes of using prior knowledge and experience, using cognitive strategies, using metacognition, and using self-motivational techniques. An example is his *FLASH* strategy for activating prior knowledge:

> Focus on topic
> Look for familiar information
> Activate knowledge and ask questions
> See what's connected
> Hypothesize. (p. 363)

Strategies such as this are embedded in instruction in all competencies and content areas. Ellis writes that the ISI model attempts "to begin the process of examining how various robust approaches (both instructive and constructive) to teaching adolescents with LD might be integrated" (Ellis, 1993b, p. 449). Indeed, the FLASH strategy described above incorporates well-documented principles of instruction in comprehension into content-area instruction.

To summarize, by introducing comprehension strategies in content-area contexts, students learn how a strategy is to be used and how the user monitors the process. Scaffolded instruction is employed throughout the instructional sequence, and each set of experiences becomes the basis for extending understanding into increasingly more sophisticated applications.

Ellis' ISI model has been widely studied by other researchers, which provides an informed basis for evaluation and subsequent revision. We will review some of the observations of other researchers that can offer a perspective for us. Montague (1993) defined two important strengths of the ISI model. First, it is a long-term, structured intervention rather than the "quick fix" that has characterized too much instruction for students with learning disabilities in the past. Second, the model is concerned with the development of metacognitive abilities in students, a critical component of reading. Montague and Hutchinson (1993) also urged Ellis to define what kinds of students will benefit from this program,

Three comments on the ISI were made by Vauras, Lehtinen, Olkinuora, and Salonen (1993). First, they suggested that Ellis provide a more comprehensive analysis of ways to maintain student motivation. Second, they suggested that Ellis incorporate ways to help adolescents extend their knowledge bases in order to learn new subject-area content more effectively. Third, Vauras et al., as well as Hutchinson (1993) and Walsh (1993), pointed out that substantial teacher education will be needed if we are to change teachers' traditional focus on teaching specific content rather than on integrating strategy instruction with content learning.

An important suggestion was that the overlap between Ellis' ISI and alternative models needs to be clarified (Scruggs & Mastropieri, 1993b; Wong, 1993). In addition, a more comprehensive evaluation of the ISI model is essential. For instance, Montague (1993) notes that "systematic component analysis, although difficult and challenging as a research endeavor, is important in understanding what works and why it works within a strategy package" (p. 435). This type of analysis of the component parts of the model would enable instruction in reading comprehension to be more effective, for teachers would have needed information for making decisions about instruction.

Ellis' revision of his ISI model (Ellis, 1993b), made in response to these comments by his peers, specifically addresses issues of motivation, evaluation, and implementation. The ISI emerges as one of the most thoroughly investigated instructional models because of the unusual amount of input from many researchers.

Inquiry-Oriented Science Learning. Although inquiry approaches in science education were widely employed in the 1960's, in recent years we have returned to content-oriented approaches that rely primarily on textbooks, in part to be able to cover more material. The heavy reading demands of textbooks require improvement in vocabulary and in reading comprehension of students with learning disabilities. When textbooks are utilized, memory-enhancing techniques such as mnemonic pictures can be helpful (Mastropieri, Scruggs, & Levin, 1987; Scruggs & Mastropieri, 1992). Elaborative mnemonic strategies employing a familiar keyword and interactive image are also recommended for students learning vocabulary and terminology in science (Konopak, Williams, & Jampole, 1991). An activity-based or hands-on model of instruction in science is recommended for students with learning disabilities instead of a textbook-oriented model (Scruggs, Mastropieri, Bakken, & Brigham, 1993; Scruggs & Mastropieri, 1993a).

Interactive Model of Teaching and Learning. An interactive instructional model that integrates text comprehension and content-area learning for adolescents with learning disabilities is presented by Bos and Anders. The comprehension instruction includes teaching both content and strategic knowledge (Bos & Anders, 1990a). The first component consists of semantic mapping and semantic feature analysis (Bos & Anders, 1987). A second component concentrates on vocabulary and reading comprehension of content area texts (Bos & Anders, 1990b; Bos, Anders, Filip, & Jaffe, 1989). Semantic mapping, semantic feature analysis, and semantic/syntactic feature analysis are utilized to improve comprehension and vocabulary, as well as to enable long-term recall of information (Bos & Vaughn, 1994). According to Bos and Anders (1990b), both models presume that "reading comprehension is a constructive process in which readers use cognitive strategies to combine information presented in the text with their hypotheses about the text meaning and their current schemata" (p. 170). In both components interactive teaching and learning is grounded in the research that substantiates the teacher serving as a mediator for learning through engaging in interactive dialogue with students.

Kansas University Strategies Intervention Model (KU-SIM). The most extensively researched strategies intervention model has been developed and validated at the University of Kansas over a period of many years. Even in the late 1970's, Alley and Deshler called for a strategic instructional approach as being best suited to the needs of students with learning disabilities. Deshler and Schumaker define learning strategies as "techniques, principles, or rules that enable a student to learn, to solve problems, and to complete tasks independently" (Deshler & Schumaker, 1986, p. 583). These innovators in the field of strategy instruction continue to extend their intervention research (Kline, Deshler, & Schumaker, 1992).

The Strategies Intervention Model designed by Deshler and Schumaker (1986) emphasizes the need to provide instruction in learning strategies that can be applied to any academic content area. Instruction is given in "how to learn." The instruction includes metacognitive strategies focused on the skills that students with learning disabilities often lack, such as word identification, reading comprehension, and organization of information. O'Shea and O'Shea (1990) refer to this Strategies Intervention Model as the "most widely applied example of metacognitive-based strategies in learning disabilities" (p. 85). Harris and Pressley (1991) suggest that "perhaps some of the most exciting work and promising results regarding maintenance and generalization are occurring in the work on learning strategies being done by Deshler, Schumaker, and their associates" (p. 398). The program not only teaches strategies, but it aims for strategy generalization, an area we know may present difficulties for the student with learning disabilities.

This model is based on the earlier Learning Strategies Curriculum, also developed at the University of Kansas, and examining its components can help us to understand the Strategies Intervention Model. The curriculum consists of a set of task-specific learning strategies for adolescents. The first strand is designed to improve reading comprehension. The six components include: (1) Word Identification Strategy, aimed at the quick decoding of multisyllable words; (2) Visual Imagery Strategy, used to form a mental picture of events described in the passage; (3) Self-Questioning Strategy, used to form questions based on the reading; (4) Paraphrasing Strategy, employed after each paragraph has been read; (5) Interpreting Visual Aids Strategy, related to diagrams, tables, and maps; and (6) Multipass Strategy, a structured approach to comprehending textbooks. The second strand aids study skills and remembering. The final strand focuses on written expression. These strategies are designed to teach the types of learning behaviors required of adolescents in order to respond to secondary curriculum demands. The authors stress that the strategies must be learned to an automatic, fluent level. They also note that student gains seem to be highly correlated with the level of staff training. The Learning Strategies Curriculum has undergone considerable testing and validation. The strategies were examined and revised individually, and now that they are used in schools around the country, additional data is being examined.

Content Enhancement Model. The content enhancement model (Lenz, Bulgren,& Hudson, 1990; Hudson, Lignugaris-Kraft, & Miller, 1993) also was developed within the programmatic research efforts at the University of Kansas. Content enhancements are instructional techniques to help students identify, organize, comprehend, and memorize important content information. They are intended to be used within an effective teaching cycle as an integrated part of the curriculum in content classes such as history and science to benefit all students. It is important to note that "domain-specific instructional routines have not emerged" (p.155). Because there do not appear to be specific techniques that work best for specific content areas, it will be helpful to have available a variety of strategies that can be generalized to several content areas.

Empirical evaluation of each of these five models is the next step, both in terms of outcomes for students and changes in teachers participating in strategic instruction. Some strategies have not yet been evaluated clinically so that we can understand their effects in controlled conditions. After that effectiveness is established, the task is still incomplete without evaluation in classroom settings. As Lenz, Bulgren, and Hudson (1990) stated, "some lines of intervention research that have proven to be effective and have had a powerful impact on performance have not yet met the test of efficiency and replicability in practice" (p.158).

Conclusion

As we continue our search for ways to provide more effective instruction in reading and other literacy skills for students with learning disabilities, the conclusions of Herber and Herber (1993) are instructive. They write:

> Students' literacy needs focus on the development of reading, writing, and reasoning at levels of sophistication sufficient to support their study of sophisticated concepts as presented in complex and, sometimes, abstract materials. Content-area teachers can serve these needs by providing instruction that integrates the teaching of course content with the teaching of appropriate literacy skills. (p. 25)

Annotated Bibliography

Aaron, P. G., & Phillips, S. (1986). A decade of research with dyslexic college students: A summary of findings. *Annals of Dyslexia, 36,* 44-65.

Aaron and Phillips review and summarize several studies of college students identified as developmentally dyslexic. Developmental dyslexia is defined as a condition of average or above-average intelligence with reading comprehension scores at least two years below expectation. The picture presented of this category of college students was consistent over all the students studied. Four symptoms were found: slow reading rate, in addition to errors in oral reading, written spelling, and written grammar. These symptoms appeared to be caused by failure to master grapheme-phoneme relationships. The students had adequate oral language skills. Because there were few differences within the group, the authors question the existence of dyslexic subtypes.

Ackerman, P. T., Dykman, R. A., & Gardner, M. Y. (1990). Counting rate, naming rate, phonological sensitivity, and memory span: Major factors in dyslexia. *Journal of Learning Disabilities, 23,* 325-327.

Ackerman, Dykman, and Gardner examine the relationship between recall (counting rate, naming rate, and memory span), phonological sensitivity and word decoding, reading comprehension, and spelling. In spite of limitations of the study, the authors found that "the most severely affected children have slow articulation and/or continuous naming rates for sequential alphanumeric stimuli" (p. 326). The slow articulation may be related to a slower rate of inner speech, providing the child with less opportunity for rehearsal of a list of sight or spelling words. The authors also suggest that slow articulation might result in more difficulty sounding out and blending words as well as comprehending what has been read.

Adams, M. J. (1990). *Beginning to read: Thinking and learning about print*. Cambridge, MA: Bradford Books/MIT Press.

Adams provides a comprehensive overview of beginning reading instruction focusing primarily on the role of phonics in learning to read. An examination of the process of skilled reading as revealed through a review of relevant research suggests that spelling, meaning and pronunciation are all important to the skilled reader in the process of word recognition. This, in turn, suggests the critical need to teach beginners spelling-sound relationships. She provides considerable detail on what should be included in instruction as well as suggested timetables for implementing the process.

Alexander, P. A., & Pate, P. E. (1991). An interactive model of word recognition: A practical stance on a relentless debate. *Journal of Reading, Writing, and Learning Disabilities International, 7*, 43-58.

Alexander and Pate advocate using both meaning-emphasis and code-emphasis approaches in teaching beginning reading, with the particular focus chosen dependent on the learner characteristics, the learning conditions, and the language processes needed. For example, they find considerable support for the notion that kindergartners benefit from programs that emphasize meaning and language while first graders need specific skill instruction. They review current research related to word recognition to support this approach and to make instructional suggestions for the teacher. "Phonological training should not be offered at the exclusion of more personal, meaning-oriented instruction, but should serve as a component of a well-rounded program" (p. 55). "It is time to move beyond the simplistic whole language versus phonics debate into a mature stage of reasoned, interactive analysis of word recognition abilities" (p. 56).

Algozzine, B., O'Shea, J. O., Stoddard, K., & Crews, W. B. (1988). Reading and writing competencies of adolescents with learning disabilities. *Journal of Learning Disabilities*, *21*, 154-160.

The researchers examined, in some detail, the performance of tenth graders in all school districts in Florida on the State Student Assessment Test-II to determine the performance of learning disabled students compared to non-learning disabled students on basic reading and writing skills. They found that students with learning disabilities performed at a lower level than regular students. Students with learning disabilities performed higher on tasks requiring literal use of communication skills of reading and writing and lower on tasks requiring application of those communication skills. In addition, employers were surveyed to determine the importance they attached to reading and writing. They gave high ratings to the skills that students with learning disabilities were able to perform.

Algozzine, B., & Ysseldyke, J. (1988). Questioning discrepancies: Retaking the first step 20 years later. *Learning Disability Quarterly*, *11*, 307-318.

Algozzine and Ysseldyke examine the historical foundations of the field of learning disabilities and provide a critical examination of theory and research. Assessment and remediation in the field has traditionally been based on two notions: first, that deficits in the psychological processes needed for success in academic tasks were presumed to be the cause of learning disabilities; and second, difficulties in performance and behavior were attributed to neurological variations in individuals. The authors examine definitions of learning disabilities, noting that students become identified as learning disabled within the process of schooling. Although definitions in the various states may differ, they contain some common elements. The definitions presume a neurological dysfunction that is evident in uneven growth patterns, is exhibited in the course of learning, is demonstrated through a discrepancy between achievement and potential, and is not due to other causes. They point out that some groups have been critical of this approach to defining learning disabilities, citing the lack of clear differences between the learning disabled and other low achievers. The authors oppose the use of discrepancy formulas to assess a learning disability because of lack of research that documents their value.

Alvermann, D.E. (1991). The Discussion Web: A graphic aid for learning across the curriculum. *The Reading Teacher*, *45*, 92-99.

This article describes the Discussion Web, "a special kind of graphic aid for teaching students to look at both sides of an issue before drawing conclusions" (p. 92). This technique is designed to be used across grade levels and curriculum areas. The Discussion Web incorporates activating background information, introducing new vocabulary, and setting purposes for reading, as well as a structured plan for discussion after reading.

Amoruso, M.S., Bryant, N.D., & Boehm, A. (in press). Teaching meaningful parts of words within sight words: A decoding strategy for LD readers. *Reading Research Quarterly*.

Amoruso, Bryant, and Boehm report on a study that investigated the effect that explicit teaching of affixes with associated meaning within sight words had on both the learning of words containing meaningful affixes and the decoding of words containing those affixes in immediate and delayed time periods. Subjects were 72 third-, fourth-, and fifth-grade readers with learning disabilities who were randomly assigned to each of three conditions. In the Affix-Meaning condition, the affixes were pointed out, the meaning taught, and the word defined] using the affix-meaning. In the Word Definition condition, the word was defined using the affix-meaning. In the Control condition, no attention was focused on the affix. All the words were taught within context. Although all students mastered 74 affixed words during three six-minute teaching sessions, the Affix-Meaning group decoded newly-presented affixed words significantly better (p < .001) across sessions and after a three-week delay. Students in the other two groups, after delay, regressed to pre-teaching decoding levels. The results indicated that teaching of affix-meaning within sight words both facilitated learning of those words and developed a compensatory strategy for decoding affixed words.

Armbruster, B.B., & Anderson, T.H. (1988). On selecting "considerate" content area textbooks. *Remedial and Special Education (RASE)*, *9*, 47-52.

These authors review the recent research on how to select content area textbooks that are easy to read, understand, and learn from. The authors focus on structure, coherence, and audience appropriateness, discussing the research basis for each and describing typical problems that students experience in reading textbooks. Specific guidelines are presented that should be helpful to teachers seeking "user-friendly" textbooks that facilitate learning from reading.

August, G. J. (1987). Production deficiencies in free recall: A comparison of hyperactive, learning-disabled, and normal children. *Journal of Abnormal Child Psychology, 15*, 429-440.

August reports on a study designed to investigate the use of organizational strategies in free recall in hyperactive, learning disabled, and normal children.   He found that hyperactive children failed to organize information spontaneously in order to recall it but were able to do so when instructed to. He concludes that this failure to organize information probably applies to other situations requiring complex cognitive strategies and is a difficulty that can be overcome.

Baca, L. M., & Cervantes, H. T. (1989). *The bilingual special education interface*, 2nd edition. Columbus, OH: Merrill.

Baca and Cervantes focus on interfacing the programs and methodologies of bilingual education and special education. They advocate an integrative model for curriculum implementation that teaches culturally and linguistically different children with exceptional needs by employing a variety of instructional strategies and materials that exhibit culturally appropriate motivation, cues, and reinforcements. The authors make specific suggestions for the assessment and instruction of the child with learning disabilities. Although acknowledging that the research findings on second language reading instruction are somewhat mixed, they support the teaching of reading to limited English proficient students in the native language before the introduction of English reading. Baca and Cervantes place the responsibility for accommodating individual differences on professionals in the school, rejecting the assumption that it is the responsibility of students to adapt to the instruction typically provided.

Baechle, C. L., & Lian, M. J. (1990). The effects of direct feedback and practice on metaphor performance in children with learning disabilities. *Journal of Learning Disabilities, 23,* 451-455.

This article reports a study that found that direct feedback and practice in small groups could increase the ability of children with learning disabilities to interpret metaphor. The authors remind us that interpretation of metaphor plays an important role in language development and that students with learning disabilities often interpret figurative expression literally rather than metaphorically.

Baker, J.M., & Zigmond, N. (1990). Are regular education classes equipped to accommodate students with learning disabilities? *Exceptional Children, 56,* 515-526.

Baker and Zigmond suggest that fundamental changes are needed in mainstream instruction if students with learning disabilities are to learn well within this setting. This study examined the educational practices in regular education classes, grades K-5, to determine changes that would be needed in order to accommodate students with learning disabilities on a full-time basis. Baker and Zigmond conclude: "The overriding impression of observers in these classrooms was of undifferentiated, large-group instruction, 'taught by the book.'. . . There were no differentiated assignments within classroom groups. This was a school with uniform expectations and practices for all students" (p. 525).

Ball, E.W., & Blachman, B.A. (1988). Phoneme segmentation training: Effect on reading readiness. *Annals of Dyslexia, 38,* 208-225.

Ball and Blachman examine the effects of seven weeks of phoneme segmentation training on groups of kindergarten children. All of the children received the same instruction in language activities and in letter names and sounds, but only part of the children received phoneme segmentation training. The results showed that phoneme segmentation training has an impact on reading skill. It also showed that this training had greater impact than did training in letter-sound correspondences without segmentation training.

Barker, T. A., Torgesen, J. K., & Wagner, R. K. (1992). The role of orthographic processing skills on five different reading tasks. *Reading Research Quarterly*, 27, 334-345.

Barker, Torgesen, and Wagner studied 87 third graders in order to "extend our knowledge concerning the independent role of orthographic skills in several different types of reading tasks" (p. 337). The five tasks were: reading of words in isolation, timed and untimed; oral and silent reading of words in context; reading of nonwords; processing of phonological information and engaging in alphabetic reading; and processing orthographic information. The authors found that "orthographic processing skill makes a significant independent contribution to each type of reading skill" (p. 342) and that "the contribution of orthographic skills varied significantly depending on whether children were reading isolated words or text. The substantially stronger relationship of orthographic ability to the text reading measures suggests that fluent access to visual word representations may play a special facilitative role in the reading of connected text" (p. 343).

Bashir, A. S., & Scavuzzo, A. (1992). Children with language disorders: Natural history and academic success. *Journal of Learning Disabilities*, 25, 53-65.

Bashir and Scavuzzo present a broad review of the role of language in education and the difficulties encountered by children with language disorders in school, particularly in reading.

Because language forms the basis for academic tasks, the results of language disorders are pervasive and long-lasting, impacting on the acquisition, organization, management, and use of knowledge as well as on social relations and cultural membership. Children with language disorders are frequently problem readers, experiencing difficulty in word recognition and/or comprehension. Suggestions are made for instructional alternatives for children with language disorders including metacognitive approaches, semantic organizers, emphasis on text structure, and a focus on vocabulary within a conceptual or experiential framework.

Bateman, B. (1991). Teaching word recognition to slow-learning children. *Reading, Writing, and Learning Disabilities, 7*, 1-16.

Bateman suggests that the term "slow-learner" includes disabled learners, because slow learners and disabled learners have common problems in reading and need similar material and instruction. She reviews research in this area and concludes that the prevailing problem is one of difficulty in acquiring and using word recognition skills. Several programs are reviewed and general principles of instruction suggested. She concludes that direct instruction is needed in phonics and in structural and contextual analysis as well as auditory blending. Instruction is not needed in visual discrimination skills.

Beech, J.R., & Awaida, M. (1992). Lexical and nonlexical routes: A comparison between normally achieving and poor readers. *Journal of Learning Disabilities, 25*, 196-206.

Beech and Awaida investigated developing readers' ability to read individual words (regular and irregular spellings) and pseudowords (without orthographic or real-word priming). Seemingly reflective of the dual-route theory of reading, the authors found that the study's 38 nine-year-old poorer readers relied more heavily upon the lexical route (sight word) than did the 40 seven- and eight-year-old reading-age-matched normally achieving readers. The poorer readers were found to have a poorer memory span, although they were slightly better at visual discrimination. According to the authors, "to compensate for poorer memory span, the poorer reader is too prone to continue with a lexical strategy for all words, or else to try to use contextual information" (p. 203). The result is that the poorer reader performs less well when decoding unfamiliar words.

Bergerud, D., Lovitt, T.C., & Horton, S. (1988). The effectiveness of textbook adaptation in life science for high school students with learning disabilities. *Journal of Learning Disabilities, 21*, 70-76.

This study explored the effectiveness of two types of text-book adaptations (graphics and study guides) compared to self-study for high school students with learning disabilities. Results indicated that students using a graphics adaptation of the text comprehended and recalled the content better than students using the study guides.

Berninger, V. W., & Abbott, R. D. (1992, April). *Redefining learning disabilities: Moving beyond IQ-achievement discrepancies to failure to respond to short-term, theory-based treatment protocols.* Paper presented at the NICHD Measurement of Learning Disabilities Conference, Bethesda, MD.

This paper presents arguments for considering alternatives to an aptitude-achievement discrepancy for defining a learning disability. The alternatives suggested by the authors include: "multivariate (on eleven developmental axes) versus univariate conceptualizations; differentiation among low functioning, underachieving, and combined low functioning and underachieving children, and 'treatment-resisting' versus 'treatment-responding' children" (p. 2). The authors offer a general model that could be used to assess the reliability and validity of response to treatment so that learning disabilities could be diagnosed in terms of "treatment resistance."

Berninger, V., Hart, T., Abbott, R., & Karovsky, P. (1992). Defining reading and writing disabilities with and without IQ: A flexible, developmental perspective. *Learning Disability Quarterly, 15*, 103-118.

Berninger, Hart, Abbott, and Karovsky challenge the definition of a learning disability as a discrepancy between IQ and achievement because it "reveals nothing about the etiology of the discrepancy, nor does it suggest an intervention for reducing it" (p. 104). The authors questioned whether "if over-achievement occurred more often than underachievement, IQ might not represent the upper limit of expected achievement as is assumed in conventional models of learning disabilities" (p. 106). The authors compare three approaches to defining disabilities based on criterion reading and writing measures and on predictor developmental measures related to reading and writing. As a result of their findings, the authors argue that a two-stage identification model is needed. Such a model relies on the use of absolute criteria, without IQ, by classroom teachers to identify low-functioning students and to place them into early intervention programs. If criteria problems persist, despite intervention, then IQ data is needed for a comprehensive assessment.

Bigsby, P. (1985). The nature of reversible letter confusion in dyslexic and normal readers: Misperception or mislabeling? *British Journal of Educational Psychology, 55*, 264-72.

Bigsby conducted an experiment with dyslexic children to determine the source of confusion in processing reversible letters. She found that the confusion was not in the visual code, thus eliminating visual perception as a source of difficulty. Rather, it appeared to be in the name code, implying a linguistic dysfunction in mislabeling the letters. Since the difficulty seems to be in the labeling, she concludes that programs remediating visual perception will not prove productive.

Billingsley, B.S., & Wildman, T.M. (1988). The effects of prereading activities on the comprehension monitoring of learning disabled adolescents. *Learning Disabilities*, *4*, 36-44.

These researchers studied the effects of prereading interventions, including self-questions and structured overviews, on the ability of adolescents with learning disabilities to monitor comprehension and to recall information later. Their results suggested that students' active involvement with text can be enhanced with a brief prereading activity that will facilitate comprehension.

Blachowicz, C.L.Z. (1991). Vocabulary instruction in content classes for special needs learners: Why and how? *Journal of Reading, Writing, and Learning Disabilities*, *7*, 297-308.

A problem-solving model of vocabulary instruction in content-area classes is proposed for students with special needs. The increased textual vocabulary loads for older learners causes particular difficulty for students with weak vocabularies. The author outlines a five-step model for this instruction and presents a sample lesson for a middle school social studies class. The steps include: establish what learners already know, highlight the new, generate possible connections between the 'known' and the 'new,' gather information to apply to the problem, and self-monitoring and consolidation. Blachowicz concludes by suggesting to us that "developing the breadth and depth of vocabulary knowledge is intimately related to learning new concepts and general problem-solving strategies. These skills can best be addressed within content classes or by the support teacher who prepares students to be mainstreamed in content-area classes" (p. 305).

Blachowicz, C.L.Z., & Lee, J.J. (1991). Vocabulary development in the whole literacy classroom. *The Reading Teacher*, *45*, 188-195.

These authors provide guidelines for effective vocabulary instruction. They recommend that teachers select vocabulary words from the context of students' reading, that they guide students to activate their prior knowledge about the words, make predictions, gather data, then reformulate what they know about a word. Teachers are urged to either model this process or provide explicit instruction in the process.

Blachowicz, C.L.Z., & Zabroske, B. (1990). Context instruction: A metacognitive approach for at-risk readers. *Journal of Reading*, 504-508.

Vocabulary instruction provided in the context of the content-area classroom was explored by the authors and a group of middle school remedial teachers over the course of a school year. This article reflects their meetings, journals, and instructional trials. They formulated and tested an approach for treating vocabulary instruction as a metacognitive problem-solving strategy. This model of instruction contains three components: (1) students must understand why and when to use context; (2) they must know what kinds of clues may be provided by context; and (3) students must know how to seek and use these clues.

Borkowski, J.G. (1992). Metacognitive theory: A framework
   for teaching literacy, writing, and math skills. *Journal of
   Learning Disabilities*, *25*, 253-257.

Borkowski develops three themes in his effort to create a
more coherent perspective on metacognitive theory. These
themes include: "(1) self-regulation as the centerpiece of
strategy-based instruction; (2) the reciprocal relationship between
self-regulated learning and beliefs about the 'self' as a learner;
and (3) 'working models' and their role in classroom teaching"
(p. 253). He reminds us that teachers urgently need explicit
examples of ways to teach children how to analyze tasks, to
activate viable strategies, to select the best strategy, and to
monitor and revise initial strategy selection. He urges additional
research to develop more precise hypotheses about self-regulation
and its interface with motivation and lower-level strategies.

Bos, C. S., & Anders, P. L. (1987). Semantic feature analysis:
   An interactive teaching strategy for facilitating learning
   from text. *Learning Disabilities Focus*, *3*, 55-59.

Results of a research study suggest that students studying
vocabulary through an interactive teaching strategy perform
better than students given direct instruction of definitions or
students using the dictionary. Bos and Anders used a semantic
feature analysis grid to help students predict the relationships
between individual words and concepts before reading. Students
participated in group discussions and shared their prior
knowledge, then they read to confirm their predictions.

Bos, C. S., & Anders, P. L. (1988). Developing higher level
   thinking skills through interactive teaching. *Journal of
   Reading, Writing, and Learning Disabilities*, *4*, 259-274.

These authors propose a complex, "interactive model for
teaching content-area concepts to students with reading [and]

learning disabilities" (p. 259). This model is based on three theoretical foundations: schema theory, a psycholinguistic model of reading, and concept learning and development theory. Bos and Anders present procedures for activating student background knowledge and for helping students to develop an understanding of the relationships among concepts. These relationships are critical for concept evaluation, synthesis, and application. The interactive teaching strategies described incorporate semantic feature analysis and semantic mapping. The authors conclude that "interactive teaching strategies can provide students with the instructional support needed to effectively learn content area concepts" (p. 271).

Bos, C. S., & Anders, P. L. (1990a). Effects of interactive vocabulary instruction on the vocabulary learning and reading comprehension of junior-high learning disabled students. *Learning Disability Quarterly*, *13*, 31-41.

Bos and Anders report that interactive vocabulary instruction was effective in improving the vocabulary and reading comprehension of junior high school students with learning disabilities. They compared definitional instruction to three interactive strategies: semantic mapping, semantic feature analysis, and semantic/syntactic feature analysis, all using content-area texts. The interactive vocabulary strategies emphasized the underlying concept represented by the words, the knowledge hypothesis, in contrast to the definition strategy which placed the major emphasis on the meanings of words. Bos and Anders conclude that "long-term learning seems to occur under conditions that provide adequate opportunities for students to (a) activate and instantiate prior knowledge, (b) share that knowledge with each other, (c) make predictions concerning the relationships among concepts, and (d) read to confirm and justify their predictions" (p. 40). These authors remind us of the need for further research to determine whether interactive techniques can be employed by practitioners, as well as researchers, with similar results.

Bos, C.S., & Anders, P.L. (1990b). Interactive teaching and learning: Instructional practices for teaching content and strategic knowledge. In T.E. Scruggs and B.Y.L. Wong (Eds.), *Intervention Research in Learning Disabilities* (pp. 166-185). New York: Springer-Verlag.

Bos and Anders present a model designed to enable text comprehension and content area learning. This interactive model for teaching and learning is based on four theoretical perspectives. Schema theory and the knowledge hypothesis emphasize the strong relationship between the activation of knowledge of a concept and comprehending text and learning content from that text. Strategic behavior involves using "the full range of language systems and strategies for interacting with text" (p. 168). The language systems include graphophonic, syntactic, and semantic. Concept learning and development theory stress the importance of relationships and organization in learning concepts, which are the substance of schemata. Finally, the sociocultural theory of cognitive development "assumes that cognitive functioning grows out of social interactions" (p. 169), including scaffolded instruction, discussion, and mediated learning. Illustrations of interactive teaching such as semantic feature analysis and semantic mapping are included. Detailed guidance is provided in how to teach these strategies using interactive teaching strategies such as activating prior knowledge, predicting, and confirming, and integrating learning. Interactive learning strategies are highlighted as ways of enabling students to generate their own charts or maps, using the same theoretical base.

The authors report on the results of a series of experiments conducted with students with learning disabilities of a variety of ages and in a variety of situations. They conclude that "at the most general level, there is support that this methodology is promising for facilitating learning disabled students' text comprehension and content learning" (p. 180).

Bos, C.S., Anders, P.L., Filip, D., & Jaffe, L. E. (1989). The effects of an interactive instructional strategy for enhancing reading comprehension and content area learning for students with learning disabilities. *Journal of Learning Disabilities*, 22, 384-390.

This study investigated the effectiveness of semantic-feature analysis (SFA), an interactive vocabulary instructional strategy, on the comprehension of social studies text by resource room students with learning disabilities. Before reading, students either completed an SFA relationship chart or used the dictionary to write definitions and sentences. Students using the SFA procedure outperformed the dictionary group. The authors conclude that "based on the active nature of learning, the dovetailing of learning strategies with interactive teaching strategies holds promise for success of students with learning disabilities" (p. 389).

Bos, C., & Vaughn, S. (1994). *Strategies for teaching students with learning and behavior problems*, 3rd Edition. Boston, MA: Allyn and Bacon.

This text provides extensive, practical information that will be helpful to teachers and to those preparing to teach students with learning and behavior problems. Information about general approaches to teaching and learning that enable a better understanding of the methods and procedures for teaching all learners is discussed. Also, the book describes methods and procedures of instruction, with a focus on which methods are most effective with what types of students, in sufficient detail that teachers will be prepared to try them. In addition, this textbook includes information about classroom management and about working with parents and professionals. Activities and appendices focused on specific academic areas have been integrated into a number of the chapters.

Braden, J. P., & Weiss, L. (1988). Effects of simple difference versus regression discrepancy methods: An empirical study. *Journal of School Psychology*, *26*, 133-142.

Because of the importance of the discrepancy between IQ and achievement in determining identification as learning disabled, Braden and Weiss compare the difference obtained based on using a simple difference (the commonly accepted method) or a regression method. They cite the available literature, which suggests that in theory a simple difference method should increase the chance of white children being identified as learning disabled and decrease the chance of black children being identified. This study investigated the results of the two methods, using second and fifth graders. The results supported the theoretical hypothesis and further found that the regression method was more likely to result in a proportional ethnic composition of groups. Since 84% of states currently use the simple difference method, the authors raise questions about the ethical and legal implications for those continuing to use a method that could be "challenged in the courts as discriminatory" (p. 141).

Brady, S. (1986). Short-term memory, phonological processing, and reading ability. *Annals of Dyslexia*, *36*, 138-153.

Brady examines the relationship between short-term memory and the phonetic coding abilities of poor readers. She reviews a considerable body of previous research in some detail and concludes that poor readers do have a difficulty in short-term memory that is specific to phonetic decoding. This was particularly evident when that task was difficult, either because of the presence of background noise or the complexity of the task itself. The difficulties experienced by poor readers in the phonological aspects of language combined with specific difficulties in short-term memory related to phonetic coding highlight the importance of this area for poor readers. The author suggests that instruction in school should focus on speech sounds and language tasks related to reading rather than such pre-reading skills as labeling and environmental sounds. She also believes "that good and poor readers use the same strategies, but poor readers are less accurate" (p. 150). It is critical to provide instruction in the phonological processes; this is where poor readers need help, not in remediating auditory or visual deficits.

Brady, S.A. (1991). The role of working memory in reading disability. In S.A. Brady and D.P. Shankweiler (Eds.), *Phonological Processes in Literacy* (pp. 129-151). Hillsdale, N.J.: Lawrence Erlbaum Associates.

Brady explores her own work and that done by others in relation to the impact of working memory and phonological processes on poor readers. She concludes that poor readers are deficient in phonological processing skills and that this limitation causes less efficient use of working memory.

Brown, A.L., & Campione, J.C. (1986). Psychological theory and the study of learning disabilities. *American Psychologist, 14*, 1059-1068.

Brown and Campione present arguments supporting the view that we should shift from diagnosing "specific and enduring cognitive deficits in the learner" (p. 1059) to analyzing "performance in basic academic disciplines" (ibid.). Stated differently, we are moving away from identifying what's wrong with the child toward looking at the difficulties the child is encountering in academic tasks. The authors trace the development of this trend in general, and they examine performance in arithmetic and reading comprehension in particular. They find that "in both arithmetic and reading . . . instruction aimed at specific error patterns or inadequate strategic procedures is less effective than instruction that creates situations in which the goal is to enhance the students' conceptual understanding of the semantics, or the meaning, of any procedures they might adopt" (p. 1064). Reciprocal teaching is seen as an effective way of achieving this. This approach also has implications for diagnosis, which should be dynamic rather than static.

Brownlee, Jr., W. A. (1988). History and the learning disabled student. *The History and Social Science Teacher, 24*(1), 28-19.

Students with learning disabilities often lack adequate schemata for comprehension, and therefore they fail to develop the strategies needed for good reading. Brownlee provides an adaptation of a semantic map to help students organize the information in a reading assignment and suggests how to model use of the map. Brownlee suggests that learning to map history reading assignments will help the student in two ways: (1) it provides a ready-made schema for organizing the structural elements of the assignment and the data contained therein, and (2) success with mapping may provide the student with the incentive to develop his or her own strategies for successful reading.

Bruck, M. (1987). The adult outcomes of children with learning disabilities. *Annals of Dyslexia, 37*, 252-263.

Bruck reviews the results of four follow-up studies of children with learning disabilities. Each study incorporates data collected in adulthood with data collected during schooling from the time the children were identified as being learning disabled. Bruck concludes that learning disabilities often persist into adulthood, being evidenced in difficulty with literacy skills and some continuing social and emotional problems, especially among females. However, the studies reported no association between childhood learning disabilities and delinquency, alcohol abuse, or drug abuse. Many of the adult subjects were well adjusted and successful in their employment and in other areas of adult life. The factors that are associated with positive adult outcomes are the severity of the childhood disability, socioeconomic status, and IQ. Bruck reports that "the most important antecedents of positive outcome are early identification accompanied by adequate intervention" (p. 262). She concludes with encouragement that when children with learning disabilities receive adequate help, learning disabilities are not necessarily a lifelong handicap.

Bruck, M. (1988). The word recognition and spelling of dyslexic children. *Reading Research Quarterly, 23,* 51-69.

Bruck studied the reading and spelling performance of 9- to 16-year-old children with dyslexia to determine whether these children used qualitatively different strategies and processes from those used by normal readers. She examined the children's use of spelling-sound and sound-spelling correspondences, their use of visual and phonological information for reading and spelling, and their use of context for reading words. She also examined the development of these strategies over the period of a school year. She found that both dyslexic and normal readers "used the same processes for word recognition . . . the same *pattern* of context effect" (p. 65) and the same use of association of sound-symbol correspondence. The children with dyslexia relied more heavily on the use of context than did normal readers, suggesting the use of a higher level skill to compensate for difficulties with a lower level skill. That finding is consistent with the comparable performance in reading comprehension demonstrated by the children with dyslexia. The data over time showed growth by the children with dyslexia at the same rate as that of the normal reading, indicating that treatment can be effective. The author suggests that the definition of dyslexia "be amended to reflect the findings that dyslexic children show essentially normal processes for reading and spelling, given their level of developing of reading and spelling skills" (p. 67).

Bruck, M., & Treiman, R. (1990). Phonological awareness and spelling in normal children and dyslexics: The case of initial consonant clusters. *Journal of Experimental Child Psychology*, *50*, 156-178.

Bruck and Treiman review the importance of phonological awareness and the difficulties experienced by students with dyslexia in this area. The issue explored in their research is whether the difficulties are due to developmental delay or to an underlying deficit. After comparing normal first and second graders with dyslexics they conclude that developmental delay seems more likely. Their spelling difficulties reflect difficulties in phonological awareness and are similar to those of younger, normal children.

Bruck, M., & Waters, G.S. (1990). An analysis of the component spelling and reading skills of good readers-good spellers, good readers-poor spellers, and poor readers-poor spellers. In T.H. Carr and B.A. Levy (Eds.), *Reading and its development: Component skills approaches* (pp. 161-206). San Diego, CA: Academic Press, Inc.

Bruck and Waters, citing the critical importance of word recognition skills for skilled reading, examined differences between good and poor readers and spellers in the sixth grade. For reading and spelling, knowledge of spelling-sound correspondences were found to be important, with automaticity a variable in success. An interesting finding was that mixed subjects were similar to poor subjects in word recognition skills and similar to good subjects in reading comprehension. Further study found that this might be due to good oral language skills. Good readers used context to aid in comprehending but not in recognizing words. Poor readers may use context for word recognition because they are not able to recognize words by decoding.

Bryan, T., Bay, M., & Donahue, M. (1988). Implications of the learning disabilities definition for the Regular Education Initiative. *Journal of Learning Disabilities, 21,* 23-28.

These authors propose that the heterogeneity of students with learning disabilities "makes it unlikely that classroom modifications alone, regardless of a teacher's pedagogical skill, will suffice to meet the complex needs of this population of children" (p. 23). They review neurological bases for learning disabilities and the wide variety of learning difficulties caused by them. In conclusion, they caution against mandating the instruction of all students with learning disabilities in any one setting.

Candler, A.C., & Keefe, C.H. (1988, March 28-April 1). *Identifying the learning disabled student with a language problem.* Paper presented at the Annual Convention of the Council for Exceptional Children, Washington, DC.

Candler and Keefe identify nine areas of difficulty for the learning disabled student with a language problem. These include difficulty with word meaning, responding inappropriately, using words inaccurately, difficulty with word finding, inventing words, inaccurate or inadequate use of referents, failure to provide appropriate information on a topic, use of immature grammatical structures, and disorganization and problems with sequencing. The authors recommend informal but structured activities to analyze students' language.

Carlisle, J.F. (1989).   Diagnosing comprehension deficits
    through listening and reading. *Annals of Dyslexia, 39,*
    159-176.

Carlisle, linking reading and listening as related receptive
language skills, reviews traditional approaches to the assessment
of comprehension performance and suggests that we need to
identify subtypes of comprehension deficits in both these skill
areas. Reading is viewed as a complex process of interrelated
comprehension skills, falling into the category of reasoning.
Based on this premise, she criticizes current tests of reading,
which "continue to treat comprehension skills as separate
diagnostic entities" (p. 163).   There are no "good" tests of
listening comprehension, although there is a serious need in this
area. She discusses and illustrates a test of comprehension of
reading and listening based on the verification of sentences as
having been part of the original text.   The sentences are
distractors. Although this test format is supported by reading
theory, it needs additional research and validation. However,
according to the author, it may become a productive way to
assess comprehension.

Carlisle, J.F. (1993).   Selecting approaches to vocabulary
    instruction for the reading disabled. *Learning Disabilities
    Research & Practice, 8,* 97-105.

In this extensive overview of vocabulary instruction,
Carlisle reviews a variety of approaches to teaching vocabulary
and presents guidelines for effective instruction. She states that
the verbal ability of the reading-disabled student will influence
the effectiveness of specific approaches to vocabulary instruction
and that this should be considered when planning instruction.
She concludes that "reading-disabled children need instructional
programs for learning word meanings, because understanding
words may support growth of comprehension skills and
knowledge of the content areas they are studying" (p. 104).

Carnine, D., Silbert, J., & Kameenui, E. J. (1990). *Direct instruction reading*, (2nd ed.). Columbus, OH: Merrill.

The authors' purpose is to help teachers learn to create an environment in which "the maximum amount of learning occurs in the shortest possible time with the least amount of resources" (p. v) and that enhances the student's self-concept. They provide in-depth procedures for teaching passage reading, including both decoding and comprehending narrative and expository material. For each topic the authors discuss specific skills and how to teach them, related research, and application exercises for the classroom.

Carr, S.C. (1991, January). *The effects of prior knowledge and schema activation strategies on the inferential reading comprehension performance of learning disabled and nonlearning disabled children.* Paper presented at the Annual Meeting of the Southwest Educational Research Association, San Antonio, TX.

This article reports a study that compared the inferential reading performance of students with learning disabilities to that of their normally achieving age-level and reading-level peers. Carr found that when children with learning disabilities have an adequately developed knowledge base, they can answer inferential questions, although not as competently as their peers. She suggests that it is beneficial to provide instructional support to help these children integrate new information with prior knowledge.

Carrasquillo, A. (1994). *Teaching English as a second language: A resource guide.* New York: Garland Publishing, Inc.

This helpful volume reviews theoretical guidelines and specific instructional techniques to assist teachers of limited

English proficient students from all language backgrounds. Carrasquillo's premise that "English as a second language often involves a link between language, ethnicity and culture, and it is manifested by diversified curricular goals and teaching patterns in the classroom" (p. xi) is reflected throughout the book.

Carrasquillo, A., & Nunez, D. (1988). *Computer-assisted metacognitive strategies and the reading comprehension skills of ESL elementary school students.* (ERIC Document Reproduction Service No. ED 301 838).

Carrasquillo and Nunez remind us that most of the software to help develop reading comprehension skills does not monitor students' use of comprehension strategies. They present the results of a study that employed the Tutorial-Direct Monitoring Strategy, derived from the work of Palincsar and Brown, to train students in the use of metacognitive strategies. Based on the findings, they suggest expanding the potential of computer-assisted instruction by using it to teach metacognitive strategies.

Carver, R.P. (1992). Commentary: Effect of prediction activities, prior knowledge, and text type upon amount comprehended: Using rauding theory to critique schema theory research. *Reading Research Quarterly, 27,* 164-174.

Carver comments on research studies by Valencia and Stallman (1989) and Johnston (1984), both related to comprehension. He proposes that prediction activities, prior knowledge, and text type become important factors in comprehension only when students are studying relatively hard material. He points out that elementary and secondary students' normal reading process, called rauding, typically is not overly demanding, and that prediction, prior knowledge, and text type may not be as important for routine reading as we have believed them to be.

Casbergue, R.M., & Greene, J.F. (1988). Persistent misconceptions about sensory perception and reading disability. *Journal of Reading, 4*, 196-203.

Casbergue and Greene provide a detailed review of the history of research investigating sensory perceptual screening and training programs designed to aid the reader with learning disabilities in learning to read and becoming proficient. The results examined are "overwhelmingly negative" (p. 201). The authors suggest that sensory and perceptual training has not been effective in overcoming reading difficulties because these programs train the eyes, not the brain, which is the critical component for reading. Unfortunately, training in this area, either in private programs or by "uninformed teachers" (p. 197), still occurs, fueled by incorrect assertions that sensory screening will identify children at risk for learning disabilities and that sensory training is needed before reading instruction can begin.

Catts, H. W. (1989). Defining dyslexia as a developmental language disorder. *Annals of Dyslexia, 39*, 50-66.

Catts critically examines prior definitions of developmental dyslexia. He cites, for example, the difficulty of an exclusionary definition that makes it difficult to identify specific individuals. If we wait until the student has a reading difficulty, we allow academic failure to occur as well as encourage lack of self-esteem and motivation. In addition, the difficulties associated with the use of discrepancy formulas are outlined in detail. The IQ score can be depressed because of lower reading abilities, less knowledge gained, and lack of world experience. Many of the tests used have been seriously questioned. He suggests, instead, a definition of developmental dyslexia that indicates a specific language disorder with "difficulties in the cognitive and metacognitive processing of phonological information" (p. 54). These may be linked to difficulties in memory processes. The difficulties may be manifested in school in problems with retrieving names and words, comprehending sentences, and decoding and recognizing words.

Chall, J.S. (1987). Reading development in adults. *Annals of Dyslexia, 37*, 240-251.

Chall reviews the stages in reading development that she has previously advanced, comparing and contrasting the development of reading in adults and children. She reviews research in the areas of beginning reading and concludes that "early systematic teaching and learning of word recognition and decoding produces better results than emphasis on meaning in the beginning" (p. 245), recognizing at the same time the need for adults to be interested in and motivated to learn reading. She documents the good news: there appear to be fewer illiterates and functional illiterates. The bad news is that there is a need for a higher level of literacy in our society today, a level that only 37% of young adults in 1986 were able to reach. She further identifies as a particular problem the number of adults who are unable to learn because of a reading disability, dyslexia, or learning disability. This group can, with proper instruction, learn to read.

Chan, L.K.S. (1991). Promoting strategy generalization through self-instructional training in students with reading disabilities. *Journal of Learning Disabilities, 24*, 427-433.

Chan identifies a major problem in the field of learning disabilities: the transfer and generalization of training in metacognitive strategies. She demonstrated the efficacy of self-instructional training in using a set of self-questions to identify the main idea in a variety of settings. She provides the questions that were used and a list of five stages for instruction, beginning with a "thinking-aloud" procedure, fading the support until the student is "using covert self-questions" (p. 430). This strategy proved more effective than the standard method of demonstration and practice.

Chan, L.K.S., & Cole, P.G. (1986). The effects of comprehension monitoring training on the reading competence of learning disabled and regular class students. *Remedial and Special Education (RASE), 7,* 33-40.

Chan and Cole accept the notion that learning disabled students "show deficiencies in spontaneous use of cognitive strategies" (p. 33). Based on this they investigated the efficacy of providing explicit training in metacognitive strategies to a group of 10- to 12-year-old students with learning disabilities. They provided training in reading-rereading or in the metacognitive strategies of self-questioning and underlining, self-questioning only, and underlining only. All three of the experimental strategies proved effective in raising the level of reading comprehension for the learning disabled. The authors conclude that the training "involved the learners in active interaction with the reading material and constant reflection on the text content" (p. 39). However, without specific instruction as to which strategy to use, transfer did not take place automatically. The control group of regular students did not show improvement after instruction in these strategies, suggesting that these students are using a cognitive strategy without instruction.

Chan, L.K.S., Cole, P.G., & Barfett, S. (1987). Comprehension monitoring: Detection and identification of text inconsistencies by LD and normal students. *Learning Disability Quarterly, 10,* 114-124.

A metacognitive strategy to help readers monitor text for internal inconsistency was investigated by Chan, Cole, and

Barfett. Readers learned a procedure for comparing one proposition or statement with others in the text in order to determine when inconsistency exists. Students with learning disabilities revealed an initial deficit in comprehension-monitoring skills; however, explicit instruction in the metacognitive strategy resulted in improved reading comprehension as well as improved comprehension monitoring.

Chan, L. K. S., Cole, P. G., & Morris, J. N. (1990). Effects of instruction in the use of a visual-imagery strategy on the reading-comprehension competence of disabled and average readers. *Learning Disability Quarterly*, *13*, 2-10.

Chan, Cole, and Morris identify poor metacognitive skills as at least partly responsible for the poor task performance and passiveness of students with learning disabilities. Based on this premise, they studied the performance of students in three training conditions: visualization instruction plus pictorial display, visualization only, and a read-reread control group. In the visualization training students were instructed to make a picture in their mind of the content of the text. The pictorial display confirmed the visualization. The approach was designed to encourage active participation on the part of the reader. The results indicated that the visualization plus pictorial display can increase comprehension, but there must be a consistent and extended effort to determine that the students begin to self-monitor and self-prompt the process of visualization.

Chiang, B., & Ford, M. (1990). Whole language alternatives for students with learning disabilities. *Learning Disabilities Forum*, *16*, 31-34.

Chiang and Ford explore two areas: theory and research related to whole language and learning disabilities and the implementation of whole language programs for students with learning disabilities. They define whole language as including the integration of the various learning processes as well as the integration of processes and content in authentic tasks of real reading and writing. A range of instructional procedures are suggested, all focused on using real, whole text, integrating reading and writing, providing students with choices, and conferencing with students for assessment and instruction. The authors note the lack of research documenting success in teaching students with learning disabilities with a whole language approach and suggest that a balanced program is needed "integrating the whole language strategies with other effective methods such as direct instruction" (p. 34).

Christensen, C. A. (1992). Discrepancy definitions of reading disability: Has the quest led us astray? A response to Stanovich. *Reading Research Quarterly, 27,* 276-280.

In this brief article, Christensen responds to Stanovich's (1991) critique of current definitions and identification practices of learning disabilities in reading. She urges that we seek specific instructional solutions to reading failure regardless of the cause, rather than focusing on whether or not a child is learning disabled.

Cicchelli, T., & Ashby-Davis, C. (1986). *Teaching exceptional children and youth in the regular classroom.* New York: Syracuse University Press.

This textbook addresses the needs of regular classroom teachers and interdisciplinary teams working with exceptional children. It suggests practical applications that can contribute to successful classroom practice. Using a team approach to teaching and learning, the authors have developed twelve self-contained modules that review the fundamentals needed by teachers. The self-instructional format of the book involves the reader in considering hypothetical cases having applications for real-life settings.

Cicchelli, T., & Baecher, R. (1989). Microcomputers in the classroom: Focusing on teacher concerns. *Educational Research Quarterly, 13*, 37-46.

This study investigated the concerns of 78 teachers about using microcomputers in their classrooms. Teachers, drawn from the elementary, junior high, and senior high school levels, completed the Stages of Concern Questionnaire that yields data on seven distinct stages of concern. After evaluating the findings, Cicchelli and Baecher suggested that inservice activities matching teachers' concern areas may reduce resistance to implementation.

Clark, D.B. (1988). *Dyslexia: Theory and practice of remedial instruction*. Parkton, MD: York Press.

Clark lays out for the reader a thorough description of the various instructional approaches recommended for teaching students who are having difficulty learning to read. It provides practical information on methods of instruction in reading, writing, and spelling, and the specific techniques that these approaches require. She presents, as well, the theory and empirical research on which these approaches are based. The book is written primarily for teachers. The last chapter addresses issues related to planning a reading curriculum; it suggests instructional components not provided in existing remedial programs that could be incorporated.

Coles, G. (1987). *The learning mystique*. New York: Pantheon.

Coles presents a broad review of many theories and issues related to learning disabilities, including, for example, the role of neurological impairment, the concept of perceptual deficits, the impact of language and memory, the role of phonological processing, and link of learning disabilities to sex and to genetics. He suggests that "complex individual attributes and social interrelationships are the starting point of many learning disabilities" (p. 136). Individual attributes include "learned academic and problem solving abilities, various prior experiences, interest, motivation, emotions, self-confidence, and attitudes" (p. 136). Coles goes on to include "powerful 'external' influences" (p. 136) such as the teacher's ability, the classroom dynamics, and the constructs of test situations. Many applications and implications of this social constructionist view of learning disabilities are explored.

Colson, S. E., & Mehring, T. A. (1990). Facilitating memory in students with learning disabilities. *Learning Disabilities Forum, 16,* 75-79.

Colson and Mehring review the difficulties experienced by learning disabled students in storing items in memory and in retrieving them efficiently when needed. Because of the fact that the concept of learning disabilities covers a wide range of difficulties, there is no general agreement on the kinds of memory problems experienced by this heterogeneous group of students. However, there is consensus on the higher incidence of memory difficulties and of an inability to use cognitive strategies. The key here may be effective instruction that provides sufficient practice and gives reasons for using the strategies. After reviewing an information processing model of human memory, the authors suggest teaching techniques and learning strategies based on a cognitive approach to instruction. This means that students are actively engaged in the process of learning, are constructing and creating forms of organization, relating new information to prior knowledge, focusing on meaning, and planning when and how to use the information.

Condus, M.M., Marshall, K.J., & Miller, S.R. (1986). Effects of the keyword mnemonic strategy on vocabulary acquisition and maintenance by learning disabled children. *Journal of Learning Disabilities, 19,* 609-613.

A keyword strategy was used to teach word meanings to twelve-year-old students with learning disabilities. The other students in the study were instructed in a control group or by utilizing picture context or sentence-experience context. Students instructed with the keyword method outperformed students assigned to the other conditions.

Council for Exceptional Children (1993). CEC policy on inclusive schools and community settings. *Teaching Exceptional Children, 25,* 1.

This policy statement on inclusion was approved at CEC's Annual Convention in 1993. It states: "CEC believes that a continuum of services must be available for all children, youth, and young adults. CEC also believes that the concept of inclusion is a meaningful goal to be pursued in our schools and communities" (p. 1).

Council for Exceptional Children, Division of Learning Disabilities (1993). *Inclusion: What does it mean for students with learning disabilities?* Reston, VA: Author.

The position of the Division of Learning Disabilities (DLD) on inclusion is reflected in the following statement: "If a continuum of service options is not available to individual students with specific learning disabilities, the intent of IDEA is not being met" (p. 1). This statement also calls for an action plan for DLD to examine research and practice on inclusion for students with learning disabilities.

Council for Learning Disabilities (1993). Position statement. *Learning Disability Quarterly, 16,* 126.

This position statement includes the following: "The Council SUPPORTS the education of students with LD in general education classrooms *when deemed appropriate* by the Individual Education Program (IEP) team. Such inclusion efforts require the provision of needed support services in order to be successful" (p. 126).

Council for Learning Disabilities, Board of Trustees (1987). The CLD position statements. *Journal of Learning Disabilities, 20,* 149-150.

In this policy statement the Board of Trustees states its position on three issues. First, it opposes instructional programs to train perceptual and perceptual-motor functions because no evidence supports their effectiveness. Second, it reaffirms the differences between (1) non-handicapped low achievers and underachievers, and (2) students with learning disabilities, for whom typical remedial programs are insufficient. Finally, the Board advocates using a broad range of diagnostic approaches in contrast to a simple discrepancy score.

Council for Learning Disabilities, Research Committee (1993). Minimum standards for the description of participants in learning disabilities research. *Journal of Learning Disabilities, 26,* 210-213.

In the interest of ensuring research validity, the CLD Research Committee has prepared these updated guidelines for participant description. The committee stresses the importance of describing participants both in the report narrative and in an accompanying table. The authors conclude: "The guidelines provided here should bring us closer to achieving the precision necessary to more fully interpret and integrate research and, ultimately, to develop better practices in applied settings" (p. 213).

Cox, A. R., & Hutcheson, L. (1988).   Syllable division: Prerequisite to dyslexics' literacy. *Annals of Dyslexia, 38,* 226-257.

Cox and Hutcheson provide a rationale for the importance of syllable division as well as specific sequential instructions for how to teach children this skill. The aim is to enable the student "to discover the new information independently" (p. 229), moving from the known to the unknown. With each stage, the steps once discovered are posted as a reference.

Crais, E.R., & Chapman, R.S. (1987).   Story recall and inferencing skills in language/learning disabled and non-disabled children. *Journal of Speech and Hearing Disorders, 52,* 50-55.

Crais and Chapman studied children's ability to recall information and draw inferences from orally presented narratives. The study included 16 nine- to ten-year-old children who were language-learning disabled and two groups of normally developing children, 16 six- to seven-year-olds and 16 nine- to ten-year-olds. Stories in fable format were used and were followed by a short series of premise and inference questions. During the retelling the children with language learning disabilities did not differ significantly from the younger age control group. However, they did perform worse on story recall and exhibited significantly more disparity between the true/false questions than their age-match controls. The authors suggest that a more extensive characterization of comprehension seems desirable. The children with language-learning disabilities seemed to have difficulty with comprehension control when answering questions that require integration of information and that change the wording of story sentences.

Cunningham, A.E (1989). Outstanding dissertation award 1987-1988. Phonemic awareness: The development of early reading competency. *Reading Research Quarterly, 24,* 471.

Cunningham compared three approaches to early reading instruction in kindergarten and first grade: a skill-and-drill group, a metacognitive group, and a control group for both kindergarten and first grade. The skill-and-drill group was trained in how to segment and blend phonemes. The metacognitive group was trained in the application, value, and utility of phonemic awareness as well as how to perform the tasks. The control group listened to stories and answered comprehension questions. In both grade levels students in the two experimental groups did better than the control group on tests of phonemic awareness. Children in first grade in the metacognitive group performed better on a transfer test than did the skill-and-drill group. The author concluded that when actually reading, it's important to have metacognitive knowledge of the task.

Darch, C., & Carnine, D. (1986). Teaching content area material to learning disabled students. *Exceptional Children, 53,* 240-246.

Darch and Carnine studied the effect of an advance organizer on literal comprehension during content-area instruction. The advance organizer was presented in the form of a visual display to fourth, fifth, and sixth graders. These authors found positive effects for students learning with the advance organizer as compared to the control group.

Darch, C., & Gersten, R. (1986). Direction-setting activities in reading comprehension: A comparison of two approaches. *Learning Disability Quarterly, 9,* 235-242.

This study compared the comprehension performance of secondary students with learning disabilities who were taught using two different approaches. The first group was given prereading activities based on a basal approach to comprehension; the second group was taught using an advance organizer in the form of an outline of the text. Students taught with the advance organizer approach performed better than the basal group on comprehension tests.

Darch, C., & Kameenui, E.J. (1987). Teaching LD students critical reading skills: A systematic replication. *Learning Disability Quarterly*, *10*, 82-91.

Darch and Kameenui contrasted two approaches to teaching three critical reading skills to elementary students with learning disabilities. The direct instruction group was trained in using specific rules and strategies to identify faulty arguments. Instruction in the discussion/workbook group encouraged student involvement through discussions on utilizing critical reading skills. Students in the direct instruction group performed better than those in the discussion/workbook group on a posttest. The authors stress that in order to achieve maximum benefits, "careful instructional programming must be systematically introduced" (p. 90).

Day, J.D., & Zajakowski, A. (1991). Comparisons of learning ease and transfer propensity in poor and average readers. *Journal of Learning Disabilities*, *24*, 421-426, 433.

Day and Zajakowski investigated differences between children with learning disabilities and average readers in reading comprehension of expository paragraphs when the topic sentence was first, last, or missing. Children were trained to find the main idea when it was either explicitly or implicitly stated. They concluded that "children with learning disabilities required significantly more instruction than average readers to reach mastery criterion on nonideal text structures" (p. 421).

DeBello, T.C. (1990). Comparison of eleven major learning styles models: Variables, appropriate populations, validity of instrumentation, and the research behind them. *Journal of Reading, Writing, and Learning Disabilities International*, *6*, 203-222.

DeBello reviews the research on eleven learning styles models. In addition to presenting an overview of each model, he compares "the elements they encompass, the populations for which they are appropriate, the reliability and validity of their instrumentation, and where they overlap and differ" (p. 203). DeBello finds that although there are many areas of overlap among the models, the multidimensional models offer a more responsive approach to the diversity of the student population. He emphasizes that there is no question that all children have individual learning styles; the question lies in how best to treat style differences in the classroom. DeBello concludes that learning styles-based programs increase student performance, and he reminds us that if we treat every child in the same way we are not being responsive to their learning styles.

DeFries, J.C., Olson, R.K., Pennington, B.F., & Smith, S.D. (1991). Colorado reading project: Past, present and future. *Learning Disabilities: A Multidisciplinary Journal*, *2*, 37-46.

This article reports information obtained in the Colorado Reading Project, a federally funded project. An extensive description is provided of the analysis of twin data which suggests a genetic etiology of reading disability. An extension of this project will be employing the methodology of behavioral genetics to address a number of questions in the field of learning disabilities, such as the relationship between mathematics disability and reading problems.

Deshler, D.D., & Schumaker, J.B. (1986). Learning strategies: An instructional alternative for low-achieving adolescents. *Exceptional Children, 25,* 583-590.

Deshler and Schumaker describe an intervention model for mildly handicapped learning disabled adolescents that is a how-to-learn approach emphasizing metacognitive learning strategies that can be generalized to any content area. The students take charge of their own learning in the process of learning the strategies and applying them. Methodology for teaching the strategies is also discussed.

Drum, P.A., & Konopak, B.C. (1987). Learning word meanings from written context. In M.G. McKeown and M.E. Curtis (Eds.), *The nature of vocabulary acquisition* (pp. 73-88). Hillsdale, NJ: Lawrence Erlbaum Associates.

Drum and Konopak consider four factors influencing expansion of vocabulary knowledge through reading. These factors include the situational context, which indicates the reader's purpose; the underlying conceptual structure of the topic of the text; the reader's prior knowledge; and the linguistic context in which the word is found. The authors note that "most word meanings are learned in context . . . but these meanings are not very precise, no more precise than the contextual information provided as clues" (p. 85). They caution that exposure to words in context may not be sufficient for building conceptual knowledge.

Dykman, R. A., & Ackerman, P. T. (1991). Attention deficit disorder and specific reading disability: Separate but often overlapping disorders. *Journal of Learning Disabilities, 24,* 96-103.

Dykman and Ackerman examined 182 children with attention deficit disorder (ADD). Each of these children was also identified by teacher ratings as belonging to one of three behavioral subgroups: ADD with hyperactivity, ADD with hyperactivity and aggressivity, and ADD without hyperactivity or aggressivity. Over half of the students were poor readers. The authors report that in their study methylphenidate ameliorated hyperactive and aggressive behavior as well as attentional difficulties. They conclude that "ADD is real, we believe, and not just the figment of frustrated teachers' imaginations. It is not difficult to understand why children who exhibit performance deficits such as revealed by our battery of tasks are not stellar performers in the classroom, even if they are not hyperactive and/or aggressive or learning disabled" (p. 101).

Eckwall, E.E., & Shanker, J.L. (1993). *Locating and correcting reading difficulties*. New York: Macmillan.

This book presents concrete procedures for locating and correcting reading difficulties that can be successfully implemented in classrooms. It stresses the importance of direct instruction, motivational learning activities, and practice in the act of reading. It also emphasizes the use of strategic approaches to teaching reading. Games and activities to strengthen reading skills are provided, and appendices include information on preparing materials for classroom use. This book is not designed to present the theoretical underpinnings of teaching reading; rather, its subject is the practice of teaching reading.

Education for All Handicapped Children Act of 1975. Public Law 94-142, 94th Congress (1975).

Under this landmark legislation, all handicapped children and youth aged three through twenty-one are entitled to a free and appropriate public education. In addition, each state is required to have a plan that complies with the federal law.

Ehri, L.C. (1987). Learning to read and spell words. *Journal of Reading Behavior*, *19*, 5-30.

Ehri reviews theory and research in the area of initial tasks in the acquisition of literacy in young children. The assumption is made that "code emphasis programs produce better beginning readers than meaning emphasis programs" (p. 5); thus the focus of attention is on how beginners process graphic cues. The author concludes that in order to acquire literacy in the beginning stages, children need to master the alphabet, since letter shapes aid in processing graphic information and the letter names can be associated with sounds. Children must also have phonemic awareness, the ability to manipulate sounds in speech, in order to master and use sound/symbol correspondences and to segment and blend sounds.

Ehri, L.C. (1989). The development of spelling knowledge and its role in reading acquisition and reading disability. *Journal of Learning Disabilities*, *22*, 356-365.

Ehri reviews her own research and that of others in order to examine the relationships between spelling and reading acquisition and disability. She concludes that there are several areas of overlap. Phonemic awareness, for example, is important for the development of skills in both areas. She theorizes that we can develop phonemic awareness in children through invented phonetic spelling, which will prepare children for reading tasks.

Ehri, L.C. (1991). Development of the ability to read words. In R. Barr, M. Kamil, P. Mosenthal, and P. D. Pearson (Eds.), *Handbook of reading research* (pp. 383-417). New York: Longman Press.

Ehri focuses on reading theories and evidence in an examination of the processes involved in developing competency in word reading abilities. Emphasis is placed on studies of normal readers rather than poor readers. Adopting Frith's (1985) three-phase scheme, Ehri describes and discusses three developmental reading phases: 1) logographic, the use of graphics; 2) alphabetic, the use of grapheme-phoneme correspondences; and 3) orthographic, the use of spelling patterns. The author points out that at any given time, learners may be in transition from one phase to the next. Her objective is to integrate these phases in an effort to provide a more coherent view of reading development. Ehri suggest that a developmental phase theory of word reading carries implications for research on beginning reading processes.

Ehri, L.C. (1992). Reconceptualizing the development of sight word reading and its relationship to recoding. In P.B. Gough, L.C. Ehri, and R. Treiman (Eds.), *Reading acquisition* (pp. 107-144). Hillsdale, NJ: Lawrence Erlbaum Associates.

Ehri critiques the dual route theory of how readers read words out of context. The dual route view is that words are read either by sight recognition or by phonological recoding. She suggests that both the sight recognition and phonological recoding routes contain important weaknesses. In this chapter Ehri proposes an alternative theory about how sight words are established in memory. She explains: "My conception of sight word reading differs from the sight word route of dual route theory in that the kind of connection enabling readers to find specific words in memory is a systematic connection between spellings and pronunciations rather than an arbitrary connection between spellings and meanings" (p. 108). In conclusion, Ehri discusses implications for instruction in sight word reading.

Ehri, L.C., & Robbins, C. (1992). Beginners need some decoding skill to read words by analogy. *Reading Research Quarterly, 27*, 12-26.

Ehri and Robbins explore the rationale behind one commonly taught strategy for beginning readers, reading unknown words by analogy to known words. The issue is whether readers need decoding skills in order to do this. They conducted a study with kindergartners and first graders to determine the role of decoding in word reading by analogy. The findings indicated that the process of reading unknown words by analogy is easier than phonologically recoding them. The findings also suggested that "in order for beginners to read words by analogy, they must possess phonological recoding skill" (p. 22). The authors examine this paradox and suggest that the beginner uses limited phonological recoding skills in analogy word reading and is not required to use complex analysis and blending skills. In fact, the strategy of reading words by analogy may be a temporary strategy or a transition to more complex recoding skills.

Elley, W.B. (1989). Vocabulary acquisition from listening to stories. *Reading Research Quarterly*, *24*, 174-187.

In two experiments conducted in New Zealand, Elley found that oral story reading provided a significant source of vocabulary acquisition, regardless of whether the reading was accompanied by an explanation of word meanings. The frequency of the word in the text, its depiction in illustrations, and the amount of redundancy in the surrounding context were the best predictors of whether a particular word would be learned.

Ellis, E.S. (1993a). Integrative strategy instruction: A potential model for teaching content area subjects to adolescents with learning disabilities. *Journal of Learning Disabilities*, *26*, 358-383.

Ellis offers a model for integrating instruction in reading strategies into content-area classrooms. His model uses scaffolded instruction, with one set of experiences being employed as a basis for the increasingly sophisticated applications that follow. Because the reading strategies are introduced in content-area classes, their utility is apparent to students. Ellis stresses that students must be taught how to use the strategy in conjunction with other known strategies and how to monitor strategy use. He recommends that each strategy be practiced in various content-learning contexts so that students will learn to generalize their use to a variety of situations.

Ellis, E.S. (1993b). Teaching strategy sameness using integrated formats. *Journal of Learning Disabilities*, *26*, 448-481.

Ellis presents the revision of his Integrative Strategy Instruction in response to critiques by other researchers (see Hutchinson, 1993; Montague, 1993; Walsh, 1993). He emphasizes that it is important that we recognize the principle that reading strategy instruction should be integrated with content-area instruction. He recommends using intrinsic motivational techniques and incorporating a number of instructional practices such as building students' background knowledge directly, using cooperative learning and other collaborative approaches to attain specific objectives, and using constructive approaches when students' understanding can be monitored closely.

Ellis, E.S., & Lenz, B.K. (1990). Techniques for mediating content-area learning: Issues and research. *Focus on Exceptional Children*, *22*, 1-16.

Ellis and Lenz incorporate the findings of research studies that focus on teaching content-area information to low-achieving students or students with learning disabilities. This article examines the mediation of content-area learning through the following means: reducing content, providing learnable text, enhancing content through study guides and graphic organizers, using technological alternatives to textbooks, and teaching learning strategies such as mnemonics, prompting strategic interaction with content, and metacognition, all to be provided during direct instruction of content-area information. The authors conclude that the acquisition of basic skills and content should be addressed in a balanced and integrated manner and that the typical predominant focus on one or the other is insufficient. They remind us that "a change toward instruction that is more learner sensitive . . . can be realized only when content-area teachers support such a change" (p. 14), and they urge that concerned regular and special educators work toward this objective.

Ellis, E. S., Lenz, B. K., & Sabornie, E. J. (1987). Generalization and adaptation of learning strategies to natural environments: Part 1. *Remedial and Special Education, 8,* 6-20.

Ellis, Lenz, and Sabornie define learning strategies as "a series of *task-specific* strategies that incorporate features of cognitive and metacognitive training" (p. 6). These strategies are usually a set of steps that cue the student through a process and are structured in such a way that the student remembers the steps to be taken. The difficulty the authors address is that of generalizing a strategy to a new situation. They examine theory and research related to ways of ensuring generalization in general and in four studies in particular. They conclude with a series of findings, including the need for explicit instruction in generalization, for the establishment of an expectation that a given strategy will be generalized, and for planned feedback to students on the results of their efforts to generalize.

Ellsworth, N.J. (1994). Critical thinking and literacy. In N. Ellsworth, C. Hedley and A. Baratta (Eds.), *Literacy: A redefinition* (pp. 91-108). Hillsdale, NJ: Lawrence Erlbaum Associates.

Ellsworth provides a rationale for including critical thinking and problem solving skills in a redefinition of literacy that will incorporate the broader understandings and competencies needed in our changing society. Next, she reports a schema-based instructional study to teach adolescents with learning disabilities to understand and solve personal problems by identifying a general problem-solving schema and applying it to reach appropriate decisions. Analysis of the data indicated that the schema-instructed group outperformed the control group. Findings support the view that instruction in application of a general schema to specific problems can improve critical thinking and decision making.

Ellsworth, N.J. (1992). Literature for the special learner: The urban, at-risk student. In C. Hedley, D. Feldman, and P. Antonacci (Eds.), *Literacy across the curriculum* (pp. 286-300). Norwood, NJ: Ablex.

This chapter presents specific suggestions for classroom teachers who wish to use literature with heterogeneous classes that include at-risk students with learning and behavioral problems. Ellsworth addresses issues of motivating students, setting priorities for instruction, individualizing instruction with a wide range of literature, and integrating direct instruction in basic skills into reading literature. Examples are given to illustrate general components of the instruction.

Elrod, G.F. (1987). Turning passive readers into active readers in content area subjects. *Reading Horizons*, 27, 197-201.

Elrod suggests a metacognitive strategy for use in secondary content-area subjects that may help turn passive readers into active readers. He writes that the strategic steps are designed to assist high school resource teachers in teaching reading while they also teach content.

Englert, C.S. (1992). Writing instruction from a socio-cultural perspective: The holistic, dialogic, and social enterprise of writing. *Journal of Learning Disabilities, 25*, 153-172.

After many years of investigating ways of teaching students with learning disabilities to write, Englert proposes that writing is "a holistic cognitive activity; cognitive processes are learned in dialogic interactions with others; cognitive development occurs in students' zones of proximal development; and knowledge construction is a social and cultural phenomenon" (p. 153). Given this perspective, Englert recommends interactive teaching that involves students in a community of writers. She concludes that "programs that emphasize writing as the mastery of series of skills or strategies, or wherein students write in private and isolated contexts" (p. 171) will not be as effective as the "social constructivism" that she espouses.

Englert, C.S., & Mariage, T.V. (1991). Making students partners in the comprehension process: Organizing the reading "posse." *Learning Disability Quarterly, 14*, 123-138.

Englert and Mariage investigated the effects of a complex metacognitive strategy they call *POSSE* on reading comprehension of expository text. *POSSE* incorporates reciprocal teaching in "prereading," "during reading," and "after reading" formats that encourages students to *P*redict, *O*rganize predictions based on text structure, *S*earch and *S*ummarize the text structure, and *E*valuate comprehension. Fourth, fifth, and sixth graders with learning disabilities showed better recall of expository ideas and knowledge of comprehension strategies than students not using the strategy.

Englert, C.S., Raphael, T.E., Anderson, L.M., Gregg, S.L., & Anthony, H.M. (1989). Exposition: Reading, writing, and the metacognitive knowledge of learning disabled students. *Learning Disabilities Research, 5*, 5-24.

This study compared the expository reading and writing performance of students with learning disabilities and its potential relationship to students' knowledge about expository texts, with that of non-disabled low- and high-achieving students. The authors found that the written recalls of students with learning disabilities were less organized and contained fewer ideas than non-disabled students. Interview data suggested that students with learning disabilities had less knowledge about processes of organizing and categorizing ideas and about processes related to monitoring and revising text on the basis of text structure. The authors suggest that "students who lack an adequate knowledge of the organizational frameworks important in reading and writing may produce less because they simply do not have a schema that prompts them to consider major groups of related ideas or ideas that instantiate the text structure schema" (p. 23).

Englert, C.S., & Thomas, C.C. (1987). Sensitivity to text structure in reading and writing: A comparison between learning disabled and non-learning disabled students. *Learning Disability Quarterly, 10*, 93-105.

Englert and Thomas review the literature on the importance and development of a knowledge of text structure in text comprehension, concluding the following: that the acquisition of this knowledge is developmental; it is critical in both reading comprehension and in writing achievement; and it is the kind of knowledge that affects performance. The authors compared the performance of third/fourth graders and sixth/seventh graders who had been identified as learning disabled as compared with low achievers and normal children in knowledge and use of text structure. They found that children with learning disabilities lacked sensitivity to the text structure, which affected their reading and writing performance. The difficulty did not seem to be due to failure to decode or use appropriate writing mechanics. Rather, it seemed due to "their failure to apply appropriate metacognitive strategies involving text structure" (p. 102). The authors suggest a possible sequence for instruction.

Farmer, M.E., Klein, R., & Bryson, S.E. (1992). Computer-assisted reading: Effects of whole-word feedback on fluency and comprehension in readers with severe disabilities. *Remedial and Special Education (RASE)*, *13*, 50-60.

Farmer, Klein, and Bryson support the notion that readers with disabilities need feedback on words in order to develop fluency and comprehension. Computer-assisted instruction is particularly useful for this since it allows for more feedback that would normally be possible in the classroom. They cite research showing the effectiveness of this on the whole word, syllable, and on-set rime level. Their own research with adolescents did not produce positive results, probably because of insufficient instruction, practice, and motivation.

Farris, P.J., & Andersen, C. (1990). Adopting a whole language program for learning disabled students: A case study. *Reading Horizons*, *31*, 5-13.

Farris and Andersen place their discussion of whole language instruction for the learning disabled in the framework of current research on the importance of students' elaboration, questioning, and use of information as well as self-monitoring these strategies and being motivated to use them. The authors compare traditional and whole language approaches to teaching the student with learning disabilities. Traditional instruction is skill oriented and structured with an emphasis on the product, not the process. Reading material is controlled in terms of length of text, sentence structure, and the number and kinds of words used. The authors related the characteristics of a whole language approach with its emphasis on process and meaning to implementation in a real classroom.

Feagans, L., & Applebaum, M. I. (1986). Validation of language subtypes in learning disabled children. *Journal of Educational Psychology, 78,* 358-364.

Feagans and Applebaum review a body of research that supports the notion that deficits or delays in language skills are common in learning disabled students. They report on a study conducted with six- and seven-year old learning disabled students to determine whether there are subtypes of language difficulties and what they are. They examined three levels of language (the syntactic, the semantic, and the discourse or narrative level) and found that the narrative level was most important for reading comprehension in school learning "and it may be much more important than the traditional building blocks of language skills, such as vocabulary and syntax" (p. 364).

Feagans, L., & Merriwether, A. (1990). Visual discrimination of letter-like forms and its relationship to achievement over time in children with learning disabilities. *Journal of Learning Disabilities, 23,* 417-425.

Feagans and Merriwether review current and past research in the area of visual discrimination and the impact it has on the acquisition and development of reading abilities. Their own research with children with learning disabilities between six and seven years of age demonstrated that these children performed poorly in reading tasks as well as in math. In addition, there may be a long-term impact on reading and comprehension. Finally, they hypothesize that a contributing factor might be the lack of strategy use on the part of the children with learning disabilities.

Feagans, L., & Short, E. J. (1986). Referential communication and reading performance in learning disabled children over a 3-year period. *Developmental Psychology*, *22*, 177-183.

Feagans and Short describe referential communication as a situation in which a speaker must convey specific information about a set of materials to a naive listener. It requires "listener competence, speaker competence, and the speaker's ability to use feedback" (p. 177). They found that students with learning disabilities had greater difficulty with the listener and the speaker roles as well as with the rephrasing tasks than did the normal group. The results further suggest that communication skills may be causally related to reading achievement for students with learning disabilities which needs further investigation.

Felton, R. H., & Brown, I.S. (1990). Phonological processes as predictors of specific reading skills in children at risk for reading failure. *Reading and Writing: An Interdisciplinary Journal*, *2*, 39-59.

Felton and Brown focused their study of the at-risk kindergartner on the relationship between phonological processing and reading. The authors found no correlation among measures of phonological awareness, phonetic recoding, and phonological recoding in lexical access. Felton and Brown further state that their data "do provide support for the importance of lexical access ability in early reading" (p. 57). However, success in early reading is not dependent solely on early literacy skills but also involves the dynamics of the classroom, the attention of the child, and the relevance of the instructional methods used.

Felton, R. H., & Wood, F. B. (1992). A reading level match study of nonword reading skills in poor readers with varying IQ. *Journal of Learning Disabilities*, *25*, 318-326.

Felton and Wood studied the ability of third- and fifth-grade poor readers (reading disabled and dyslexic) to read nonwords. They found that compared to nondisabled first graders, the target group was more impaired on nonword reading. Thus, Felton and Wood suggest that there is a need for decoding assessment and intervention with poor readers because the evidence points to deficits in phonological coding that are not related to IQ. They also point out that more research is needed to identify factors that are critical in discovering the relationship between decoding and word identification and in defining reading disabilities and developing instruction.

Feuerstein, R., Jensen, M., Hoffman, M. B., & Rand, Y. (1985). Instrumental enrichment, an intervention program for structural cognitive modifiability: Theory and practice. In J. W. Segal, S. F. Chipman, and R. Glaser (Eds.), *Thinking and learning skills. Volume 1: Relating instruction to research* (pp. 43-82). Hillsdale, NJ: Lawrence Erlbaum Associates.

This chapter reports "an intervention program designed to help its recipients learn to learn and to reach higher levels of thinking" (p. 43). The primary goal is to enhance the capacity of low-functioning adolescents. These authors presume that the lack of Mediated Learning Experience [MLE] in which an adult mediates a stimulus prior to its perception by the child causes a reduced modifiability when individuals are confronted with new stimuli. Instrumental Enrichment is designed to provide MLE experiences to adolescents who have not received sufficient MLE interactions previously. The content-free program, using a series of instruments focusing on individual, specific skills, is described in detail. The results of studies conducted on the effectiveness of the Instrumental Enrichment program are included.

Fleischner, J.E., Nuzum, M.B., & Marzola, E.S. (1987). Devising an instructional program to teach arithmetic problem-solving skills to students with learning disabilities. *Journal of Learning Disabilities, 20,* 214-217.

These authors report a process designed to develop and test an instructional program to teach arithmetic story problem-solving to students with learning disabilities. They write that "some students who have adequate reading and computation skills lack the procedural, process, and task-specific knowledge necessary to solve these problems" (p. 217). The literature they review on information processing, instructional theory, and mathematics education provides helpful guidelines for teachers.

Fowler, A.E. (1988). Grammaticality judgments and reading skill in grade 2. *Annals of Dyslexia, 38,* 73-94.

Fowler explored the relationship between the ability to judge the grammaticality of sentences as well as the ability to restate grammatically incorrect sentences and reading ability in second graders. She found that poor readers could identify whether a sentence was incorrect but could not manipulate the components and restate the sentence correctly. She concluded that "it is not basic lexical and syntactic knowledge that is lacking in poor readers, but metalinguistic ability, the most unnatural skill of extracting and manipulating phonemic elements, or perhaps a broader underlying deficit in phonological processing" (p. 91). In addition, "the basic syntactic structures are intact" (p. 91), but when heavy demands are placed on short-term memory, the poor reader has difficulty manipulating the sentence. It is the lower-level processes of short-term memory, decoding, and basic phonological processes that cause difficulties in reading, including comprehension.

Frankenberger, W., & Fronzaglio, K. (1991). A review of states' criteria and procedures for identifying children with learning disabilities. *Journal of Learning Disabilities, 24,* 495-500.

This study investigated changes in states' definitions and/or eligibility criteria for learning disabilities and whether increases in students identified as learning disabled may have resulted from the criterion used in quantifying an ability/achievement discrepancy. Results indicated that 40% of states had revised their guidelines between 1988 and 1990. It also revealed that a significant relationship existed between the criterion employed in determining a discrepancy and a state's yearly increase in students with learning disabilities.

Freebody, P., & Byrne, B. (1988). Word-reading strategies in elementary school children: Relations to comprehension, reading time, and phonemic awareness. *Reading Research Quarterly, 23,* 441-452.

Freebody and Byrne examined prior research and the results of their own study with normal second- and third-grade students in an effort to clarify the role of reading words by decoding and/or recognizing sight words. They found that "failure to acquire and use efficient decoding skills will begin to take a toll on reading comprehension by Grade 3" (p. 441). Students who rely on sight work recognition and do not develop decoding skills will face potential reading difficulties as the text becomes more complex and academic demands of reading become heavier.

Freund, L.A. (1987). Classification/categorization model of instruction for learning disabled students. *Journal of Reading, Writing, and Learning Disabilities International, 3,* 309-319.

Freund describes research and an instructional model to teach classification and categorization skills to students with learning disabilities. She writes: "Practitioners are encouraged to include instruction in classification and categorization as an integral part of the curriculum, rather than as a separate sequence of 'thinking skills' objectives apart from the classroom content" (p. 317).

Frith, U. (1986).   A developmental framework for developmental dyslexia. *Annals of Dyslexia*, *36*, 69-81.

The framework provided by Frith for understanding developmental dyslexia is that of normal literacy development. Developmental is defined by the author as including both intrinsically motivated change (maturation) and extrinsically motivated skill acquisition. In order to understand the process here, we need to look at the literacy-related errors made by dyslexics and try to determine whether they occur because of an inability to use a strategy or an ability to use a strategy, but poorly, or whether the errors occur because of inappropriate efforts to compensate. Frith proposes a three-stage model by which the normal child acquires literacy: through instant word recognition (logographic), letter-sound by letter-sound analysis (alphabetic), or instant recognition of the morphemic parts of a word using letter order (orthographic). Progress thorough the stages may be uneven with compensatory strategies used as transitions and with each stage building on the prior one. The implications of this for developmental dyslexia are several. First, developmental dyslexia must be limited to the disorder and should not include developmental delay because these latter problems will not continue after the initial stages of reading acquisition. In addition, the later in the stage that the disorder occurs, the less serious is the disorder because the child will already have a growing base of knowledge and skills that can be used. Frith further distinguished developmental dyslexia from acquired dyslexia, which can occur during any aspect of learning to read. Examples are provided to illustrate the stages.

Fulk, B.J.M., Mastropieri, M.A., & Scruggs, T.E. (1992). Mnemonic generalization training with learning disabled adolescents. *Learning Disabilities Research and Practice*, 7, 2-10.

This study investigated the effect of intensive generalization training focused on the development of complex mnemonic strategies. These strategies were learned in order to facilitate the ability of students with learning disabilities to transfer the strategy to independent use. One-on-one training sessions including learning vocabulary, science, and social studies yielded better results than students not taught the mnemonic strategies. The authors point out that classroom-based research is needed to examine the effectiveness of more intensive, long-term instruction.

Furlong, M.J., (1988). An examination of the simple difference score distribution model in learning disability identification. *Psychology in the Schools*, 25, 132-143.

Furlong describes the simple difference score distribution model and examines the mandated implementation of this method in California. A potential problem with this method is the risk of "potential biases against subgroups in the LD referral population" (p. 133). He found that referral status of students was a better predictor of placement than was the discrepancy score.

Gajria, M., & Salvia, J. (1992). The effects of summarization instruction on text comprehension of students with learning disabilities. *Exceptional Children*, 58, 508-516.

Students in grades 6-9 with learning disabilities showed improved reading comprehension after they learned a metacognitive strategy for summarizing expository text. The students were given direct instruction on five rules of summarization. Usage of the strategy was maintained over time, and students reported that they employed the strategy in other settings.

Garcia, E.E. (1994). "Hispanic" children: Effective schooling practices and related policy issues. In N. Ellsworth, C. Hedley, and A. Baratta (Eds.), *Literacy: A Redefinition* (pp. 77-87). Hillsdale, NJ: Erlbaum.

In introducing guidelines for instruction of Hispanic children, Garcia presents demographic information for the United States and for California that documents the need for our attention. He provides a case study of two elementary schools, grades K-5, over a two-year period that illustrates effective instructional practices. Elements of this model include: good communication between teacher and students, student collaboration, and instruction of basic skills and academic content organized around themes that were usually selected by students in consultation with the teacher. The child-centered curriculum that ensued seemed to enhance motivation for student learning. Garcia concludes that "academic learning has its roots in language experiences and processes of communication . . . opportunities for speaking, listening, reading, and writing along with native language scaffolding to help guide students through the learning process" (p. 85).

Garner, R., Alexander, P.A., & Hare, V.C. (1991). Reading comprehension failure in children. In B.Y.L. Wong (Ed.), *Learning about learning disabilities* (pp. 284-309). New York: Academic Press.

Garner, Alexander, and Hare (1991) remind us that many factors besides poor decoding skills can cause reading comprehension problems. These authors include the following additional causes: "confusion about task demands, insufficient domain knowledge, insufficient comprehension monitoring, low self-esteem, and low interest in task" (p. 283). They correctly point out the interrelated nature of all of the causes of comprehension failure.

Gaskins, R. W., Gaskins, J. C., & Gaskins, I. (1992). Using what you know to figure out what you don't know: An analogy approach to decoding. *Reading and Writing Quarterly: Overcoming Learning Difficulties, 8,* 197-221.

Gaskins, Gaskins, and Gaskins developed a program for poor readers based on theory and research. Poor readers need a strategy beyond use of context to read words. They need explicit instruction on word parts, a basic sight vocabulary, as well as phonological awareness and sound-symbol association skills. They can benefit from the analogous word strategy used by good readers. Above all, poor readers need to become flexible in their approach to identifying words. The article contains a thorough description of the program.

Gelzheiser, L. M. (1987). Reducing the number of students identified as learning disabled: A question of practice, philosophy or policy? *Exceptional Children, 54,* 145-150.

Gelzheiser points out that "because of rising identification rates and evidence of overidentification, it has been suggested that those who fail to meet expectations be accommodated by modifying classroom instruction" (p. 145). She goes on to present arguments that support the idea that the accommodation of exceptional students in the mainstream should be facilitated.

Gerber, P. J., & Reiff, H. B. (1991). *Speaking for themselves: Ethnographic interviews with adults with learning disabilities.* Ann Arbor, MI: University of Michigan Press.

Gerber and Reiff interviewed in depth nine adults with learning disabilities in this ethnographic study. Although some are unemployed and some are successful professionals, the persistence of learning disabilities into these individuals' adult lives is striking. Subjects described the disabling impact of failure that begot more failure in their educational, social/emotional, and vocational growth. They also explored the assistance and compensatory strategies that seemed most effective: having sufficient early successes, family and school support, and exceedingly hard work. Speaking for themselves, these interviewees provide direction for professionals working with students with reading and learning disabilities.

German, D., Johnson, B., & Schneider, M. (1985). Learning disability versus reading disability: A survey of practitioners' diagnostic populations and test instruments. *Learning Disability Quarterly, 8,* 141-157.

German, Johnson, and Schneider surveyed reading resource professionals and learning disabilities professionals, including both self-contained and resource professionals, to determine the differences and similarities in assessments of reading disorders by these groups. The authors point out that the learning disabilities specialists work with a group of students presumed to follow the guidelines of PL 94-142. Therefore, those students are generally of average or above average intelligence, while those of below-average intelligence or from non-English speaking backgrounds might be more likely to be referred to reading specialists. Both groups of professionals identified language deficits as a matter of concern but generally did not use language tests in the assessment of process. Perceptual and motor tests were more likely to be used by learning disabilities specialists than by reading specialists. Both groups used reading tests to identify reading strengths and weaknesses.

Gibbs, D.P., & Cooper, E.G. (1989). Prevalence of communication disorders in students with learning disabilities. *Journal of Learning Disabilities*, 22, 60-63.

Gibbs and Cooper investigated the prevalence of articulation, language, voice, fluency, and hearing problems among eight- to twelve-year-old children with learning disabilities. They reported that language deficits were found in more than 90% of the children; however, only 6% were receiving the services of a speech-language pathologist. In addition, the authors found that the prevalence of these problems was neither sex nor age related, suggesting that children do not outgrow these difficulties.

Glowacki, J. (1990). Literature especially with remedial readers. *Journal of Reading*, *33*, 553-554.

In this brief article, Glowacki offers suggestions for incorporating literature into the daily reading instruction of junior high school remedial students. She suggests that teachers read aloud to their students and that they match students' interests when helping them select literature to read.

Graham, L., & Wong, B. Y. L. (1993). Comparing two modes of teaching a question-answering strategy for enhancing reading comprehension: Didactic and self-instructional training. *Journal of Learning Disabilities*, *26*, 270-279.

Graham and Wong, using both average and poor readers in fifth and sixth grade, investigated two issues: whether the use of a specific metacognitive question answering strategy (QAR) would increase comprehension, and whether self-instruction or didactic training in the strategy would be more effective. They found that the use of the strategy did increase comprehension and that the self-instructional training was more effective than the didactic for both the immediate task and for maintaining strategy use.

Graham, S., & Harris, K. R. (1990). Self-instructional strategy development. *Learning Disabilities Forum, 16,* 15-22.

Graham and Harris identify strategy instruction as one of the most important instructional procedures for use with learning disabled students. They base this conclusion on research that has demonstrated that learning disabled students can learn to use strategies that they might not discover or use by themselves "since they often employ ineffective strategies or fail to engage in these processes at all" (p. 15). While there is lack of agreement on one particular method of instruction, they suggest that instruction should provide students with mastery of the strategy, knowledge of its use and significance, and self-regulatory skills in strategy development and use. Using written expression as the example, the authors provide a detailed description with a "metascript" of how to provide this kind of instruction to students.

Graham, S., & Harris, K.R. (1994). Cognitive strategy instruction: Methodological issues and guidelines in conducting research. In S. Vaughn and C. Bos (Eds.), *Research issues in learning disabilities: Theory, methodology, assessment, and ethics* (pp. 146-162). New York: Springer-Verlag.

Graham and Harris summarize what we know about cognitive strategy instruction as well as providing guidelines for conducting research. They discuss which strategies should be studied, how they should be taught, and how strategy instruction should be evaluated. Graham and Harris conclude that although cognitive strategy instruction is not common in either special or regular classrooms, it offers significant educational promise.

Graham, S., & Johnson, L. A. (1989). Research-supported teacher activities that influence the text reading of students with learning disabilities. *Learning Disabilities Forum*, *15*, 27-30.

This article discusses instructional procedures that increase fluency and/or comprehension for students with learning disabilities. The authors remind us of several requisites for success. First, materials should be attractive and at the students' instruction level to avoid frustration. Second, deductive text organization (main idea plus supportive details) is easier to comprehend than inductive organization (main idea later in text or to be inferred). Third, illustrations containing information that can be used to obtain the desired outcome assist the reader. Principles of teaching and learning that are discussed include previewing text, activating prior knowledge, making predictions, setting goals through an introduction of key concepts and new vocabulary, using advanced organizers, and text summary.

Graves, A. W. (1986). Effects of direct instruction and metacomprehension training on finding main ideas. *Learning Disabilities Research*, *1*, 90-100.

Graves conducted a research study that investigated the effect of direct instruction alone and direct instruction plus self-monitoring on the ability of students with learning disabilities to find the main idea. Results suggested that direct instruction plus self-monitoring was most effective but that direct instruction alone was more effective than the control condition. Graves reminds us that metacognitive strategies can help students with learning disabilities to improve their reading comprehension.

Graves, M.F. (1987). The roles of instruction in fostering vocabulary development. In M.G. McKeown and M.E. Curtis (Eds.), *The nature of vocabulary acquisition*

(pp. 165-184).   Hillsdale, NJ: Lawrence Erlbaum
Associates.

Graves discusses a variety of roles that instruction can play
in fostering students' vocabulary development. He lists three
goals of vocabulary instruction (learning words, learning to learn
words, and learning about words), and he notes that instruction
directed at any of these three goals will foster achievement in the
others as well.   Graves reminds us of the need to promote
students' desire to acquire word meanings, and motivation is an
important part of the long-term comprehensive plan of instruction
that he proposes. Both contextual learning and direct instruction
in word meanings are important in this model.

Gresham, F.M., & Reschley, D.J. (1988).   Issues in the
conceptualization, classification, and assessment of social
skills in the mildly handicapped.   In T.R. Kratochwill
(Ed.), *Advances in school psychology* (pp. 203-247).
Hillsdale, NJ: Lawrence Erlbaum Associates.

These authors examine the relevance of social skills for
mainstreaming learners with mild disabilities.   They conclude
that social competence should receive more emphasis in the
identification and placement of students and that assessment of
these skills should be conducted routinely during the evaluation
of students with disabilities.

Griffey, Jr., Q.L., Zigmond, N., & Leinhardt, G. (1988). The
effects of self-questioning and story structure training on
the reading comprehension of poor readers. *Learning
Disabilities Research, 4*, 45-51.

Griffey, Zigmond, and Leinhardt review the importance of
metacomprehension, "defined as the active monitoring of the
reading process, the awareness of the state of reading
comprehension, and the application of strategies to remediate

comprehension failures" (p. 45). They review some of the strategies good readers use to comprehend text, including summarizing text, altering reading pace, rereading new material, and self-generating questions. All of these strategies require the active participation of the reader in the task of comprehending. Then, the authors remind us that students with learning disabilities are frequently characterized as poor readers. The results of a study constructed with elementary students with learning disabilities suggest the usefulness of providing direct instruction in using self-generated questions to identify the elements of story grammar for learning disabled students. The combination of two metacognitive strategies (knowledge and use of story structure) appears to be "a potentially valuable addition to the classroom teacher's repertoire of instructional methods for enhancing the reading comprehension of LD readers" (p. 50).

Griffin, C.C., Simmons, D.C., & Kameenui, E.J. (1991). Investigating the effectiveness of graphic organizer instruction on the comprehension and recall of science content by students with learning disabilities. *Journal of Reading, Writing, and Learning Disabilities International*, 7, 355-376.

Griffin, Simmons, and Kameenui examined the effect of graphic organizers on fifth- and sixth-grade resource room students' acquisition and recall of science content from mainstream text. No difference was found between the mastery of students in the graphics organizer group and the control group. The investigators suggest two likely reasons that may inform us of important principles. First, the mainstream science textbook was used, and the resource room students' reading levels were considerably lower; the investigators concluded that in future studies, the textual material should be appropriate for the reading level of students. Second, they concluded that the graphic organizers had not depicted sufficiently explicitly the linkages among ideas.

Groff, P. (1991). Word recognition and critical reading. *Journal of Reading, Writing, and Learning Disabilities International, 7,* 17-31.

Groff asserts that automatic word recognition is so important to critical reading that we must provide direct instruction in it, not leave it to chance. The reader has to be able to read individual words in order to critique the author's message. Because of this conviction, Groff concludes that "direct, systematic, and intensive instruction in word recognition is called for. The whole language argument to the contrary is unsound, and thus must be rejected" (p. 29).

Groshong, C.C. (1988, February). *Teaching group participation skills to the learning disabled: A key to effective mainstreaming.* Paper presented at the International Conference of the Association for Children and Adults with Learning Disabilities, Las Vegas, NV.

Groshong used Junior Great Books discussions to teach critical thinking skills and independent learning behaviors to fifth grade students with learning disabilities. In this paper she suggests a series of skills hierarchies in the areas of listening, group interaction, discussion, and thinking that would be helpful to teachers interested in using this type of instruction. Groshong reports that establishing an effective group interaction structure appears to be the most important factor in achieving progress in building discussion skills.

Groteluschen, A.K., Borkowski, J.G., & Hale, C. (1990). Strategy instruction is often insufficient: Addressing the interdependency of executive and attributional processes. In T.E. Scruggs and B.Y.L. Wong (Eds.), *Intervention research in learning disabilities* (pp. 81-101). New York: Springer-Verlag.

Groteluschen, Borkowski, and Hale recognize the need for strategy instruction for students with learning disabilities who frequently do not engage in strategy use and application in new tasks. The authors present their model of metacognition, which, based on "improving performance through the deliberate use of a strategy" (pp. 81-82), forms the basis for the discussion. The transfer of strategies is particularly difficult for students with learning disabilities. Extensive training is not the answer. Self-attribution, self-esteem, and locus of control are all an important part of the development of strategy use and transfer. The authors review suggestions for developing these variables. In addition, students need to assume executive control of the process. Studies in this area are also examined.

Gurney, D., Gersten, R., Dimino, J., & Carnine, D. (1990). Story grammar: Effective literature instruction for high school students with learning disabilities. *Journal of Learning Disabilities*, *23*, 335-342.

This study investigated the effectiveness of story grammar instruction in teaching comprehension of literature to adolescents with learning disabilities. The story grammar technique that they used was an adaptation of similar techniques that have been employed at the elementary school level. The investigators were particularly interested in improving students' ability to make sophisticated inferences about character, plot, and motivation. Although the sample was small, the findings of the study suggest that comprehension of adolescents can be improved by learning story grammar.

Hallahan, D.P. (1992). Some thoughts on why the prevalence of learning disabilities has increased. *Journal of Learning Disabilities*, *25*, 523-528.

Hallahan explores possible reasons for the increase in the identification of children with learning disabilities. He presents the logic of critics who maintain that these children are "more a myth than a reality" (p. 523) as well as that of others who argue that at least some of the increased identification probably represents students who are genuinely in need of learning disabilities services.

Hammill, D.D. (1993). A brief look at the learning disabilities movement in the United States. *Journal of Learning Disabilities, 26,* 295-310.

In this article Hammill reviews the development of the learning disabilities movement in the United States. He begins with ideas that contributed to its theoretical basis. Next, he discusses the events between 1963 and 1990 that established learning disabilities as a recognized field. Finally, Hammill provides a glimpse into the future. This organized and informative presentation illuminates a complex, and, at times, contradictory venture.

Haney, G., & Thistlethwaite, L. (1991). A model critical reading lesson for secondary high-risk students. *Journal of Reading, Writing, and Learning Disabilities, 7,* 337-354.

This article defines critical reading, discusses associated frameworks, and lists considerations for changing topics and reading materials. The authors present an example of a critical reading lesson and suggest guidelines for teachers working with students with learning disabilities on critical reading skills. In conclusion, Haney and Thistlethwaite state that they believe the success the students experienced is in large part due to the fact that the investigators "made the process less abstract by providing a visual map that allowed the students to 'see' the steps of the strategy as parts of an integrated process" (p. 350).

Hargis, C.H., Terhaar-Yonkers, M., Williams, P.C., & Reed, M.T. (1988). Repetition requirements for word recognition. *Journal of Reading, 31,* 320-327.

Hargis, Terhaar-Yonkers, Williams, and Reed (1988) studied how rapidly students with learning disabilities were able to recognize words and how many repetitions it took to make that recognition automatic under different conditions. The conditions explored the interaction between the meaningfulness of the word itself, the use of context in the process of identification, and the decodability of the word. They cite several useful conclusions. Words presented in context as well as those that were meaningful required fewer repetitions for mastery. Decodability was important but not as important as the other two variables. The interactions were particularly interesting. Low-imagery words with little concrete meaning required context with substantial repetition for mastery. It is important to remember that many of the basic words children need to learn are low-imagery words. High-imagery, decodable words required the fewest repetitions for mastery. The problem is compounded because one way to read words in context is to read text. Poor readers can't read text, so they don't get the repetition. The teacher's role is to ensure that students with learning disabilities encounter words in a variety of readable text, whether written by others, by the teacher, or by peers.

Harris, K.R., & Pressley, M. (1991). The nature of cognitive strategy instruction: Interactive strategy construction. *Exceptional Children, 57,* 392-404.

Harris and Pressley discuss and illustrate the basis and nature of good cognitive strategy instruction and its contribution to the education of students with learning disabilities. They make the point that both teachers and students are constructing knowledge during strategy instruction. In addition, they examine the nature of good cognitive strategy instruction and provide illustrations of several models of instruction in the areas of reading comprehension, writing, and memory. Maintenance, generalization, and teacher implementation of these strategy instructional approaches are also examined. Harris and Pressley conclude that "good strategy instruction entails making students aware of the purposes of strategies, how and why they work, and when and where they can be used" (p. 401).

Haskell, D.W., Foorman, B.R., & Swank, P.R. (1992). Effects of three orthographic/phonological units on first-grade reading. *Remedial and Special Education (RASE)*, *13*, 40-49.

Haskell, Foorman, and Swank examine the effects of instruction in whole word recognition, phoneme-grapheme correspondence and use, and onset-rime recognition and use. The latter was included because it appeared from the research literature to be easier for beginners than the use of individual phonemes and could be generalized to other words, as compared to the limited generalization of whole words. The authors found that normal first graders in the onset-rime group were more successful than the other two groups and were more accurate on exception words. "A potential advantage of the onset-rime level of instruction . . . may be that it gives students more flexibility than they would get from individual phoneme instruction when reading exception words" (p. 46).

Healy, J.M., & Aram, D. M. (1986). Hyperlexia and dyslexia: A family study. *Annals of Dyslexia*, *38*, 237-252.

Healy and Aram examine the possibility of genetic transmission of hyperlexia in which very young children can read but not comprehend advanced text, and they relate this to the transmission of dyslexia. They write that "developmental dyslexia may be defined as a complex of disorders which affect information processing strategies related to encoding or comprehension of written language, particularly manifest in reading, writing or spelling problems" p. 241. Also, the authors remind us that "several comprehensive studies . . . have confirmed genetic transmission of dyslexia, probably of several different forms, with a sex-related difference in expression" (p. 241). Healy and Aram conclude that hyperlexia is a sex-influenced family-transmitted developmental disorder of reading and language.

Hedley, C.N., Hedley, W.E., & Baratta, A.N. (1994). Visual thinking and literacy. In N. Ellsworth, C. Hedley, and A. Baratta (Eds.), *Literacy: A redefinition* (pp. 109-126). Hillsdale, NJ: Lawrence Erlbaum Associates.

Visual thinking or imagery is an important means of critical thinking and problem solving. This chapter first presents an historical overview of visual thinking in which the authors conclude that verbal thinking appears to have eclipsed visual thinking in recent times. It then goes on to discuss how we learn through imagery and imagination and to examine ways in which teachers can use these applications in their classrooms.

Henry, M.K. (1988). Beyond phonics: Integrated decoding and spelling instruction based on word origin and structure. *Annals of Dyslexia, 38,* 258-275.

According to Henry, dyslexic students must be taught letter-sound correspondences, common word divisions, syllables and morphemes, and word origin in order to facilitate their ability to decode the printed word into a series of sounds that is a real word. Henry found that students had little knowledge of the structural components of words. Further, she found it was common for a student to recognize the correct spelling for a dictated word but to have trouble spelling the word from dictation. Henry cites the Stanford Project as having successfully combined language-based decoding and spelling curriculum.

Findings indicated that students who are dyslexic benefitted greatly from the discussions and that the lessons, based on word origin and structure, helped students understand that words of different origin may have different patterns. Henry identifies a need for morphemic structural analysis because "phonics" only offers a help for short, regular words.

Herber, H.L., & Herber, J.N. (1993). *Teaching in content areas with reading, writing, and reasoning*. Boston, MA: Allyn and Bacon.

This book presents ways to teach the content of academic subjects while simultaneously teaching the relevant reading, writing, and reasoning skills. Herber and Herber write, "We take as our first premise the belief that subject-area teachers are interested principally in teaching their course content, the substance of their disciplines" (p. v). The reality of their assumption, the basis for the book, allows them to address in practical terms ways in which classroom teachers from the intermediate grades through college can incorporate instruction in needed literacy skills to support the teaching of course content.

Herr, C. M. (1988). Strategies for gaining information. *Teaching Exceptional Children*, *20*, 53-55.

This brief article directed at classroom teachers suggests using advance organizers to teach self-questioning summarization and paraphrasing strategies in content areas to readers with learning disabilities. Herr provides examples from science, history, and English.

Hicks, J.S. (1988). Using microcomputers to teach reading, writing, and spelling to the special child. In C.N. Hedley and J.S. Hicks (Eds.), *Reading and the special learner* (pp. 215-230). Norwood, NJ: Ablex.

Hicks suggests practical ways for classroom teachers to use computers to instruct students with mild disabilities in the language arts, from the preschool level on up. He also comments on the need for teacher training that will prepare teachers who are competent and comfortable with this technology.

Hicks, J.S. (1993). A whole language approach to teaching reading to the special learner. In A. Carrasquillo and C. Hedley (Eds.), *Whole language and the bilingual learner*. Norwood, NJ: Ablex.

Hicks concludes that "the use of the whole language approach in the area of semantics, or extracting meaning from either oral or written language, is highly applauded" (p. 179). He presents reasons for incorporating a whole language approach and reviews some of the problems that he sees with instructional methods favored in the past.

Higgins, K., & Boone, R. (1991). Hypermedia CAI: A supplement to an elementary school basal reader program. *Journal of Special Education Technology, 11,* 1-15.

This article reports results from the first year of a three-year study of the effects of hypermedia computer-assisted instructional reading materials for grades K-3. The hypermedia materials were planned to enable the participation of both students with and without disabilities, and they provided students additional information about words and concepts from their basal text. The results of the investigation suggest that this is a promising tool for poor readers.

Hill, L.B., & Hale, M.G. (1991). Reading Recovery: Questions classroom teachers ask. *The Reading Teacher, 44,* 480-483.

Hill and Hale describe the Reading Recovery program in some detail, comparing it to other approaches used in teaching beginning reading. In other programs, first the child learns a letter and then the sound of the letter. These are taught in a prescribed sequence. In Reading Recovery, first the child hears the sound in a word and then identifies the symbol. The sounds and symbols are taught according to the needs of the text and the child, not according to a set sequence. "Reading recovery children are taught to use cues and strategies rather than to memorize skills in order to read fluently" (p. 481). The emphasis is on providing a broad approach to teaching reading to at-risk first graders.

Hittleman, D.R. (1988). Using literature to develop daily-living literacy: Strategies for students with learning difficulties. *Journal of Reading, Writing, and Learning Disabilities International, 4,* 1-12.

Hittleman discusses practical ways in which literature based on real-life situations and problems can be used to help students improve daily-living literacy skills. He also applies this instructional technique to actual daily-living materials such as election ballots and sales slips; he stresses that the actual material should be used instructionally rather than a watered-down version from a workbook.

Ho, H.Z., Gilger, J. W., & Decker, S. N. (1988). A twin study of Bannatyne's "genetic dyslexic" subtype. *Journal of Child Psychology and Psychiatry as Allied Disciplines, 29,* 63-72.

This study evaluated Bannatyne's proposed "genetic dyslexic" subtype of reading disability. The authors clarify that "dyslexia may be defined as an unexpected difficulty in the development of reading and spelling that occurs in the absence of lowered intelligence, socioeconomic disadvantage, primary emotional disturbance, peripheral sensory deficits, or gross neurological impairment" (p. 63). Dyslexia is synonymous with reading disability, specific reading disability, developmental dyslexia and specific developmental dyslexia. There is much evidence that dyslexia is "a heterogeneous disorder with different subtypes" (p. 63).

Little known about these subtypes. Bannatyne identified one subtype that was found to run in families and assumed to be genetic. These authors obtained data from 60 pairs of twins in which at least one twin had a reading disorder. Results suggest, but do not provide conclusive evidence, a genetic etiology. The authors conclude that "individuals with this particular profile may constitute a specific subtype of reading disability" (p. 63).

Hodgson, J. (1992). The status of metalinguistic skills in reading development. *Journal of Learning Disabilities*, *25*, 96-101.

Hodgson reacts to Sawyer's article, which stresses the critical importance of phonological abilities, particularly segmentation of phonemes, words, and sentences, in the hierarchy of early reading stages. He reviews evidence suggesting that metaphonological abilities are not necessary and/or sufficient to ensure the development of reading competence. Reading development "may intimately involve more abstract elements of the linguistic system" (p. 100).

Hollingsworth, P.M., & Reutzel, D.R. (1988). Whole language with LD children. *Academic Therapy*, *23*, 477-488.

Hollingsworth and Reutzel suggest that we use practices consistent with whole language theory in order to enable students with language learning disabilities to become competent users of language as a communication medium. To educate this population, approaches must be interdisciplinary. Historically, instruction for students with learning disabilities was reserved for the special education and remedial reading teachers. The instruction used generally broke down reading and writing skills into subsets and subskills. The authors cite research that raises questions about this approach. For example, children lose sight of the holistic nature of reading and writing when they only practice subskills and when reading consists of worksheets. An analogy is made to the process a child uses to learn oral language in which learning is based on real experiences and built on the child's strengths. Many suggestions are made to implement this view of reading instruction in a classroom setting.

Horn, C.C., & Manis, F.R. (1985). Normal and disabled readers' use of orthographic structure in processing print. *Journal of Reading Behavior, 17,* 143-161.

Horn and Manis review the relationship between the ways in which different models of reading view print processing, particularly the use of orthographic structure. In their study, the authors examined the use of orthographic structure by disabled and nondisabled fifth- and sixth-grade students as well as a group of nondisabled third graders. They found that disabled students relied more on orthographic structure to read words than did nondisabled students of the same age and to the same extent that younger nondisabled students did. They concluded that students did this "to compensate for deficiencies in other aspects of word recognition" (p. 158), supporting Stanovich's (1980) interactive-compensatory hypothesis.

Horton, S.V., & Lovitt, T.C. (1989). Using study guides with three classifications of secondary students. *Journal of Special Education, 22,* 447-462.

Horton and Lovitt report the findings of two studies that examined the effectiveness of study guides in increasing the comprehension of learning disabled, remedial, and regular education students in secondary science and social studies classes. The results suggest that students using study guides produced higher performance than those not using the guides.

Horton, S. V., Lovitt, T. C., & Christensen, C. C. (1991). Matching three classifications of secondary students to differential levels of study guides. *Journal of Learning Disabilities, 24,* 518-529.

This article presents a study in which remedial, nondisabled, and learning disabled students enrolled in social studies and science classes were assigned to differential levels of study guides. Multilevel study guides containing different levels of referential cues were found to be more effective than single-level study guides that did not contain referential cues. These effects applied to all groups of students on both factual and interpretive questions. The authors suggest practical guidelines for matching students with appropriate levels of study guides.

Horton, S.V., Lovitt, T.C., & Givens, A. (1988). A computer-based vocabulary program for three categories of student. *British Journal of Educational Technology, 19,* 131-143.

Two experiments tested the effects of computer-based instruction on the vocabulary achievement of high school learning disabled students, remedial readers, and general education students. The remedial students and those with learning disabilities made significant gains on computer items after only one or two sessions.

Horton, S.V., Lovitt, T.C., Givens, A., & Nelson, R. (1989). Teaching social studies to high school students with academic handicaps in a mainstreamed setting: Effects of a computerized study guide. *Journal of Learning Disabilities, 22,* 102-107.

Reading and Learning Disabilities

This study investigates the effects on textbook comprehension of a computerized study guide in comparison to a notetaking condition. Subjects were remedial students and students with learning disabilities enrolled in a geography class. Both groups of students achieved higher performance using a computerized study guide than did those taking notes.

Houck, C.K. (1987). Teaching LD adolescents to read. *Academic Therapy*, 22, 229-237.

Houck recognizes the difficulty of teaching adolescent students with learning disabilities because of their history of failure, with its concomitant decline in self-esteem and motivation. She provides numerous suggestions for structuring an educational environment with suitable materials and instructional strategies. She advocates the use of direct instruction, student involvement, and the monitoring of outcomes.

Howell, M.J., & Manis, F.R. (1986). Developmental and reader ability differences in semantic processing efficiency. *Journal of Educational Psychology*, 78, 124-129.

This study, conducted with second-third and fifth-sixth grade students found that readers with learning disabilities required more time than normal readers to retrieve categorical information from memory. The authors concluded that the differences obtained were due to speed of processing, not to failure to categorize and organize information in semantic memory. This lack of speed did not seem to be limited to the processing of words but also was evident in the semantic processing of picture information.

Hudson, P., Lignugaris-Kraft, B., & Miller, T. (1993). Using content enhancement to improve the performance of adolescents with learning disabilities in content classes. *Learning Disabilities Research & Practice*, *8*, 106-125.

This article describes content enhancements, which are techniques used by the teacher to help students identify, organize, comprehend, and memorize critical content information. Content enhancements have been found to benefit all students in content-area classes such as history and science. This article describes each type of content enhancement and reviews its use with secondary students with learning disabilities. The content enhancements discussed include visual displays, advance organizers, study guides, mnemonics, peer mediation, audiotapes, and computer-assisted instruction. The authors conclude that "content enhancements and effective teaching practices can be used throughout an effective instructional cycle to improve the performance of all students in content classes" (p. 125).

Hughes, C.A., & Smith, J.O. (1990). Cognitive and academic performance of college students with learning disabilities: A synthesis of the literature. *Learning Disability Quarterly*, *13*, 66-79.

Hughes and Smith examined the finding of 26 studies of the cognitive and academic performance of college students with learning disabilities. They reviewed, in some detail, implications for the academic areas. They determined that the "reading problems characteristic of school-aged students with learning problems are found to persist into young adulthood. The areas of greatest difficulty appear to be comprehension and reading rate" (p. 71).

Hurford, D.P. (1990). Training phonemic segmentation ability with a phonemic discrimination intervention in second- and third-grade children with reading disabilities. *Journal of Learning Disabilities*, *23*, 564-569.

Hurford reports a study using children chosen from classrooms comprised of learning disabled or reading disabled students. The purpose of the study was to determine whether phonemic discrimination training might aid phonemic segmentation ability. The results indicated that in order to teach phonemic segmentation we need to teach phonemic discrimination first. The author also suggests that we might combine direct instruction in the skills and interaction with meaningful text.

Hurford, D.P., Darrow, L.J., Edwards, T.L., Howerton, C.J., Mote, C.R., Schauf, J.D., & Coffey, P. (1993). An examination of phonemic processing abilities in children during their first-grade year. *Journal of Learning Disabilities, 26,* 167-177.

Hurford et al. review research concerned with the role of phonological processing in beginning reading and the potential difference for reading disabled, garden-variety poor readers, and normal first-grade readers. The results indicated that there were few differences between reading disabled and garden-variety poor readers but that "both performed differently than the children without reading disabilities" (p. 167). The study demonstrated that it was possible to identify these children early in their school careers. The implications of the study are clearly identified. Children who are potentially at-risk for reading difficulties should receive instruction in phonological processing skills.

Hutchinson, N.L. (1993). Integrative strategy instruction: An elusive ideal for teaching adolescents with learning disabilities. *Journal of Learning Disabilities, 26,* 428-432.

Hutchinson comments on Ellis' (1993a) model for Integrative Strategy Instruction in this article. She suggests that Ellis' model requires validation and that Ellis should address the question of how one successfully implements educational change. She concludes that "integrative strategy instruction remains an elusive ideal for teaching adolescents with learning disabilities" (p. 431).

Idol, L. (1987a). A critical thinking map to improve content area comprehension of poor readers. *Remedial and Special Education (RASE)*, *8*, 28-40.

Idol taught secondary students to use a mapping strategy for thinking critically about expository text in U.S. government and history. The teacher modeled the strategy, then led students in completing the map, then encouraged students to complete the map independently. After this instruction, participants performed better on comprehension of passages from a different social studies text and on a test of reading comprehension.

Idol, L. (1987b). Group story mapping: A comprehension strategy for both skilled and unskilled readers. *Journal of Learning Disabilities*, *20*, 196-205.

Idol's study focuses on the manner in which students can be taught comprehension using a schema-based approach in large group instructional situations. She demonstrates the success of story mapping in groups of learning-disabled, low-achieving, and high-achieving students.

Idol, L., & Croll, V. J. (1987). Story-mapping training as a means of improving reading comprehension. *Learning Disability Quarterly*, *10*, 214-229.

Idol and Croll advocate providing instruction in using a story map to organize and store information about narrative texts. They cite previous research to support the efficacy of this approach, which relates to the reader's prior knowledge of text structure. Direct instruction was used with five students in the procedure. The results indicated an improvement in "comprehension on daily reading lessons" (p. 257). The improvement was maintained when the students no longer used the mapping strategy.

Individuals with Disabilities Education Act (IDEA). Public Law
    101-476 (1990).

IDEA is a reauthorization of the earlier *Education for All Handicapped Children Act* (1975). It employs the terms "disabilities" rather than "handicaps" and "individuals" rather than "children." In addition to retaining the mandates of the earlier law, it recognizes new categories of disabilities such as autism and requires transition plans for adolescents with disabilities.

Ingram, C.F., & Dettenmaier, L. (1987). LD college students
    and reading problems. *Academic Therapy*, *22*, 513-519.

Ingram and Dettenmaier address two issues of importance to those planning programs for college students with learning disabilities: 1) What are the characteristics of these students? 2) Should we remediate their difficulties or provide instruction in compensatory strategies? A review of the student profiles at a major university showed that these students had average intelligence with performance scores on the WAIS-R significantly higher than the verbal scores. They generally had low reading achievement and did not do well in college courses where the ability to read was important for success in gathering and understanding information. They also demonstrated a lack of attention based on an analysis of the arithmetic, digit symbol, information and digit span subtests of the WAIS-R. This cluster, frequently used to discriminate children with learning disabilities, was also found useful in discriminating these young adults with learning disabilities from normal students. In addition, there appeared to be difficulties in remembering and using mnemonic strategies. Students frequently failed to decode words automatically. The authors conclude that it was useful to provide compensatory strategies such as asking for help in reading and note-taking by getting aid from a peer, using a tape recorder or getting assistance from a special services center.

Isaacson, S.L. (1992). Volleyball and other analogies: A response to Englert. *Journal of Learning Disabilities, 25,* 173-177.

In responding to Englert's (1992) article in which she places writing in a sociocultural perspective, Isaacson reaffirms her general philosophy as well as her success in providing students both with an understanding of how texts are organized and with procedural knowledge about writing. He concludes that Englert's strategies are "exciting in their effects" (p. 177) and that "students with and without learning disabilities can benefit from learning text structures and cognitive strategies" (p. 177).

Iversen, S., & Tunmer, W.E. (1993). Phonological processing skills and the Reading Recovery program. *Journal of Educational Psychology, 85,* 112-126.

Iversen and Tunmer investigated whether systematic instruction in word analysis skills in conjunction with a Reading Recovery program would enhance the acquisition of reading skills for at-risk students. The investigators did not use a skill-and-drill approach but rather a metacognitive approach. They used phonograms and an onset-rime strategy with words that came from stories already read. The teacher modeled the strategy; the child made words with magnetic letters. The approach required two phonological processing skills: phonological awareness and phonological recoding. Emphasis was placed on the transfer to unknown words, on "developing metacognitive knowledge and strategies for identifying and spelling unfamiliar words, not on 'knowing' a particular list of words" p. 118. The authors found that children in the modified Reading Recovery program reached a stage of discontinuing the program faster than standard Reading Recovery students and learned to read "much more quickly" (p. 123).

Jansky, J. J. (1986). Language and the developing child: Pivotal ideas of Katrina de Hirsch. *Annals of Dyslexia, 36,* 196-214.

Jansky reviews the long career and many contributions made by de Hirsch to the field of dyslexia, including, for example, her emphasis on organizational problems with language as well as the many aspects of the concept of maturational lag. She reminds us of de Hirsch's focus on the possibility of prediction of failure and the need for intervention.

Jenkins, J. R., Heliotis, J., Haynes, M., & Beck, K. (1986). Does passive learning account for disabled readers' comprehension deficits in ordinary reading situations? *Learning Disability Quarterly, 9,* 69-76.

Jenkins, Heliotis, Haynes, and Beck identify critical characteristics of the learning disabled reader, which include "problems in focusing and sustaining attention" (p. 69) and passivity, which may result in failure to choose, use, and monitor appropriate learning strategies. The present study was designed to investigate these two issues using reading tasks in an elementary school environment with individual or group instruction. An additional individual condition required that the student restate the text that had been read, a condition designed to encourage attention and self-monitoring. The results were inconclusive and did not demonstrate a consistent or strong difference between regular and disabled readers in the different conditions. The authors suggest this may have been due to methodological considerations. However, there did seem to be some indication that restating text was helpful to both groups, for the groups appeared to "comprehend more when they employ a strategy for monitoring their attention and comprehension, such as [the] restatement procedure" (p.75).

Jenkins, J. R., Heliotis, J. D., Stein, M. L., & Haynes, M. C. (1987). Improving reading comprehension by using paragraph restatements. *Exceptional Children, 53,* 54-59.

These investigators examined a metacognitive strategy that taught elementary school students with learning disabilities to summarize as they read. Students wrote brief restatements of the important ideas of paragraphs as they were reading. All of the students demonstrated better comprehension after the training than did the control students.

Jenkins, J.R., Matlock, B., & Slocum, T.A. (1989). Two approaches to vocabulary instruction: The teaching of individual word meanings and practice in deriving word meaning from context. *Reading Research Quarterly, 24,* 215-235.

This experiment with fifth-grade students compared teaching individual word meanings with practice in deriving word meaning from context. The authors conclude that "instruction in individual meanings effectively taught specific word meanings, whereas the training in deriving meaning improved students' ability to derive word meanings" (p. 215). They also report that additional practice on individual meanings led to higher levels of mastery of the specific words taught. Finally, they report that considerable practice was required for students to learn to derive meaning. The authors suggest that both types of instruction hold potential for adding to students' vocabulary and that employing both techniques may be more effective than relying exclusively on either strategy.

Jenkins, J.R., Pious, C.G., & Jewell, M. (1990). Special education and the Regular Education Initiative: Basic assumptions. *Exceptional Children, 56,* 479-491.

The authors examine basic assumptions of the Regular Education Initiative, and several partnership models are discussed. They infer that "teachers and specialists form a partnership, but the classroom teachers are ultimately in charge of the instruction of all children in their classrooms, including those who are not succeeding in the mainstream" (p. 479).

Johns, J.L. (1991). Helping readers at risk: Beyond whole language, whole word, and phonics. *Journal of Reading, Writing, and Learning Disabilities, 7,* 59-67.

Johns identifies "a recurring debate between meaning-based (whole language) and phonics-based (code emphasis) approaches to teaching reading" (p. 59) and concludes that we need to go beyond this debate and provide excellent instruction for all students, including those at risk. We need to establish a positive, caring relationship, encourage and enable them to read and reread text, and use appropriate level materials which are of interest. It is especially important to unify the act of reading and provide instruction in the whole process, not only in isolated pieces of it. In an example of a child with word reading problems, the author points out that the teacher must provide instruction, modeling strategies so that the child can acquire a set of strategies to use in pronouncing and understanding words.

Johnson, D. (1988). Specific developmental disabilities of reading, writing and mathematics. In J.F. Kavanagh and T.J. Truss, Jr., (Eds), *Learning disabilities: Proceedings of The National Conference* (pp. 79-163). Parkton, MD: York Press.

Johnson reviews recent research findings in important areas in the field of learning disabilities. These areas include current issues related to incidence and identification; assessment; causes of learning disabilities; the prognosis for students with learning disabilities; and research on reading, writing, and mathematics disabilities. She urges research to help differentiate students with learning disabilities from other underachievers, and she reminds us of the importance of research related to the etiology of learning disabilities. Johnson recommends that future research reports specify clearly the subjects and the settings in which the research was conducted. Finally, the author writes that "every effort should be made to integrate theory and practice" (p. 143) in order to improve the education of children with learning disabilities.

Jones, B.H., (1986). The gifted dyslexic. *Annals of Dyslexia*, *36*, 301-317.

Jones explores the characteristics of and the difficulties experienced by one of the least studied groups of students, the gifted dyslexic. She found "the dyslexic student frequently does not read, spell, listen or get his thoughts on paper at the level his intelligence predicts. His organization skills are frequently poor" (p. 305). The author provides guidance in developing a diagnostic profile and suggests suitable tests, instructional procedures, and other sources of information. The examples of cases and of written work are helpful.

Jones, K. M., Torgesen, J. K., & Sexton, M. A. (1987). Using computer guided practice to increase decoding fluency in LD children: A study using the Hint and Hunt I Program. *Journal of Learning Disabilities*, *20*, 122-128.

Jones, Torgesen, and Sexton identify the need for practice and mastery of both speed and accuracy in word identification. Because this is hard to accomplish in a classroom setting, they investigated the effect of a computer program with elementary school students with learning disabilities that provided instruction in phonics. They found a substantial increase in speed and accuracy as well as in the ability to generalize to words on a paper copy. There was also increased speed of paragraph reading, i.e. increased fluency.

Jordan, B. T., & Jordan, S. G. (1990). Jordan left-right reversal test: An analysis of visual reversals in children and significance for reading problems. *Child Psychiatry and Human Development, 21,* 65-74.

Jordan and Jordan identify the "controversial" connection between reading and reversals and review research from the Jordan Left-Right Reversal Test. They report that studies using their test indicate that "learning disabled children and a group of below average readers made significantly more errors, indicating that visual reversals are dysfunctional for reading skills" (p. 65).

Kamhi, A. G. (1992). Response to historical perspective: A developmental language perspective. *Journal of Learning Disabilities, 25,* 48-52.

Kamhi asserts that an historical perspective on learning disabilities does not enable us to understand the nature of students with dyslexia. Rather, we need to define and describe it. He suggests that exclusionary definitions tell us what it is not, not what it is. "The deficits displayed by individuals with dyslexia do not extend too far into general domains of cognitive functions, such as reasoning, problem solving, and comprehension" (p. 51). Kamhi concludes that it is "a developmental language disorder" (p. 50) with a particular difficulty in encoding and retrieving phonological information. He suggests that teachers focus on word recognition skills, which are fairly limited, using direct instruction with a multisensory component.

Kauffman, J.M., Gerber, M.M., & Semmel, M.I. (1988). Arguable assumptions underlying the Regular Education Initiative. *Journal of Learning Disabilities, 21*, 6-11.

These authors present arguments in rebuttal of several basic assumptions of advocates of the Regular Education Initiative. They urge that additional research be conducted to help us understand how teaching in classrooms that incorporate a broad range of individual differences can be organized to maximize every student's learning.

Kavale, K. A. (1987). Theoretical issues surrounding severe discrepancy. *Learning Disabilities Research, 3*(1), 12-20.

Kavale explores issues related to the discrepancy criteria for identification of learning disabilities. Discrepancy refers to the difference between actual achievement and expected achievement. He concludes that "discrepancy alone cannot diagnose LD; it can only indicate that a primary symptom is present. Discrepancy may be a necessary condition for LD but it is hardly sufficient" (p. 19). Kavale suggests that cognitive, linguistic, and social factors need to be a part of the framework for assessment, a framework in which discrepancy plays a role, but is not the only variable.

Kavale, K. (1990a). Effectiveness of special education. In T.B. Gutkin and C.R. Reynolds (Eds.), *Handbook of school psychology* (pp. 868-896). New York: Wylie Press.

In this carefully researched chapter, Kavale explores the effectiveness of several procedures and techniques related to special education using meta-analysis to summarize statistically a variety of studies in several research domains. In the area of process training, only psycholinguistic training was effective. Perceptual-motor training and modality training were not effective, and Kavale points out that instructional time should be spent in other ways. He suggests that the best setting for placement of a child with special needs is a complex issue, and we do not have clear answers at this time. Of the medically based interventions, stimulant drugs appear to be an effective intervention for hyperactivity. In contrast, diet therapy, such as the Feingold diet, is not supported by research findings. In conclusion, Kavale suggests that the effective schooling research needs to be better integrated into special education practice.

Kavale, K.A. (1990b). Variances and verities in learning disabilities interventions. In T.E. Scruggs and B.Y.L. Wong (Eds.), *Intervention research in learning disabilities* (pp. 3-33). New York: Springer-Verlag.

Using meta-analysis, Kavale synthesizes the results of a number of research studies about learning disabilities in this chapter. He points out that the various ways of structuring research studies have made it difficult to integrate the results of different studies, and he urges attention to this problem in the future. Kavale reports that psycholinguistic training can be helpful for students but that perceptual-motor and modality training show no benefits. Stimulant medication is effective for treating hyperactivity, but diet therapy has not proved to be useful. Kavale notes that research findings are not clear regarding the best placement of students with learning disabilities and that more investigation is needed in this area. He stresses that "contextual appraisal" is important, because what works in one situation does not necessarily work in another. He suggests that the following components of effective schooling need to be incorporated: "(1) clearly defined curriculum, (2) focused instruction, (3) consistent behavior management, (4) close monitoring of performance, and (5) strong instructional leadership" (p. 22).

Keogh, B.K. (1988). Perspectives on the Regular Education Initiative. *Learning Disabilities Focus, 4*, 3-5.

Keogh reports on a symposium she chaired on the Regular Education Initiative that was sponsored by the Division of Learning Disabilities, Council for Exceptional Children. She acknowledges that special educators need to evaluate programs and demonstrate which practices work and why. However, Keogh also reminds us that competently administered special education programs can provide educational, personal, and social benefits. She questions the potential of regular education to incorporate students with learning problems and she seeks evidence that would demonstrate this capability.

Keogh, B. K., & Weisner, T. (1993). An ecocultural perspective on risk and protective factors in children's development: Implications for learning disabilities. *Learning Disabilities: Research and Practice, 8*, 3-10.

This article reports ongoing efforts to specify risk conditions or variables that affect the development of at-risk children and their families. Keogh and Weisner propose an ecocultural perspective employing four predictive models of risk. Among other conclusions to date, they have found that "risk and protective factors have their locus in the child, family, and social context; both risk and protective factors must be taken into account in diagnosis and intervention planning" (p. 3). One conclusion they draw from this finding is that interventions that include the family, rather than our current almost exclusive focus on the individual child, may be more effective. One objective of their continuing research is to identify which factors are amenable to change, for this could affect both assessment and intervention planning.

Kershner, J.R., Cummings, R.L., Clarke, K.A., Hadfield, A.J., & Kershner, B.A. (1990). Two-year evaluation of the Tomatis Listening Training Program with learning disabled children. *Learning Disability Quarterly, 13*, 43-53.

These authors report the results of a follow-up study of the Tomatis Program, a process-oriented, neuro-psychological training program. Findings had been reported after one year, and similar findings are reported here after a two-year period. This study failed to support the purported remedial effectiveness of the Tomatis Program in training auditory processes.

Kinder, D., Bursuck, B., & Epstein, M. (1992). An evaluation of history textbooks. *Journal of Special Education, 4,* 472-491.

A study of textbook readability is reported in this article. Ten eighth-grade history texts were evaluated in terms of global coherence, local coherence, questioning techniques, and vocabulary development. Results of the study confirm the importance of careful textbook selection and the need to consider a broader range of criteria than traditional readability. Although each of the texts evaluated was highly recommended, significant differences among them existed in most of the areas examined. Instructional implications of these results are discussed and should be of interest to teachers seeking the most appropriate textbooks for their students.

Kletzien, S. B. (1991). Strategy use by good and poor comprehenders reading expository text of differing levels. *Reading Research Quarterly, 26,* 67-86.

Kletzien reviews previous literature on the role of knowledge and control of reading strategies in text comprehension. In an experiment with good and poor high school readers, she found that both groups were aware of various strategies but used only a few: using key vocabulary, rereading, making inferences, and using prior knowledge. For more difficult passages, recognizing passage and sentence structure were also used. The differences between the groups related to their ability (or willingness) to try a variety of strategies and also their persistence in trying strategies even when they were faced with frustration material. These differences were not evident with independent-level material but were evident with instructional-level material. Good readers recognized that they needed to utilize a variety of strategies, particularly organizational strategies. This might be attributed to an unwillingness to take the risk of attempting difficult text on the part of acknowledged poor readers.

Kline, F. M., Deshler, D. D., & Schumaker, J.B. (1992). Implementing learning strategy instruction in class settings: A research perspective. In M. Pressley, K. R. Harris, and J. T. Guthrie (Eds.), *Promoting academic competence and literacy in school* (pp. 361-406). San Diego, CA: Academic Press.

This chapter identifies barriers to the implementation of learning strategy instruction and evaluates the effects of specific interventions designed to surmount these barriers. It also discusses the program at Kansas University Institute for Research in Learning Disabilities in terms of research methodology and the instructional methods employed to teach learning strategies for students with learning disabilities. The authors conclude that school personnel must make changes if learning strategy instruction is to be implemented successfully.

Konopak, B. C., Williams, N. L., & Jampole, E. S. (1991). Use of mnemonic imagery for content learning. *Journal of Reading, Writing, and Learning Disabilities, 7,* 309-320.

This descriptive study investigates the use of the keyword method, an elaborative mnemonic strategy to improve recall, with middle school students with learning disabilities. This strategy uses imagery to link prior knowledge with new information to facilitate learning. The study was conducted with small groups of resource room students studying rock formations in science. Although students were interested in the strategy and they did improve, the results were not as positive as in previous studies of the keyword method. The authors concluded that "these students needed additional instruction in developing and applying the keyword method to content information" (p. 317).

Koskinen, P.S., Wilson, R.M., Gambrell, L.B., & Neuman, S.B. (1993). Captioned video and vocabulary learning: An innovative practice in literacy instruction. *The Reading Teacher*, *47*, 36-43.

These authors report that captioned video is an innovative and promising approach for improving motivation, vocabulary, and reading comprehension. They note that the multisensory presentation is appealing to students, and they offer specific suggestions for getting started with captioned video. The authors conclude that "even though there are substantial differences between reading printed text and reading screen text, below-average readers appear to benefit from the multifaceted support provided by captioned video" (p. 41).

Kuder, S.J. (1990). Effectiveness of the DISTAR reading program for children with learning disabilities. *Journal of Learning Disabilities*, *23*, 69-71.

Kuder compares the results of two approaches to teaching reading to elementary school students with learning disabilities with a mean age of eight years, ten months. The DISTAR group used only the DISTAR program with no other outside materials. The basal group used basal readers and supplemental materials. The program was maintained for two years. At the end of the first year Kuder found no difference in the two groups on reading achievement as measured by the Woodcock Reading Mastery Test. When the groups were retested at the end of the second year, the author found the DISTAR group and the basal group had made similar improvements, except that the DISTAR group scored better in the word attack skills subtest. Kuder reviewed research literature on DISTAR and did not find consistent support for its use with students with learning disabilities.

Kuder, S.J. (1991). Language abilities and progress in a direct instruction reading program for students with learning disabilities. *Journal of Learning Disabilities, 24*, 124-127.

Kuder explores the question of why direct instruction programs work well with some students with learning disabilities and not with others. Why the mixed reviews? He studied 26 students with learning disabilities from an inner city who had received instruction in a DISTAR program. He found that "success in a direct instruction reading program was related to the language abilities of inner city students with reading disabilities. Specifically, improvements in word attack were related to phonological abilities, while progress in word comprehension was related to syntactic knowledge" (p. 126). Kuder suggests that specific language skill instruction (phonological and syntactic awareness) be provided in conjunction with reading instruction.

Lapadat, J.C. (1991). Pragmatic language skills of students with language and/or learning disabilities: A quantitative synthesis. *Journal of Learning Disabilities, 24*, 147-158.

The relationship of pragmatic language ability to academic and social behavior is of interest to teachers working with students with learning disabilities. This article reports a study that used meta-analysis procedures to evaluate 33 studies including a total of 825 students with language disorders or learning disabilities. "Students with language and/or learning disabilities demonstrated consistent and pervasive pragmatic deficits in conversation compared to non-disordered peers across settings, conversational partners, age groups, and types of pragmatic skills measured . . . . Furthermore, these pragmatic deficits appeared to be more attributable to underlying language deficits than to insufficient social knowledge" (p. 147). Lapadat concludes that students with learning disabilities could also be described as language disordered, a difficulty that we would expect to be manifested in different ways as students progress through school.

Laughton, J., & Morris, N. T. (1989).   Story grammar knowledge of learning disabled students.   *Learning Disabilities Research, 4*, 87-95.

Laughton and Morris report the results of a study to determine whether elementary school learning disabled and non-learning disabled students differ in their inclusion of basic story grammar components in written narratives. They found that in grades 3, 4, and 5 there were important differences, but differences were not evident in grade 6. The authors recommend further investigation of effective instruction in story grammar for students with learning disabilities in the early grades.

Learning Disabilities Association (1993). Position paper on full inclusion of all students with learning disabilities in the regular classroom. *LDA Newsbriefs, 28*(2), 1.

In its statement on inclusion, the LDA writes: "LDA believes that decisions regarding educational placement of students with disabilities must be based on the needs of each individual student. . . . LDA believes that the placement of ALL children with disabilities in the regular classroom is as great a violation of IDEA as is the placement of ALL children in separate classrooms on the basis of their type of disability" (p. 1).

Lee, R. F., & Kamhi, A. G. (1990). Metaphoric competence in children with learning disabilities. *Journal of Learning Disabilities, 23,* 471-482.

These authors examined metaphoric competence in two groups of nine- to eleven-year-old students with learning disabilities and one group of non-disabled peers. One group of students with learning disabilities had a history of spoken language impairments, and students in this group consistently performed less well than the group of students with learning disabilities without language impairments. This group, in turn, performed less well than the non-disabled children. Students with poor performance produced a higher proportion of literal responses than the other children. The authors remind us that "the novelist Walker Percy once pointed out that a metaphor is always wrong, literally speaking: It says that one thing is another, as in the suggestion that love is a rose or life's a beach. What is worse, he adds, is that oftentimes the best metaphors are the ones that are most wrong. For children with language and learning impairments, this almost seems unfair" (p. 481).

Lenchner, O., Gerber, M. M., & Routh, D. K. (1990). Phonological awareness tasks as predictors of decoding ability: Beyond segmentation. *Journal of Learning Disabilities, 23,* 240-247.

Lenchner, Gerber, and Routh reviewed training studies and found that "phonological awareness training affected reading performance, especially if it involved training in both segmentation and blending and direct instruction in letter-sound correspondence" (p. 241). In their own study of third- and fourth-grade students they found that ability in blending, manipulating phonemes and segmenting phonemes was the best predictor of success in decoding.

Lenz, B.K., Bulgren, J., & Hudson, P. (1990). Content enhancement: A model for promoting the acquisition of content by individuals with learning disabilities. In T.E. Scruggs and B.Y.L. Wong (Eds.), *Intervention research in learning disabilities* (pp. 122-165). New York: Springer-Verlag.

These authors define content enhancement as instruction to a heterogeneous group of students in which both group and individual needs are met, the integrity of the content is maintained, and instruction promotes effective learning. Content enhancements consist of carefully planned instructional routines and devices that are designed for use by content-area teachers. The theoretical underpinnings of this model of instruction are reviewed, and specific guidelines for planning and utilizing content enhancements are discussed that should be helpful to teachers.

Lenz, B. K., & Hughes, C. A. (1990). A word identification strategy for adolescents with learning disabilities. *Journal of Learning Disabilities, 23,* 149-163.

Lenz and Hughes report on the results of a study in which adolescent students with learning disabilities were taught a strategic, problem solving approach to word identification. The students were taught seven steps to be used which included the use of context, application of structural analysis rules, and the use of resources such as the teacher. The procedure was taught through direct instruction. The authors found that instruction reduced oral reading errors and increased comprehension for most students.

Leong, C. K. (1988). A componential approach to understanding reading and its difficulties in preadolescent readers. *Annals of Dyslexia, 38,* 95-119.

Leong cites "the complexity and richness of reading" (p. 96) and uses this premise for an examination of the interrelatedness of components in preadolescent reading. The components he studies are: orthographic/phonological, morphological, and sentence and paragraph comprehension. He says that these components had "mutually reinforcing and mutually facilitating effects" (p. 114).

Leong, C. K. (1989). Productive knowledge of derivational rules in poor readers. *Annals of Dyslexia, 39,* 94-115.

In this study Leong examined 75 poor readers in grades 4, 5, and 6 to determine their knowledge of derivational morphology. The results indicated a developmental trend, with readers using "different mechanisms in producing derived or base forms of words according to the complexity of the orthographic and/or phonological changes needed in the derivational process" (p. 94). The results confirmed the need for direct instruction in word parts, morphemes, and rules.

Leong, C. K., Simmons, D.R., & Izatt-Gambell, M. A. (1990). The effect of systematic training in elaboration on word meaning and prose comprehension in poor readers. *Annals of Dyslexia, 40,* 192-215.

The authors propose that proficiency in reading results from the interaction of word knowledge and discourse processing. These are defined and explained. Word knowledge requires the use of both internal and external contextual cues; discourse processing requires training in prose comprehension, word knowledge, and the use of appropriate strategies. Leong, Simmons, and Izatt-Gambell describe two training studies designed to explore the effectiveness of training in word knowledge through elaboration and in text comprehension. In spite of the limitations of the studies, the authors conclude that teaching word knowledge from context can be effective for poor readers as well as teaching learning strategies such as self-questioning. Both studies support direct, explicit teaching as being important for poor readers.

Lerner, J.W. (1987). The Regular Education Initiative: Some unanswered questions. *Learning Disabilities Focus, 3,* 3-7.

Lerner poses the following questions that the Regular Education Initiative (REI) does not address: 1) Will services for students with learning disabilities be eliminated? 2) Is a label or is school failure the real stigma? 3) Are all learning disabled children "mildly handicapped?" 4) Why should the current special education system be dismantled? and 5) Should special education be responsible for solving all school problems? She urges the involvement of regular educators in the discussion of the REI, for their effective instructional participation will be required for success.

Lerner, J.W. (1993). *Learning disabilities: Theories, diagnosis & teaching strategies* (6th ed.). Boston, MA: Houghton Mifflin Company.

In this classic text on learning disabilities, Lerner writes: "The condition of learning disabilities is perplexing: although such students are not blind, many do not see as normal students do; although they are not deaf, many do not listen or hear normally; although they are not retarded in mental development, they do not learn. Many of these students exhibit other behavior characteristics that make them disruptive in the classroom and at home. Such individuals are the concern of this book" (p. xix). Indeed, this quotation captures the spirit of this volume. Lerner reviews the history of learning disabilities, emerging directions in the field, the assessment-teaching process, theoretical perspectives, and research-based instruction. Case studies provide practical applications of the principles presented.

Lerner, J. W., Cousin, P. T., & Richeck, M. (1992). Critical issues in learning disabilities: Whole language learning. *Learning Disabilities Research & Practice, 7,* 226-230.

This article reflects the current controversy over the effectiveness of whole language instruction for students with learning disabilities. Cousin and Richeck, interviewed by Lerner, define whole language instruction, describe how it differs from other instructional approaches, and review the role of phonics and instructional materials. Cousin and Richeck suggest that whole language may enable the student with learning disabilities to become an active learner, acquiring and using strategies while, at the same time, reading meaningful text. However, they caution that "students with special learning needs require more support from teachers and should receive more demonstrations of the uses of oral and written language. Children with learning disabilities require specific instruction on developing their strategic abilities as they read and write" (p. 228). They also emphasize the need for direct instruction in skills, using a careful, structured approach. The conclusion suggests that "children with learning disabilities need many types of instruction" (p. 229).

Lerner, J. W., & Lowenthal, B. (1989). Attention Deficit Disorders: New responsibilities for the special educator. *Learning Disabilities: A Multidisciplinary Journal, 4,* 1-8.

This article provides some basic information about four aspects of attention deficit disorders (ADD): characteristics, historical perspectives, assessment, and treatment. The authors point out that students with ADD are eligible for services under one of the existing categories of IDEA or under Section 504 of the Rehabilitation Act. Treatment including medication, educational intervention, behavior management, and family training and counseling is recommended.

Leshowitz, B., Jenkens, K., Heaton, S., & Bough, T.L. (1993). Fostering critical thinking skills in students with learning disabilities: An instructional program. *Journal of Learning Disabilities, 26,* 483-490.

This article reports positive results of a study to enhance the critical thinking skills of middle and high school students with learning disabilities by having them learn and apply the principles of scientific inquiry. Student-teacher dialogues were employed to engage students in critical inquiry. Using brief magazine articles and advertisements, students identified the principal claim made in an article or advertisement, graphed the data, and evaluated the claim based on the data. The overall performance of students with learning disabilities exceeded that of a control group of regular education students who had not received the instruction.

Leverett, R.G., & Diefendorf, A.O. (1992). Students with language deficiencies. *Teaching Exceptional Children, 24,* 30-35.

This brief article offers practical suggestions for classroom teachers who are working with students who exhibit language difficulties. The authors focus on ways of providing specific information related to vocabulary within the context of the student's reading. They suggest using a "marginal gloss," which is a method of providing assistance with difficult vocabulary or other aspects of reading right on the margin of the text.

Levy, B.A., & Hinchley, J. (1990). Individual and developmental differences in the acquisition of reading skills. In T. Carr and B.A. Levy (Eds.), *Reading and its development: Component skills approaches* (pp. 81-128). San Diego, CA: Academic Press.

Levy and Hinchley, using a sample of 345 children in grades 3 through 6, studied a range of reading skills, chosen after a review of models of reading in order to compare good and poor readers. The results were remarkably consistent. Poor readers were less sensitive to phonemes, had smaller memory spans, were slower in naming tasks, were more confused by phonemes when the task was to read for meaning, and made less use of text structure than good readers. They also found that a reader who understood the text could decode the words; ability to decode rapidly did not ensure comprehension.

Liberman, I.Y. (1990). Phonology and beginning reading revisited. In C. von Euler (Ed.), *International symposium series: Brain and reading* (pp. 207-220). Hampshire, England: Macmillan.

Liberman reviews the differences between listening and reading, the relevance of phonological structure in language, and the development of the awareness of it in young children. She concludes that "most problems in learning to read and write stem from deficits in the language faculty, not from deficiencies of a more generally cognitive or perceptual sort" (p. 207). The author suggests that children, particularly those with phonological deficits, need direct instruction in the alphabetic principles of language. She makes the point that reliance on "'whole language' and 'language experience' approaches are likely to be disastrous" (p. 214).

Liberman, I. Y., & Liberman, A. M. (1990). Whole language vs. code emphasis: Underlying assumptions and their implications for reading instruction. *Annals of Dyslexia*, *40*, 51-76.

Liberman and Liberman critically examine the premises of a whole language approach to reading instruction, concluding that learning to read is not like learning to speak, that it does not progress as a natural, biological process and that it requires learning certain alphabetic principles that are specific to reading and developed for that purpose. Children need to "understand the alphabetic principle, the insight that words are distinguished from each other by the phonological structure that the alphabet represents" (p. 58). The authors review research to support the difficulties beginning readers can experience through a lack of phonological awareness and the effectiveness of instruction. The approaches taken by the proponents of whole language are identified and critiqued.

Liberman, I.Y., Shankweiler, D., & Liberman, A.M. (1989). The alphabetic principle and learning to read. In D. Shankweiler and I.Y. Liberman (Eds.), *Phonology and reading disability: Solving the reading puzzle* (pp. 1-33). Ann Arbor, MI: University of Michigan Press.

Liberman, Shankweiler, and Liberman present a detailed review of the role of phonological awareness in the mastery of the alphabetic principle for beginning readers. They also suggest that difficulties in accessing and manipulating phonemes and deficits in working memory contribute to the problems encountered by some readers. Specific suggestions for direct instruction are included.

Lipsky, D.K., & Gartner, A. (1987). Capable of achievement and worthy of respect: Education for handicapped students as if they were full-fledged human beings. *Exceptional Children, 54*, 69-74.

These authors comment to Madeline Will's proposal of the Regular Education Initiative. They write that "the establishment of a separate system of education for the disabled is an outgrowth of attitudes toward disabled people. . . . There is no compelling body of evidence that segregated special education programs have significant benefits for students" (p. 72).

Lipson, M. Y., & Wixson, K. K. (1986). Reading disability research: An interactionist perspective. *Review of Educational Research*, 56, 111-136.

Lipson and Wixson identify three approaches to understanding reading disabilities. The first, a medical model, is based on the identification of a neurological dysfunction, which they believe applies to an "extremely small" percent of the population. The second model, a deficit model, has become a search for deficits within the individual as well as environmental and emotional factors.

A third model is suggested by Lipson and Wixson, a model that will take into account the interactive nature of reading. They review a substantial body of research for both good and poor readers and conclude that "the necessity for identifying the 'disability' is eliminated, and our attention is refocused on how each child performs under different conditions and which set of conditions is most likely to facilitate learning" (pp. 120-121). This set of conditions requires a search for the most productive interaction between the reader, the text and the context. The issue is not that of defining disability; it is that of determining how to instruct.

Lipson, M.Y., & Wixson, K.K. (1991). *Assessment and instruction of reading disability: An interactive approach*. New York: Harper Collins.

Lipson and Wixson review reading models and related research and conclude that reading is an interactive process. With this as a framework they examine a variety of assessment procedures for evaluating the learner and the context in which the learning takes place. Instructional procedures are suggested for all aspects of the reading process.

Lovitt, T., & Horton, S. V. (1987). How to develop study
   guides. *Journal of Reading, Writing, and Learning
   Disabilities International*, *3*, 333-343.

Lovitt and Horton are concerned that many students with
learning disabilities have comprehension difficulties because they
do not know how to read textbook materials for which they are
responsible. These authors recommend that teachers develop
study guides. They also provide detailed procedures and helpful
guidelines for developing and using such guides with students in
content-area subjects.

Lundberg, I., Frost, J., & Petersen, O. (1988). Effects of an
   extensive program for stimulating phonological awareness
   in preschool children. *Reading Research Quarterly*, *23*,
   263-284.

Lundberg, Frost, and Petersen provided phonological
awareness training to preschoolers without providing training in
reading. The program used games and exercises that helped
children discover the structure of the language. They found the
program affected metalinguistic skills such as rhyming tasks and
"tasks involving word and syllable manipulation" (p. 263).
There was a "dramatic" effect on sound segmentation. They
concluded that "phonemic awareness can be developed outside
the context of the acquisition of an alphabetic writing system"
(p. 263) but we need to provide explicit instruction.

Lyon, G. R. (1985). Identification and remediation of learning
   disability subtypes: Preliminary findings. *Learning
   Disabilities Focus*, *1*, 21-35.

Lyon reports on prior research and an extensive effort to
identify learning disability subtypes and to relate reading
instruction for each type to a particular method. The author
identifies many of the difficulties inherent in this kind of

research, including, for example, the difficulty in controlling for the amount and kind of prior and present reading instruction and the instructional procedures and materials used by the teacher outside of the experimental situation. He concludes that "these investigations have taught us more about what to do and what not to do in future studies than about the relationships between subtype learning characteristics and magnitude of response to different teaching methods" (p. 33). Because it seems clear that readers with learning disabilities do possess different characteristics and difficulties they will require different approaches to the instruction, but the particular paths are not clearly established in the research literature.

Lyon, G. R. (1991). *Research in learning disabilities: Research directions (Tech. Rep.).* Bethesda, MD: National Institutes of Child Health and Human Development.

This paper reviews the NICHD-sponsored multidisciplinary research efforts funded in 1989 and 1990 as well as the five dyslexia program projects funded in 1979, 1986, and 1987. It concludes with recommendations for future research directions in the area of learning disabilities.

Lyon, G. R., Gray, D.B., Kavanagh, J. F., & Krasnegor, N. A. (1993). *Better understanding learning disabilities: New views from research and their implications for education and public policies.* Baltimore, MD: Paul Brookes.

The chapters in this book are focused on 1) identifying the major reasons for the persistent difficulty of the field of learning disabilities in establishing a reliable and valid definition and classification system, and 2) identifying the conditions that must be in place if the field is to establish a firm definitional, theoretical, conceptual, and methodological base. The editors comment on the need for such investigation in the preface: "Much of our research thinking about learning disabilities is based on information obtained from ambiguously defined samples of children with school-identified learning disabilities who have been measured by technically inadequate tests at a single point in time. . . . The result is that the field of learning disabilities lacks a logically consistent, easily operationalized, and empirically valid definition and classification system. Therefore it is extremely difficult to make solid predications about the behavior and learning outcomes of youngsters with learning disabilities" (p. 9). This volume brings together the thinking of a number of researchers on approaches to solving these problems.

Lyon, G.R., & Moats, L.C. (1988). Critical issues in the instruction of the learning disabled. *Journal of Consulting and Clinical Psychology, 36*, 830-835.

Lyon and Moats present a selective review of research-based literature focusing on the various models of learning disabilities because these models form the framework for the assessment and instruction of students. These models include: medical and psychoeducational, neuropsychological, behavioral, linguistic, and cognitive. In each instance the authors explore the theories behind the model and as well as the instructional approaches that are used. They conclude that we need research methodologies and teaching strategies that are "dynamic, fluid, and flexible" (p. 834).

Lyons, C. A. (1991). Reading Recovery: A viable prevention of learning disability. *Reading Horizons, 31*, 385-408.

Lyons identifies the increase in the number of students classified as learning disabled in recent years as a major strain on school resources. Citing positive effects of Reading Recovery on at-risk and learning disabled students, Lyons illustrates the program with a case study. Learning disabled students fail to use the multiple cuing system of meaning and language structure as well as visual/auditory information. The author compares the isolated skill approach of traditional remediation with the holistic reading/writing framework of Reading Recovery. The former focuses on the code, the latter on meaning. The Reading Recovery program is explained and illustrated in detail. It is seen as a viable way of preventing reading failure, thus reducing the strain on school resources as well as the strain imposed on students.

Lysynchuk, L., & Pressley, M. (1990). Vocabulary. In M. Pressley and Associates (Eds.), *Cognitive strategy instruction that really improves children's academic performance* (pp. 71-80). Cambridge, MA: Brookline Books.

Lysynchuk and Pressley begin by reminding us that "although vocabulary instruction appears to be a key element in education, there is very little research examining the vocabulary instruction currently taking place in schools" (p. 71). They discuss the importance of such instruction and recommend the keyword method, which is a technique based on mental imagery that facilitates associations between prior knowledge and new vocabulary. The authors conclude that "mnemonic techniques positively affect remembering, but do not permit learners to infer the meanings of undefined vocabulary words" (p. 77).

Majsterek, D. J., & Wilson, R. (1989). Computer-assisted instruction for students with learning disabilities: Considerations for practitioners. *Learning Disabilities Focus, 5,* 18-27.

These authors point out that for computer-assisted instruction to be effective, we must use good software. They write: "Practitioners interested in using CAI to build speed and accuracy in basic skills are encouraged to consider two factors in selecting and using software with their pupils: the technical and instructional adequacy of the programs and the appropriateness of the materials for each student's individual educational plans" (p. 18). They conclude by suggesting sources of software reviews and criteria for software evaluation.

Malone, L. D., & Mastropieri, M.A. (1992). Reading comprehension instruction: Summarization and self-monitoring training for students with learning disabilities. *Exceptional Children, 58,* 270-279.

Malone and Mastropieri review possible sources of difficulty in reading for students with learning disabilities, particularly in the area of comprehension. They focus on research related to the effects of training in isolated strategies and in "packages" of strategies. The authors report on their own research with three groups of students with learning disabilities in grades 6, 7, and 8. They were trained in a summarization strategy, in both a summarization strategy and a self-monitoring strategy, or in a traditional approach emphasizing vocabulary. The summarization and the summarization plus self-monitoring were more effective in recall of text than the traditional approach. They hypothesize that in comparing summarization and summarization plus self-monitoring, the difficulty of the text may be a critical variable, with more difficult text requiring the addition of the self-monitoring component.

Manis, F. R., Szeszulski, P. A., Holt, L. K., & Graves, K. (1990). Variation in component word recognition and spelling skills among dyslexic children and normal readers. In T. H. Carr and B. A. Levy (Eds.), *Reading and its development: Component skills approaches* (pp. 207-259). San Diego, CA: Academic Press.

Manis et al. review the "dual-access" model of word recognition in which the reader has visual access to a word, recognizing it from its orthographic features and phonological access, recognizing it from its letters and sounds. Comparing normal readers with dyslexic readers in elementary school the researchers found that dyslexic readers were more dependent on phonological cues to decode words than good readers but that they knew less about sound-symbol correspondence than good readers.

Mann, V. A., & Brady, S. (1988). Reading disability: The role of language deficiencies. *Journal of Consulting and Clinical Psychology, 56,* 811-816.

Mann and Brady explore the role of language as a variable in reading disability, focusing primarily on language processing and phonological awareness. Several difficulties in processing language are examined. These include "working memory, speech perception, naming ability, and sentence comprehension" (p. 813). The authors conclude that a problem with phonological representation may be the basis for many difficulties in reading. They present several instructional applications.

Manolakes, G. (1988). Comprehension: A personal experience in content area reading. *The Reading Teacher, 42,* 200-202.

Recognizing the problem good adult readers have in experiencing and understanding difficulties in reading, particularly reading comprehension, Manolakes leads us through a unique activity. We read an article on electronics, identify the sources of our difficulties, and answer the comprehension questions. As Manolakes points out, this is not a happy experience. Even though we can answer many of these comprehension questions, our lack of prior knowledge prevents real comprehension.

Marzola, E. S. (1988). Interrogating the text: Questioning strategies designed to improve reading comprehension.

Journal of Reading, Writing, and Learning Disabilities, 4,
243-258.

Marzola reviews studies examining the use of questioning
strategies in helping students with learning disabilities to improve
their reading comprehension. In looking at Question Answer
Relationships (QARs), ReQuest, and Reciprocal Teaching,
Marzola differentiates between teacher-generated questions and
student-generated questions. She concludes that self-questioning
"comprehension strategies spontaneously used by good readers
can be taught to poor readers" (p. 253).

Mastropieri, M. A., & Peters, E. E. (1987). Increasing prose
    recall of learning disabled and reading disabled students
    via spatial organizers. *Journal of Educational Research,*
    80, 272-76.

Mastropieri and Peters report that junior high school
students who studied spatially organized illustrations prior to
hearing a related prose passage had better recall of the content
and illustrations than students who studied a randomized list.
The authors suggest that "these findings . . . support the
contention that after exposure to a spatial organizer, recall is
facilitated through the formation of a cognitive representation
which learners can then use as a vehicle for storing related
semantic content" (p. 276). They suggest further investigation
of this strategy.

Mastropieri, M.A., Scruggs, T.E., & Fulk, B.J. (1990).
    Teaching abstract vocabulary with the keyword method:
    Effects on recall and comprehension. *Journal of Learning*
    Disabilities, 23, 92-107.

Mastropieri, Scruggs, and Fulk review the relationships
between language and memory, pointing out that students with
learning disabilities may be deficient in both the structure of

semantic memory (the way information is stored and organized) and the process of semantic memory (what is done with the information). The authors propose the use of a keyword method (a common word and related picture cue the meaning of the target word) to meet both of these difficulties. In the research reported in this article, the keyword method was effective with the recall of abstract words and with the application of the strategy to the words in different contexts.

Mastropieri, M. A., Scruggs, T. E., & Levin, J. R. (1987). Learning-disabled students' memory for expository prose: Mnemonic versus nonmnemonic pictures. *American Educational Research Journal*, *24*, 505-519.

These authors examine the effects of mnemonic pictures and non-mnemonic pictures as a memory aid for students with learning disabilities. Both included pictorial representations in the text, but only the mnemonic picture condition provided direct mnemonic links to aid in remembering. A third group, a control, was instructed without use of any pictures. Both mnemonic and non-mnemonic pictures aided recall, but the mnemonic picture condition was more effective.

Mather, N. (1992). Whole language reading instruction for students with learning disabilities: Caught in the cross fire. *Learning Disabilities Research and Practice*, *7*, 87-95.

Mather identifies "the role of explicit, skill-by-skill decoding instruction" (p. 87) as the key distinction between the whole language approach, which emphasizes meaning, and a basic skill approach, which emphasizes word structure. She points out that students who do not "intuitively develop knowledge of the alphabetic principle may require more explicit instruction in the letter-sound relationships" (p. 89) and that these students will not progress beyond the stage of acquiring some sight words without explicit, direct instruction. Mather suggests using a metacognitive approach, helping "children understand how phonemic knowledge is related to learning to read" (p.91), in teaching decoding. She also recommends providing the minimum of decoding instruction needed for mastery while immersing children in literature.

Mather, N. & Kirk, S. A. (1985). The type III error and other concerns in learning disability research. *Learning Disability Research, 1,* 56-64.

Mather and Kirk review the definition of learning disabilities provided in PL 94-142 and a clarification by Kirk and Chalfant. The authors suggest that there are two kinds of learning disabilities: developmental learning disabilities in which basic processes are involved, and academic learning disabilities in which the problems are associated with performance in academic areas. The first can certainly lead to the second. In this article the authors focus on the existence of perceptual difficulties and modality preference as variables in learning disabilities and academic performance. They note that much of the research has refuted these notions, but teachers can identify the existence of these elements in practice. They suggest that this discrepancy is due to errors in research.

McCormick, S. (1992) Disabled readers' erroneous responses to inferential comprehension questions: Description and analysis. *Reading Research Quarterly, 27,* 54-77.

McCormick reports a study of the reasons for erroneous responses to inference questions by 80 fifth grade disabled readers. She found that "greater proportions of errors were found in 3 of 7 categories: (a) integration of text and prior information, (b) ability to write intended responses, and (c) recall of text cues" (p. 54). Of 26 subcategories of sources of error, "4 accounted for 54% of incorrect responses: (a) overreliance on background knowledge, (b) underdeveloped written responses, (c) answers unrelated to main points in the selection, and (d) answers too specific to reflect global constructs" (ibid.). In concluding, McCormick offers suggestions for assessment and instruction that will help instruct readers to make inferential responses to text.

McKeown, M. G., & Beck, I. (1988). Learning vocabulary: Different ways for different goals. *Remedial and Special Education (RASE)*, *9*, 42-46.

This article offers suggestions for vocabulary instruction that will improve comprehension. The features of this program include providing multiple exposures to words in various contexts and engaging students in thinking actively about word meanings. McKeown and Beck favorably compare the effects of an instructional program incorporating these features with instruction based on learning definitions. They remind us that the characteristics of the learners, the nature of the words taught, and the goal of instruction should guide the development of instructional activities.

McKeown, M.G., Beck, I.L., Sinatra, G.M., & Loxterman, J. A. (1992). The contribution of prior knowledge and coherent text to comprehension. *Reading Research Quarterly*, *27*, 78-93.

This study investigated the contributions of background knowledge and considerate (easy to read) text to comprehension. Four segments of a fifth-grade social studies textbook and four revised versions, designed to improve text coherence, were used. The authors provided students with relevant background knowledge, then tested the effects of this knowledge through their comprehension of the two versions of the text. Students who read the revised text showed better recall than students who read the original text. The authors discuss the teacher's role in mediating learning from textbooks in content area-instruction.

McKinney, J. D., Osborne, S. S., & Schulte, A. C. (1993). Academic consequences of learning disability: Longitudinal prediction of outcomes at 11 years of age. *Learning Disabilities Research and Practice, 8,* 19-27.

These authors report a research study that investigated academic achievement of children with learning disabilities over a five year period. The children were identified in the first and second grades, and they were compared to average-achieving children who were followed for the same time period. The findings indicate that, with the exception of IQ, different variables predicted the achievement of children with learning disabilities than that of average children. "Teacher perceptions of intelligence, measured IQ, grade retention, and teacher perceptions of task-oriented behavior predicted [achievement] for children with learning disabilities" (p. 19). This study is one component of a larger longitudinal study, the Carolina Longitudinal Learning Disabilities Project, which is also discussed in this article.

McLeskey, J. (1992). Students with learning disabilities at primary, intermediate, and secondary grade levels: Identification and characteristics. *Learning Disability Quarterly, 15,* 13-19.

This study produced descriptive information about 790 students with learning disabilities, K-12, who were identified during the 1987-88 school year in Indiana. McLeskey reports that identification peaked in first grade, and that 58% were retained prior to being identified. By the end of grade 5, 76% of the students had been identified. He points out that some evidence suggests retention might be used as a remedial measure prior to labeling a student as learning disabled, and he suggests additional research in this area.

Melekian, B. A. (1990). Family characteristics of children with dyslexia. *Journal of Learning Disabilities, 23*, 386-391.

A review of 249 children with severe dyslexia demonstrated that their families were generally of low-occupational status and were poorly educated. Additionally, these children were predominantly the oldest child in a large family. Parental age and matrimonial status seemed unimportant.

Meltzer, L. J., Solomon, B., Fenton, T., & Levine, M.D. (1989). A developmental study of problem-solving strategies in children with and without learning difficulties. *Journal of Applied Developmental Psychology, 10*, 171-193.

Meltzer, Solomon, Fenton, and Levine, using the term "learning difficulties" rather than the term "learning disabilities," review the significance of problem solving in learning, the development of strategy use, and the patterns of strengths and weaknesses that were exhibited by learning disabled students. The results of their study indicated that students with learning difficulties exhibited "significantly weaker problem-solving strategies" (p. 189) than did normal students. These strategies included difficulties organizing information using a plan, shifting among strategies, and attending to information that is significant.

Mercer, C.D. (1992). *Students with learning disabilities,* 4th ed. New York: Maxwell Macmillan International.

Mercer provides a comprehensive coverage of the field of learning disabilities in this introductory text. He presents a broad range of theories and practices – behavioral, medical, and psychological – that are important background for teachers. The history of the field, definitions and characteristics, assessment, instructional practices, and needs of families are among the topics he addresses.

Mercer, C. D., Hughes, C., & Mercer, A. R. (1985). Learning disabilities definitions used by state educational departments. *Learning Disability Quarterly, 8,* 45-55.

Mercer, Hughes, and Mercer trace the development of the definitions of learning disabilities from PL 91-320, the Learning Disabilities Act of 1969, to the present. They present the results of a survey of definitions, practices and procedures from the various states conducted in 1983. Results of this survey indicated that 72% of the states use a definition based on the 1977 definition which forms the basis for defining students with learning disabilities under PL 94-142. Although the majority of the states include a reference to the basic psychological processes involved in using language, few states include this in identification criteria. "The academic component continues to be a basic factor in defining and identifying LD" (p. 50). The authors conclude: "Considering the youth of the learning disabilities field, it is not surprising that definitions are controversial and tentative. This condition very likely reflects our present state of knowledge" (p. 54).

Mercer, C.D., & Mercer, A.R. (1993). *Teaching students with learning disabilities.* New York: Macmillan.

This book is a comprehensive, practical text devoted to good instructional practices for teachers working with students with learning difficulties. The authors state that "the primary purpose of this book is to prepare teachers . . . for the challenges of individualized programming for students with learning or behavioral problems" (p. viii). They define individualized programming as the student working on appropriate tasks over time under effective motivational conditions. In keeping with the purpose of the book, Mercer and Mercer provide an overview of theory and practice in assessment, classroom management, instructional materials, developing social and emotional behavior, and teaching academic skills.

Moats, L. C., & Lyon, G. R. (1993). Learning disabilities in the United States: Advocacy, science, and the future of the field. *Journal of Learning Disabilities, 26,* 282-294.

This article presents a history of learning disabilities in the United States. It describes the complex relationships that have existed among the social and political forces that have molded the field, advocacy, research, and instructional practices. Moats and Lyon offer a clear rationale for establishing clinical and scientific validation of learning disabilities. They conclude: "To preserve the gains we have made in public recognition of LD, program funding, and legal safeguards, we need to redouble our efforts to put science in the driver's seat" (p. 291).

Montague, M. (1988, October). *Story Grammar and Learning Disabled Students' Comprehension and Production of Narrative Prose.* Paper presented at the Annual Meeting of the Florida Reading Association, Orlando, FL.

Montague compares three groups of learning disabled students to three groups of non-learning disabled students from grades 4 to 11 in order to identify the role and level of the use of story grammar in comprehension of text and the writing of the student's own text. She found that "LD students have acquired a rudimentary but perhaps not fully developed schema for narrative prose" (p.1). These students had knowledge of story grammar and were able to use it in comprehending and writing text. However, compared to NLD students, they "manifest deficiencies in relation to activation of prior knowledge, conceptual knowledge, and strategic knowledge" (p. 6). In addition, stories "written by LD students are incohesive, unorganized, and incomplete in relation to episodic structure" (p. 7). Thus, the implication of this study is that students with learning disabilities have the basis of story grammar; however, they do not make sufficient use of it because of problems with cognitive tasks and information processing.

Montague, M. (1993). Student-centered or strategy-centered instruction: What is our purpose? *Journal of Learning Disabilities, 26,* 433-437.

In this article, Montague presents her reactions to Ellis' Integrative Strategy Instruction model for teaching content to students with learning disabilities. She comments favorably upon the fact that Ellis' model emphasizes the development of metacognitive abilities and that it is a long-term, structured intervention, rather than the haphazard "quick fix" that is too often tried. She notes that this model has not been systematically validated and urges additional research to do so, pointing out that it is important to understand what works and why it works within a strategy package.

Montague, M., Maddux, C. D., & Dereshiwsky, M. I. (1990). Story grammar and comprehension and production of narrative prose by students with learning disabilities. *Journal of Learning Disabilities, 23,* 190-197.

Montague, Maddux and Dereshiwsky review theory and research on the role of story grammar in reading comprehension and writing, as well as the role of metacognition in processing text. In their study of students with learning disabilities in grades 4-5, 7-8, 9-10, the results substantiated the "hypothesis that students with LD have acquired a rudimentary, but not fully developed, schema for narrative prose" (p. 195). The authors identify the need to provide direct instruction in story grammar and teach students strategies for applying story grammar to comprehending and producing narrative text.

Morais, J. (1987). Segmental analysis of speech and its relation to reading ability. *Annals of Dyslexia, 37,* 126-141.

Morais establishes the importance of segmental awareness in the acquisition of reading in an alphabetic system. This awareness does not appear to be related to maturation but rather to instruction and experiences in learning to read. He cites a series of studies to show that "awareness of phonemic segments is the main, the characteristic effect of alphabetic literacy" (p. 129). When initial reading instruction focuses on phonics, the teacher makes this part of the instruction. However, when reading focuses on whole words, students generally are not made aware of phonemic segments. He further demonstrates a relationship between segmentation of phonemes and success in reading. The ability to perform segmental analysis is specific to reading but has, underlying it, a general analytic ability. Dyslexic students are frequently unable to perform segmental analysis but do demonstrate abilities to perform other analytic tasks. Thus, it is not clear what causes this difficulty in dyslexic students.

Morais, J. (1991). Constraints on the development of phonemic awareness. In S.A. Brady and D.P. Shankweiler (Eds.), *Phonological Processes in Literacy* (pp. 5-27). Hillsdale, NJ: Lawrence Erlbaum Associates.

Morais reviews a large body of research in the area of phonemic awareness with several conclusions. Phonemic awareness, sensitivity to the phonemic structure of words, is needed in order to develop initial literacy. Rhyming ability does not appear to foster literacy and does not seem to foster phonemic awareness. What is required is specific instruction in phonemic awareness that includes phoneme-grapheme correspondences. Poor readers rely heavily on context as an aid to decoding, and they need to have other strategies available.

Morrison, D. C., & Hinshaw, S. P. (1988). The relationship between neuropsychological/perceptual performance and socioeconomic status in children with learning disabilities. *Journal of Learning Disabilities, 21*, 124-128.

Morrison and Hinshaw examined a battery of tests and collected data from a variety of sources to determine the relationship between variables frequently associated with learning disabilities. The results of their study suggested that low socioeconomic status was associated with low intelligence and low academic achievement. However, it was not associated with the neuropsychosocial/perceptual dysfunctions found in the group of children with learning disabilities. The authors point out the limited sample used did not include inner-city and non-Caucasian children.

Morrison, G. M., MacMillan, D. L., & Kavale, K. (1985). System identification of learning disabled children: Implications for research sampling. *Learning Disability Quarterly, 8*, 2-10.

Morrison, MacMillan, and Kavale examine the process of identifying a learning disability in some detail in order to highlight the pitfalls as well as the implications for understanding research using samples from this population. Variables that influence initial referrals are teacher and peer biases and tolerances. The referral system is characterized as uncertain and variable, "a variability that works against the identification of children with characteristics that match theoretical definitions" (p. 4). This, in turn, affects the sampling procedures used in research studies and the appropriate interpretation of results.

Naslund, J. C., & Samuels, S. J. (1992). Automatic access to word sounds and meaning in decoding written text. *Reading and Writing Quarterly: Overcoming Learning Difficulties, 8,* 135-156.

Naslund and Samuels review the concept of automaticity and its relation to decoding words. Fluency in reading depends on access to the words in an immediate fashion and with "a minimum of conscious effort and conscious control" (p. 135). The authors investigate how automaticity is developed. The traditional limited-resource model is examined and the many problems with it explored. They suggest that the automatization is not a rote process but rather one of memory retrieval. They relate this to the act of reading and suggest that "phonological, lexical, and syntactical components" (p. 148) are all involved in developing automaticity.

Neuman, S. B., & Koskinen, P. (1992). Captioned television as comprehensible input: Effects of incidental word learning from context for language minority students. *Reading Research Quarterly, 27,* 94-106.

Extending their line of research in the effects of captioned television on the reading comprehension of poor readers, Neuman and Koskinen apply this intervention with bilingual students. They report it to be effective with this population in facilitating the incidental learning of new words as well as in improving reading comprehension.

Newby, R. F., Caldwell, J., & Recht, D. R. (1989). Improving the reading comprehension of children with dysphonetic and dyseidetic dyslexia using story grammar. *Journal of Learning Disabilities, 22,* 373-380.

Newby, Caldwell, and Recht describe an instructional procedure used with two subtypes of dyslexic students.

Dysphonetic dyslexia refers to difficulties with "sequential phonetic processing of written text" (p. 373), while dyseidetic dyslexia refers to difficulty with whole word identification. The instructional program for teaching story grammar that is described by the authors emphasized comprehension and built on strengths, using procedures and materials commonly found in schools. The results demonstrated that strategy instruction is effective for dyslexic students and that they "can effectively use metacognitive methods to organize their understanding of reading material" (p. 378). The authors were not sure whether it was important to match the specific strategy with the specific subtype or whether the metacognitive strategy training itself was sufficient.

Nicholson, T., Bailey, J., & McArthur, J. (1991). Context cues in reading: The gap between research and popular opinion. *Journal of Reading, Writing, and Learning Disabilities International, 7,* 33-41.

Nicholson, Bailey, and McArthur investigated whether children relied on context as an aid in reading words. Their results confirmed findings in previous studies that "the poor readers made more use of context than did the good readers" (p. 38). The authors suggest that their study extends our understanding of the use of context by identifying the conditions in which the use of context is a useful strategy. The use of context to improve decoding skills is useful. The use of context to compensate for poor decoding skills is not useful, for if students do that, they will not learn decoding in the long run. The authors express concern about whole language programs that "put excessive emphasis on the use of context as a strategy for recognizing words" (p. 40).

Oberlin, K. J., & Shugarman, S. L. (1989). Implementing the Reading Workshop with middle school LD readers. *Journal of Reading, 32,* 682-687.

Oberlin and Shugarman describe the procedures and effectiveness of a Reading Workshop approach used with middle school students with learning disabilities. In contrast to the traditional remedial approach "in which the instruction focuses solely on word recognition and isolated comprehension skills, a focus which may not produce skilled readers" (p. 682), the Reading Workshop focuses on the development of the qualities of a good reader. The procedures that are directed toward this goal include reading mini-lessons in "literacy conventions," teacher modeling of good reading behaviors, sustained silent reading of student-selected text, and readers' dialogue journals. All of these activities are designed to develop "positive reading attitudes, high levels of book involvement and high achievement in reading skills" (p. 682). Results from attitude tests indicated improved reading attitudes and increased level of book involvement. These results were substantiated by teacher observation.

O'Connor, R. E., Jenkins, J. R., Cole, K. N., & Mills, P. E. (1993). Two approaches to reading instruction with children with disabilities: Does program design make a difference? *Exceptional Children, 59*, 312-323.

O'Connor, Jenkins, Cole, and Mills cite the effectiveness of DISTAR with disadvantaged students but the lack of research showing its effectiveness with young children with learning disabilities. To investigate this issue they studied children predicted to fail or with documented learning disabilities. There were two groups, one used DI Reading Mastery 1, based on DISTAR, which provides direct, sequential instruction of phonics. The other group was taught Superkids, which does not follow a strict sequence of phonics instruction and which uses a "more relaxed attitude toward strategic learning approaches" (p. 313). According to the results, both groups improved over the year. When tested a year later, there was still no advantage for either group. The authors suggest that there are many unanswered questions, which means that we must be cautious in proposing programs.

Ohanian, S. (1990).   P.L. 94-142: Mainstream or quicksand? *Phi Delta Kappan*, *4*, 217-222.

Concerns about what happens to students who have been mainstreamed are the focus of Ohanian's article. She suggests that many are "drowning," lacking the help that they need in order to grow and learn, both academically and socially. Ohanian uses specific cases to illustrate her points.   In conclusion, she writes that "we are very reluctant to admit that some people should be allowed – even encouraged – to be different. . . . Maybe we should spend less time on labels and more time providing meaningful alternatives for all students who don't flourish in the mainstream" (p. 222).

Olson, M.W., & Gee, T.C. (1991). Content reading instruction in the primary grades: Perceptions and strategies. *The Reading Teacher*, *45*, 298-307.

Olson and Gee recommend strategies for primary-grade children to improve reading comprehension. Strategies they discuss include semantic mapping, self-questioning (KWL), concrete manipulatives and experiences, expository paragraph frames, visual imagery, and group summarizing.

Olson, R., Wise, B., Conners, F., & Rack, J. (1990). Organization, heritability, and remediation of component word recognition and language skills in disabled readers. In T. H. Carr and B. A. Levy (Eds.), *Reading and its development: Component skills approaches* (pp. 261-322). San Diego, CA: Academic Press.

In studying disabled readers these authors found evidence that phonological coding difficulties might be heritable, while difficulty with orthographic coding (sight words) was probably related to reading experiences. "Reading generally improves with greater exposure to print, even in children with severe phonological deficits" (p. 303). They developed a computer program designed to get students to read more and to receive immediate feedback on word recognition and decoding skills. Because they found students had difficulty blending segmented phonemes, they gave feedback on whole words, syllables, and subsyllables. The children read interesting stories containing target words. The feedback on whole words was the least effective. The feedback on the various segmented conditions was about equally effective. The authors suggest advantages to the use of a computer for this instruction: the computer is always enthusiastic and patient and always teaches the way it is programmed to do.

O'Shea, D. J., & O'Shea, L. (1990). Theory-driven teachers reflecting on developments in reading instruction. *Learning Disabilities Forum*, *16*, 80-91.

O'Shea and O'Shea suggest that the experienced teacher must be knowledgeable and reflective about learning disabilities as well as reading theory and practice in order to make the decisions needed for effective instruction. To this end, they review various theories of learning disabilities and related reading practices, including the psychoneurological, the psychological processing, the behavioral, the cognitive, and the holistic theory.

O'Shea, L. J., Sindelar, P. T., & O'Shea, D. J. (1987). The effects of repeated readings and attentional cues on the reading fluency and comprehension of learning disabled readers. *Learning Disabilities Research*, *2*, 103-109.

O'Shea, Sindelar, and O'Shea studied the effects of rereading and attentional cues on reading fluency and comprehension on third-grade students with learning disabilities. They found that rereading had a positive effect on performance in both tasks. Attentional cueing (remember as much as you can about the story) had a positive effect on comprehension, but attentional cueing for fluency (read quickly and correctly) did not.

O'Sullivan, P.J., Ysseldyke, J.E., Christenson, S.L., & Thurlow, M.L. (1990). Mildly handicapped elementary students' opportunity to learn during reading instruction in mainstream and special education settings. *Reading Research Quarterly*, 25, 131-146.

This study should be of interest to all teachers, both in the mainstream and in special education. These researchers estimated "what proportion of classroom time was *academic engaged time*, or time on task, and what proportion was *academic responding time*, in which students were given the opportunity to respond. Students were actively engaged and actively responding for significantly higher proportions of time in special education reading classes than in regular reading classes. However, because less time was spent overall in special education reading classes, the absolute time spent actively engaged and actively responding in special education classes was about the same as (or slightly less than) in regular classes" (p. 131). This documents the need to improve instruction in all classrooms.

Palincsar, A.S., & Brown, D.A. (1987). Enhancing instructional time through attention to metacognition. *Journal of Learning Disabilities, 20,* 66-75.

Palincsar and Brown identify two components to metacognition: the knowledge we possess about our cognitive activity, and our ability to regulate it. The authors review appropriate research, concluding that by teaching strategies we can close the gap between good and poor readers, including those identified as learning disabled. Traditionally, we have examined the basic processes involved and concluded that students with learning disabilities are deficient in their basic processing abilities. This approach has had limited value in planning useful instructional programs. Palincsar and Brown conclude, on the basis of the research reviewed, that we should use a metacognitive approach, teaching students to use and monitor appropriate strategies. In a detailed review of metacognitive instructional programs designed to enhance memory, improve text comprehension, writing and math problem solving, they conclude that it is beneficial to provide explicit strategy instruction. Appropriate metacognitive strategies for improving text comprehension included self-correction of errors, self-generation of questions, and strategic study of strategies such as Informed Strategies for Learning. The studies reviewed demonstrate that strategy instruction can be successful and beneficial. However, metacognitive instruction has not been widely implemented in special education classrooms. It remains "a challenge that special educators have not yet been observed to embrace" (p. 74).

Palincsar, A. S., & Klenk, L. (1992). Fostering literacy learning in supportive contexts. *Journal of Learning Disabilities, 25,* 211-225.

Palincsar and Klenk describe programs implemented in classrooms with students identified as learning disabled and/or emotionally disturbed. These programs are grounded in metacognitive theory and emphasize the importance of intentional learning for at-risk children. They suggest that students with learning disabilities have difficulty with intentional learning because they do not understand the nature of learning and lack the strategies and motivation to learn. Palincsar and Klenk suggest the use of reciprocal teaching as a means to overcome these difficulties.

The authors also suggest "redefining the contexts of early literacy learning" (p. 213). Frequently children read little text, are bored, and spend time on low-level skills, not on reading and writing for meaning. The authors described a program on which they were still compiling data. In conjunction with a standard program that includes phonics instruction, children read stories around a theme and wrote using invented spelling; Palincsar and Klenk remind us that reading and writing are social interactive processes. So far they have found that the children are more inclined to take risks given this instruction and that their understanding of print is improving.

Paris, S.G., & Oka, E.R. (1989). Strategies for comprehending text and coping with reading difficulties. *Learning Disability Quarterly, 12,* 32-42.

Paris and Oka discuss the power of metacognitive strategies to help students with learning disabilities comprehend text and manage reading problems. They recommend that students be taught how and when to use specific strategies and "how to set goals, persevere, and make accurate attributions while reading" (p. 32). They argue that difficulties with reading often become roadblocks to learning and motivation because children who cannot read as expected become frustrated. These authors present specific directions for *cognitive coaching* that should be helpful to teachers who wish to teach students with learning disabilities to apply metacognitive comprehension strategies.

Pehrsson, R. S., & Denner, P. R. (1988). Semantic organizers: Implications for reading and writing. *Topics in Language Disorders, 8,* 24-37.

Pehrsson and Denner review applications of semantic organizers to help students comprehend text better and improve their writing. They explain why "every semantic organizer has both a verbal (semantic) component and a graphic-structure (organizer) component" (p. 27). The authors suggest that this approach is both preventative and remedial.

Perfetti, C.A. (1991). On the value of simple ideas in reading instruction. In S.A. Brady and D.P. Shankweiler (Eds.), *Phonological Processes in Literacy* (pp. 211-218). Hillsdale, N.J.: Lawrence Erlbaum Associates.

Through a series of imaginative examples, Perfetti leads us to the conclusion that "reading is a matter of decoding words" (p. 213). To add comprehension to the picture is to talk about language. He explores the dimensions of the alphabetic principle and decoding. Readers must be able to decode new words in order to read text. Children need direct instruction in phonemic awareness and in the alphabetic principle in order to learn to read. Comprehension requires mastery of all language systems as well as non-linguistic knowledge.

Phillips, S. E., & Clarizio, H. F. (1988). Limitations of standard scores in individual achievement testing. *Educational Measurement Issues and Practice*, *7*, 8-15.

Phillips and Clarizio examine the advantages, disadvantages and limitations of using status standard scores, developmental standard score scales, and grade equivalent scores for individual and group achievement tests for identifying students with learning disabilities. They do not question the use of a discrepancy formula for this purpose but rather examine how to determine the achievement part of the formula. They conclude that the widely used status standard score has serious limitations. Further study is needed in these areas.

Pinnell, G. S. (1989). Reading Recovery: Helping at-risk children learn to read. *The Elementary School Journal*, *90*, 161-183.

Pinnell describes the origin of the Reading Recovery program, its purposes and procedures, evaluation results to date, and the illustrative progress of one particular child. The emphasis in this program is on communicating and constructing meaning. The focus in instruction is on teaching at-risk students the strategies that good readers use, including: operating on print, self-monitoring, cross-checking, searching for cues, and self-correcting. Traditional remedial programs do not provide opportunities to develop strategies, instead emphasizing individual units of words and letters rather than meaning.

Pressley, M. (1990). Getting started teaching strategies. In M. Pressley and Associates (Eds.), *Cognitive strategy instruction that really improves children's academic performance* (pp. 179-188). Cambridge, MA: Brookline Books.

In this concluding chapter of his book, Pressley presents specific guidelines for teachers wishing to get started in teaching strategies. These guidelines include: 1) select a few strategies to teach; 2) use powerful methods of teaching; 3) motivate students to use the strategies they are taught; 4) encourage students to believe that they can become good information processors; and 5) following the initial success in teaching strategies, extend the approach in the curriculum.

Pressley, M., & Associates (1990). *Cognitive strategy instruction that really improves children's academic performance*. Cambridge, MA: Brookline Books.

This volume provides practical help for teachers who would like to learn how to teach students, both in regular and special education, how to learn more effectively. The chapters cover decoding, reading comprehension, vocabulary, spelling, writing, and mathematics. Pressley writes that "cognitive strategy instruction is not suggested as a substitute for content teaching, but rather a complement to it. Our view is that good thinking consists not only of using the right procedures but coordinating use of effective strategies with a well developed knowledge base" (p. 5).

Pressley, M., Levin, J.R., & McDaniel, M.A. (1987). Remembering versus inferring what a word means: Mnemonic and contextual approaches. In M.G. McKeown and M.E. Curtis (Eds.), *The nature of vocabulary acquisition* (pp. 107-128). Hillsdale, NJ: Lawrence Erlbaum Associates.

This chapter presents both research-based theory and specific guidelines for instruction in remembering and inferring word meanings. "The distinction between remembering and inferring processes is important because we emphasize that effective vocabulary-inferring processes and effective vocabulary-remembering strategies are complementary vocabulary-acquisition components, with one's strength being the other's weakness, and vice versa. In particular, we propose here that learning from context and the use of mnemonic techniques . . . are potentially effective vocabulary-inferring and vocabulary-remembering components, respectively" (pp. 107-8). The authors point out that if one's objective is to maximize remembering vocabulary, then a mnemonic approach is to be preferred. On the other hand, if the objective is to enhance pronunciation, syntax, spelling, and motivation, then other strategies such as inferring word meanings from context should be considered.

Pressley, M., Scruggs, T. E., & Mastropieri, M. A. (1989). Memory strategy research in learning disabilities: Present and future directions. *Learning Disabilities Research, 4,* 68-77.

These authors argue that "for practical as well as scientific reasons, a solid foundation of laboratory research on strategy use is needed before issues of classroom applications and materials modifications can be addressed" (p. 68). They discuss major research questions regarding learning disabilities and memory strategy instruction, and they present a proposed model for an efficient sequence of research in memory strategy instruction.

Putnam, M.L. (1993). Readability estimates of content area textbooks used by students mainstreamed into secondary classrooms. *Learning Disabilities: Research and Practice, 3*, 53-59.

Mastering expected reading in content-area classes is a frequent source of difficulty for students with learning disabilities. Putnam reports a study of the level of difficulty of texts frequently used in 7th- and 10th-grade English, science, social studies, and mathematics classes, utilizing the average of three widely-used formulas – the Flesch Index, the FOG Index, and the Dale-Chall Readability Formula. He found that 7th grade texts tend to be written at a higher grade level, while 10th grade text were written at a comparatively lower level. Social studies texts were among the most difficult to read. These findings clarify one reason that mainstreamed students with poor reading comprehension have particular difficulty in content-area classes. Putnam suggests that teachers determine the readability level of texts and make an appropriate match between the text and the student's skill level.

Rack, J. P., Snowling, M. J., & Olson, R. K. (1992). The nonword reading deficit in developmental dyslexia: A review. *Reading Research Quarterly, 27*, 28-53.

"Dyslexia is typically defined as a reading and spelling problem that cannot be accounted for by sensory or neurological damage, lack of educational opportunity, or low intelligence . . . . The concept of dyslexia, as defined in this way, has been surrounded by controversy since its first use" (p. 29). The authors examine two inconsistent hypotheses: that dyslexics have a deficit in phonological language skills and that dyslexics are deficient in both phonological skills and word-specific skills. The authors state that dyslexia is a deficit on the word level with comprehension less impaired, and that impairment is probably due to problems with word recognition. They explore issues of word recognition and decoding for both adults and developing readers and conclude that even with stage models of reading, both perform important functions.

A review of research using reading-level match comparisons is presented and considered from the perspective of a deficit or a delay in phonological skills. The results are summarized as being strongly in support of the deficit hypothesis. Rack, Snowling, and Olson also make a number of other important points. There is an open question as to "whether there are additional non-phonological cognitive abilities that might influence the developmental path taken by different individuals" (p. 50). In addition, the authors emphasize the need to consider the use of phonological skills, not as an either/or matter, but on a continuum depending on the difficulty of the word, the student's level of skills, and the stage of reading development.

Reetz, L. J., & Hoover, J. H. (1992). The acceptability and utility of five reading approaches as judged by middle school LD students. *Learning Disabilities Research and Practice, 7,* 11-15.

Reetz and Hoover investigated the reactions to instruction of middle school students with learning disabilities who had word identification problems. The five types of instruction used were: language experience, direct instruction, multisensory learning, neurological impress, or a basal reader. The response to the first four was equally acceptable. The response to the basal reader was the most favorable. The authors suggest that this may be because the students viewed the basal approach as the most socially acceptable. They also suggest that "it may be important to acquaint students with the importance of remedial methods for meeting their individual needs when these materials diverge from the familiar" (p. 14).

Reid, R., & Harris, K.R. (1993). Self-monitoring of attention versus self-monitoring of performance: Effects on attention and academic performance. *Exceptional Children, 60*, 29-40.

Reid and Harris stress the importance of self-monitoring behavior and cite evidence to demonstrate that students with learning disabilities may not have developed these behaviors. They review literature on two kinds of self-monitoring behaviors: self-monitoring of attention (SMA) and self-monitoring of performance (SMP). The authors studied the effects of instruction in both types of monitoring in learning spelling words compared to a spelling study procedure (SSP). Both types of monitoring increased the on-task behavior of the subjects. The effect on spelling mastery was more complex. "Spelling achievement was significantly lower in SMA and in SSP, and spelling maintenance was significantly lower in SMA than in SSP and SMP" (p. 29). These finding led the authors to conclude that instruction in self-monitoring behavior must be linked to the task, the learner, and the outcome desired.

Reiff, H.B., Gerber, P.J., & Ginsberg, R. (1993). Definitions of learning disabilities from adults with learning disabilities: The insiders' perspectives. *Learning Disability Quarterly, 16*, 114-126.

These authors asked 71 successful adults who had been identified as learning disabled while in school to define the term "learning disabilities." In so doing, participants contributed conceptualizations about learning disabilities that were a product of their years of personal experience. Some of their definitions stressed difference rather than disability, such as: "Can't learn the way everyone else learns" (p. 122). Others explicitly dismissed the idea of disability: "Not a disability as long as you realize that you will have to work a little bit harder than other people" (p. 122). Finally, some focused on poor teaching: "Not a learning disability but a teaching disability" (p. 122). The authors point out that the skewed nature of the participants, for many of them may be gifted although learning disabled, limits the generalizability of the findings. In addition, participants' perceptions represent only those adults who have been successful. The authors conclude that learning disabilities necessitate alternative approaches if one is to achieve vocational success.

Reinking, D. (1993). A new focus for the National Reading Research Center. *The Computing Teacher*, *20*(6), 29-31.

In this brief article, the author reports a new educational research agenda driven by changes in technology that affect the nature of teaching, learning, and literacy. Reinking reminds us that "computers are changing the nature of literacy. For example, growing evidence suggests that reading and writing electronic texts is not the same as reading and writing text on paper" (p. 30). The new research agenda will focus on school-based research, teachers as researchers, developing engaged readers, and research that is expected to make a noticeable contribution to improving literacy nationally.

Reynolds, M.C., Wang, M.C., & Walberg, H.J. (1987). The necessary restructuring of special and regular education. *Exceptional Children*, *53*, 391-398.

These authors suggest "Rights Without Labels" guidelines based on a three-step approach to effective services: 1) pre-referral screening and intervention; 2) the inclusion of curriculum-based assessment procedures; and 3) reallocation of resources to facilitate providing effective services in the mainstream. They write: "The categories used in special education for mildly handicapped students are not reliable nor valid. . . . It is recommended that a program of pilot projects be initiated in conjunction with regular educators to redesign categorical programs and policies" (p. 391).

Rhodes, L.K., & Dudley-Marling, C. (1988). *Readers and writers with a difference: A holistic approach to teaching learning disabled and remedial students.* Portsmouth, NH: Heinemann.

After reviewing the history of learning disabilities and the various definitions and extrinsic and intrinsic etiologies that have been suggested, Rhodes and Dudley-Marling conclude that the important issue is how to identify effective teaching strategies. They advocate a holist approach in which learning is placed in a meaningful context, and the parts are not isolated but are taught and learned within that context. Holistic approaches encourage active learning and build on strengths. The holistic approach is documented in this book in many ways. For example, to overcome limitations of standardized tests, the authors provide specific guidance in assessment through observation of the child as he/she reads and writes. Many specific suggestions are made to develop readers who view reading as actively constructing meaning, using knowledge of language and text conventions as well as world knowledge.

Richardson, S. O. (1989). Specific developmental dyslexia: Retrospective and prospective views. *Annals of Dyslexia, 39,* 3-23.

Richardson presents a detailed review of the history of dyslexia over the past few centuries, examining oral and written language as well as perceptual-motor processes. She concludes that because of the heterogeneous nature of the disability, all disciplines must work together. She advocates providing instruction in decoding because our language is phonetically based. In addition, because reading is essentially gaining meaning from text, she advocates comprehension instruction incorporating "speaking, writing, spelling and reading activities as part of a total language arts approach" (p. 19).

Rickelman, R.J., & Henk, W.A. (1991). Parents and computers: Partners in helping children learning to read. *The Reading Teacher, 44,* 508-509.

This brief article offers rules of thumb for parents who are interested in using computers educationally at home to improve reading. These guidelines include: (1) be aware of hardware requirements; (2) preview the software; (3) provide software that is at a level the child can use independently; (4) select programs that will be used frequently; (5) do not view a computer as a replacement for books; (6) work with the child; and (7) use the school for support.

Rinehart, S.D., Barksdale-Ladd, A., & Welker, W.A. (1991). Effects of advance organizers on text recall by poor readers. *Reading, Writing, and Learning Disabilities, 7,* 321-335.

These researchers investigated the effects of building or activating prior knowledge before reading. Varied presentations of advance organizers were studied in content-area classrooms. An oral delivery of the advance organizer by the teacher, followed by whole-group discussion, was effective in improving text recall.

Ripich, D. N., & Griffith, P. L. (1988). Narrative abilities of children with learning disabilities and non-disabled children: Story structure, cohesion, and propositions. *Journal of Learning Disabilities, 21,* 165-173.

Ripich and Griffith examine the abilities of students with learning disabilities to retell simple stories using story grammar and to generate stories. "Story grammar refers to the macrostructure of text organization, the top-down level of processing" (p. 165-166). Prior research has indicated that students with learning disabilities could use this set of organizational rules to retell text. The results of this study found that students did make use of story grammar and that, with increasing age, they recalled more details. The authors suggest the need for instruction and guidance for students with learning disabilities in this area.

Rogan, L.L., & Hartman, L.D. (1990). Adult outcomes of learning disabled students ten years after initial follow-up. *Learning Disabilities Focus, 5*, 91-102.

This article presents data from a second follow-up of young adults who had been identified as learning disabled while they were in school. The sample was varied; some were college graduates, some high school graduates, and some had attended high school self-contained special education classes. The authors conclude that "among the variables contributing to a favorable outcome were intensive effective intervention during the elementary and middle school years, ongoing supportive tutoring or resource help during mainstream school attendance, counseling or therapy when needed, consistent parental understanding and support, and the absence of severely complicating neurological and emotional problems" (p. 91). As we seek to improve educational programs for students with learning disabilities, long-term data such as this offers valuable information.

Rogers, T. (1991). Dyslexia: A survivor's story. *Journal of Learning Disabilities, 24*, 121-123.

Rogers reflects on his personal experiences with dyslexia. He traces his failure as an elementary school student without appropriate help, his successful learning at the Gow School, a private school for boys with dyslexia, and finally his marginal struggle at a prestigious private high school where, once more, the assistance he needed was lacking. Remembering his experiences at the Gow School he writes: "I tasted for the first time a sense of worth and of being accepted for who I was and for what I could do" (p. 123). Rogers' contribution offers substance to our understanding that effective, early intervention is important for students with learning disabilities.

Roller, C.M. (1990). Commentary: The interaction of knowledge and structure variables in the processing of expository prose. *Reading Research Quarterly, 25,* 79-89.

Roller suggests that the interaction between knowledge and structure may explain many of the conflicting findings in research on text processing. She concludes that "text structure is most important when the subject matter is moderately unfamiliar to the reader, because the reader can use knowledge of the structure to construct the relations between the concepts in the text" (p. 79). Because it is from this type of reading that readers acquire most new knowledge, utilizing text structure to aid comprehension is an important skill even though it is not needed in most everyday reading.

Rose, D., Meyer, A., & Pisha, B. (1994). Out of print: Literacy in the electronic age. *Literacy: A redefinition.* Hillsdale, NJ: Lawrence Erlbaum Associates.

These authors clarify the limitations of print and the advantages of electronic multimedia in teaching children to read and in teaching content. They highlight technology's ability to promote active engagement of learners, to aid in including students with all levels of disabilities in regular classrooms, and to individualize instruction. "Adapting the pace of instruction, the time allotted to individual tasks, or trying out a different explanation are all methods of individualizing instruction. Such methods place great burdens on the teacher" (p. 56). They go on to explain ways in which electronic multimedia perform these adaptations well.

Roser, N. L., Hoffman, J. V., & Farest, C. (1990). Language, literature, and at-risk children. *The Reading Teacher, 43*, 554-559.

This article reports the authors' attempts to include quality literature in a traditional reading/language arts program for students at risk who also have limited English proficiency. They include specific steps that they followed to create and implement the program that should be helpful to teachers with similar interests. The authors conclude: "Our results indicate that a literature-based program can be implemented successfully in schools that serve at-risk students" (p. 559).

Ross, J. M., & Smith, J. O. (1990). Adult basic educators' perceptions of learning disabilities. *Journal of Reading, 33*, 340-347.

Ross and Smith cite the growing acceptance of the reality that learning disabilities extend across the life span and are a concern for educators of adults as well as for educators of children. The estimate of the number of learning disabled adults in adult basic education and high school equivalency programs is uncertain as best, but it is high. There is little information available about these adults and few programs designed to take their needs into account. A survey of attitudes and knowledge of teachers and administrators in adult programs showed variations in the definition of learning disabilities and identification procedures. There was general concern about the lack of services available to adults with learning disabilities. The authors suggest a multilevel service model designed to provide inservice training, consultation to teachers, and direct services to adults.

Rottman, T. R., & Cross, D. R. (1990). Using informed strategies for learning to enhance the reading and thinking skills of children with learning disabilities. *Journal of Learning Disabilities, 23,* 270-278.

Rottman and Cross review the research related to metacognition, reading, and students with learning disabilities. They also present information on Informed Strategies for Learning, a program designed to "instruct children about the existence and use of reading strategies" (p. 271). They report on a study in which this program was used with students with learning disabilities. The results were generally positive, although the authors are cautious because of the difficulties of field-based research.

Ryan, E. B., Short, E. J., & Weed, K. A. (1986). The role of cognitive strategy training in improving the academic performance of learning disabled children. *Journal of Learning Disabilities, 19,* 521-529.

Ryan, Short and Weed advocate addressing issues of cognitive processing in providing remediation for learning disabled students. They characterize the learning disabled as passive learners who don't organize information or use strategies. They review difficulties in metacognition and metamemory. In looking specifically at reading behavior, the authors find a failure to monitor comprehension, over-reliance on decoding, and inadequate knowledge and use of processing strategies. In addition, learning disabled students lack motivation and attribute their difficulties to external causes. The authors explore the dimensions of cognitive behavior modification and cite its effectiveness. They state that "poor comprehenders have been assisted substantially by strategy training" (p. 524), citing the use of mental imagery, self-questioning and paraphrasing as effective strategies to help the reader become active. In addition, they report that metacognitive training significantly increased strategy awareness and comprehension of text. Numerous studies and strategies are reviewed.

Salend, S.J. (1994). *Effective mainstreaming: Creating inclusive classrooms* (2nd ed.). New York: Macmillan.

Salend writes, "This book is intended to assist you in meeting the challenges of implementing effective mainstreaming and creating inclusive classrooms in your school" (p. iii). Given the major efforts to accomplish these objectives today, Salend addresses an important topic as he translates research into practice to expand the range of students being accommodated in the mainstream classroom setting. Specific ways of determining and meeting the diverse educational needs of students are presented within the context of the mainstream setting. Modifying instruction in reading, writing, social studies, science, and mathematics receives special attention. Salend also offers guidelines for modifying the classroom environment and classroom behavior.

Salvia, J., & Ysseldyke, J.E. (1991). *Assessment in special and remedial education*, (5th ed.). Boston, MA: Houghton Mifflin.

The objective of this basic text in assessment is to provide teac_ers with the information needed to understand the results of assessment instruments and to use them in making appropriate educational plans for their students. The authors write: "Decisions regarding the most appropriate environment and the most appropriate program for an individual should be data-based decisions. . . . However, misuse and misunderstanding of tests may well occur unless teachers are informed consumers and users of tests" (p. xii). This comprehensive book covers principles of formal and informal assessment, basic concepts of measurement, the assessment of intelligence and other processes, assessment of academic skills, and applying assessment information to educational decision making.

Samuels, S. J. (1987). Information processing abilities and reading. *Journal of Learning Disabilities*, *20*, 18-22.

Samuels presents the LaBerge and Samuels model of reading as a way of understanding the difficulties students may have learning to read. The model includes four elements: attention, visual memory, phonological memory, and semantic memory. Of these, the element of attention has been cited as the major source of difficulty, particularly because of the limited capacity to process information. When decoding is not automatic, attention is not available for comprehending the text.

Samuels discusses a series of experiments with boys in grades three through six comparing learning disabled and normal students to determine differences in attention as a possible cause of difficulties for students with learning disabilities. He found no difference in the two groups, suggesting that "the low academic achievement of the learning disabled is not necessarily the result of attention deficits" (p. 21). He suggests using an information processing approach as the basis for determining causes of their difficulty in reading.

Sawyer, D. J. (1992). Language abilities, reading acquisition, and developmental dyslexia: A discussion of hypothetical and observed relationships. *Journal of Learning Disabilities*, *25*, 82-95.

Sawyer reviews research in the areas of language abilities and reading acquisition, focusing primarily on the beginning stages of reading. She relates Frith's three stages of reading to the development of language and to the acquisition and use of strategies. The three stages focus on recognizing whole words, decoding words through the use of phonemes, and reading words through the use of larger units. Developmental dyslexia is seen as a failure in the development and use of cognitive abilities in moving from one stage to another. In addition, the author suggests that developmental dyslexia may be "apparent" when there is a mismatch between the child's abilities and instruction or "true" dyslexia that is the result of biological impairment. Suggestions for remediation are made for both conditions.

Schunk, D.H., & Rice, J.M. (1987). Enhancing comprehension skill and self-efficacy with strategy value information. *Journal of Reading Rehabilitation, 19,* 285-302.

Schunk and Rice report two investigations that examine the effects of providing poor readers with minimal information that strategy use improves performance. In both studies, the children were given instruction on strategies to help them find main ideas. The findings of both studies suggest that poor readers may not benefit from the minimal strategy value information that was provided in this study. The authors remind us that previous investigations have indicated that multiple sources of strategy value information are effective in improving comprehension and promoting self-confidence.

Schunk, D.H., & Rice, J.M. (1992). Influence of reading-comprehension strategy information on children's achievement outcomes. *Learning Disability Quarterly, 15,* 51-64.

Schunk and Rice suggest that information about the usefulness of comprehension strategies will benefit poor readers. They conducted two experiments. In the first experiment, two groups of poor readers received instruction on finding main ideas. One group was also given information regarding the value of using comprehension strategies, which produced good results. In the second experiment, one group was taught how to modify the strategy in addition to the conditions of Experiment 1. This procedure produced the strongest results of all. The authors conclude that strategy value information "enhances comprehension self-efficacy, skill, strategy use, and transfer of achievement outcomes" (p. 61). These findings should be of interest to classroom teachers who may integrate information about the value of learning strategies with their instruction of these strategies themselves.

Scott, J.A., Hiebert, E.H., & Anderson, R.C. (1994). Research as we approach the millennium: Beyond *Becoming a Nation of Readers*. In F. Lehr and J. Osborn, *Reading, language, and literacy: Instruction for the twenty-first century* (pp. 253-282). Hillsdale, NJ: Lawrence Erlbaum Associates.

"The rhetoric surrounding emergent literacy instruction has changed significantly since the publication of *Becoming a Nation of Readers . . . .* Research that documents intensive focused instruction as part of classroom practice for beginning readers would integrate the three areas that often have been studied separately over the past several years – whole language, phonemic awareness, and early interventions" (p. 272).
These authors examine the issues of motivation, comprehension, and emergent literacy as they focus our attention on new directions for research in reading instruction.

Scruggs, T. E., Bennion, K., & Lifson, S. (1985). Learning disabled students' spontaneous use of test taking skills on reading achievement tests. *Learning Disability Quarterly, 8*, 205-210.

Scruggs, Bennion and Lifson compare strategies used by third grade learning disabled and normal students in taking reading achievement tests. They found that students with learning disabilities made less use of appropriate reasoning strategies, particularly in inferential comprehension items, and that when they did use reasoning strategies, they were less successful with them. The fact that they had inappropriately high levels of confidence in their ability to use reasoning strategies suggests a lack in the area of metacognitive abilities. The authors conclude that the problem is in reading comprehension, not in test-taking skills. "Strategy training in such areas could lead to improved reading comprehension as well as improved test-taking skills, particularly since selecting and implementing appropriate strategies has been found to improve general cognitive functioning" (p. 210).

Scruggs, T.E., & Mastropieri, M.A. (1986a). Academic characteristics of behaviorally disordered and learning disabled students. *Behavioral Disorders, 23*, 184-190.

Children in grades 1-3 who were behaviorally disordered or learning disabled were compared, and the authors report that there were few differences in their academic performance. They also discuss the pros and cons of cross-categorical placement for these two groups of students.

Scruggs, T. E., & Mastropieri, M. A. (1986b). Improving the test-taking skills of behaviorally disordered and learning disabled children. *Exceptional Children, 53*, 63-68.

Scruggs and Mastropieri attribute many of the difficulties students with learning disabilities experience in school to their failure to use "appropriate learning and problem-solving strategies" (p. 63). This includes an inability to attend to the critical components of a task and to select appropriate academic and problem-solving strategies. Ineffective test-taking strategies reflect difficulties in these problem-solving strategies. They found that appropriate test-taking strategies could be taught to third and fourth grade students with learning disabilities and behavior disorders with improved performance on the word study skills subtest but not the reading comprehension subtest. They suggested that the difficulties in the reading comprehension subtest were probably due to inappropriate reading and reasoning strategies.

Scruggs, T.E., & Mastropieri, M.A. (1990). The case for mnemonic instruction: From laboratory research to classroom applications. *Journal of Special Education, 24*, 7-31.

These authors review a decade of their own experimental investigations and those of others concerning memory-enhancing strategy use. They report concurrent investigations of both content and vocabulary acquisition. In each case, special education students learned better when they employed mnemonic strategies. Scruggs and Mastropieri recommend the use of these strategies by special education teachers in their instruction.

Scruggs, T.E., & Mastropieri, M.A. (1992). Classroom applications of mnemonic instruction: Acquisition, maintenance, and generalization. *Exceptional Children, 58*, 219-229.

Scruggs and Mastropieri describe a study conducted to investigate the effectiveness of mnemonic training on the learning of science content by students with learning disabilities. Mnemonic pictures representing the content formed the basis for the training. The authors "found that mnemonic instruction can produce strong and lasting effects on the acquisition and maintenance of science content" (p. 227).

Scruggs, T.E., & Mastropieri, M.A. (1993a). Current approaches to science education: Implications for mainstream instruction of students with disabilities. *Remedial and Special Education (RASE)*, *14*, 15-24.

These authors suggest that different approaches to science education can differentially enhance or inhibit the success of mainstreamed students with disabilities. They discuss four domains of school functioning: language and literacy, cognitive-conceptual, psycho-social, and sensory-physical abilities. The authors make the point that mainstream curriculum approaches, including textbook-content approaches and activity-inquiry approaches, interact with these four areas of disability. Scruggs and Mastropieri conclude that it is not clear that either approach is better suited for all mainstreamed students; rather, the particular needs of individuals, the content of the lessons, and the attributes of the teacher should determine the selection of the type of instruction.

Scruggs, T.E., & Mastropieri, M.A. (1993b). Special education for the twenty-first century: Integrating learning strategies and thinking skills. *Journal of Learning Disabilities*, *26*, 392-398.

Responding to Ellis' Integrative Strategy Instruction (ISI) model, Scruggs and Mastropieri comment that although it is not empirically validated as a model, a number of the components have been validated, and the model appears to be coherent and logically sound. They suggest that Ellis specify how ISI differs from other models and how it is similar, pointing out that the proposals of a number of researchers need to be synthesized to produce a documented body of interventions that can be recommended to the classroom teacher.

Scruggs, T.E., & Mastropieri, M.A. (1994).   Issues in conducting intervention research: Secondary students. In S. Vaughn and C. Bos (Eds.), *Research issues in learning disabilities: Theory, methodology, assessment, and ethics* (130-145). New York: Springer-Verlag.

The authors remind us that little intervention research has been conducted to identify methods for improving programs for students with learning disabilities. Because interventions should be well-grounded in theories of learning as well as the characteristics of students with learning disabilities, experiments should first be conducted in controlled environments; if this is successful, the experiment should then be evaluated in classrooms. The authors discuss research designs that they have found useful in their own classroom intervention research. They stress the importance of good design, and they remind us that an inadequate research design can invalidate the most promising efforts.

Scruggs, T.E., Mastropieri, M.A., Bakken, J.P., & Brigham, F.J. (1993). Reading versus doing: The relative effects of textbook-based and inquiry-oriented approaches to science learning in special education classrooms. *Journal of Special Education, 27,* 1-15.

This article reports an investigation of mnemonic instruction of science content with secondary students with mild disabilities. In addition to basic mnemonic instruction, students were also taught to generate and draw their own mnemonic pictures. The findings suggest that mnemonic instruction produces better performance. In addition, students were able to generate and apply their own mnemonic strategies to new content. The authors suggest that these results should not be interpreted to mean that mnemonic instruction can be employed to meet all instructional objectives in science. However, "when the instructional objectives involve the acquisition and retention of discriminations, concepts, facts, rules, or procedures, mnemonic instruction may very well be the optimal procedure" (p. 228).

Seidenberg, P. L. (1989). Relating text-processing research to reading and writing instruction for learning disabled students. *Learning Disabilities Focus*, 5, 4-12.

This article proposes that the concepts derived from research on text processing can provide a foundation for the design of more effective instruction for students with learning disabilities. The literature reviewed focused on two areas: first, cognitive processes in which learners perform complex reading and writing tasks; and second, the importance of text structure types. Recommendations for instructional practice are also offered.

Shafrir, U., Siegel, L.S., & Chee, M. (1990). Learning disability, inferential skills, and postfailure reflectivity. *Journal of Learning Disabilities*, 23, 506-513.

Citing the "growing body of data [that] points to deficits in metacognitive processes as possible contributors to learning disabilities" (p. 506), Shafrir, Siegel, and Chee compared normally achieving children and children with learning disabilities to determine their inferential skills and their ability to monitor and detect errors in their performance. Both areas were found to be a major source of difficulty. However, the authors point out that the population is heterogeneous, and it is important to look at each child's abilities.

Shapiro, S., & Welch, M. (1991). Using poetry with adolescents in a remedial reading program: A case study. *Reading Horizons*, 31, 318-331.

This article presents a case study of a fifteen-year-old boy with severe learning disabilities. He attended a university-based reading clinic for several semesters, and he finally experienced reading and writing success through the use of poetry – his own and that of others – for instruction.

Shaywitz, B., Shaywitz, S., & Fletcher, J. (1992). The Yale Center for the Study of Learning and Attention Disorders. *Learning Disabilities: A Multidisciplinary Journal, 3,* 1-12.

This article describes the work of the Yale Center for the Study of Learning and Attention Disorders. Its primary mission is to develop a comprehensive classification system. These researchers write: "It is hypothesized that there are three major influences on learning – cognitive, attentional, and behavioral" (p. 1). They conclude by discussing subtypes of disorders and appropriate interventions.

Shepherd, M.J. (1988). Discussion: Review of research on specific reading, writing, and mathematics disorder. In J.F. Kavanagh and T.J. Truss, Jr. (Eds.), *Learning disabilities: Proceedings of the National Conference* (pp. 164-167). Parkton, MD: York Press, Inc.

This response to recent research in the field of learning disabilities presents a critique that stimulates our thinking. Shepherd questions the label "learning disabled" because of its broad implications, and she suggests that the term "specific developmental disorders" might be more appropriate. In addition, she addresses one of the difficulties of research in the field: "The problem with the research conducted over the past twenty years . . . is that we cannot summarize findings across studies" (p. 165). Given this restriction, it is difficult to base practice on theory.

Shinn, M. R., Tindal, G. A., Spira, D., & Marston, D. (1987). Practice of learning disabilities as social policy. *Learning Disability Quarterly, 10,* 17-28.

These authors point out that in spite of the uncertainties as to what constitutes learning disabilities, we have in PL 94-142 a major social policy in place, one that costs a great deal of money to implement. In an effort to identify the reality of how we are providing assessment and services, the authors examined regular education students, Chapter 1 students, and students with learning disabilities. In terms of achievement, they ranked from high to low, with students with learning disabilities consistently lower than the other two groups. The authors suggested that there may be a possibility that "lack of success in the classroom may be the basis for LD social policy" (p. 24).

Shinn, M. R., Ysseldyke, J. E., Deno, S. L., & Tindal, G. A. (1986). A comparison of differences between students labeled learning disabled and low achieving on measures of classroom performance. *Journal of Learning Disabilities, 19*, 545-552.

Shinn, Ysseldyke, Deno, and Tindal identify several problems related to the definition and identification of learning disabled students. These include the failure of research to support the use of discrepancy formula or scatter analysis of scores and the lack of consensus among professionals in the identification process. Further, there has been a failure to distinguish between learning disabled students and low achieving students as well as a misclassification of students using the federal definition. This study examined the difference between students with learning disabilities and low-achieving students based on classroom performance. "No meaningful differences" (p. 545) were found in their performance on norm-referenced tests; however, their performance in the classroom revealed significant differences in reading, spelling and spelling accuracy. The authors state that teacher referrals are frequently based on classroom performance and that the formal diagnosis made confirms that referral.

Siegel, L. S., & Linder, B. A. (1984). Short-term memory processes in children with reading and arithmetic learning disabilities. *Developmental Psychology, 20*, 200-207.

Siegel and Linder review theory and research supporting the difficulties in short-term memory often experienced by learning disabled students. Children with a learning disability have more difficulty with phonemic coding in reading as well as with awareness of the phonological aspects of short-term memory tasks. However, since the use of phonetic codes appears to develop over time, the authors suggest that there is evidence of a developmental delay rather than a deficit.

Siegel, L. S., & Ryan, E. B.(1988). Development of grammatical-sensitivity, phonological, and short-term memory skills in normally achieving and learning disabled children. *Developmental Psychology, 24*, 28-37.

Because of the close relationship between grammatical, phonological, and short-term memory skills and the development of reading abilities, the authors studied these skills in normal children, reading disabled, arithmetic disabled, and attention deficit disordered children from seven to fourteen years old. The disabled population was all identified as learning disabled. Siegel and Ryan found a significant lag in grammatical skills for the reading disabled but not for the other groups studied. "These findings clearly support the idea that reading disability represents a language disorder" (p. 34). In addition, there was a dramatic difference between the reading disabled and all other students in phonics and phonological processing. Reading disabled students also demonstrated poorer short-term memory than the other groups of students. The Attention Deficit Disorder (ADD) students performed less well on reading text than on reading individual words, suggesting that prose may require more attention than individual words. The authors conclude that in remediating a reading disability, we need to develop these particular areas.

Silliman, E. R. (1989).   Narratives: A window on the oral substrate of written language disabilities. *Annals of Dyslexia, 39*, 125-139.

Silliman presents a wide-ranging review of the transition from a language learning disability exhibited in the narrative structures used in oral language to a learning disability exhibited in literacy learning. She identifies several implications. The difficulties experienced may be organizational in nature; there may be a lack of content knowledge, which, in turn, hinders the processing strategies that can be used; and there may be a lack of metacognitive strategies.

Silver, A.A. (1994).   Biology of specific (developmental) learning disabilities. In N. Ellsworth, C. Hedley, and A. Baratta (Eds.), *Literacy: A redefinition* (pp. 187-212). Hillsdale, NJ: Erlbaum.

Silver writes: "This chapter reviews some of the known and some of the speculative data relating to learning disabilities that the neuroscientist can offer to the educator and to suggest ways in which that information can contribute to education for the future" (p. 187).   Silver discusses neuropsychological processing defects and their effect on learning to read, recent medical tools for assessment such as magnetic resonance imaging and positron emission scanning, and the familial and heritable basis of specific learning disabilities. He concludes that effective education for children with specific learning disabilities may depend on their unique pattern of disabilities and abilities.

Silver, A.A., & Hagin, R.A. (1990). *Disorders of learning in childhood*. New York: Wiley.

This unusual text presents a comprehensive overview of learning disorders. This overview provides "a clinically based classification of learning disorders; offers general principles of diagnosis and management from biological, psychological, educational, and social perspectives; and describes the categories of children with learning disorders most frequently seen in clinics and classrooms" (vii), all perspectives that should form the basis for educational decisions appropriate to the child's needs. It represents an unusual integration of the theory and practice of education, child psychiatry, and the neurosciences. Silver and Hagin offer specific suggestions for the education of children with learning disorders.

Silver, L. (1990). Attention-Deficit Hyperactivity Disorder: Is it a learning disability or a related disorder? *Journal of Learning Disabilities*, *23*, 393-397.

Silver addresses the issue of Attention Deficit-Hyperactivity Disorder (ADHD) as it relates to learning disabilities and school services. He points out that "between 15% and 20% of children and adolescents with learning disabilities will have ADHD" (p. 396). He reminds us that the treatment of learning disabilities and ADHD is quite different. Special education is the preferred treatment for a learning disability. However, for ADHD the treatment includes behavioral management, family counseling, and the use of medications. Medication decreases hyperactivity, impulsivity, and distractibility in approximately 80% of children and adolescents with ADHD. Silver reminds us that "if these treatment interventions control the behaviors (hyperactivity, distractibility, impulsivity), the child or adolescent can function in the classroom like a nondisabled individual" (p. 396).

Simmonds, E.P.M. (1992). The effects of teacher training and implementation of two methods for improving the comprehension skills of students with learning disabilities. *Learning Disabilities Research and Practice, 7,* 194-198.

Simmonds examines the effectiveness of teaching 24 resource room teachers to implement Question Answer Relationships (QARs), which are self-questioning metacognitive strategies. The students with whom the strategy was employed ranged from first through ninth grades. The results suggest that teachers learned the strategy well, that the QARs were easily adapted to content-area reading, and that they improved the question-recognition and location performance of students with learning disabilities.

Simmons, D.C., Fuchs, D., & Fuchs, L.S. (1991). Instructional and curricular requisites of mainstreamed students with learning disabilities. *Journal of Learning Disabilities, 24.* 354-360.

These authors discuss fundamental changes of instruction and curricula that will be required in mainstream reading classes if students with learning disabilities are to be successfully integrated. They point out that the commercial curricula that form the basis of reading instruction in mainstream classes do not meet the needs of poor readers such as students with learning disabilities.

Simmons, D. C., & Kameenui, E. J. (1986). Articulating learning disabilities for the public: A case of professional riddles. *Learning Disability Quarterly, 9,* 304-314.

Simmons and Kameenui reviewed articles on learning disabilities that appeared in the popular press from 1963 to 1984. They found "among the most durable and frequently reported conceptions of LD is the assumption that the source of a learning disability resides within the individual and is the result of a neurophysiological disorder" (p. 311). Instructional techniques frequently described included teaching to strengths and weaknesses and using multisensory techniques, often with an emphasis on phonics.

Simmons, D. C., & Kameenui, E. J. (1990). The effect of task alternatives on vocabulary knowledge: A comparison of students with and without learning disabilities. *Journal of Learning Disabilities, 23,* 291-297

This article reports a research study of the vocabulary knowledge of ten- and twelve-year-old students with learning disabilities. These authors report that, compared to normally achieving students, "students with learning disabilities are (a) significantly less able to construct fully specified responses to [vocabulary] production tasks, (b) comparable in their ability to use pictorial responses to demonstrate vocabulary knowledge not accessible in production tasks, and, (c) when equated in reading achievement, only ten-year-olds are significantly poorer in composite vocabulary knowledge" (p. 291). Simmons and Kameenui conclude with the need to determine the nature of these differences, the ways and conditions in which students know and don't know.

Sinatra, R. (1992). Using meaningful contexts to build poor readers' sight vocabularies. *Reading and Writing Quarterly: Overcoming Learning Difficulties, 8,* 179-195.

Sinatra identifies word recognition as the largest single problem faced by children in a university reading clinic. Based on this experience and on the research literature, he makes several suggestions for effective instruction. To build sight vocabulary for children having difficulties we must "deemphasize the child's perspective of reading as being a word-centered process to one that emphasizes reading as being a meaning-centered process" (pp. 179-180). The words must be presented in a meaningful context. The author describes four ways of approaching instruction that will provide a context for the student: children's literature, a thematic approach, language experience, and interactive computer software programs. These approaches capitalize on the strategy children with learning disabilities often use, that of gaining access to the word through meaning. Direct teaching of words or phonemes occurs only in the context of reading, not in isolation.

Sinatra, R. C., Berg, D., & Dunn, R. (1985). Semantic mapping improves reading comprehension of learning disabled students. *Teaching Exceptional Children*, *17*, 310-314.

Sinatra, Berg, and Dunn advocate the use of semantic mapping as a strategy to improve comprehension and recall of text because it enables the student to organize information and link it to prior knowledge. These are areas of considerable difficulty for many learning disabled students. In addition, it draws on the non-verbal strengths they often have. The authors present an overview of theory and research supporting their premises. A detailed description is provided of two kinds of maps – one based on class, example, and attribute relationships and the other on story grammar as well as the instructional procedures used. The maps were constructed by the students before reading a selection. The specific, concrete visual organizer appeared to aid in vocabulary understanding and recall, but, more significantly, in comprehending through explicit construction and visualization of "the organization of the relationships among the concepts and ideas" (p. 313).

Snider, V. E., & Tarver, S. G. (1987). The effect of early reading failure on acquisition of knowledge among students with learning disabilities. *Journal of Learning Disabilities*, *20*, 351-356.

Snider and Tarver use Chall's five stages of reading development as the basis for their analysis of the effects of early reading failure on the learning disabled student. It is critical to recognize, according to the authors, that the stages are hierarchical so that success in one depends on mastery of the prior stage. Failure to acquire accuracy in decoding and fluency in reading, common difficulties for students with learning disabilities, suggests that they will not acquire the knowledge base that they need for comprehension of difficult text. The implications for instruction include the need for direct instruction in phonics in order to ensure automatic decoding skills, in vocabulary and general information, and in reasoning skills. In addition, instruction should be provided in metacognitive skills and study skills for older students.

Snyder, B.L., & Pressley, M. (1990). Introduction to cognitive strategy instruction. In M. Pressley and Associates (Eds.), *Cognitive strategy instruction that really improves children's academic performance* (pp. 7-26). Cambridge, MA: Brookline Books.

Snyder and Pressley discuss ways that research and theory contribute to the development of strategy instruction for classroom use. They write that "a good strategy user is one who possesses a variety of strategies and uses these procedures to meet cognitive challenges. These strategies include 'tricks' that aid in the performance of very specific tasks" (p. 8). They point out that strategies are typically integrated into higher-order sequences to achieve complex cognitive goals; they are seldom used in isolation.

Spear, L.C., & Sternberg, R.J. (1987). An information-procession framework for understanding reading disability. In S. J. Ceci (Ed.), *Handbook of cognitive, social, and neuropsychological aspects of learning disabilities, Vol. II*, pp. 3-31. Hillsdale, NJ: Erlbaum.

Spear and Sternberg, citing the complexity of reading and of remediating a reading disability, explore the implications for a reading disability of two models of information processing, top-down and bottom-up. They examine the models in terms of reading, language, and memory. The authors conclude that the problem areas seems to be verbal and cognitive, nonverbal, or perceptual. The authors apply this framework to a discussion of word-level reading problems for disabled readers and make general suggestions for the teacher.

Speece, D. L. (1987).   Information processing subtypes of
    learning-disabled readers. *Learning Disabilities Research*,
    2(2), 91-102.

Speece acknowledges the possibility that there may be a variety of causes of reading problems in learning disabled students, including linguistic processes, memory deficits, and verbal deficits. However, she focuses on cognitive information processing deficits. She compared learning disabled readers to normally achieving readers nine or ten years of age. She examined sustained attention, encoding, short-term memory capacity, memory organization and speed of recoding, all with verbal stimuli. The results indicated that not only do the learning disabled differ from normal readers, but they differ from each other. However, "several subtype patterns support current hypotheses that link information-processing deficits with reading failure but none received unqualified support" (p. 91). In addition, she points out that the Woodcock Reading Mastery Test appeared to measure global reading skill, not reading differences. She also indicates an important direction for future research: perhaps we should be examining skilled reading and the processing skills needed for that in exploring the information processing skills of the learning disabled.

Spekman, N.J., Goldberg, R.J., & Herman, K.L. (1993).   An
    exploration of risk and resilience in the lives of individuals

with learning disabilities. *Learning Disabilities Research and Practice*, *8*, 11-18.

Learning disabilities are examined as a risk factor in this article, and the view is presented that learning disabilities should be viewed in interaction with other risk factors specific to the individual as well as environmental factors. The authors also examine underlying principles of resilience in individuals and their impact on those with learning disabilities. They suggest that education should focus on successful adaptation and competence within a life-span perspective because learning disabilities remain into adulthood.

Spekman, N.J., Herman, K.L., & Vogel, S.A. (1993). Risk and resilience in individuals with learning disabilities: A challenge to the field. *Learning Disabilities Research and Practice*, *9*, 59-65.

This article presents the report of a symposium on risk and resilience in individuals with learning disabilities. The major themes of the symposium were research, direct services, and social policy, and each is reviewed by these authors. They conclude with a plea for funding of longitudinal research projects and projects to translate research findings into practice.

Stahl, S. (1994). Separating the rhetoric from the effects: Whole language in kindergarten and first grade. In F. Lehr and J. Osborn (Eds.), *Reading, language, and literacy: Instruction for the twenty-first century* (pp. 101-114). Hillsdale, NJ: Lawrence Erlbaum Associates.

Stahl explores issues related to whole language for kindergarten and first grade students. To write this chapter, he analyzed data from 51 studies of reading instruction. He concludes that an early emphasis on decoding leads to higher achievement; however, he suggests that this can be accomplished within the context of reading stories. He reminds us that "good phonics instruction can also involve direct instruction. However, direct instruction of phonics seems most effective when it is well integrated into a reading program that also stresses meaningful interactions with text and writing" (p. 112). Thus, Stahl provides a practical guide for instruction.

Stahl, S. A., & Erickson, L. G. (1986). The performance of third grade learning disabled boys on tasks at different levels of language: A model-based exploration. *Journal of Learning Disabilities, 19,* 285-290.

Stahl and Erickson explore three possible causes of difficulties experienced by students with learning disabilities in reading and in language tasks. The three causes reflect three different theoretical models. In the first model, students with learning disabilities experience difficulties because of a general language difficulty, "a lack of awareness of the nature of language (metalinguistic awareness)" (p. 285), a position supported by many in the field. In the second model, the difficulty is caused by slowness in speed-of-processing, a position supported by research documenting slowness in reading tasks. In the third model, the rule-abstraction model, students with learning disabilities fail to abstract rules in linguistic situations. In comparing the performance of learning disabled and normal readers, the authors found that the rule-abstraction model accounted for more of the differences in the groups as shown, for example, by the learning disabled students' difficulties in retelling stories using elements of story grammar. This suggests the need for direct instruction in rules relating to reading. We are currently doing this in decoding programs like DISTAR but need to extend it to comprehension. However, the other two models also accounted for some of the differences between groups, suggesting that they may account for some of the difficulties of subgroups of students with learning disabilities.

Stahl, S.A., & Miller, P.D. (1989). Whole language and language experience approaches for beginning reading: A quantitative research synthesis. *Review of Educational Research, 59,* 87-116.

Stahl and Miller report the effects of whole language and language experience approaches on beginning reading achievement. They conducted a quantitative synthesis of 5 large federal studies and 46 additional studies that compared basal reading approaches to whole language or language experience approaches. Their findings suggest that, overall, the two approaches were approximately equal in their effects. However, several differences were noted.

> First, whole language/language experience approaches may be more effective in kindergarten than in first grade. Second, they may produce stronger effects on measures of word recognition than on measures of reading comprehension. Third, more recent studies show a trend toward stronger effect for the basal reading program relative to whole language/language experience methods. Fourth, whole language/language experience approaches produce weaker effects with populations labeled specifically as disadvantaged than they do with those not specifically labeled. (p. 87)

The authors suggest that whole language/language experience approaches might be employed for teaching print concepts and expectations about reading, but that more direct approaches might be used to help students master word recognition skills that are prerequisite to effective comprehension.

Stahl, S.A., & Shiel, T.G. (1992). Teaching meaning vocabulary: Productive approaches for poor readers.

Reading and Writing Quarterly: Overcoming Learning Disabilities, 8, 223-241.

These authors describe three productive approaches to vocabulary instruction for poor readers: teaching children to derive word meanings from context; teaching word parts such as roots, prefixes, and suffixes; and teaching words as part of semantic groups. They suggest a two-track approach to vocabulary instruction for poor readers. First, basic skills could be taught in a remedial setting and second, active involvement in vocabulary discussions could be included in their instruction in regular classes.

Stainback, S., & Stainback, W. (1992). Schools as inclusive communities. In S. Stainback & W. Stainback (Eds.), *Controversial issues confronting special education: Divergent perspectives* (p. 29-43). Boston, MA: Allyn and Bacon.

Stainback and Stainback present a rationale for full inclusion of all students in the educational mainstream. They assert that inclusion holds benefits for students, avoids the ill effects of segregation, and promotes equality. In response to the question of whether or not mainstreaming will work, they respond: "Where it is not working, we should be asking what is preventing it from working and what can be done about it" (p. 41).

Stanovich, K. E. (1988). The right and wrong places to look for the cognitive locus of reading disability. *Annals of Dyslexia*, 38, 154-177.

Stanovich, equating reading disability and dyslexia, examines the impact of cognitive research in the field of reading on our concept of reading disability. He cites research supporting a wide range of cognitive deficits, including phonological, syntactic, comprehension, rule learning, memory, and metacognition. However, it is the failure of processes at the word level that are indicative of a reading disability. "An early specific deficit in the area of phonological processing might lead to a cascade of interacting cognitive deficits that become more pervasive as schooling progresses" (p. 161). He characterizes learning disabilities not as a discrete entity, but, instead, as a graded continuum. Thus, learning disabilities are not like measles but rather like obesity. They are both health problems. Obesity, like learning disabilities, is on a continuum; it is difficult to say exactly how many people are obese because it depends on where you decide obesity begins.

Stanovich, K. E. (1991). Discrepancy definitions of reading disability: Has intelligence led us astray? *Reading Research Quarterly, 26,* 7-29.

Stanovich, using the terms "reading disability" and "dyslexia" interchangeably, raises serious questions about the present practice of using the discrepancy between intelligence and achievement as a basis for the identification of students with learning disabilities. He suggests, instead of this practice, that we "measure the discrepancy between reading ability and listening comprehension" (p. 20).

The author examines research comparing dyslexics and garden-variety poor readers and concludes that "it is surprisingly difficult to demonstrate cognitive differences between poor readers of differing IQs" (p. 15). It is reading skill and reading ability that differentiate the two groups. In addition, he states that there are "no good data indicating that discrepancy-defined dyslexics respond differently to various educational treatments than do garden-variety readers of the same age" (p. 15). Stanovich suggests that we need more evidence before we can be certain that there are reading-related cognitive differences between dyslexics and garden-variety poor readers and that different instruction is needed for the two groups.

Stanovich, K. E. (1992). Response to Christensen. *Reading Research Quarterly, 27*, 279-280.

Stanovich writes: "There are, in my judgment, enough suggestive data to justify – scientifically – the search for a cognitively and neurologically distinct subgroup of poor readers if, as I argued in my review, different aptitude benchmarks are used for the differentiation" (p. 279). He points out that he does not believe that a constructivist framework precludes the usefulness of neurological analysis. At the same time, Stanovich concludes: "I have no lack of sympathy for analyses that set educational achievement differences in a social and political context" (p. 280).

Sternberg, R.J. (1987). Most vocabulary is learned from context. In M.G. McKeown and M.E. Curtis (Eds.), *The nature of vocabulary acquisition* (pp. 89-106). Hillsdale, NJ: Lawrence Erlbaum Associates.

Sternberg suggests that all students be taught to use context, independently, to acquire word meanings in all of their reading. His rationale is that most vocabulary is learned from context, and that therefore readers should learn to make better use of it. He reminds us that the learning-from-context method is best for teaching students how to learn, not for teaching specific word meanings; and he notes that more direct methods, such as the keyword method, are more effective for the latter purpose. In conclusion, Sternberg states that we need to employ both types of instruction.

Stirling, E. G., & Miles, T. R. (1988). Naming ability and oral fluency in dyslexic adolescents. *Annals of Dyslexia, 38*, 50-72.

Stirling and Miles examine the role of oral language in the dyslexic. The authors cite previous research documenting the "increasing awareness of possible deficiencies in the oral language of dyslexic children, though it is by no means certain how widespread they are nor what form they take" (p. 53). In testing dyslexic adolescent boys, they found that the subjects were significantly weaker in oral language than non-dyslexic boys. The various weaknesses indicated to Stirling and Miles a "linguistic uncertainty" (p. 65) which is not limited to written language but also applies to oral language. This is significant because oral language forms the foundation for written language.

Stone, W.L., & LaGreca, A.M. (1990). The social status of children with learning disabilities: A reexamination. *Journal of Learning Disabilities, 23,* 32-37.

Stone and LaGreca report the results of a study of the specific types of peer status problems of children with learning disabilities. They found that these children obtain lower sociometric scores than their nondisabled peers, that they are disproportionately overrepresented in the rejected and neglected sociometric groups, and that they are underrepresented in the popular and average groups. Over half of the total sample of children with learning disabilities fell into one of the low status categories. The authors conclude by urging that longitudinal studies be conducted to learn more about the effects of various intervention strategies.

Stump, C.S., Lovitt, T.C., Fister, S., Kemp, S.K., Moore, R., & Schroeder, B. (1992). Vocabulary intervention for secondary-level youth. *Learning Disability Quarterly, 15,* 207-222.

These researchers report a study that introduced precision-teaching of vocabulary to regular and special education teachers over a two-year period. The teachers, in turn, employed this approach with students in their classrooms. These authors report that this approach for teaching vocabulary was effective. The majority of students demonstrated increased accuracy and fluency on timed vocabulary quizzes, and both teachers and students endorsed this method.

Swanson, H. L. (1986). Do semantic memory deficiencies underlie learning disabled readers' encoding processes? *Journal of Experimental Child Psychology, 41,* 461-488.

Swanson investigated the "extent to which learning disabled readers' atypical encoding related to their deficiencies in semantic memory" (p. 461). He found that students with learning disabilities produced lower scores on recall and organization measures than did skilled readers. All groups benefitted from instructions that oriented them to the task. However, during these instructions, students with learning disabilities had more difficulty attending to the task. Overall, the inadequate structure and organization of semantic memory appears to play a significant part in the disabled readers' difficulties in encoding. The author concludes that "the to-be-recalled word has a representation in semantic memory, perhaps in the form of a set of qualitatively different features – orthographic, phonemic and semantic. Disabled readers' encoding of words fails to effectively activate a subset of those features" (p. 485).

Swanson, H. L. (1987). Information processing theory and learning disabilities: An overview. *Journal of Learning Disabilities, 20,* 3-7.

Swanson describes information processing as a series of stages that include three components: memory, strategies, and monitoring of the strategies. His concern with much of the previous work done in the field of information processing and the student with learning disabilities is that it has focused on "isolated components and strategies" (p. 5), missing the critical element, the need to integrate components. "Learning disabilities is not simply a deficiency in a certain cognitive area, but rather represents poor coordination of several mental components and/or cognitive areas involved in information processing" (p. 5). However, the cognitive area alone is not sufficient to explain learning disabilities. It requires a recognition and understanding of the role of the child's experience, the context in which learning occurs, and the interaction between these two and the information components.

Swanson, H. L. (1988). Memory subtypes in learning disabled readers. *Learning Disability Quarterly*, *11*, 342-357.

Citing the conflicting research results regarding memory performance and the learning disabled, Swanson reviews research on memory and suggests that two components are important for this current study: structural resources – the prior knowledge a reader can access when needed – and semantic processing – relating or grouping items that go together. The author reports that students with learning disabilities exhibited a range of memory deficits. An important finding was that over 50% of the students with learning disabilities studied had difficulty forming multiple connections between information in memory and new information from the material used in the task.

Swanson, H.L. (1989). Phonological processes and other routes. *Journal of Learning Disabilities*, *22*, 493-497.

Swanson reviews Siegel's (1989) proposal that phonological processes are the key to understanding and instructing readers who are experiencing difficulty. He cites research findings showing difficulties in semantic processing and findings demonstrating the importance of lexical access to words as well as phonological access. He concludes that there is certainly some confusion about phonological processes being solely responsible for reading difficulties.

Swanson, H. L. (1990). Instruction derived from the strategy deficit model: Overview of principles and procedures. In T.E. Scruggs and B.Y.L. Wong (Eds.), *Intervention research in learning disabilities* (pp. 34-65). New York: Springer-Verlag.

Swanson puts intervention strategies for learning disabled students into a broad perspective of "higher order cognitive processing," identifying the difficulties experienced in strategy acquisition and use as overriding problems that may relate to and influence isolated processing difficulties such as phonological coding. Swanson provides a detailed review of research in this area, particularly concentrating on his own research. Detailed guidance is provided for designing instruction.

Swanson, H.L., Christie, L., & Rubadeau, R.L. (1993). The relationship between metacognition and analogical reasoning in mentally retarded, learning disabled, average, and gifted children. *Learning Disabilities Research & Practice, 8,* 70-81.

Swanson, Christie, and Rubadeau review the role of metacognition in cognitive processing as well as that of analogical problem-solving ability. In a study designed to determine if there is a link between the two, they gave a metacognitive questionnaire and a series of analogical reasoning tasks to groups of students who were identified as mentally retarded, learning disabled, normally achieving, or gifted. The findings were complex, dealing with each group and with the interrelations between the two variables. However, the authors generally conclude that "LD children's performance reflects specific-processing interdependence related to the metacognition of strategy variables and analogical reasoning" (p. 80).

Swanson, H.L., & Ransby, M. (1994). The study of cognitive processes in learning disabled students. In S. Vaughn and

C. Bos (Eds.), *Research issues in learning disabilities* (pp. 246-275). New York: Springer-Verlag.

Swanson and Ransby present a detailed review of four approaches used in thinking about the cognitive processes of students with learning disabilities. These include global structures and processes, cognitive correlates, domain-specific processing, and stage-sequence processing.

Swanson, H.L., Reffel, J., & Trahan, M. (1991). Naturalistic memory in learning-disabled and skilled readers. *Journal of Abnormal Child Psychology, 19*, 117-147.

Swanson, Reffel, and Trahan report the findings of a series of three studies designed to extend our knowledge of the memory difficulties associated with students with learning disabilities by studying their performance on naturalistic memory tasks. Detailed results are reported for all three studies. In general, the authors confirm the relationship between memory and reading, conclude that students with learning disabilities exhibit difficulty with naturalistic and laboratory memory tasks, and suggest that the problem may lessen as children get older.

Symons, S., McGoldrick, J.A., Snyder, B.L., & Pressley, M. (1990). Reading comprehension. In M. Pressley and Associates (Eds.), *Cognitive strategy instruction that really improves children's academic performance* (pp. 45-70). Cambridge, MA: Brookline Books.

This chapter describes comprehension strategies that can be taught to elementary-school children, with an emphasis on those that can be taught in less than ten hours of class time. The authors present a rationale for each strategy, specific guidelines for instruction, and the research evidence that underlies each. The strategies discussed include summarization, mental imagery, representational imagery, question generation, story grammar, and activating prior knowledge. The authors conclude that "students who use these strategies should remember more of the text because they would have constructed a rich representation of text while performing the activities" (p. 65).

Thomas, C. C., Englert, C. S., & Gregg, S. (1987). An analysis of errors and strategies in the expository writing of learning disabled students. *Remedial and Special Education (RASE)*, 8, 30-46.

Thomas, Englert and Gregg cite research supporting the notion that students with learning disabilities are not sensitive to the importance of text structure and of main ideas and details. Their writing strategies reflect this, demonstrating a "chaotic . . . associative, knowledge-telling process" (p. 21). Expository text, according to the authors, presents three major sources of difficulty. First, the text structure may be "unfamiliar, variable, or ill-defined" (p. 21). Second, the writer must remember the text structure and what has been said. Third, the writer must know a variety of text structures and be able to signal their use to the reader. The authors studied the expository writing strategies of students in grades 3 and 4, and 6 and 7. The errors of redundancy, irrelevancy, early termination, and mechanical problems suggest a lack of sensitivity to text structure and a failure to monitor the process of generation of expository text. Extended instruction in the process of writing and in the use of writing strategies is needed in order to overcome these difficulties.

Thornburg, D.G. (1991). Strategy instruction for academically at-risk students: An exploratory study of teaching "higher-order" reading and writing in the social studies. *Journal of Reading, Writing, and Learning Disabilities, 7,* 377-406

Thornburg reports on a training study conducted with at-risk seventh-grade students who were given direct instruction in the use of higher-order cognitive strategies in a social studies class. Background is provided on the importance of strategy generalization and the difficulty for at-risk students in accomplishing this task. The "cognitive apprenticeship" program is an example of the application of this framework using higher-order strategies and problem solving and reasoning in specific curricular areas. Teacher training workshops and student strategies are explained in some detail. The results of the training study were generally positive, indicating that "these types of instructional supports would appear to have considerable promise in encouraging students to use cognitive strategies that, until recently, were thought to be beyond their reach" (p. 401).

Torgesen, J. K. (1986). Computers and cognition in reading: A focus on decoding fluency. *Exceptional Children, 53,* 157-162.

Torgesen supports the contribution of cognitive research in setting directions for reading instruction. He points out, however, that "the ability to engage in complex, higher level processing strategies is directly dependent on the efficiency with which lower level processes are executed" (p. 158). The implication for reading instruction is clear. Word recognition must occur fluently and accurately in order for comprehension to occur. Evidence is cited to demonstrate that difficulties in word recognition are experienced by young learning disabled children and that this difficulty can continue through high school. The author advocates the use of computers to build fluency using Perfetti's model of word recognition through recognition of whole units and common letter patterns and through analysis of individual letters and sounds. A review of a relevant but admittedly incomplete research base suggests computers may be an effective way to provide practice with Perfetti's model to develop fluency.

Torgesen, J. K. (1988).   Studies of children with learning
    disabilities who perform poorly on memory span tasks.
    Journal of Learning Disabilities, 21, 605-612.

Torgesen reports on a series of studies examining the
processing difficulties experienced by children with learning
disabilities who exhibit memory deficits.   The studies
documented difficulty in coding, or representing, the
phonological features of language. In academic tasks this was
seen as difficulty in becoming fluent in word identification or
analysis. This is particularly significant in the beginning stages
of reading in which the emphasis is on identifying and decoding
words.

Torgesen, J. (1991).   Learning disabilities: Historical and
    conceptual issues. In B.Y.L. Wong (Ed.), *Learning about
    learning disabilities* (pp. 3-39).   San Diego, CA:
    Academic Press.

This chapter provides an overview of the field of learning
disabilities. Torgesen describes the current status of the field;
he presents a brief historical perspective that focuses on the
development of the guiding assumptions of the field; and he
discusses problems to be solved in the future.

Torgesen, J.K. (1994). Learning disabilities theory: Issues and
    advances. In S. Vaughn and C. Bos (Eds.), *Research
    issues in learning disabilities: Theory, methodology,
    assessment, and ethics* (pp. 3-21). New York: Springer-
    Verlag.

This chapter addresses issues that are important for the
discussion of learning disabilities theory, elements that should be
included in any theory of learning disabilities. Torgesen reviews
the two most completely developed current theories of learning
disabilities.   The first theory is that of nonverbal learning

disabilities, and the second is the theory of phonological reading disabilities. Torgesen concludes by suggesting that a small percentage of school-age children fall into either of these categories, and that "both scientific integrity and advancement of theory will be best served by careful discipline in our claims about the extent of these problems in samples of school aged children" (p. 17).

Torgesen, J. K., Dahlem, W. E., & Greenstein, J. (1987). Using verbatim text recordings to enhance reading comprehension in learning disabled adolescents. *Learning Disabilities Focus, 3*(1), 30-38.

This article reports three experiments that examined the effects on adolescents with learning disabilities of using verbatim text recordings to increase their comprehension and learning of information from textbooks. The authors report that when students completed a worksheet as they read, in addition to using supplemental auditory tapes, they showed gains in performance on weekly comprehension tests. When the supplemental tapes were used without the worksheet, improvement was not shown.

Torgesen, J. K., Waters, M.D., Cohen, A.L., & Torgesen, J.L. (1988). Improving sight-word recognition skills in LD children: An evaluation of three computer program variations. *Learning Disability Quarterly, 11*, 125-132.

Torgesen, Waters, Cohen, and Torgesen studied the effectiveness of three computer programs designed to teach sight words to students with learning disabilities in grades 1 to 3. The three programs were: graphics only, graphics plus synthetic speech, and synthetic speech only. All three approaches resulted in significant growth in the speed and accuracy of word recognition. The authors caution that any learning that takes place as a result of the computer program must be reinforced in real text in the classroom.

Trabasso, T. (1994). The power of the narrative. In F. Lehr and J. Osborn (Eds.), *Reading, language, and literacy: Instruction for the twenty-first century* (pp. 187-200). Hillsdale, NJ: Lawrence Erlbaum Associates.

This chapter examines narrative text from a psychological and educational perspective. The author reminds us of the importance of the ability to make inferences, for with them we often achieve coherence in understanding text. Trabasso also demonstrates that self-questioning strategies can aid comprehension and recall.

Treiman, R., & Hirsh-Pasek, K. (1985). Are there qualitative differences in reading behavior between dyslexics and normal readers? *Memory and Cognition, 13,* 357-364.

Treiman and Hirsh-Pasek compared the performance in reading individual real and nonsense words of a group of boys who had been identified as dyslexic with a younger group of normal children. The reading level of both groups was the same. They found in examining the dyslexic students that "their reading performance was quantitatively different from that of normal children in that it lagged behind, but it did not appear to be qualitatively different" (p. 363). This finding supports the developmental-lag hypothesis for dyslexia rather than the rule-deficiency hypothesis or the extreme-individual-difference hypothesis. The authors do not accept the finding that all dyslexic students are deficient in phonological processes. They also suggest that "the remedial methods found to be appropriate for children who are labeled as dyslexic may also be appropriate for children who are depressed in reading because of low intelligence or poor education" (p. 363).

U.S. Department of Education (1991, September 16). *Policy memorandum: Clarification of policy to address the needs of children with Attention-Deficit Disorders within general and/or special education.*

U.S. Department of Education (1992). *To assure the free appropriate public education of all children with disabilities.* Fourteenth Annual Report to Congress on the Implementation of the Individuals with Disabilities Act. Washington, D.C.: U.S. Government Printing Office.

The annual report to Congress provides a wealth of current facts and figures about the demographics and the education of individuals with disabilities. This is a widely used source of information regarding students with learning disabilities.

U.S. Office of Education (1977, December 29). Education of handicapped children. Assistance to the states: Procedures for evaluating specific learning disabilities. *Federal Register, Part III.* Washington, DC: U.S. Department of Health, Education and Welfare.

Vacca, R. T., & Padak, N. D. (1990). Who's at risk in reading? *Journal of Reading, 33,* 485-488.

Vacca and Padak explore the concept of the "at risk" student, citing the personal and societal effects of students who don't learn effectively, drop out of school, and become economically marginal citizens. Because literacy is so important, they identify what it means to be at risk in reading. The lack of control and the sense of "learned helplessness" are significant elements. These students often have a lack of knowledge of the reading process, a low self-image, little interest in reading, and a limited repertoire of strategies.

Van Bon, W.H.J., Boksebeld, L.M., Freide, T.A.M.F., & van den Hurk, A.J.M. (1991). A comparison of three methods of reading-while-listening. *Journal of Learning Disabilities, 24,* 471-476.

Van Bon, Boksebeld, Freide, and van den Hurk compared the effects of three different approaches used with students with learning disabilities: reading while listening using different texts each session; reading while listening with the same text repeated; reading while listening, using different texts with the listeners identifying errors in the reading in their copies of the story. Reading while listening under all conditions produced positive results. "Texts and single words from the preceding training session are read faster in the testing sessions than words not practiced before" (p. 475). The authors conclude that we need more research in order to explore why the conditions yielded similar results.

Van Daal, V.H.P., & van der Leij, A. (1992). Computer-based reading and spelling for children with learning disabilities. *Journal of Learning Disabilities, 25,* 186-195.

Van Daal and van der Leij, using the premise that learning to spell helps the child move from implicit phonological awareness to explicit phonological awareness, report on a study with children with written language disorders who were trained to spell using a computer. Three conditions were used. The group taught to read the word and copy it from the screen using the keyboard made fewer spelling errors and read the practiced words faster than the group who wrote the words from memory. Both of these groups outperformed the group who only read the word on the screen. All groups could receive speech feedback as needed. Van Daal and van der Leij conclude that computer instruction could provide the kind of processing required to improve both spelling and reading problems.

Vaughn, S., & Hogan, A. (1990). Social competence and learning disabilities: A prospective study. In H.L. Swanson and B.K. Keogh (Eds.), *Learning disabilities: Theoretical and research issues* (pp. 175-191). Hillsdale, NJ: Lawrence Erlbaum Associates.

This chapter reviews the literature as it pertains to four essential components of social competence: positive relations with others, accurate/age-appropriate social cognition, absence of maladaptive behaviors, and effective social behaviors. In addition, the authors report initial findings from a prospective study of the social competence of students with learning disabilities. Vaughn and Hogan conclude that "hypotheses suggesting that the social competence difficulties of LD students can be explained solely by teachers' perceptions, withdrawal from the regular classroom, and being labeled LD are inaccurate" (p. 187) because children who are later identified as learning disabled show patterns "demonstrating risk for social competence problems as early as 6 weeks into their first formal schooling, kindergarten" (p. 187).

Vaughn, S., Hogan, A., Kouzekanani, K., & Shapiro, S. (1990). Peer acceptance, self-perceptions, and social skills in LD students prior to identification. *Journal of Educational Psychology, 82,* 1-6.

This article reports an investigation of the social status and social skills of 239 kindergartners. The children were later identified as learning disabled, low achieving, average achieving, or high achieving. The findings revealed that students later identified as learning disabled differed from their peers on social variables and attention problems. The authors suggest that the later social difficulties of students identified as learning disabled are probably not solely a function of a history of low teacher acceptance and of low achievement.

Vauras, M., Lehtinen, E., Olkinuora, E., & Salonen, P. (1993). Devices and designs: Integrative Strategy Instruction from a motivational perspective. *Journal of Learning Disabilities, 26,* 384-393.

Responding to Ellis' Integrative Strategy Instruction model, these authors pinpoint the problem of knowledge acquisition in adolescents with learning disabilities. Because these students' knowledge base is meager, learning content involves some form of instructional "bootstrapping." The article also discusses the importance of changing teachers' habitual instructional orientation of teaching content to an orientation of focusing on strategic instruction of content. Finally, these authors point out that sufficient attention has not been paid to "the motivational and emotional prerequisites for and consequences of new instruction" (p. 384).

Vogel, S. A., & Walsh, P. C. (1987). Gender differences in cognitive abilities of learning-disabled females and males. *Annals of Dyslexia, 37,* 142-165.

Vogel and Walsh administered the Wechsler Adult Intelligence Scale to 28 "college-able" females and 21 "college-able" males with learning disabilities in order to identify any cognitive differences between the two groups. Some highlights of the study include the finding that males with learning disabilities exhibited higher visual-spatial abilities than did the females and the finding that females with learning disabilities performed at a lower level on the subtest demonstrating information and background knowledge. It may be that the lack of information acquired in school by females is due to "the cumulative effect of the reading difficulties" (p. 160). The authors also suggest that the lack of general information in students with learning disabilities may be caused by the difficulty that they have in "spontaneously generating strategies to attend to, learn, and organize information, and therefore have problems recalling information" (p. 160). Finally, they describe these students' potential and real difficulties in shifting strategies and remembering information.

Wagner, M. (1990, April). *The school programs and school performance of secondary students classified as learning disabled: Findings from the National Longitudinal Transition Study of Special Education Students.* Paper presented at the meeting of the American Educational Research Association. Boston, MA.

This report from the National Longitudinal Transition Study addresses the characteristics of secondary students with learning disabilities, school programs for them, and their school performance. The majority of secondary students with learning disabilities spend the majority of their instructional time in regular education classes, they are usually held to the same grading standards as non-disabled students, and they typically are not provided direct services beyond what is available through their special education classes. In addition, this report points out that regular education teachers are not routinely provided with substantial direct support for the instruction of students with learning disabilities. In conclusion, Wagner states that "encouraging greater instruction of students with disabilities in regular education classes, without serious attention to the instruction that goes on in those classes, would seem simply to encourage greater rates of academic failure" (p. 28).

Waldron, K. A., Saphire, D. G., & Rosenblum, S. A. (1987). Learning disabilities and giftedness: Identification based on self-concept, behavior, and academic patterns. *Journal of Learning Disabilities, 20,* 422-427.

Waldron, Saphire and Rosenblum document the difficulties of identifying the learning disabled/gifted child. Gifted children are often self-critical of their accomplishments. Gifted children with learning disabilities are even more self-critical. Their self-concept is low, and they are not able to perform academically at a level they deem appropriate. The result is frequently asocial behavior. Teachers of the gifted who are also trained in identifying learning disabilities may be able to identify and teach these children effectively.

Walker, S. C., & Poteet, J. A. (1989). Influencing memory performance in learning disabled students through semantic processing. *Learning Disabilities Research, 5,* 25-32.

Walker and Poteet report results of a study with 4th- and 5th-grade students with and without learning disabilities that focuses on levels of processing. The authors conclude that "one method of improving the memory performance of LD students may be simply to add as much semantic context to a learning activity as possible rather than relying solely on rote learning with many repetitions" (p. 30). They add an important point to this: "Whenever possible, new information should be tied to previous learning to assist students in creating naturally occurring semantic relationships that will aid in later recall" (p. 31).

Walsh, J. (1993). The promise and pitfalls of integrated strategy instruction. *Journal of Learning Disabilities, 26,* 438-442.

Responding to Ellis' Integrated Strategy Instruction (ISI), Walsh points out that the instructional strategies in this model have their roots in cognitive strategy research. He suggests that if cognitive strategy instruction in content-area classes is to be shifted to the mainstream, teachers will need to be trained to assess student cognition using multiple methods. Walsh concludes by reminding us that the most important challenge for Ellis and the ISI model is to provide empirical support for its effectiveness.

Wasik, B.A., & Slavin, R.E. (1993). Preventing early reading failure with one-to-one tutoring: A review of five programs. *Reading Research Quarterly, 28*, 179-200.

Wasik and Slavin review the long-term effectiveness of five programs designed to prevent early reading failure that are used with students with learning disabilities: Reading Recovery, Success for All, Prevention of Learning Disabilities, The Wallach Tutoring Program, and Programmed Tutorial Reading. Reading Recovery is based on the view that reading is an act of constructing meaning. Word identification is taught as needed in the context of text. Success for All is a comprehensive reading program using real text and teaching word identification skills systematically. Tutorial help is provided for any child who is falling behind. Prevention of Learning Disabilities advocates identifying skills needed for reading (prereading, word attack, comprehension, and study skills) and teaching those with which the child is having a problem. The program focuses on perceptual analysis of print, decoding and oral language proficiency. The Wallach Tutoring Program emphasizes systematic instruction in essential subskills of reading. Phonics is taught outside the context of connected text. Programmed Tutorial Reading identifies and isolates specific sight word and decoding skills outside the realm of connected text. Research studies related to the programs are reviewed. The broader programs, using certified teachers, had greater impact.

Weinstein, G., & Cooke, N.L. (1992). The effects of two repeated reading interventions on generalization of fluency. *Learning Disability Quarterly, 15*, 21-28.

Weinstein and Cooke found that repeated reading developed fluency in students with learning disabilities who were beginning readers. They note that it is important for the student to establish a way of judging when fluency is sufficient to move to the next text. They suggest focusing on fluency improvement and using that rather than a fixed-rate criterion. The latter may take longer to achieve, with less generalization to fluency.

Werner, E.E. (1993). Risk and resilience in individuals with learning disabilities: Lessons learned from the Kauai longitudinal study. *Learning Disabilities Research and Practice*, *8*, 28-34.

This article reports results of an unusual longitudinal investigation that traces the risk and resilience in individuals with learning disabilities in Kauai. Werner reports that most made a successful adaptation to adult life. Marriage, divorce, and employment rates resembled those of the cohort as a whole, and the proportion of mental health difficulties declined from adolescence to adulthood. The author concludes that the positive outcomes for these individuals are, at least in part, the result of "protective buffers and mechanisms that operated in the lives of vulnerable children and youth who succeeded against the odds" (p. 32). Werner explains that self-esteem and self-efficacy are promoted through supportive relationships, and all of the youngsters with learning disabilities who overcame the odds had at least one person in their lives with whom they had established a close bond. In young adulthood, the opening up of opportunities for education, vocational improvement through the Armed Forces, and active involvement in a church provided structure and assistance.

White, T.G., Sowell, J., & Yanagihara, A. (1989). Teaching elementary students to use word-part clues. *The Reading Teacher*, *42*, 302-308.

White, Sowell, and Yanagihara advocate direct instruction in the identification and meaning of a limited number of useful affixes as well as the application to unfamiliar words. The approach is suggested for all students. The authors provide detailed suggestions for the 19 affixes to be taught as well as the sequence and methods of instruction.

Whitmire, B.M., & Stone, C.A. (1991). Visual imagery skills and language abilities of normal and language-learning disabled children. *Learning Disability Quarterly, 14,* 49-59.

Whitmire and Stone identify and describe one subcategory of learning disabilities: language learning disabled (LLD). They review past research and describe their own, concluding that these children not only operate at an earlier level of development, often with complex difficulties, but they also "have been found to be less proficient in the use of various forms of nonverbal representation" (p. 49), including visual imagery. In examining the relationship between difficulties in language and in visual imagery, the researchers found that vocabulary knowledge seemed to be significant. The authors suggest the need for further research to determine if during reading instruction, LLD children should engage in imaging as well as develop language skills.

Will, M. (1986). Educating children with learning problems: A shared responsibility. *Exceptional Children, 52,* 411-416.

Will, Assistant Secretary of Education, proposed an initiative that was based on the premise that the current special education system contains several flaws: 1) many youngsters with learning problems are not eligible for special education services; 2) there is a tendency to equate poor performance with a handicap; 3) rather than emphasizing early prevention, special education students are usually identified after failure; and 4) the special education system does not lead to cooperative school-parent relationships. The Regular Education Initiative proposed by Will suggested that students be educated in regular education

classrooms based on their individual needs, that early
identification and intervention be emphasized, that curriculum-
based assessment procedures be employed, and that the research
of the effective schools programs be implemented.   Will
concluded that to resolve the barriers inherent in the current
system will require a partnership across professional and
institutional boundaries.

Williams, J.P. (1988). Identifying main ideas: A basic aspect of
     reading comprehension. *Topics in Language Disorders, 8,*
     1-13.

This article provides a critique of current instruction in
textual main idea identification and notes that a lack of consensus
on definition and an inconsistency within lessons add to student
difficulty.   Williams suggests a more explicit use of text
structure for determining important ideas, and she discusses the
theory of macrostructure and textual hierarchy.   She points out
that it is important for students to know that different genres
have different types of information and that texts contain
different cues as to important ideas.   She also reviews studies
that suggest that direct instruction of main idea comprehension
is effective.

Williams, J.P. (1991). Comprehension by learning-disabled and
     non-disabled adolescents of personal/social problems
     presented in text. *American Journal of Psychology, 104,*
     563-586.

Williams reports results of a study of adolescents who read
and retold short problem narratives and answered questions.
When a statement of the character's priority for action was
included in the text, even the poorest readers showed this
sensitivity to text structure.   Measures of idea units recalled,
problem-schema components reported, and error rate reflected
students' overall reading ability.   However, overall student

reading ability was not reflected in the degree to which extraneous information was incorporated into the problem representations. Students with learning disabilities "made more importations and more implausible importations than did non-disabled students. . . . Only proficient readers showed awareness of the source of the information (text or extratext) on which their predications were based" (p. 563).

Williams, J.P. (1993). Comprehension of students with and without learning disabilities: Identification of narrative themes and idiosyncratic text representations. *Journal of Educational Psychology*, *85*, 631-641.

This article reports the results of a study of adolescent students with learning disabilities' reading comprehension of a story and the identification of story theme. Students with learning disabilities performed below the level of their peers without disabilities and at the same level as younger students without learning disabilities. However, on the measure of incipient awareness of theme, the students with learning disabilities scored below the younger students without learning disabilities. Williams suggests that students with learning disabilities have "specific difficulty with 'getting the point,' perhaps because they build up less effective text representations through the inappropriate use of background knowledge or intrusion of personal points of view" (p. 631).

Williams, J.P. (1994). Twenty years of research on reading: Answers and questions. In F. Lehr and J. Osborn (Eds.), *Reading, language, and literacy: Instruction for the twenty-first century* (pp. 59-73). Hillsdale, NJ: Lawrence Erlbaum Associates, Inc.

In this chapter, Williams reviews the research evidence that supports an emphasis on phonics as one part of beginning reading instruction. She points out that findings from a variety of research approaches support the importance of a knowledge of phonics, which, in turn, strengthens the case for instruction in decoding. The research approaches on which she draws include basic research, applied research, method comparisons, survey data, and observational studies. Williams goes on to review two promising research topics related to phonological structure: phonemic skills and spelling. She concludes that "to be a proficient reader, one must have these skills [phonics and decoding], regardless of how one acquires them. And many children do not seem able to acquire them without careful, explicit, structured lessons" (p. 70).

Winne, P.H., Graham, L., & Prock, L. (1993). A model of poor readers' text-based inferencing: Effects of explanatory feedback. *Reading Research Quarterly, 28,* 52-66.

These authors report that poor third- to fifth- grade readers were able to make low-level text-based inferences from passages read to them. It appeared that explicit feedback resulted in better inference-making than less specific feedback. In the explicit feedback condition, tutors added routine feedback to students' answers by explaining and demonstrating the process for combining information about the problem, the rule that solved the problem, and the critical fact employed to create an inference. The authors found that students had lacked procedural knowledge that they needed. They conclude that "teaching low-achieving readers to discriminate and use text clues that aid inferencing . . . is a facet of comprehension instruction that has received relatively less attention than instruction designed to activate students' background knowledge about topics addressed in text" (p. 64).

Winograd, P., & Niquette, G. (1988). Assessing learned helplessness in poor readers. *Topics in Language Disorders, 8,* 38-55.

Winograd and Niquette review research findings on the relationships between learned helplessness and reading difficulties, and they review ways of assessing learned helplessness and of remediating these difficulties. They suggest that it is important to obtain information from the child regarding perception of the sources of success or failure, and they provide some examples to illustrate how this might be done. Their suggestions for remediation are straightforward. Children need to be interested in what they are reading, and the authors suggest using interesting text, not skills worksheets. The atmosphere must be noncompetitive and nonthreatening, with reading done for an authentic purpose.

Wong, B. Y. L. (1986). Metacognition and special education: A review of a view. *Journal of Special Education, 20,* 9-29.

Wong provides a thorough, extensive, and readable review of research on the relevance of a cognitive approach for learning disabled and educable mentally retarded students, the contributions of metacognition to the field, the impact of metacognition on remediation, and the constraints in applying metacognitive theory to understanding special education students. The author views the growth of interest in and information about metacognition as helpful in understanding and remediating the difficulties encountered by students with learning disabilities. Metacognition does not, however, account for decoding difficulties, increase deficient content knowledge or provide affective training.

Wong, B.Y.L. (Ed.). (1991a). *Learning about learning disabilities.* San Diego, CA: Academic Press.

This textbook provides a balanced focus on research and practical issues. It reviews three areas: 1) conceptual, historical, and research aspects of learning disabilities; 2) assessment and instructional aspects of learning disabilities; and 3) understanding learning disabilities through a life-span approach.

Wong, B.Y.L. (1991b).   The relevance of metacognition to learning disabilities.   In B.Y.L. Wong (Ed.), *Learning about learning disabilities* (pp. 231-258).   New York: Academic Press.

Wong discusses the research that has demonstrated that teaching students metacognitive strategies enhances their reading comprehension.   Wong extends this with a rationale for the relevance of metacognition to learning disabilities.   She reminds us of the research on metacognitive skills in reading that discriminates among younger readers, poor readers and skilled readers.   She concludes by stating that practical applications of metacognitive strategies to teaching students with learning disabilities are still at an early stage.   However, ongoing research lends promise for progress in the near future.

Wong, B.Y.L. (1992a).   *Contemporary intervention research in learning disabilities: An international perspective.*   New York: Springer-Verlag.

This book addresses two issues: 1) that there is great need for theories and models of intervention, and 2) that strategy instruction needs maintenance and generalization in academic school settings.   The feature that most prominently distinguishes this volume reporting research on learning disabilities from others is the inclusion of research from other countries to gain an international perspective.   The chapters reflect the areas of cognition, program intervention, social skills, families with a learning disabled child, socioemotional coping, and a history of the field.

Wong, B.Y.L. (1992b). On cognitive process-based instruction: An introduction. *Journal of Learning Disabilities, 25,* 150-152, 172.

Wong defines cognitive processed-based instruction as "teaching through modeling and thinking aloud the cognitive processes that underlie the acquisition of knowledge, or the execution of a task, or the solving of a problem in a specific academic domain" (p. 150). We need to examine what the "expert" does and then develop instructional approaches. She traces the history of the development of this type of instruction and contrasts it with the process training advocated by Kirk.

Wong, B.Y.L. (1993). Pursuing an elusive goal: Molding strategic teachers and learners. *Journal of Learning Disabilities, 26,* 354-357.

Wong, in this introduction to a discussion of cognitive strategy and content-area instruction by a number of researchers in the field, writes that "cognitive or learning strategies can be defined as behaviors of a learner that are intended to influence how the learner processes information" (p. 354). She reviews the movement toward anchoring cognitive strategy instructional research in specific content domains, reminding us that general strategy knowledge interacts with domain-specific knowledge. Wong introduces Ellis' Integrated Strategy Instruction model and the reactions to it that are presented by other researchers. In conclusion, Wong urges research to determine the efficacy of the various models of strategy instruction reviewed in this series and to determine which parts are effective and why.

Wong, B. Y. L., Wong, R., Perry, N. and Sawatsky, D. (1986). The efficacy of a self-questioning summarization strategy for use by underachievers and learning disabled adolescents in social studies. *Learning Disabilities Focus, 2,* 20-34.

The authors describe a strategy to summarize the main ideas of paragraphs, a strategy that was effectively transferred to new content materials by students with learning disabilities through the use of a self-questioning strategy. The emphasis on cognitive and metacognitive strategy training "appears to benefit LD students because it shifts the focus from ability (structural) deficits that may well defy remediation to increasing cognitive and metacognitive skills" (p. 21). A review of previous research in these areas is included. Specific procedures and materials used are also described.

Wood, T. A., Buckhalt, J. A., & Tomlin J. G. (1988). A comparison of listening and reading performance with children in three educational placements. *Journal of Learning Disabilities, 21,* 493-496.

Wood, Buckhalt and Tomlin studied the performance of learning disabled, mildly mentally retarded, and normal readers to compare listening and reading performance. The study included students from 9 to 15 years old. They found that all students performed better on listening tasks than on reading tasks, but students with learning disabilities demonstrated a higher discrepancy than the other two groups. The results suggest the need to investigate "the relationship of modality strength to the development of reading skills" (p. 496) because students with learning disabilities appear to have "less difficulty with auditory process than with visual processing and auditory-visual integration" (p. 496).

Yopp, H. K. (1992). Developing phonemic awareness in young children. *The Reading Teacher, 45,* 696-703.

Yopp defines phonemic awareness as "an understanding that speech is composed of individual sounds" (p. 696). It requires the ability to "analyze or manipulate the units of speech" (p. 696), a particularly difficult task in view of the abstract nature of these units. Many students entering school have difficulty in this area. Yopp reviews considerable research documenting the relationship between reading acquisition and phonemic awareness. Citing evidence to support the view that training in phonemic awareness can be effective, the author presents and illustrates a variety of activities that can be used for instruction.

Ysseldyke, J.E., Thurlow, M.L., & Bruininks, R.H. (1992). Expected education outcomes for students with disabilities. *Remedial and Special Education (RASE), 13,* 19-30.

These authors urge that we examine the extent to which students with disabilities achieve the objectives set for other students. They discuss current practices in the assessment of educational outcomes and suggest that students with disabilities have not been included. Major considerations in developing a comprehensive system of outcome indicators are reviewed. In conclusion, the authors remind us that, in the process, we must remember that we are dealing with students.

Zivian, M. T., & Samuels, M. T. (1986). Performance on a word-likeness task by normal readers and reading-disabled children. *Reading Research Quarterly, 21,* 150-160.

Zivian and Samuels examine the notion of developmental delay for reading disabled students. Developmental delay suggests that all readers go through the same steps, moving in the same direction. "Individual differences in rate of development should not affect the final level of development attained" (p.151). Based on prior research, which suggested that reading disabled students could not process aural information as well as other students, the authors studied children ages 8 to 11 to determine the effects of three modes of presentation: reading, listening, and reading plus listening, both on their ability to make judgments on real words and pseudowords. The results indicated that although reading-disabled children can integrate auditory and visual information, they do not show an increase in knowledge of the orthographic structure of words. This suggests that they may not be simply developmentally delayed.

Author Index

Subject Index

SOURCE BOOKS ON EDUCATION

BILINGUAL EDUCATION
A Source Book for Educators
by Alba N. Ambert and Sarah Melendez

TEACHING SCIENCE TO YOUNG CHILDREN
A Resource Book
by Mary D. Iatridis

SPECIAL EDUCATION
A Source Book
by Manny Sternlicht

COMPUTERS IN THE CLASS-ROOM . . . WHAT SHALL I DO?
A Guide
by Walter Burke

SCHOOL PLAY
A Source Book
by James H. Block and Nancy R. King

COMPUTER SIMULATIONS
A Source Book to Learning in an Electronic Environment
by Jerry Willis, Larry Hovey,
and Kathleen Hovey

PROJECT HEAD START
Past, Present, and Future Trends in the Context of Family Needs
by Valora Washington
and Ura Jean Oyemade

ADULT LITERACY
A Source Book and Guide
by Joyce French

MATHEMATICS EDUCATION IN SECONDARY SCHOOLS AND TWO-YEAR COLLEGES
A Source Book
by Louise S. Grinstein
and Paul J. Campbell

BLACK CHILDREN AND AMERICAN INSTITUTIONS
An Ecological Review and Resource Guide
by Valora Washington
and Velma LaPoint

SEXUALITY EDUCATION
A Resource Book
by Carol Cassell and Pamela M. Wilson

REFORMING TEACHER EDUCATION
Issues and New Directions
edited by Joseph A. Braun, Jr.

EDUCATIONAL TECHNOLOGY
Planning and Resource Guide Supporting Curriculum
by James E. Eisele and Mary Ellin Eisele

CRITICAL ISSUES IN FOREIGN LANGUAGE INSTRUCTION
edited by Ellen S. Silber

THE EDUCATION OF WOMEN IN THE UNITED STATES
A Guide to Theory, Teaching, and Research
by Averil Evans McClelland

MATERIALS AND STRATEGIES FOR THE EDUCATION OF TRAINABLE MENTALLY RETARDED LEARNERS
by James P. White

RURAL EDUCATION
Issues and Practice
by Alan J. DeYoung

EDUCATIONAL TESTING
Issues and Applications
by Kathy E. Green

THE WRITING CENTER
New Directions
edited by Ray Wallace
and Jeanne Simpson

TEACHING THINKING SKILLS
Theory and Practice
by Joyce N. French and Carol Rhoder

TEACHING SOCIAL STUDIES TO THE YOUNG CHILD
A Research and Resource Guide
by Blythe S. Farb Hinitz

TELECOMMUNICATIONS
A Handbook for Educators
by Reza Azarmsa

CATHOLIC SCHOOL EDUCATION IN THE UNITED STATES
Development and Current Concerns
by Mary A. Grant and Thomas C. Hunt

DAY CARE
A Source Book
Second Edition, by Kathleen Pullan
Watki and Lucius Durant, Jr.

SCHOOL PRINCIPALS AND CHANGE
by Michael D. Richardson, Paula M.
Short, and Robert L. Prickett

PLAY IN PRACTICE
A Systems Approach to Making Good Play Happen
edited by Karen VanderVen, Paul Niemiec, and Roberta Schomburg

TEACHING SCIENCE TO CHILDREN
Second Edition
by Mary D. Iatridis with a contribution by Miriam Maracek

KITS, GAMES AND MANIPULATIVES FOR THE ELEMENTARY SCHOOL CLASSROOM
A Source Book
by Andrea Hoffman and Ann Glannon

PARENTS AND SCHOOLS
A Source Book
by Angela Carrasquillo and Clement B. G. London

PROJECT HEAD START
Models and Strategies for the Twenty-First Century
by Valora Washington and Ura Jean Oyemade Bailey

INSTRUMENTATION IN EDUCATION
An Anthology
by Lloyd Bishop and Paula E. Lester

TEACHING ENGLISH AS A SECOND LANGUAGE
A Resource Guide
by Angela L. Carrasquillo

SECONDARY SCHOOLS AND COOPERATIVE LEARNING
Theories, Models, and Strategies
by Angela L. Carrasquillo

THE FOREIGN LANGUAGE CLASSROOM
Bridging Theory and Practice
edited by Margaret A. Haggstrom, Leslie Z. Morgan, and Joseph A. Wieczorek

READING AND LEARNING DISABILITIES
Research and Practice
by Joyce N. French, Nancy J. Ellsworth, and Marie Z. Amoruso